JOHNNY CASH

I SEE A DARKNESS

A GRAPHIC NOVEL BY REINHARD KLEIST

JOHNNY CASH

I SEE A DARKNESS

Abrams ComicArts, New York

Thanks for all the support, not only for this book:

Michael Groenewald, Claudia Jerusalem-Groenewald, Richard Weize, Franz Dobler, Basti "Vadda Cash" Krondorfer, Erika and Lothar Kleist.

Bettina Oguamanam, Sylvia Schuster, Carlsen Comics, Martin Rabitz, Ron Rineck, Butch-Meier-Band, Steffen "Doc" Mittelstedt, David Fernandez, Christian Vagt, Helmut, Fil, Mawil, Andi Michalke, Naomi Fearn, Jo Werth, K77, Möbel Olfe, Keb-up 1 at Rosenthaler Platz for moral support, Greg Dulli for Love (Demo), the immortal johnny-cash-club at gayromeo.de.

Uli, Oli, Basti, Roland Heinrich and Oldrik the bassist, The Crooked Jades: Megan Adie, Carley Wolf, Jeff Kazor, Adam Tanner, Erik Pearson, Digger Barns, Pencil Quincey.

– *Reinhard Kleist*

Cataloging-in-Publication Data has been applied for and may be obtained from the Library of Congress.

ISBN 978 0 8109 8463 9

English language version © 2009 SelfMadeHero, a division of Metro Media Ltd (www.selfmadehero.com). First published in German by Carlsen Verlag GmbH in 2006. Copyright text and illustrations © 2006 by Carlsen Verlag GmbH, Hamburg. All rights reserved

Translated from the German edition by Michael Waaler c/o Parkbench Publishing Services
Layout: Andy Huckle

Printed and bound in China
10 9 8 7 6 5 4 3 2 1

Abrams ComicArts books are available at special discounts when purchased in quantity for premiums and promotions as well as fundraising or educational use. Special editions can also be created to specification. For details, contact specialmarkets@abramsbooks.com or the address below.

115 West 18th Street
New York, NY 10011
www.abramsbooks.com

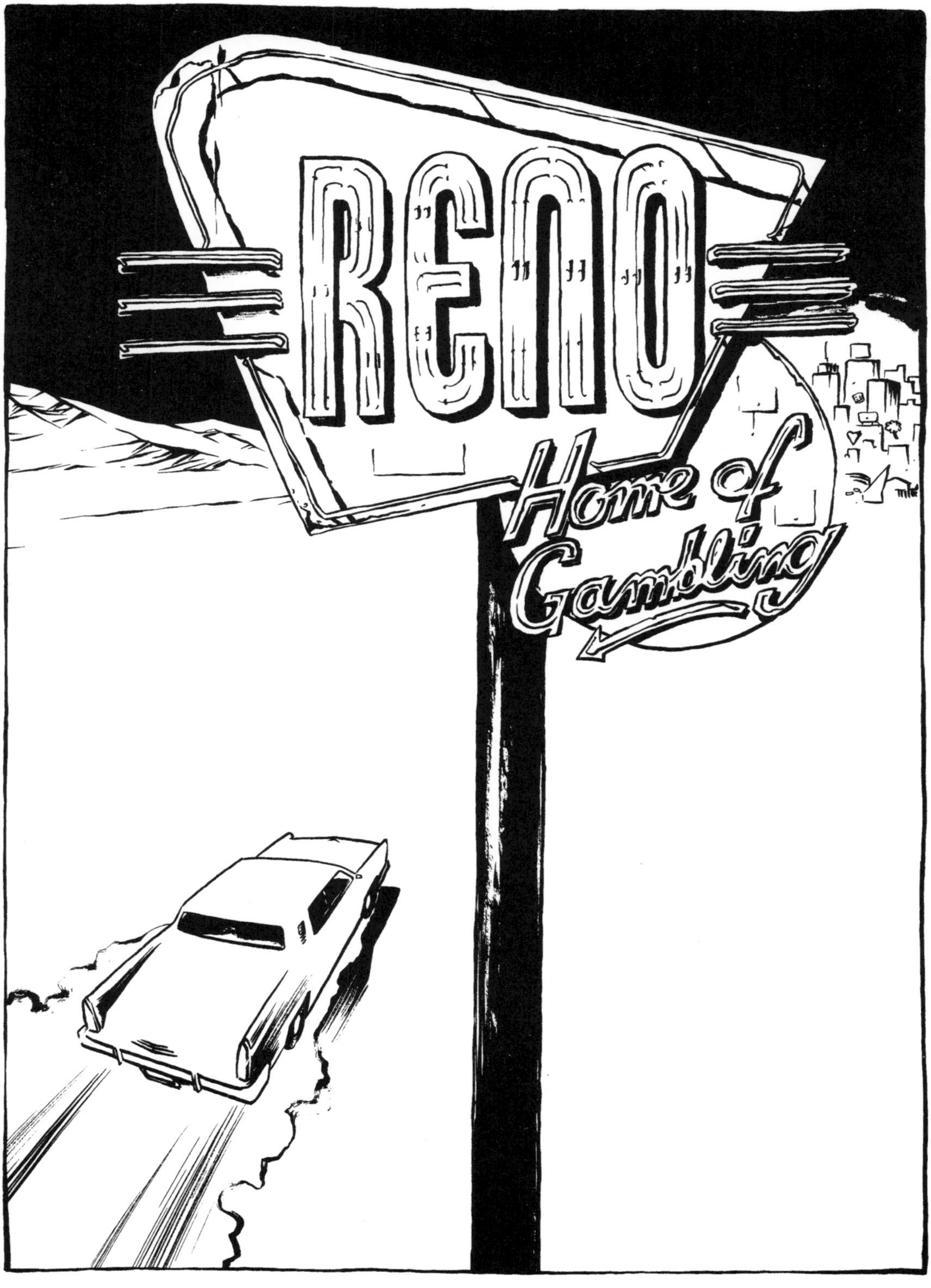
RENO
Home of Gambling

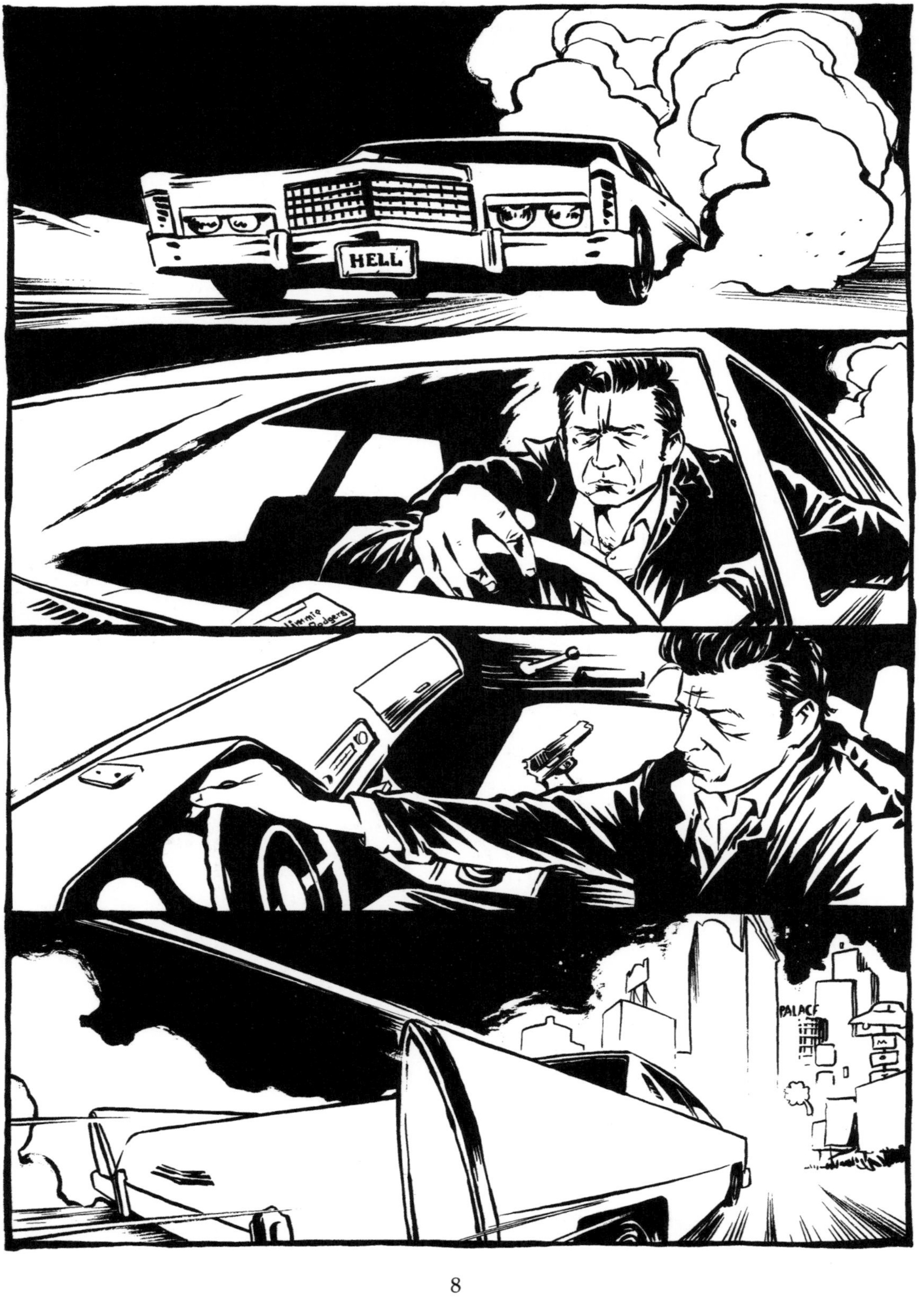
HELL
PALACE

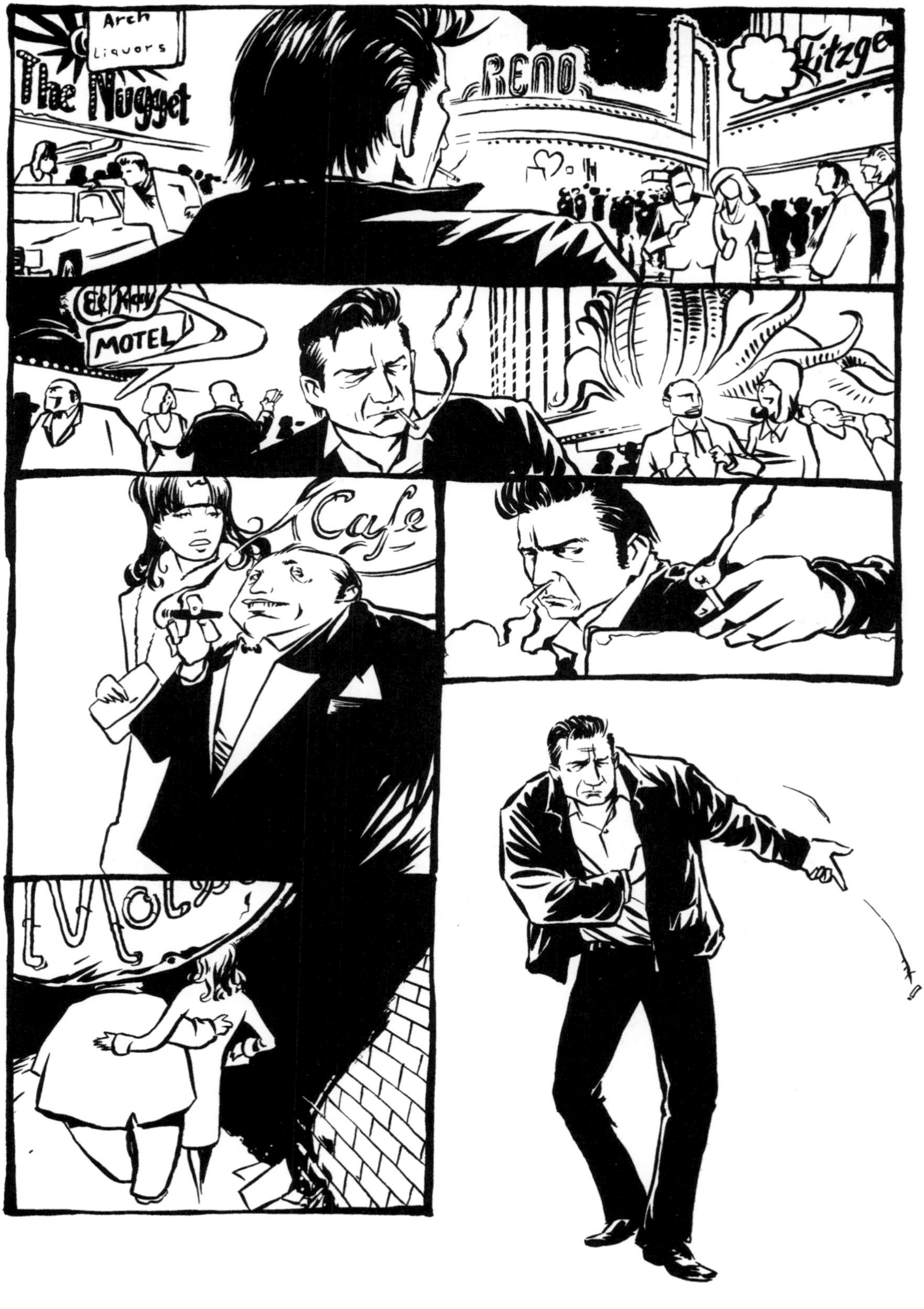
Arch
Liquors
The Nugget
RENO
Fitzge
MOTEL
Cafe

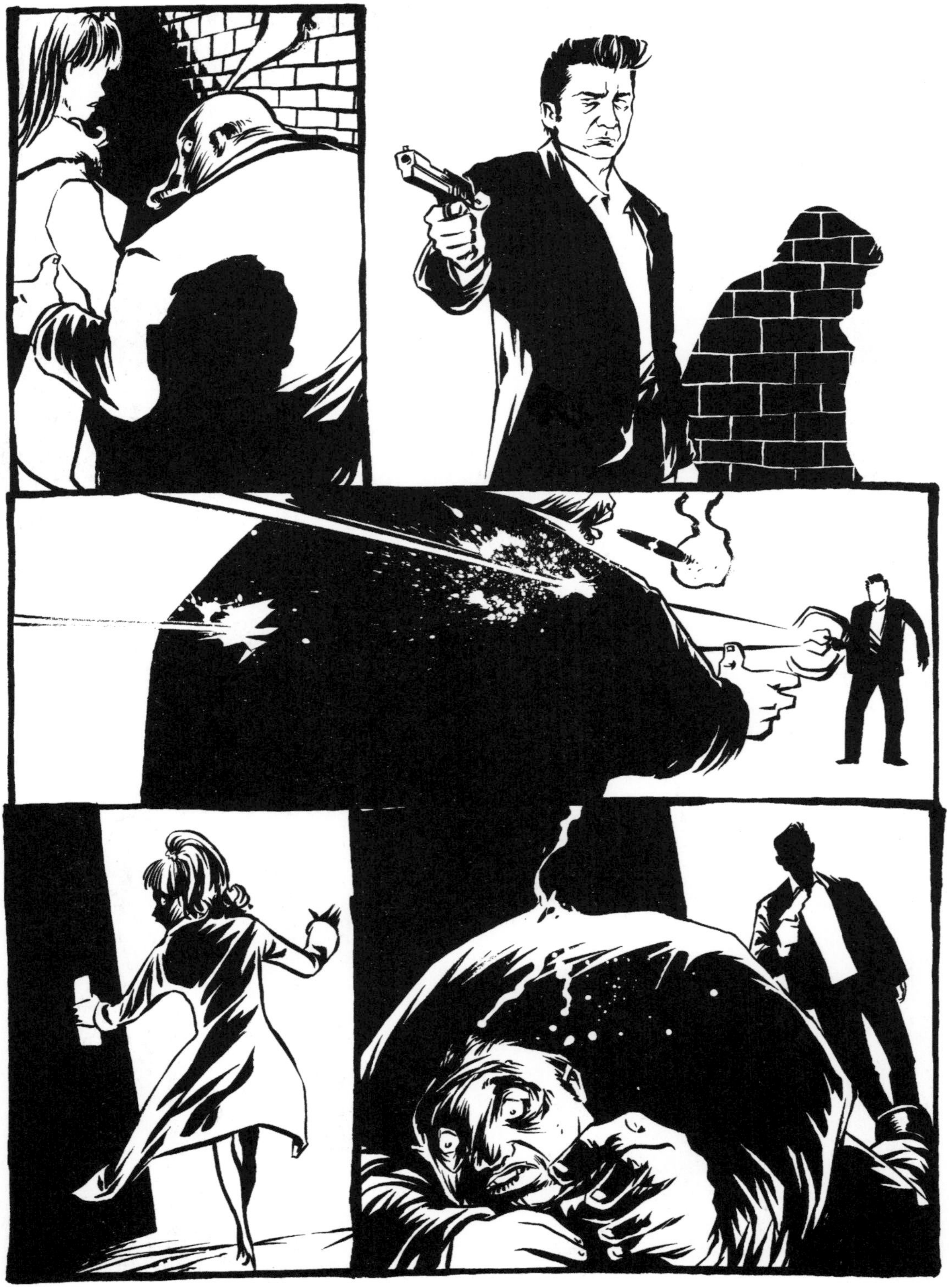

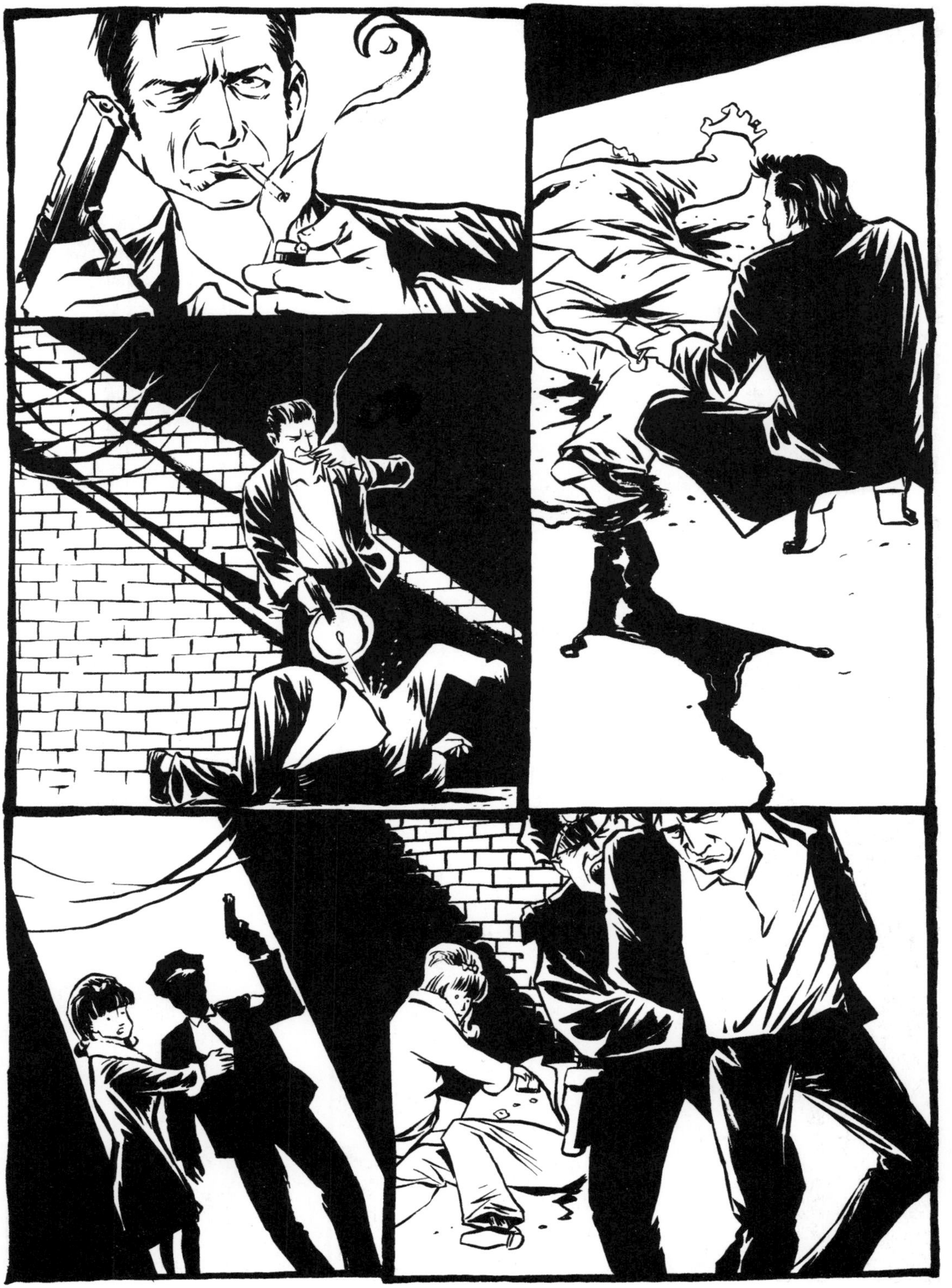

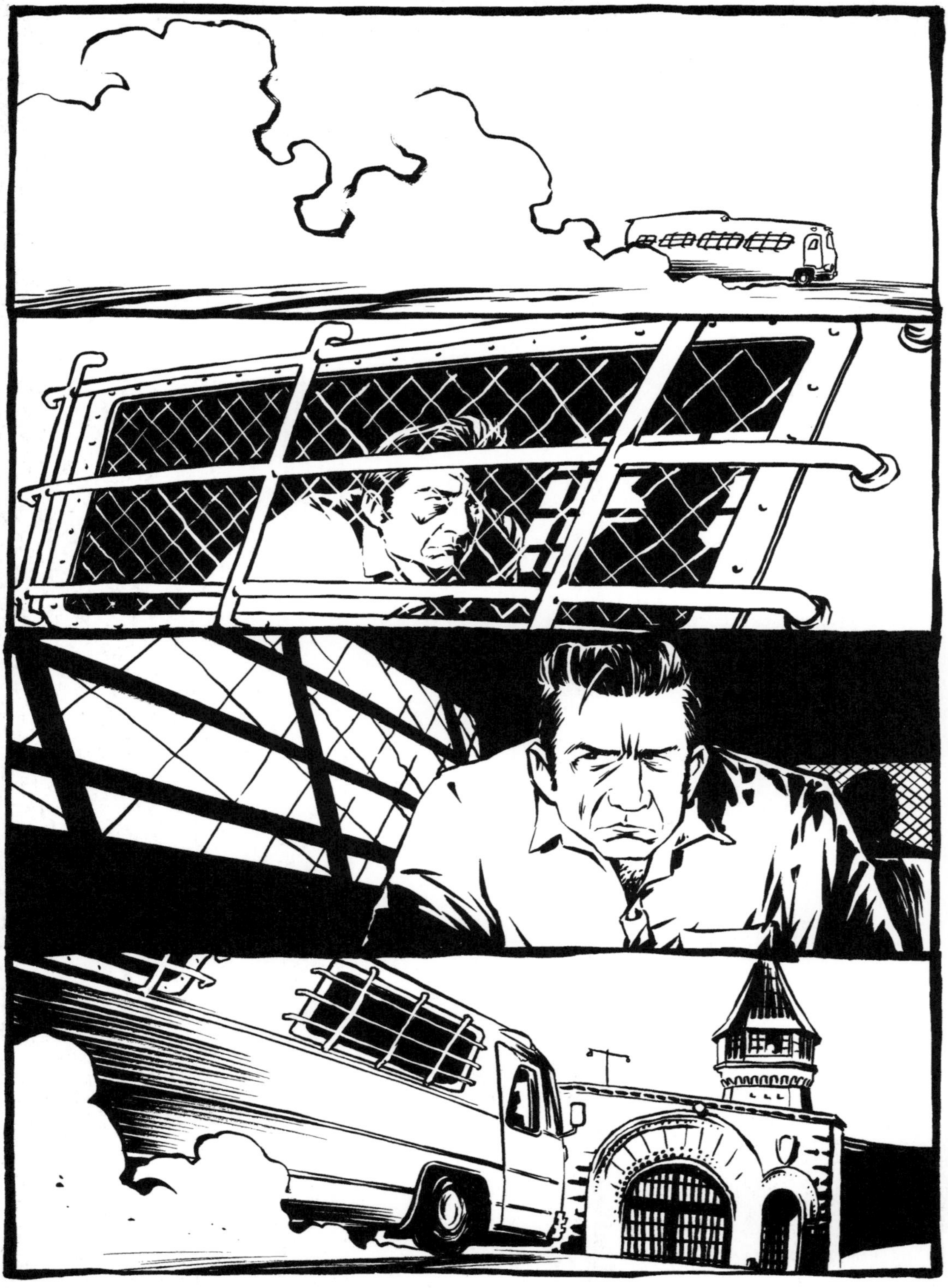

CHAPTER 1
1935-1956

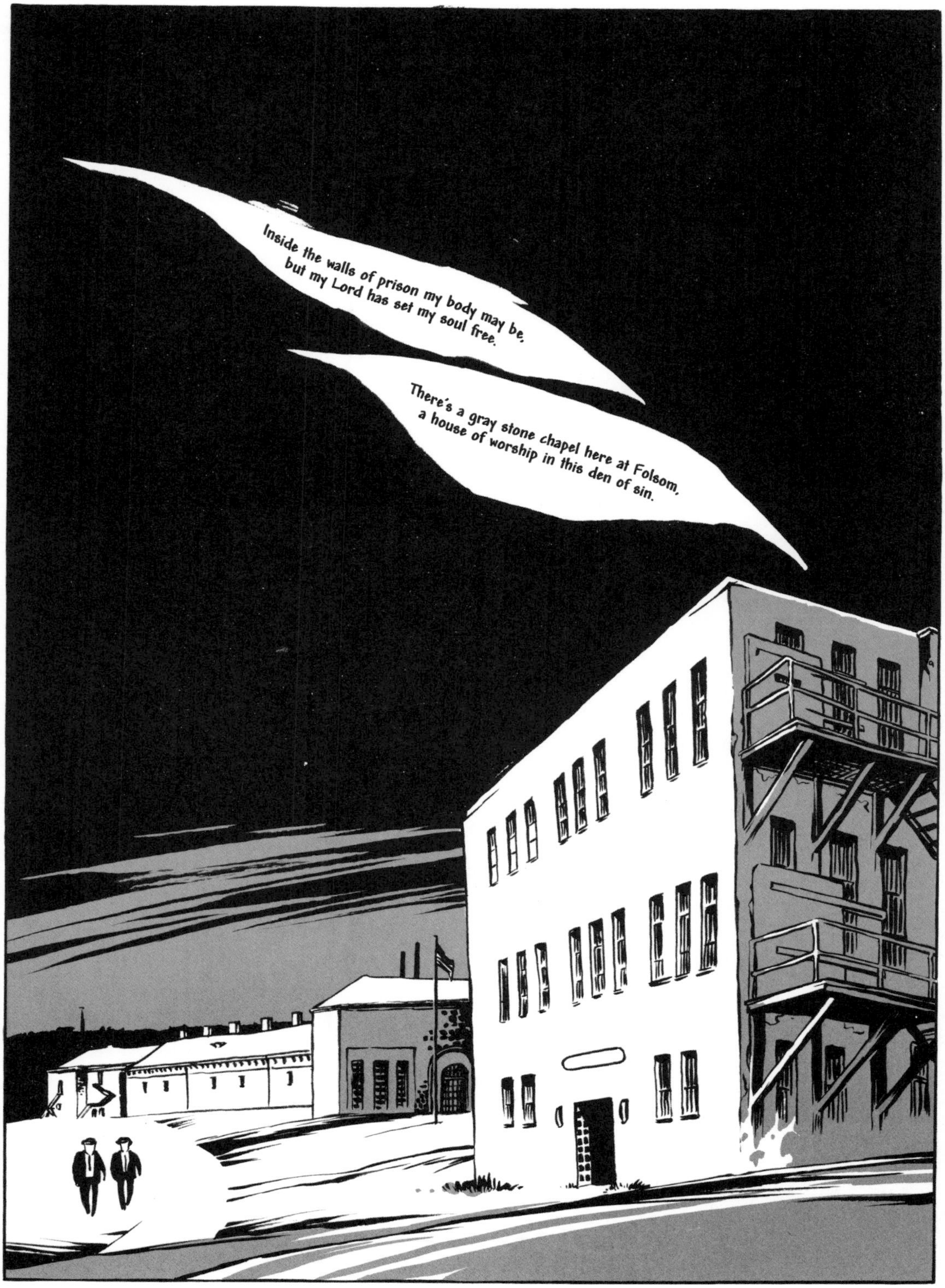
Inside the walls of prison my body may be, but my Lord has set my soul free.
There's a gray stone chapel here at Folsom, a house of worship in this den of sin.

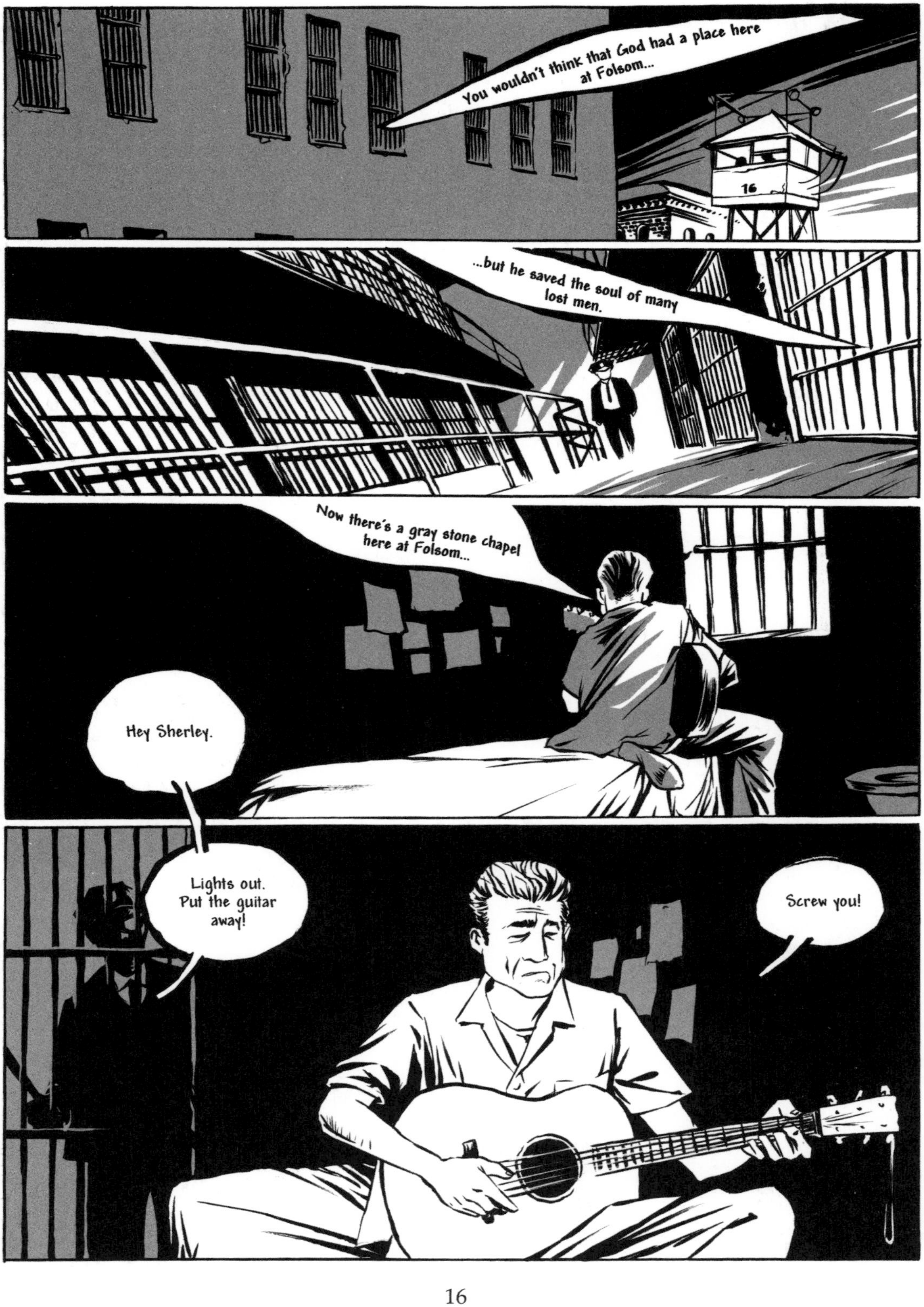
You wouldn't think that God had a place here at Folsom...
16
...but he saved the soul of many lost men.
Now there's a gray stone chapel here at Folsom...
Hey Sherley.
Lights out. Put the guitar away!
Screw you!

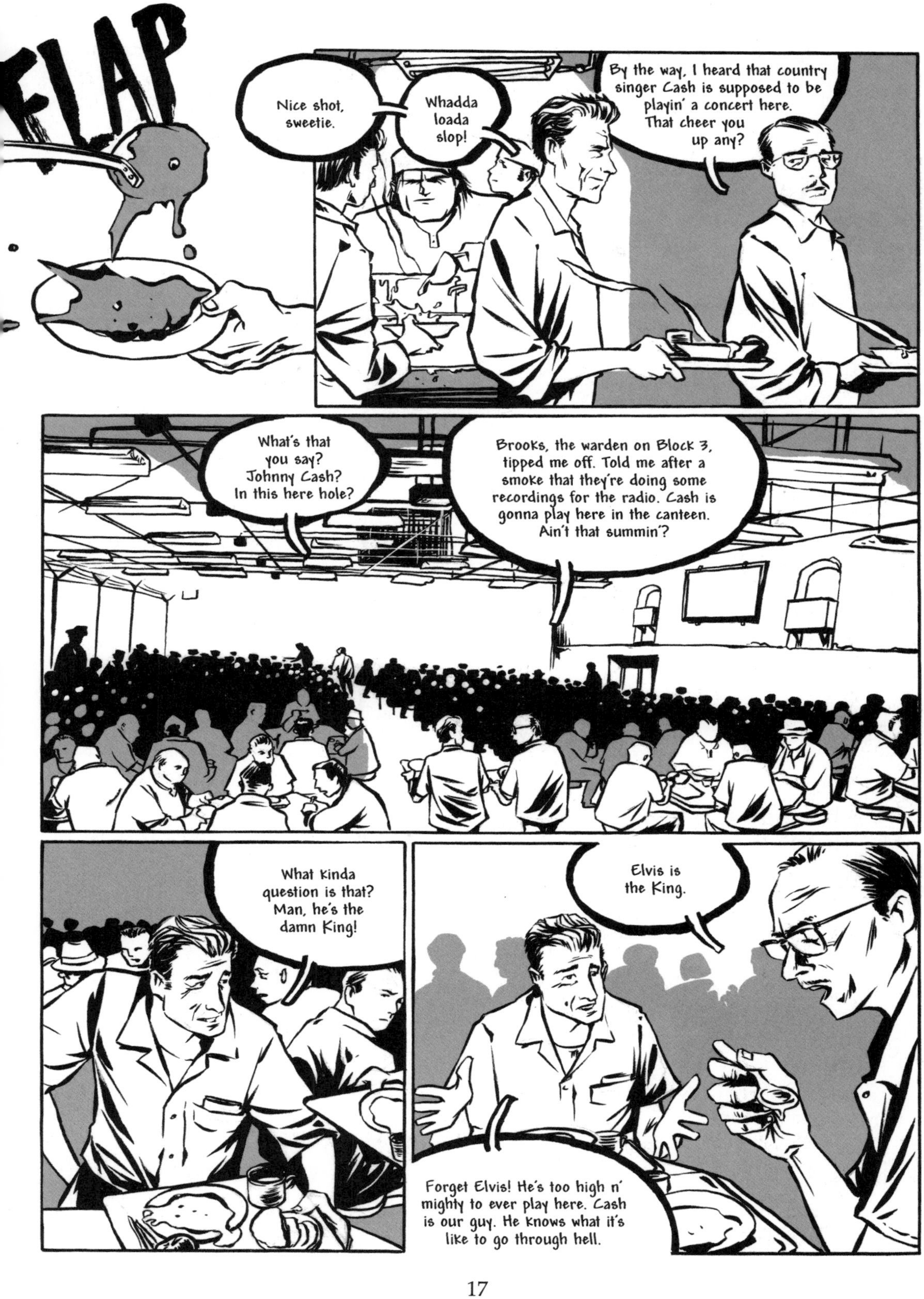
FLAP
Nice shot, sweetie.
Whadda loada slop!
By the way, I heard that country singer Cash is supposed to be playin' a concert here. That cheer you up any?
What's that you say? Johnny Cash? In this here hole?
Brooks, the warden on Block 3, tipped me off. Told me after a smoke that they're doing some recordings for the radio. Cash is gonna play here in the canteen. Ain't that summin'?
What kinda question is that? Man, he's the damn King!
Elvis is the King.
Forget Elvis! He's too high n' mighty to ever play here. Cash is our guy. He knows what it's like to go through hell.

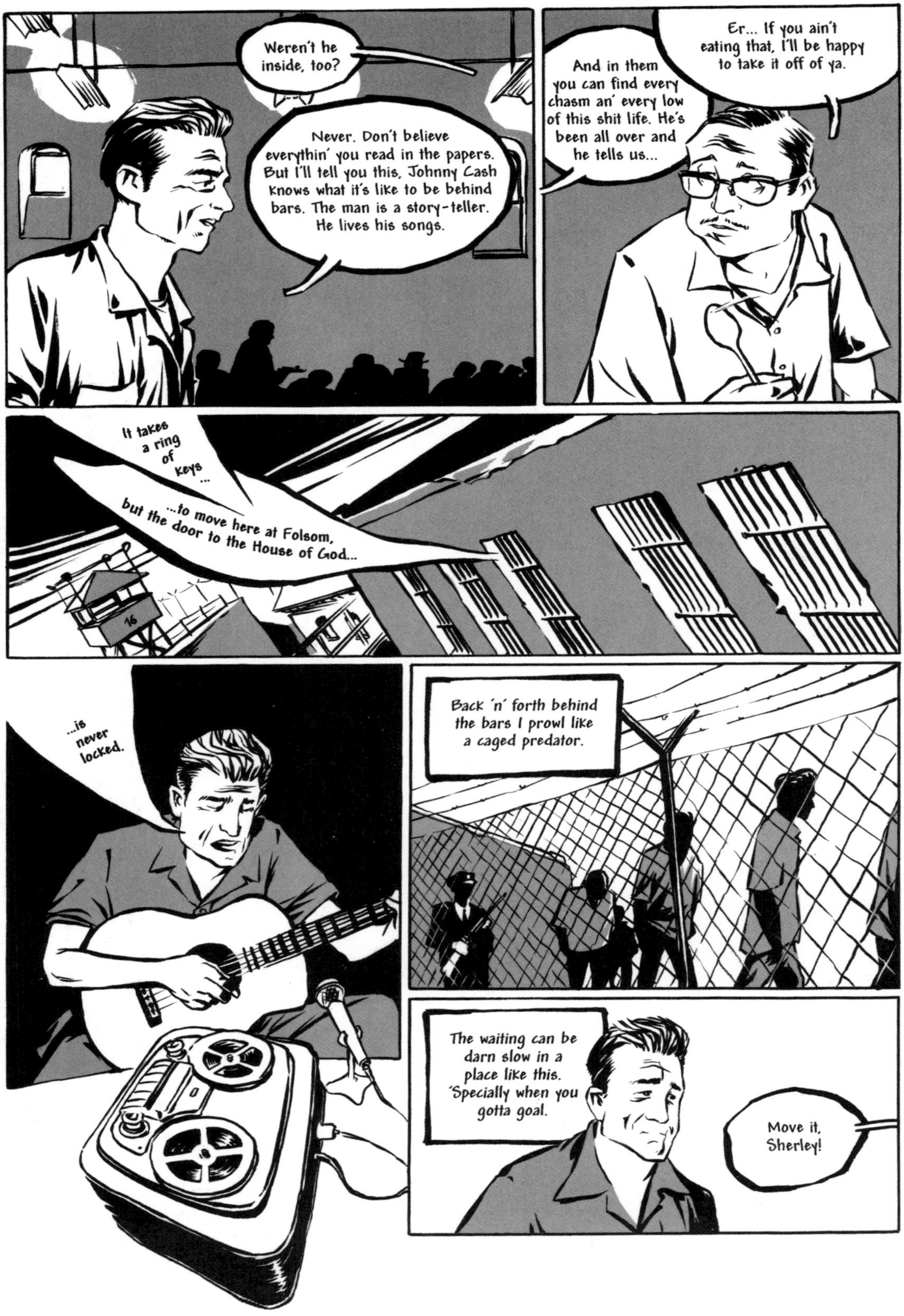
Weren't he inside, too?
Never. Don't believe everythin' you read in the papers. But I'll tell you this, Johnny Cash knows what it's like to be behind bars. The man is a story-teller. He lives his songs.
And in them you can find every chasm an' every low of this shit life. He's been all over and he tells us...
Er... If you ain't eating that, I'll be happy to take it off of ya.
It takes a ring of keys ...
...to move here at Folsom, but the door to the House of God...
...is never locked.
Back 'n' forth behind the bars I prowl like a caged predator.
The waiting can be darn slow in a place like this. 'Specially when you gotta goal.
Move it, Sherley!

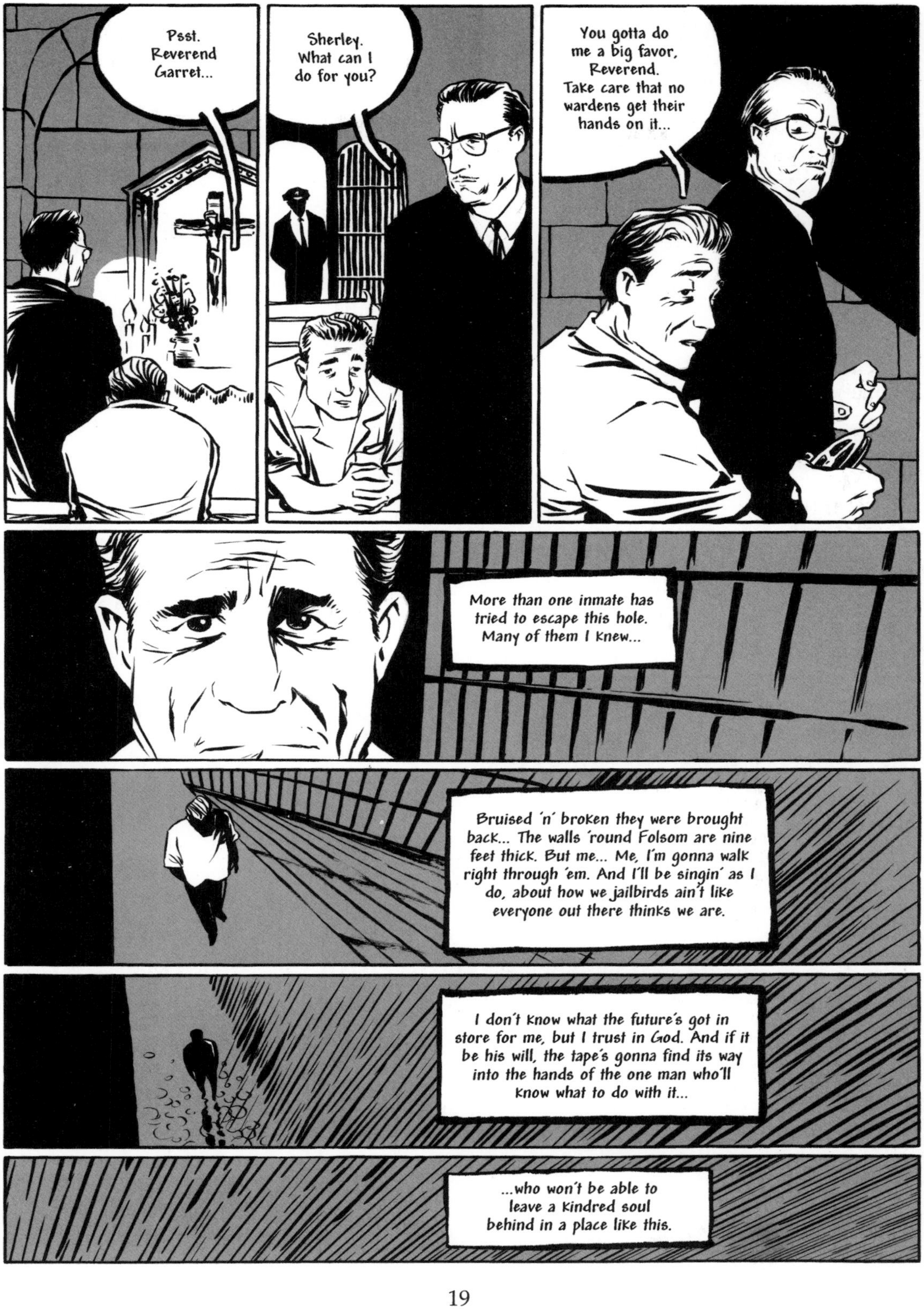
Psst. Reverend Garret...
Sherley. What can I do for you?
You gotta do me a big favor, Reverend. Take care that no wardens get their hands on it...
More than one inmate has tried to escape this hole. Many of them I knew...
Bruised 'n' broken they were brought back... The walls 'round Folsom are nine feet thick. But me... Me, I'm gonna walk right through 'em. And I'll be singin' as I do, about how we jailbirds ain't like everyone out there thinks we are.
I don't know what the future's got in store for me, but I trust in God. And if it be his will, the tape's gonna find its way into the hands of the one man who'll know what to do with it...
...who won't be able to leave a kindred soul behind in a place like this.

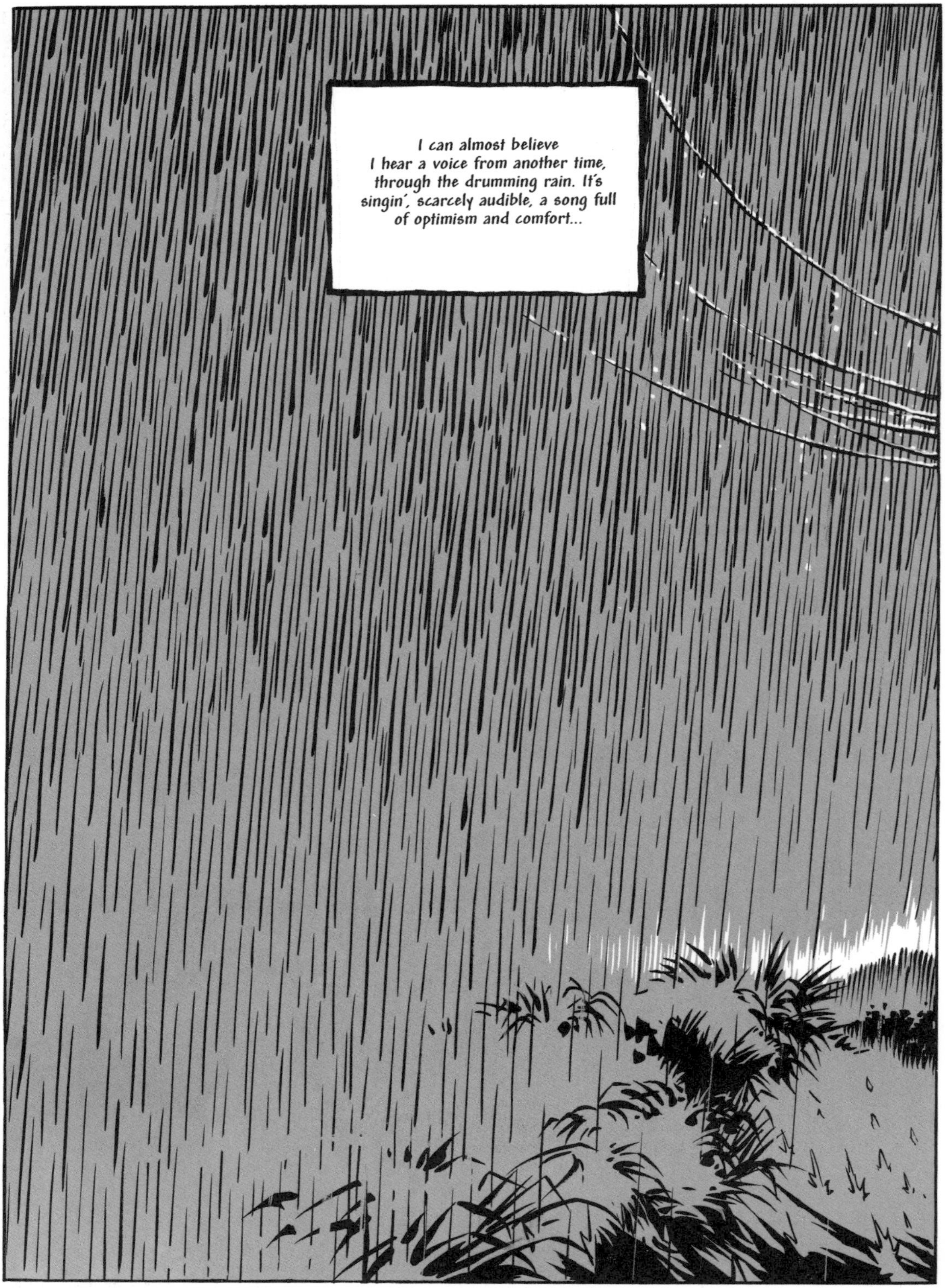
I can almost believe I hear a voice from another time, through the drumming rain. It's singin', scarcely audible, a song full of optimism and comfort...

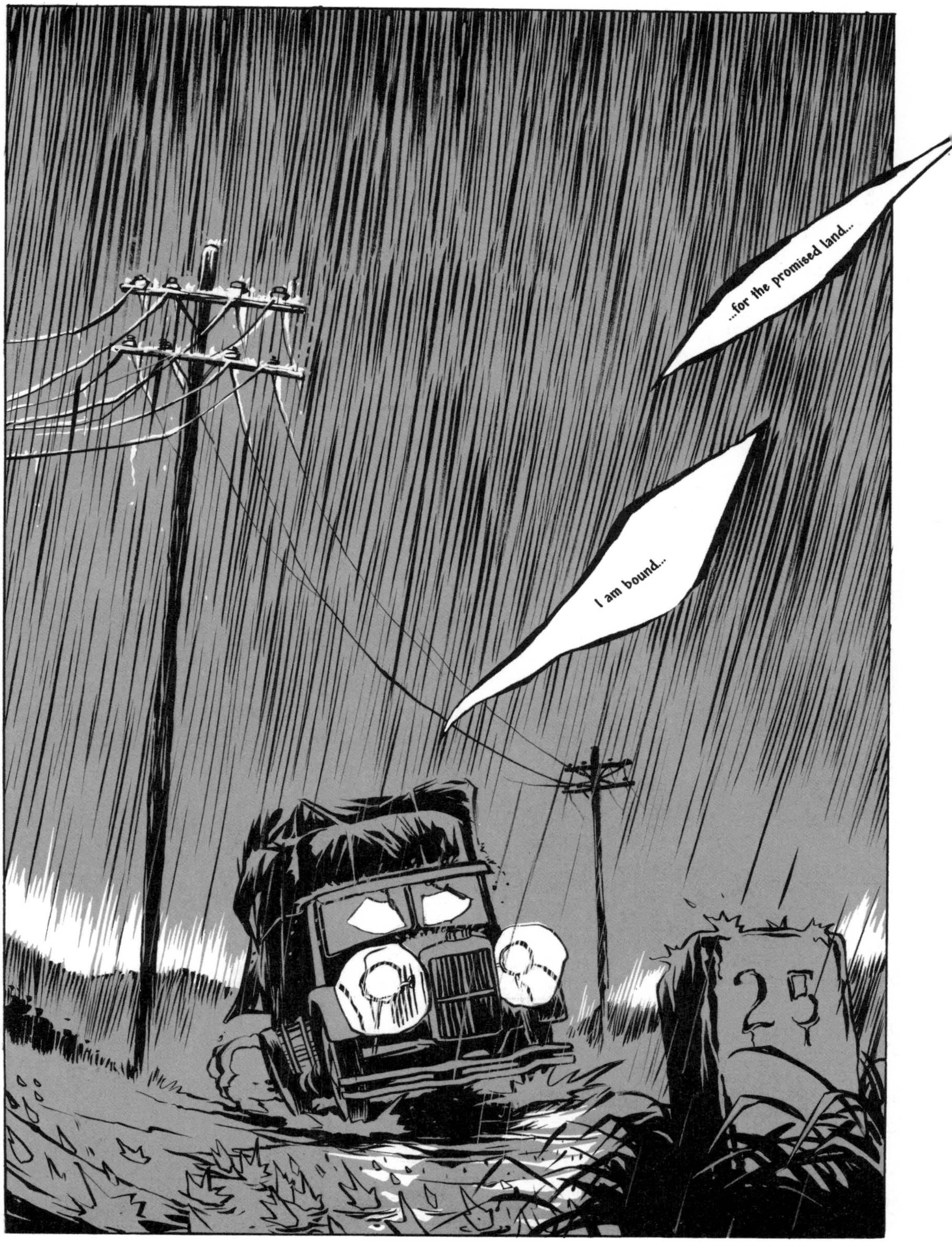
I am bound...
...for the promised land...
25

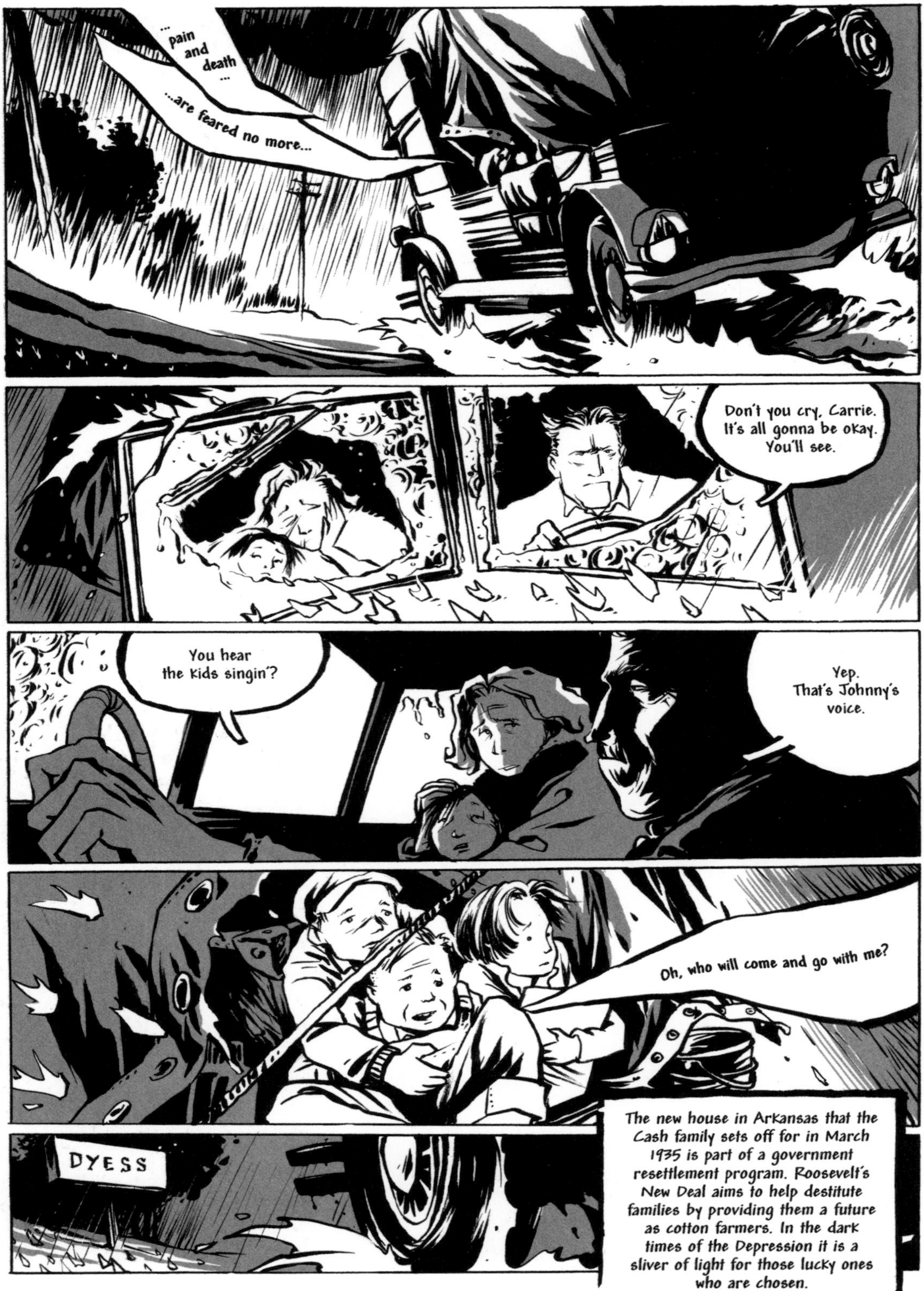
... pain and death ... ...are feared no more...
Don't you cry, Carrie. It's all gonna be okay. You'll see.
You hear the kids singin'?
Yep. That's Johnny's voice.
Oh, who will come and go with me?
DYESS
The new house in Arkansas that the Cash family sets off for in March 1935 is part of a government resettlement program. Roosevelt's New Deal aims to help destitute families by providing them a future as cotton farmers. In the dark times of the Depression it is a sliver of light for those lucky ones who are chosen.

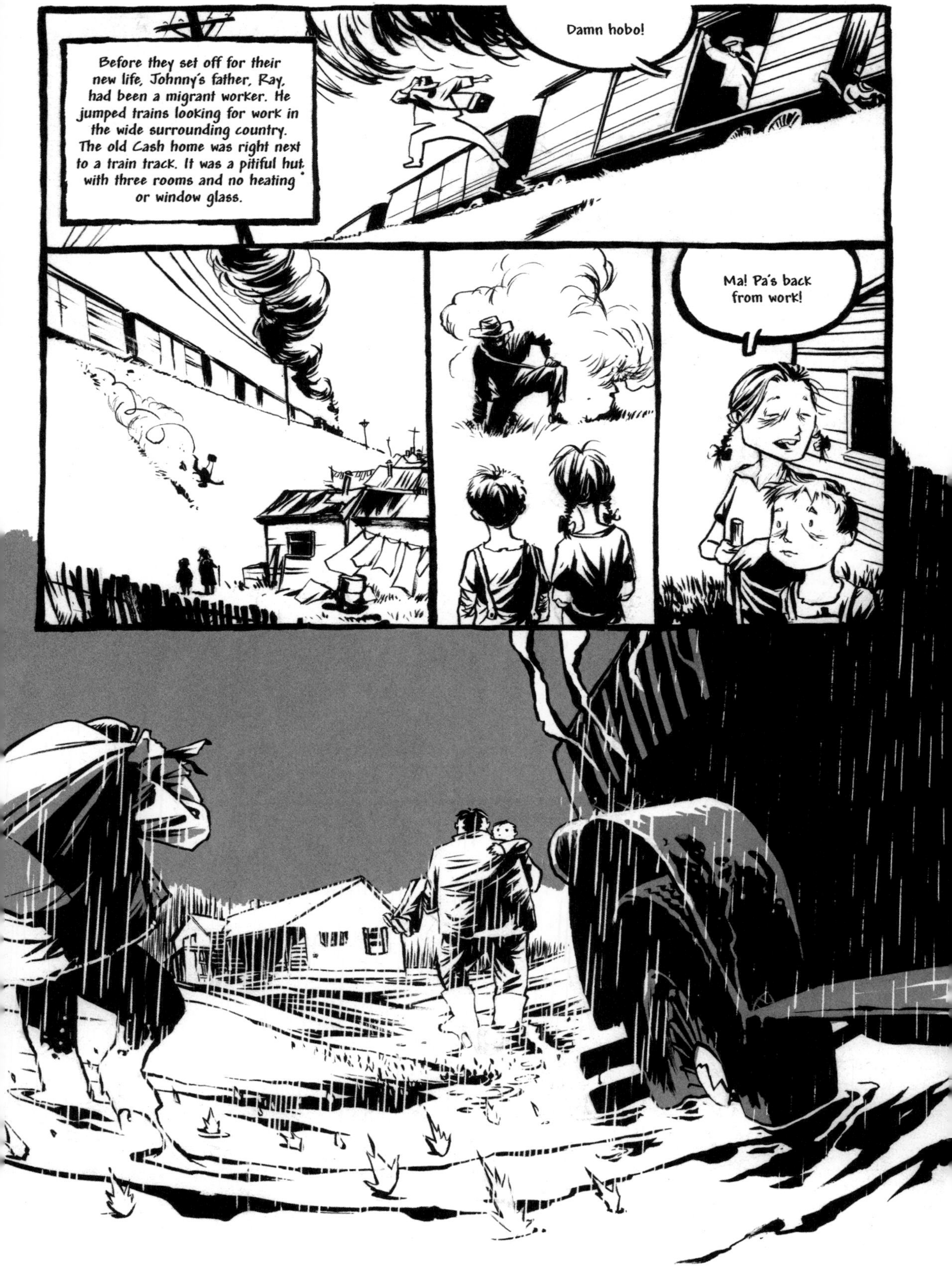
Before they set off for their new life, Johnny's father, Ray, had been a migrant worker. He jumped trains looking for work in the wide surrounding country. The old Cash home was right next to a train track. It was a pitiful hut with three rooms and no heating or window glass.
Damn hobo!
Ma! Pa's back from work!

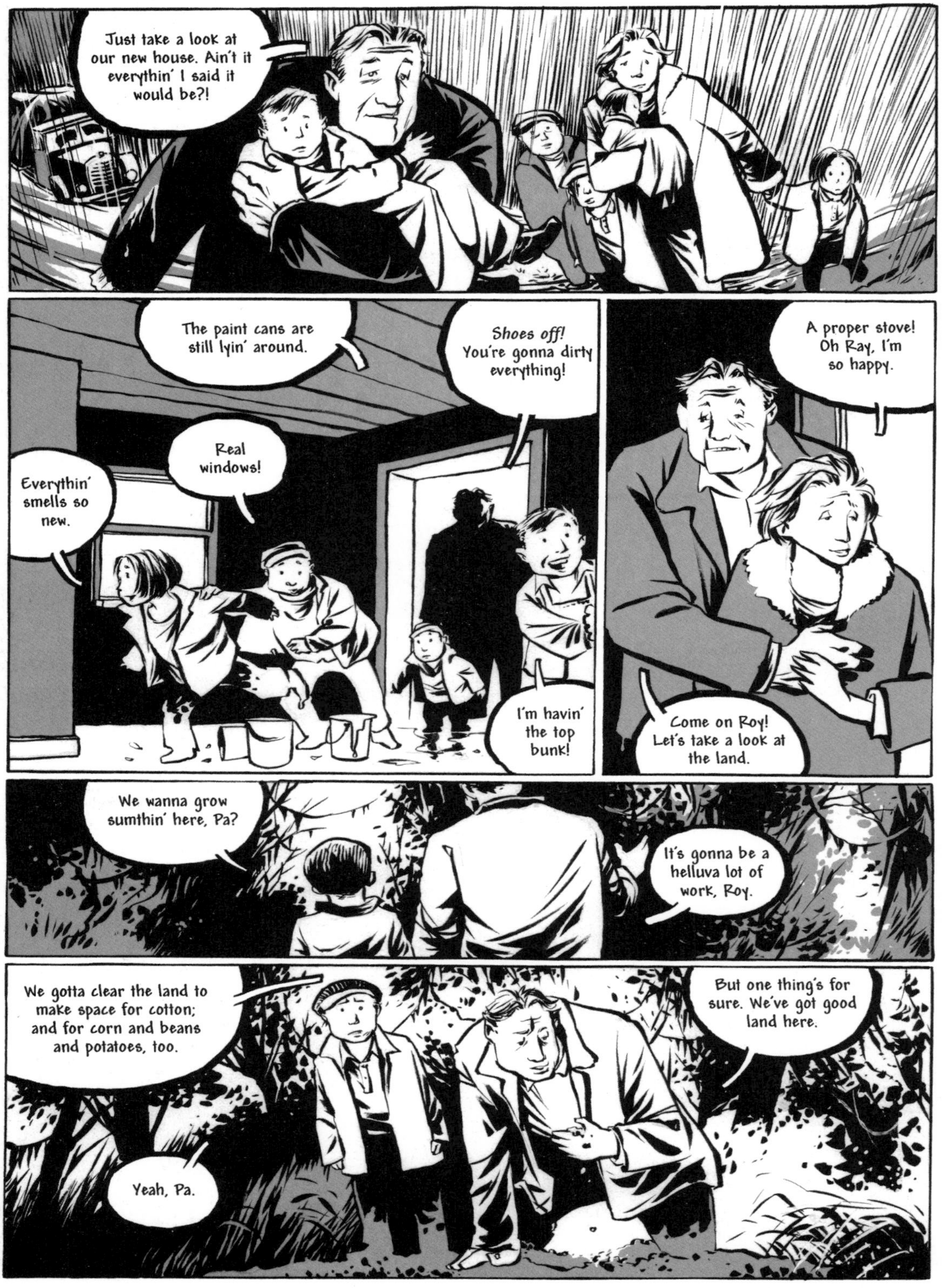
Just take a look at our new house. Ain't it everythin' I said it would be?!
The paint cans are still lyin' around.
Shoes off! You're gonna dirty everything!
Real windows!
Everythin' smells so new.
I'm havin' the top bunk!
A proper stove! Oh Ray, I'm so happy.
Come on Roy! Let's take a look at the land.
We wanna grow sumthin' here, Pa?
It's gonna be a helluva lot of work, Roy.
We gotta clear the land to make space for cotton; and for corn and beans and potatoes, too.
But one thing's for sure. We've got good land here.
Yeah, Pa.

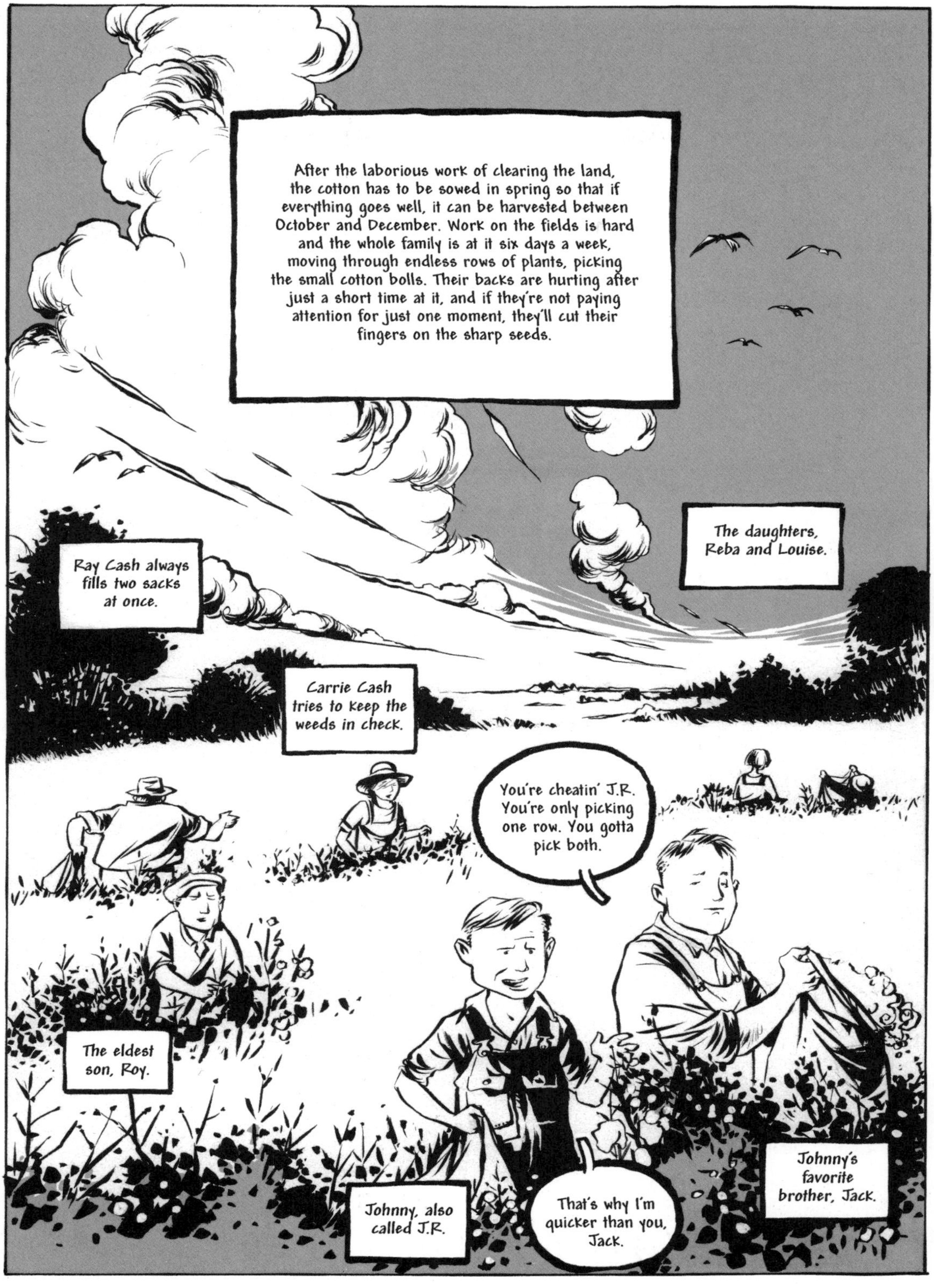
After the laborious work of clearing the land, the cotton has to be sowed in spring so that if everything goes well, it can be harvested between October and December. Work on the fields is hard and the whole family is at it six days a week, moving through endless rows of plants, picking the small cotton bolls. Their backs are hurting after just a short time at it, and if they're not paying attention for just one moment, they'll cut their fingers on the sharp seeds.
Ray Cash always fills two sacks at once.
The daughters, Reba and Louise.
Carrie Cash tries to keep the weeds in check.
You're cheatin' J.R. You're only picking one row. You gotta pick both.
The eldest son, Roy.
Johnny's favorite brother, Jack.
Johnny, also called J.R.
That's why I'm quicker than you, Jack.

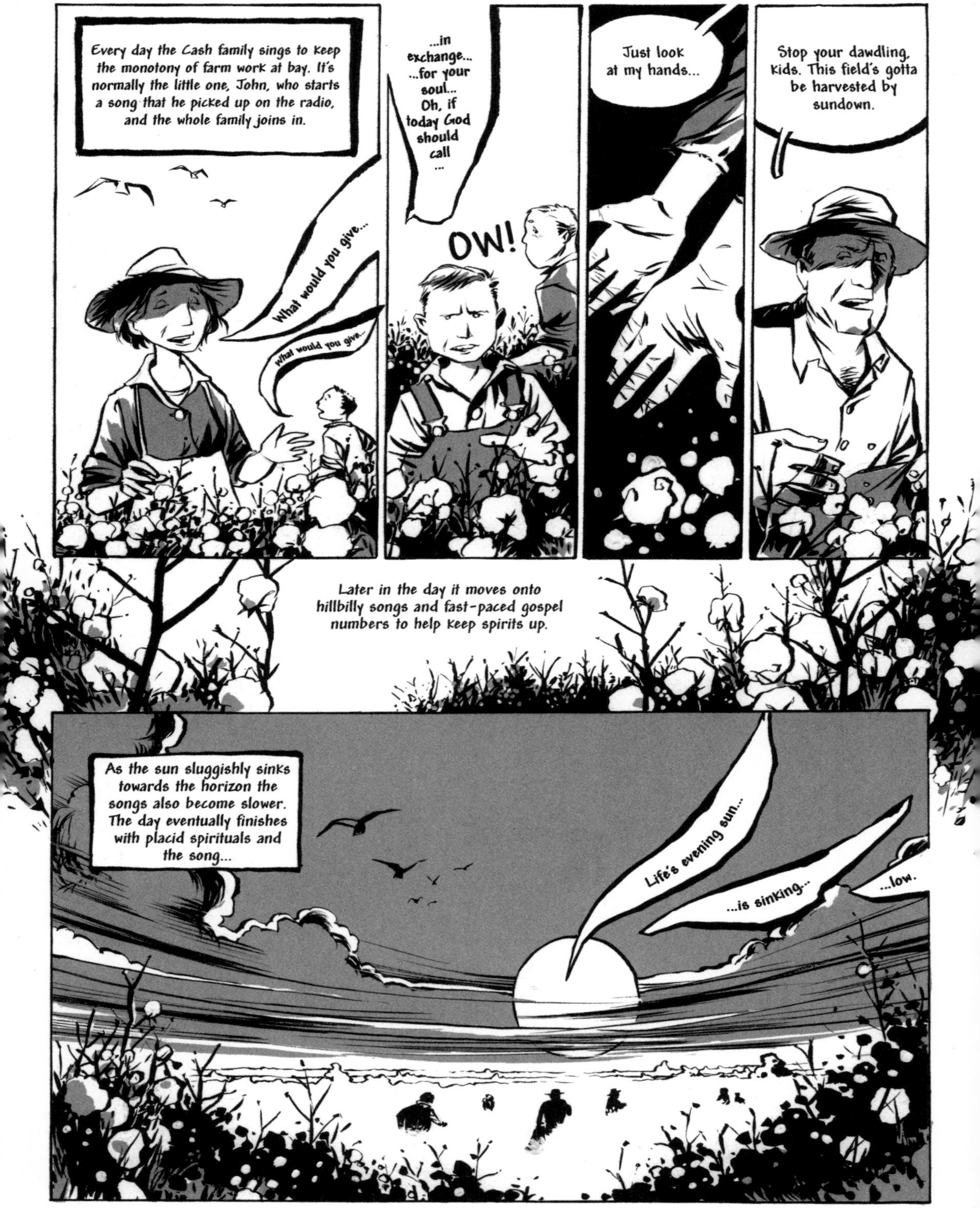
Every day the Cash family sings to keep the monotony of farm work at bay. It's normally the little one, John, who starts a song that he picked up on the radio, and the whole family joins in.
What would you give...
what would you give...
...in exchange... ...for your soul... Oh, if today God should call ...
OW!
Just look at my hands...
Stop your dawdling, kids. This field's gotta be harvested by sundown.
Later in the day it moves onto hillbilly songs and fast-paced gospel numbers to help keep spirits up.
As the sun sluggishly sinks towards the horizon the songs also become slower. The day eventually finishes with placid spirituals and the song...
Life's evening sun...
...is sinking...
...low.

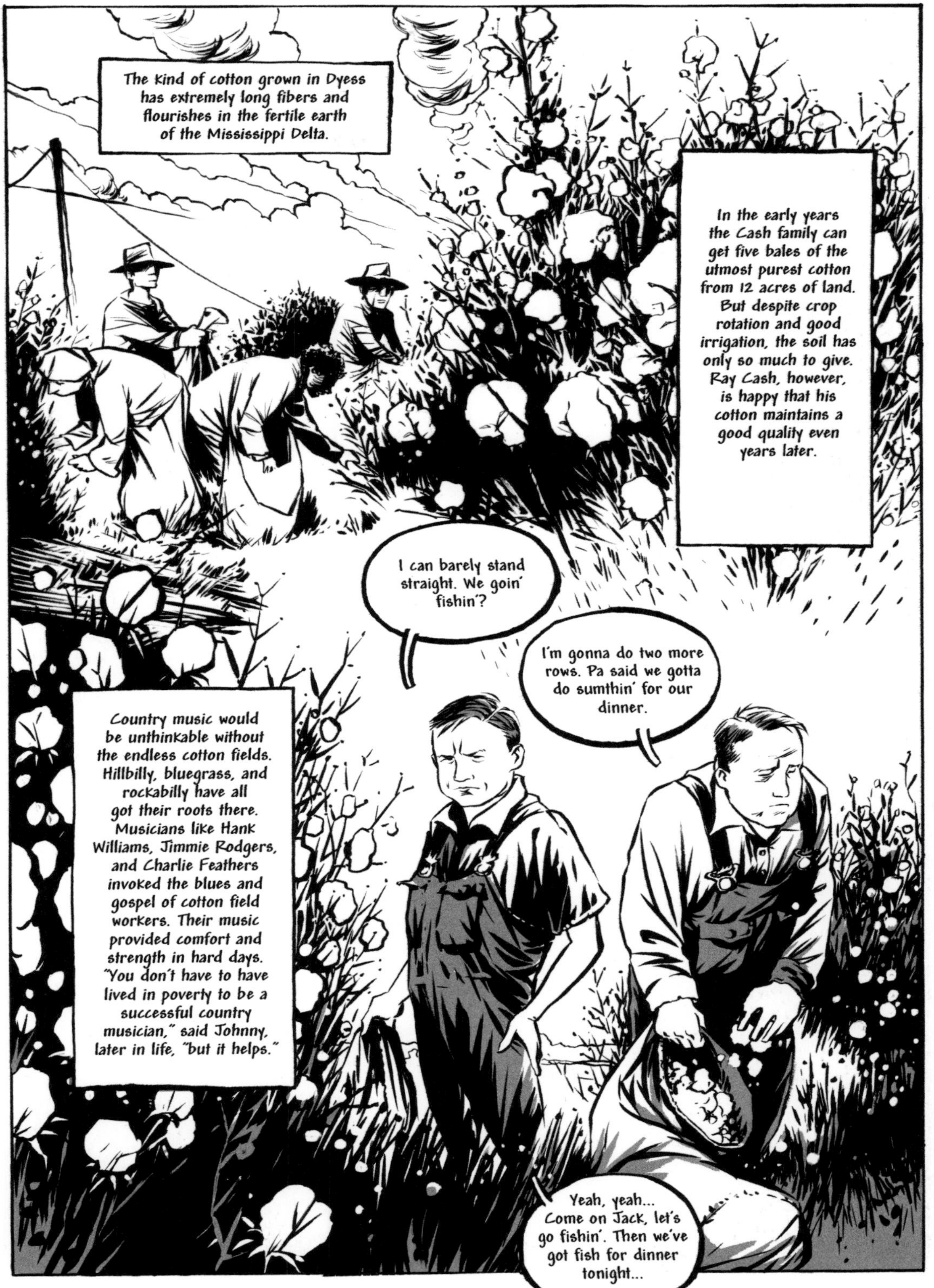
The kind of cotton grown in Dyess has extremely long fibers and flourishes in the fertile earth of the Mississippi Delta.
In the early years the Cash family can get five bales of the utmost purest cotton from 12 acres of land. But despite crop rotation and good irrigation, the soil has only so much to give. Ray Cash, however, is happy that his cotton maintains a good quality even years later.
Country music would be unthinkable without the endless cotton fields. Hillbilly, bluegrass, and rockabilly have all got their roots there. Musicians like Hank Williams, Jimmie Rodgers, and Charlie Feathers invoked the blues and gospel of cotton field workers. Their music provided comfort and strength in hard days. "You don't have to have lived in poverty to be a successful country musician," said Johnny, later in life, "but it helps."
I can barely stand straight. We goin' fishin'?
I'm gonna do two more rows. Pa said we gotta do sumthin' for our dinner.
Yeah, yeah... Come on Jack, let's go fishin'. Then we've got fish for dinner tonight...

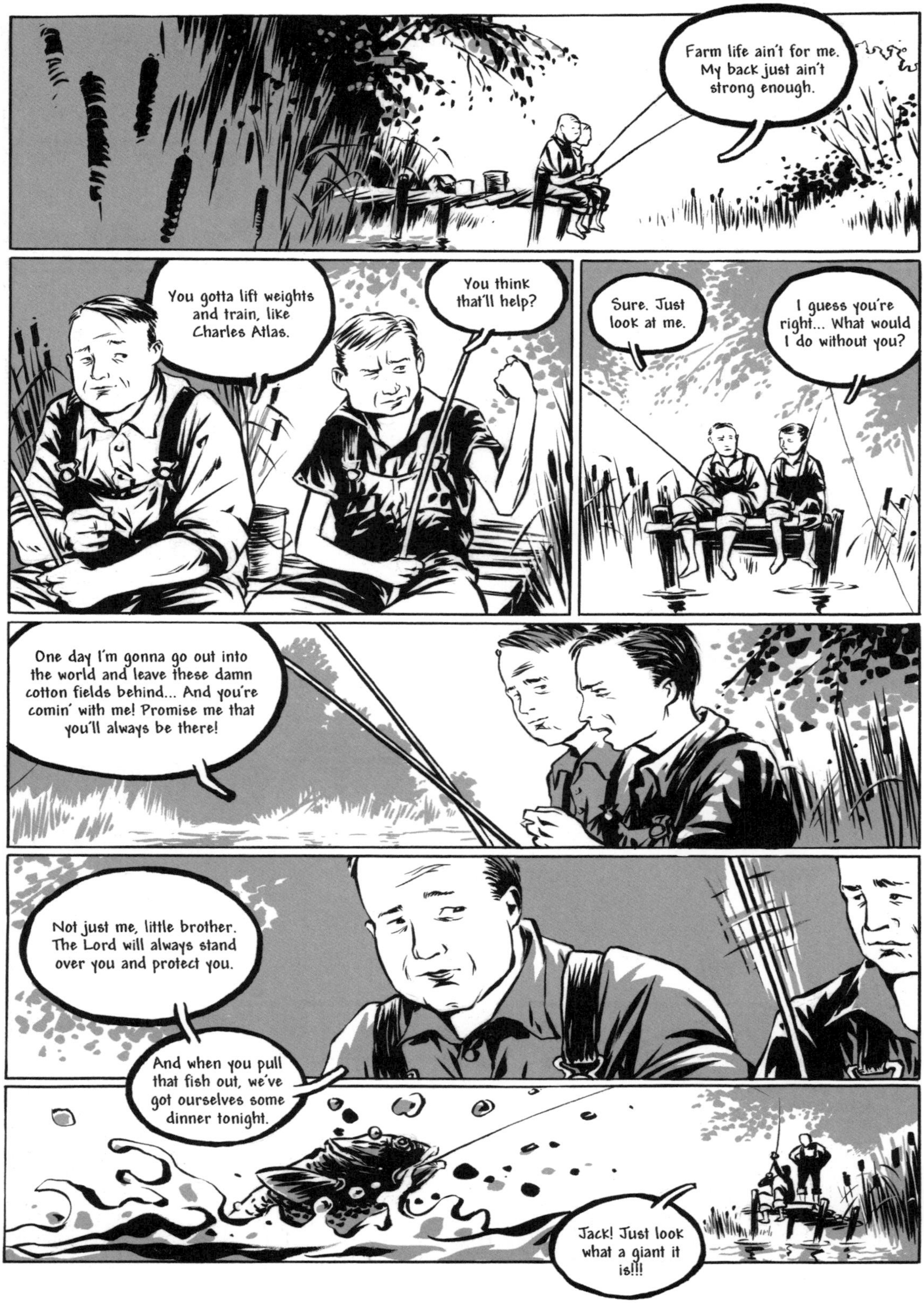

Farm life ain't for me. My back just ain't strong enough.
You gotta lift weights and train, like Charles Atlas.
You think that'll help?
Sure. Just look at me.
I guess you're right... What would I do without you?
One day I'm gonna go out into the world and leave these damn cotton fields behind... And you're comin' with me! Promise me that you'll always be there!
Not just me, little brother. The Lord will always stand over you and protect you.
And when you pull that fish out, we've got ourselves some dinner tonight.
Jack! Just look what a giant it is!!!

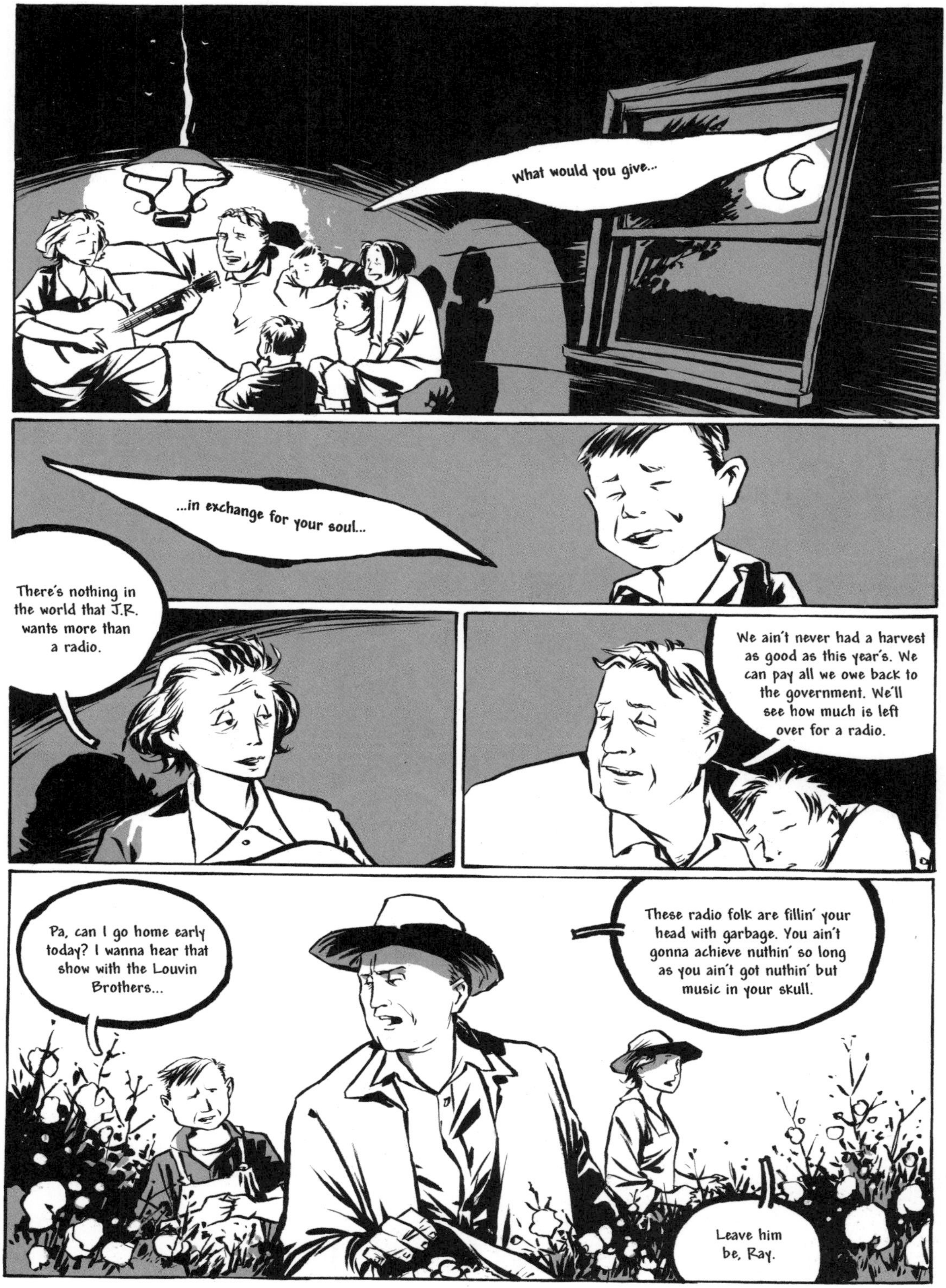
What would you give...
...in exchange for your soul...
There's nothing in the world that J.R. wants more than a radio.
We ain't never had a harvest as good as this year's. We can pay all we owe back to the government. We'll see how much is left over for a radio.
Pa, can I go home early today? I wanna hear that show with the Louvin Brothers...
These radio folk are fillin' your head with garbage. You ain't gonna achieve nuthin' so long as you ain't got nuthin' but music in your skull.
Leave him be, Ray.

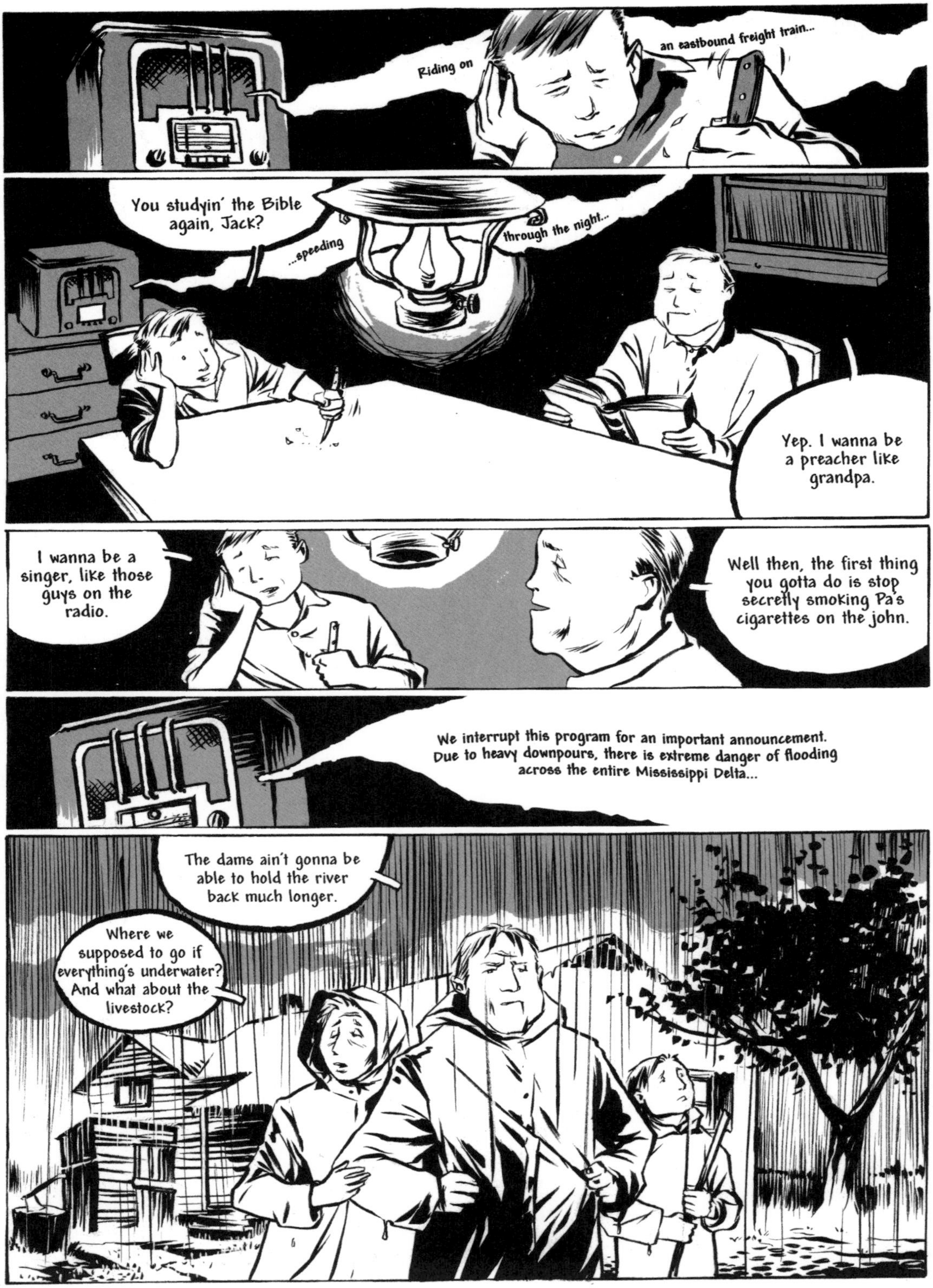
Riding on
an eastbound freight train...
You studyin' the Bible again, Jack?
...speeding
through the night...
Yep. I wanna be a preacher like grandpa.
I wanna be a singer, like those guys on the radio.
Well then, the first thing you gotta do is stop secretly smoking Pa's cigarettes on the john.
We interrupt this program for an important announcement. Due to heavy downpours, there is extreme danger of flooding across the entire Mississippi Delta...
The dams ain't gonna be able to hold the river back much longer.
Where we supposed to go if everything's underwater? And what about the livestock?

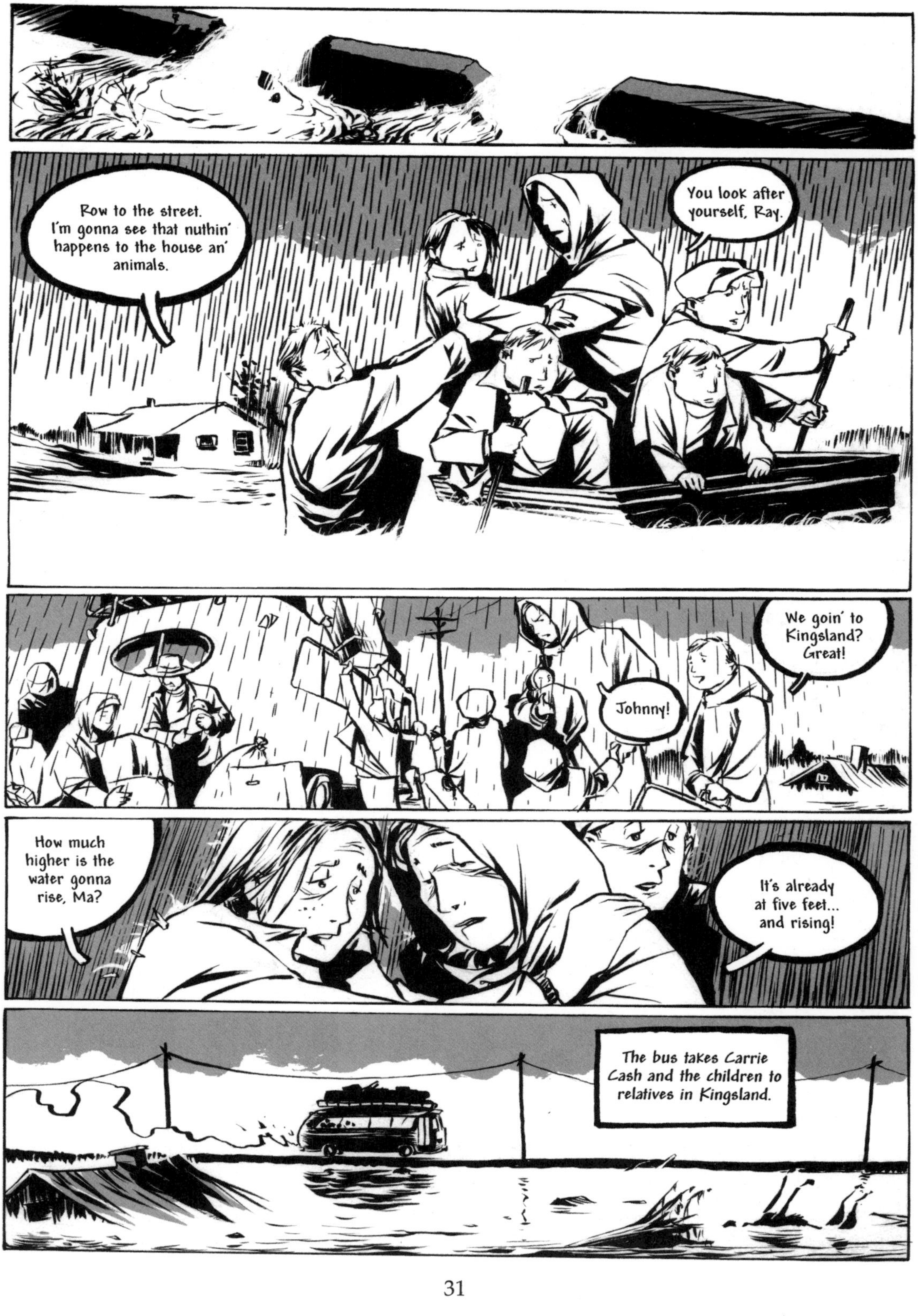
Row to the street. I'm gonna see that nuthin' happens to the house an' animals.
You look after yourself, Ray.
Johnny!
We goin' to Kingsland? Great!
How much higher is the water gonna rise, Ma?
It's already at five feet... and rising!
The bus takes Carrie Cash and the children to relatives in Kingsland.

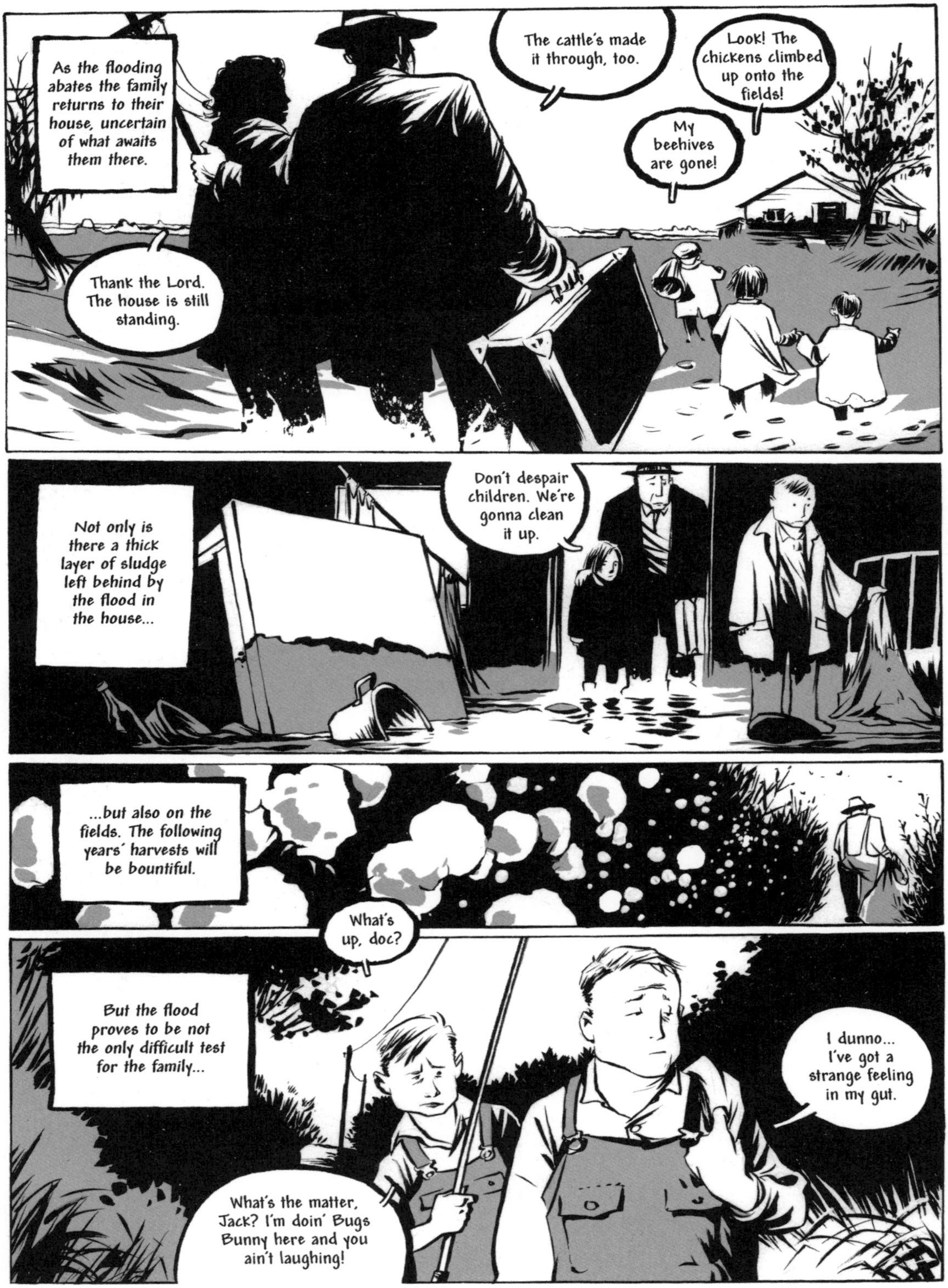
As the flooding abates the family returns to their house, uncertain of what awaits them there.
The cattle's made it through, too.
Look! The chickens climbed up onto the fields!
My beehives are gone!
Thank the Lord. The house is still standing.
Not only is there a thick layer of sludge left behind by the flood in the house...
Don't despair children. We're gonna clean it up.
...but also on the fields. The following years' harvests will be bountiful.
What's up, doc?
But the flood proves to be not the only difficult test for the family...
I dunno... I've got a strange feeling in my gut.
What's the matter, Jack? I'm doin' Bugs Bunny here and you ain't laughing!

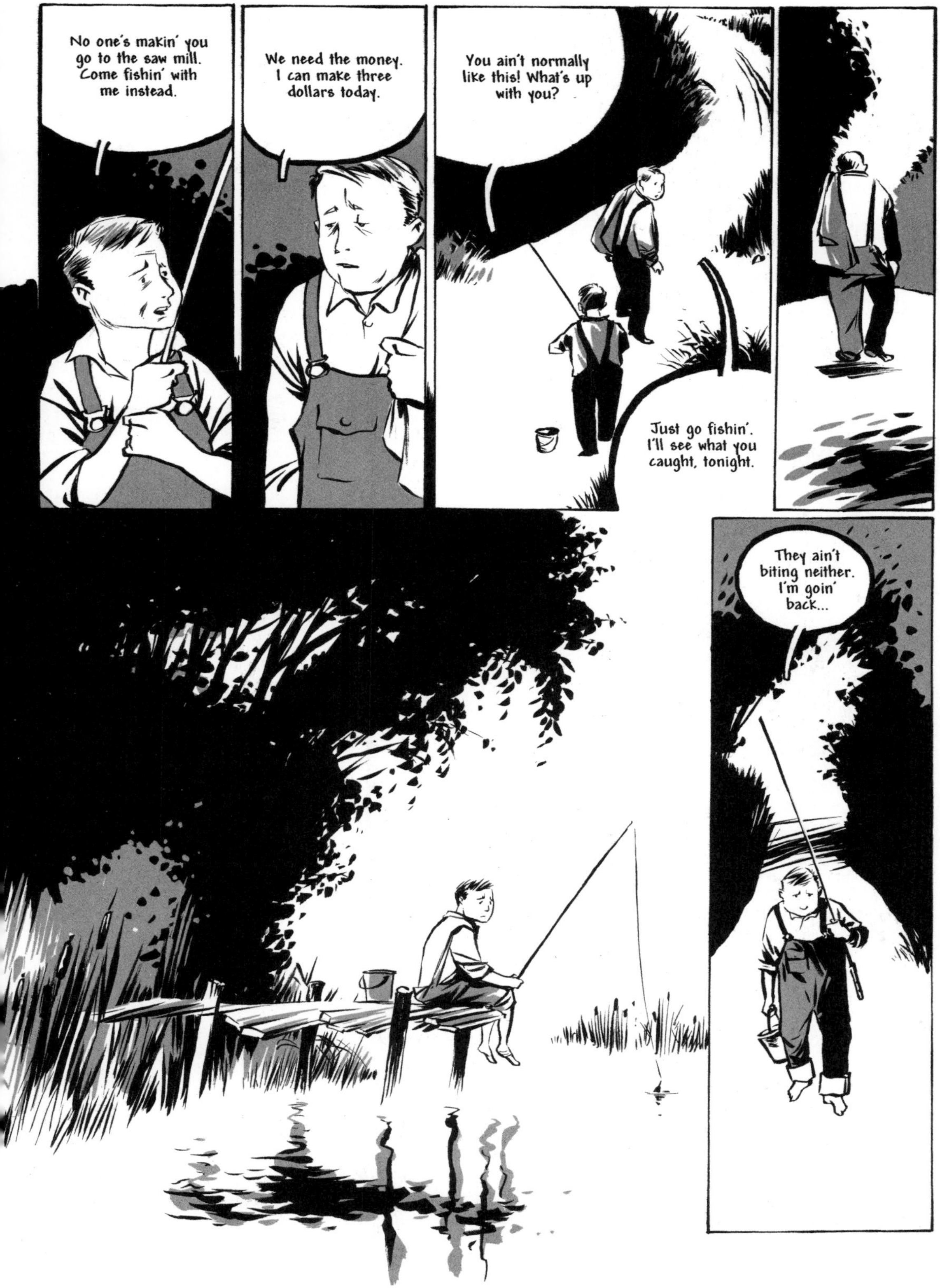
No one's makin' you go to the saw mill. Come fishin' with me instead.
We need the money. I can make three dollars today.
You ain't normally like this! What's up with you?
Just go fishin'. I'll see what you caught, tonight.
They ain't biting neither. I'm goin' back...

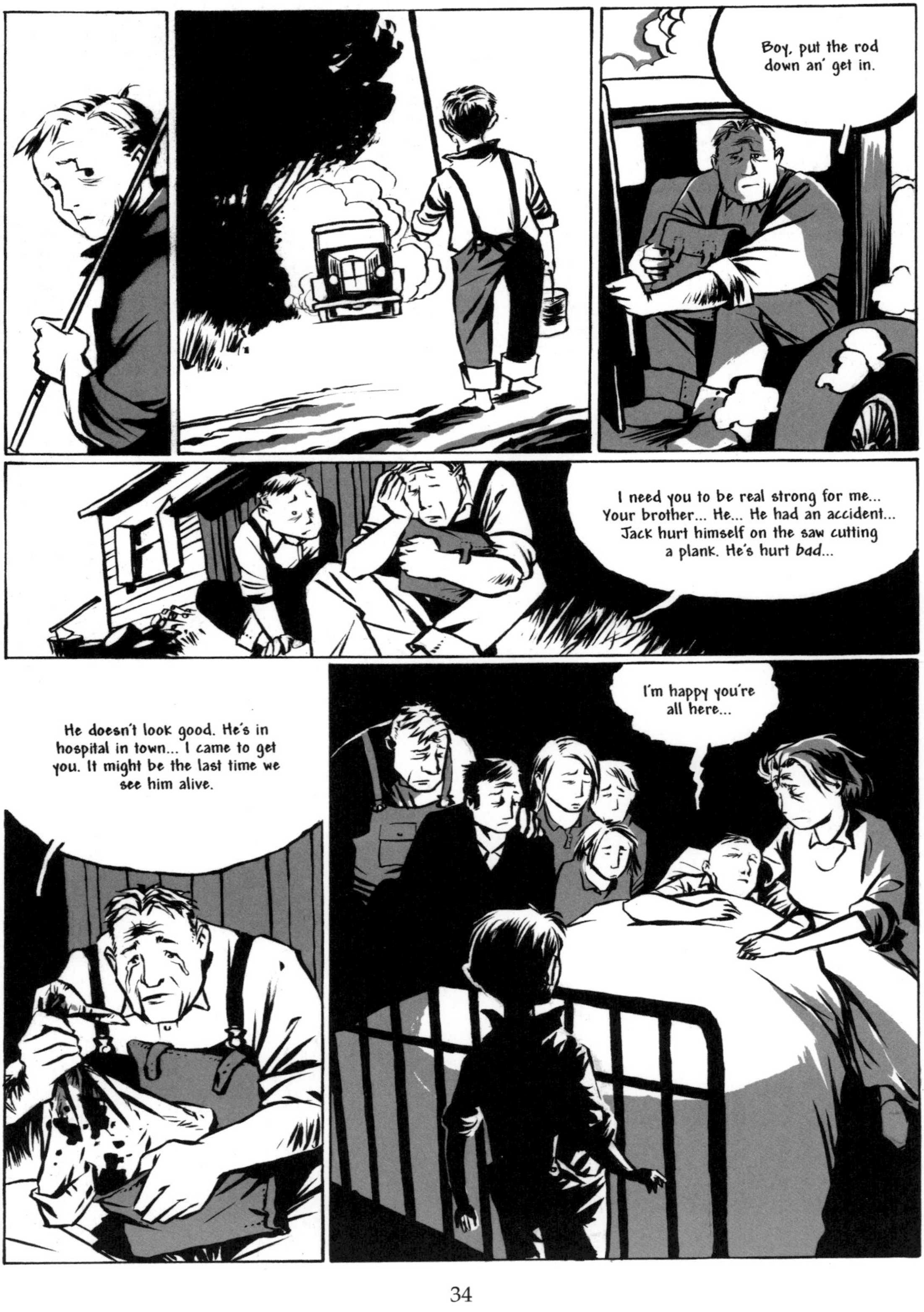
Boy, put the rod down an' get in.
I need you to be real strong for me... Your brother... He... He had an accident... Jack hurt himself on the saw cutting a plank. He's hurt *bad*...
He doesn't look good. He's in hospital in town... I came to get you. It might be the last time we see him alive.
I'm happy you're all here...

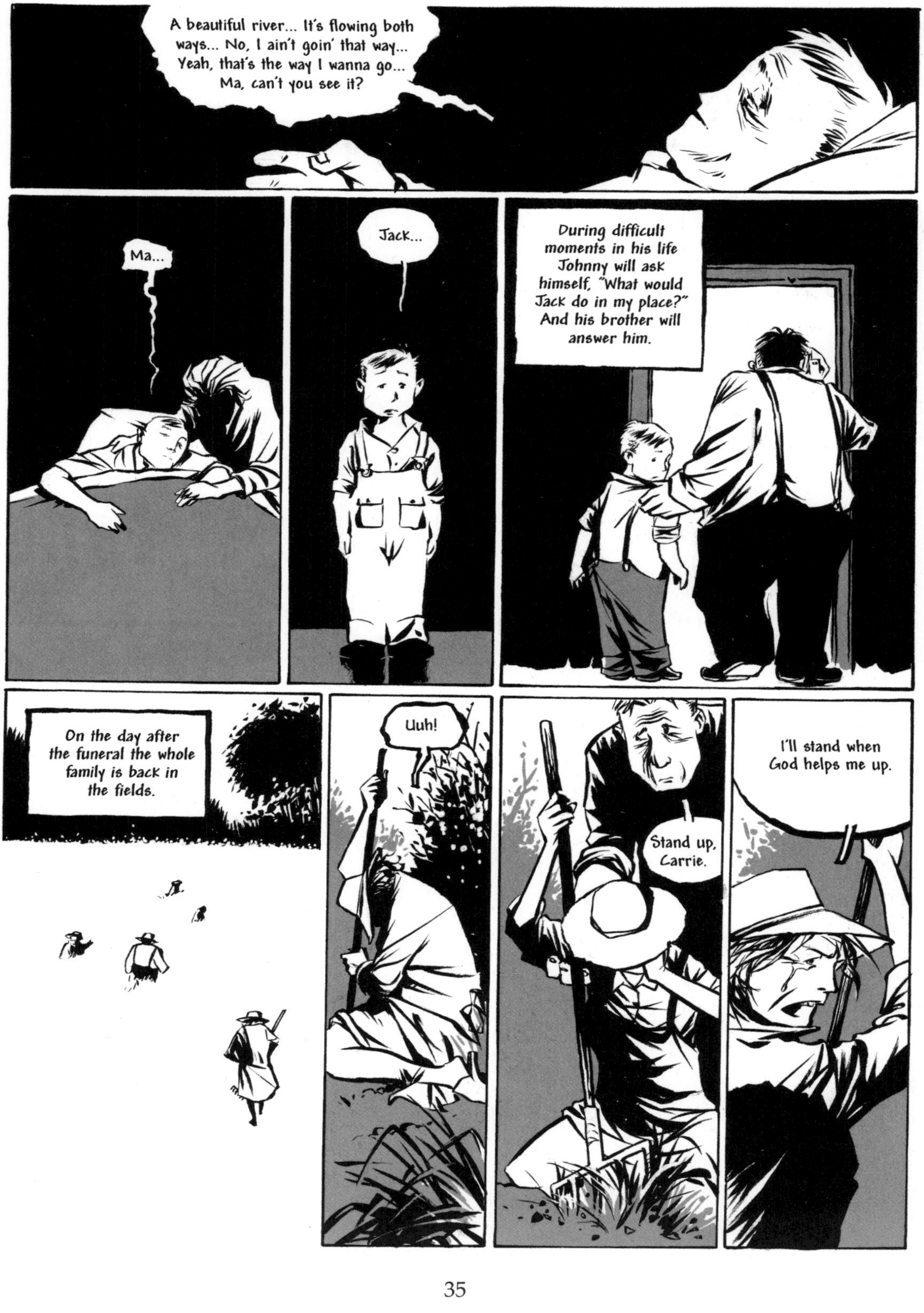
A beautiful river... It's flowing both ways... No, I ain't goin' that way... Yeah, that's the way I wanna go... Ma, can't you see it?
Ma...
Jack...
During difficult moments in his life Johnny will ask himself, "What would Jack do in my place?" And his brother will answer him.
On the day after the funeral the whole family is back in the fields.
Uuh!
Stand up, Carrie.
I'll stand when God helps me up.

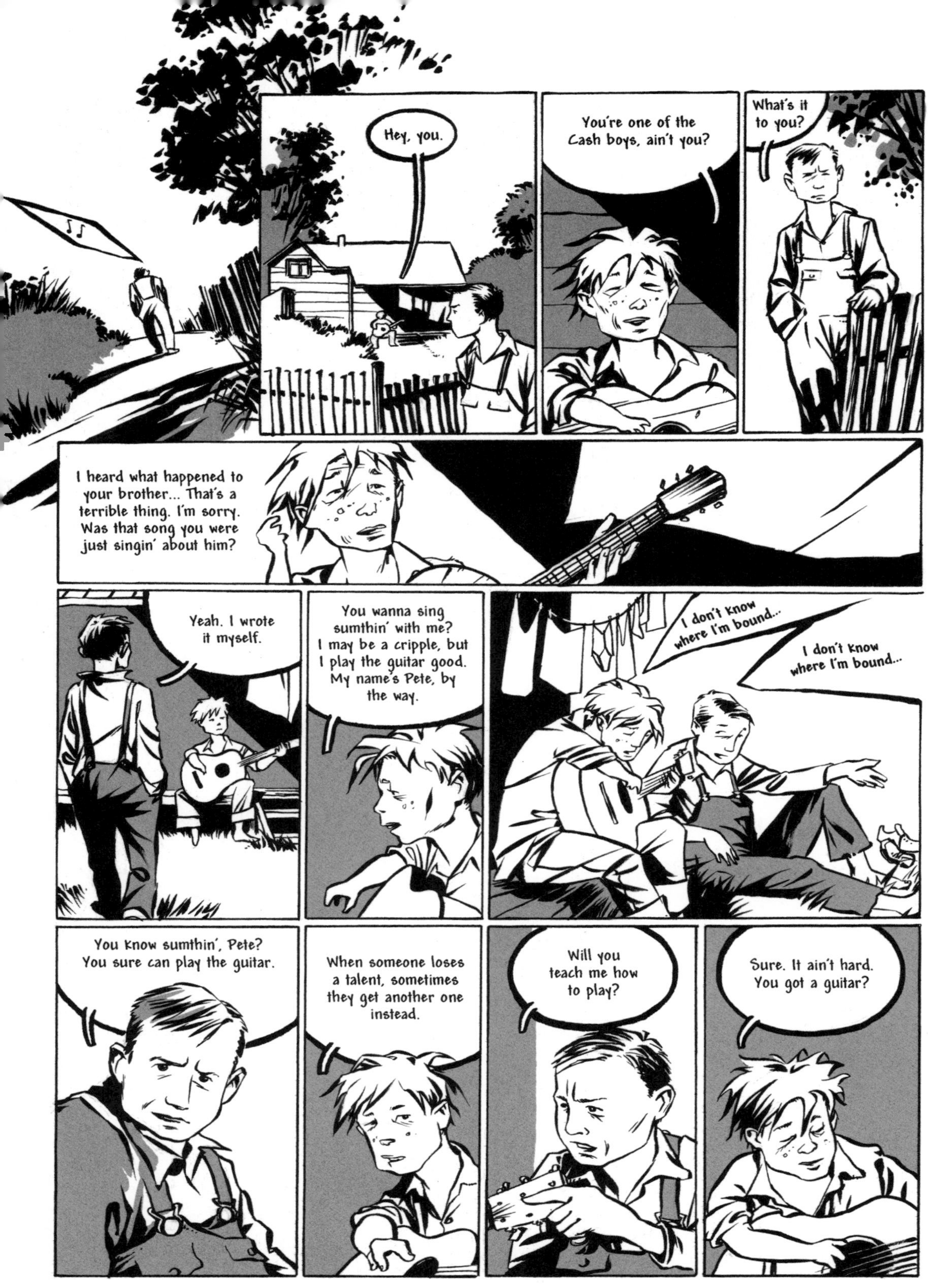
Hey, you.
You're one of the Cash boys, ain't you?
What's it to you?
I heard what happened to your brother... That's a terrible thing. I'm sorry. Was that song you were just singin' about him?
Yeah. I wrote it myself.
You wanna sing sumthin' with me? I may be a cripple, but I play the guitar good. My name's Pete, by the way.
I don't know where I'm bound...
I don't know where I'm bound...
You know sumthin', Pete? You sure can play the guitar.
When someone loses a talent, sometimes they get another one instead.
Will you teach me how to play?
Sure. It ain't hard. You got a guitar?

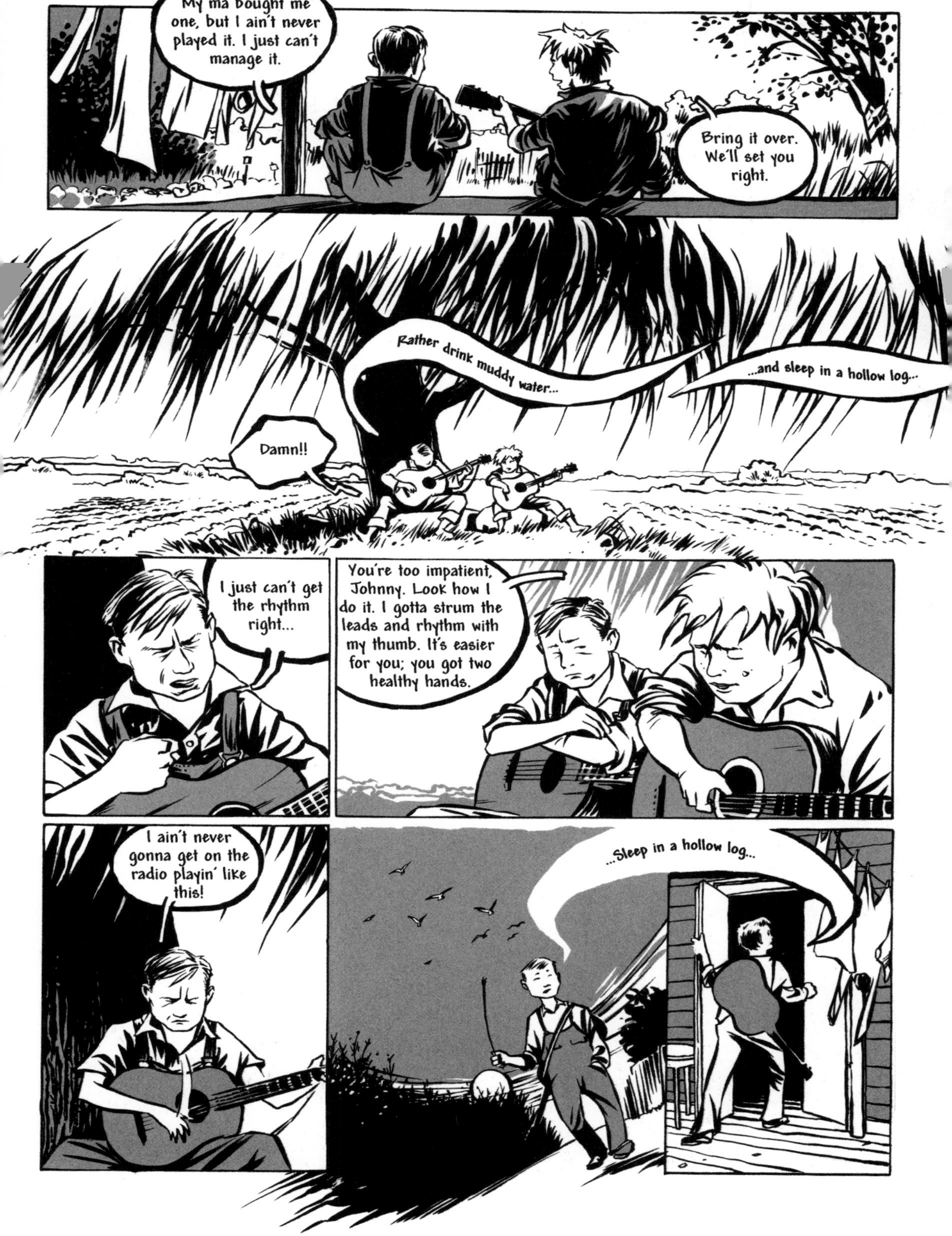
My ma bought me one, but I ain't never played it. I just can't manage it.
Bring it over. We'll set you right.
Rather drink muddy water...
...and sleep in a hollow log...
Damn!!
I just can't get the rhythm right...
You're too impatient, Johnny. Look how I do it. I gotta strum the leads and rhythm with my thumb. It's easier for you; you got two healthy hands.
I ain't never gonna get on the radio playin' like this!
...Sleep in a hollow log...

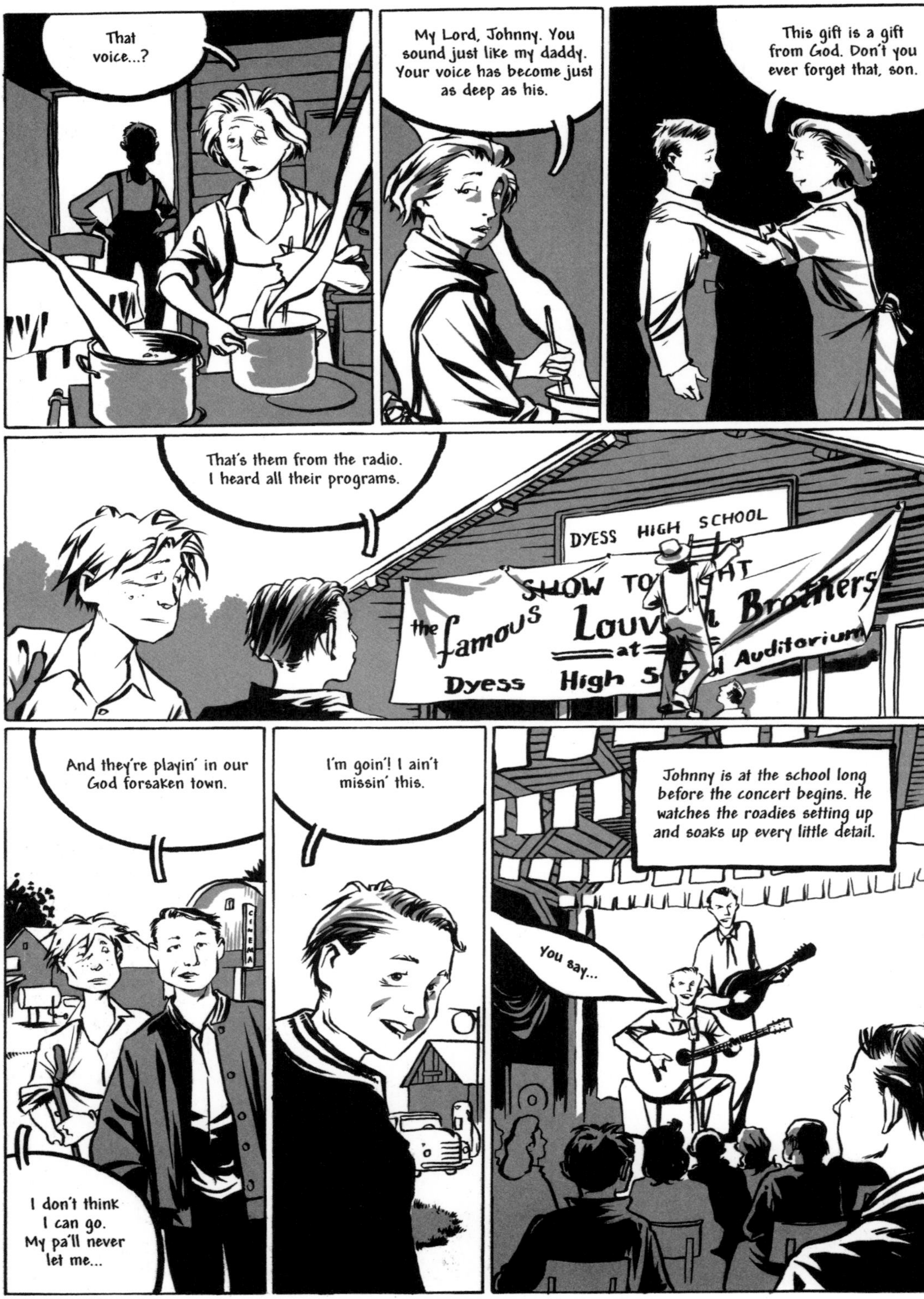
That voice...?
My Lord, Johnny. You sound just like my daddy. Your voice has become just as deep as his.
This gift is a gift from God. Don't you ever forget that, son.
That's them from the radio. I heard all their programs.
DYESS HIGH SCHOOL
the famous Louv
Brothers
at
Dyess High S
Auditorium
And they're playin' in our God forsaken town.
I don't think I can go. My pa'll never let me...
CINEMA
I'm goin'! I ain't missin' this.
Johnny is at the school long before the concert begins. He watches the roadies setting up and soaks up every little detail.
You say...

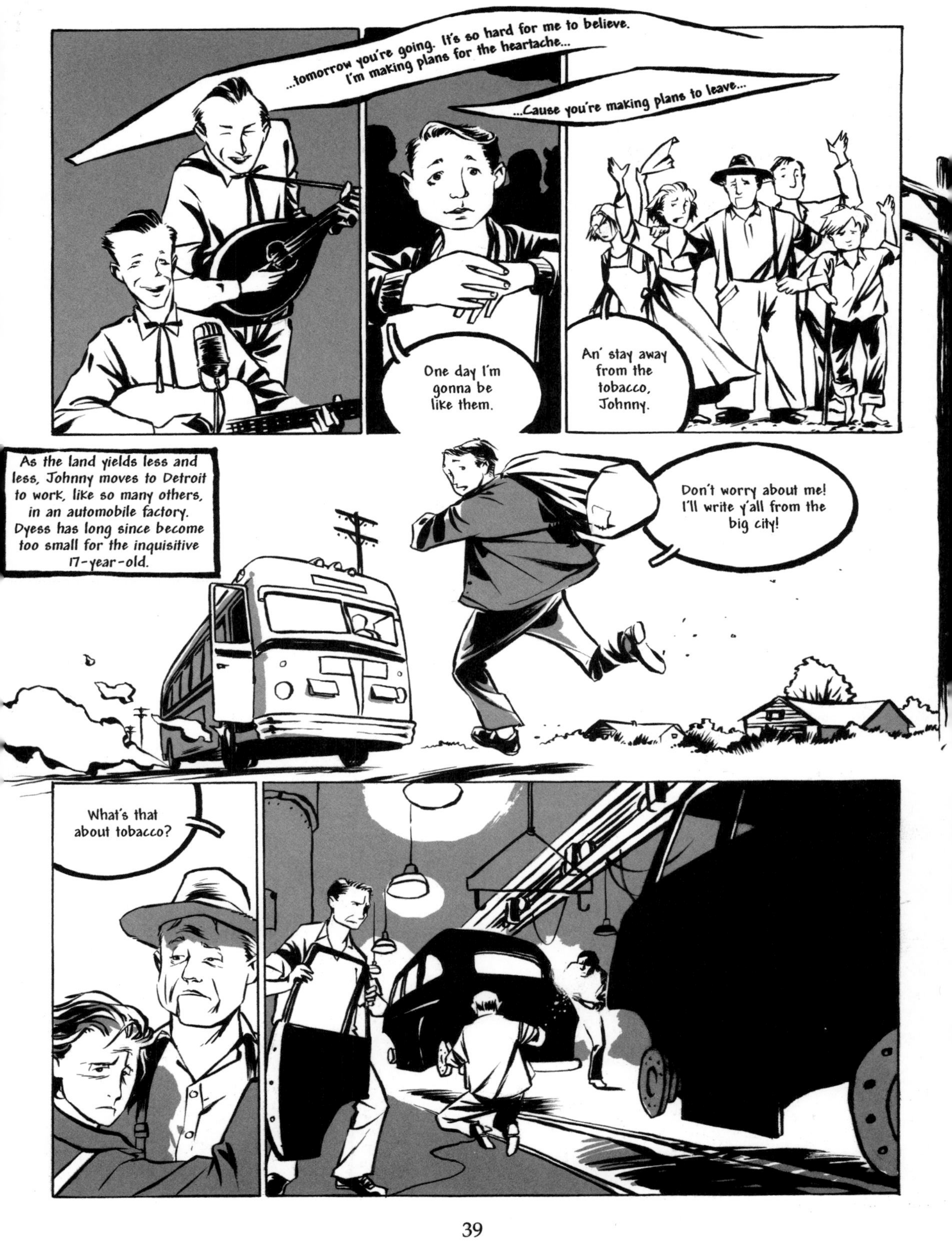
...tomorrow you're going. It's so hard for me to believe.
I'm making plans for the heartache...
...Cause you're making plans to leave...
One day I'm gonna be like them.
An' stay away from the tobacco, Johnny.
As the land yields less and less, Johnny moves to Detroit to work, like so many others, in an automobile factory. Dyess has long since become too small for the inquisitive 17-year-old.
Don't worry about me! I'll write y'all from the big city!
What's that about tobacco?

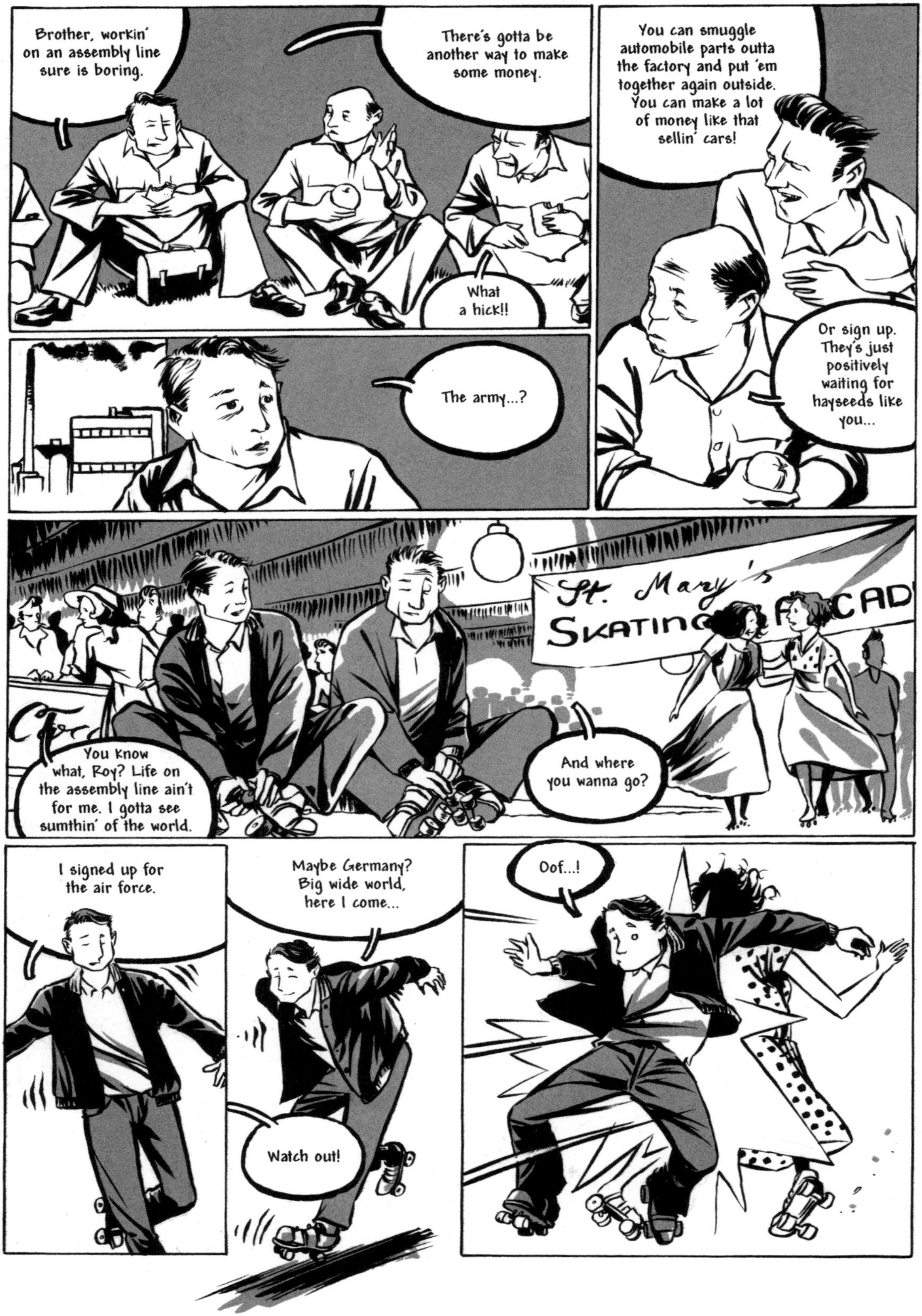

Brother, workin' on an assembly line sure is boring.
There's gotta be another way to make some money.
What a hick!!
You can smuggle automobile parts outta the factory and put 'em together again outside. You can make a lot of money like that sellin' cars!
The army...?
Or sign up. They's just positively waiting for hayseeds like you...
St. Mary's Skating
You know what, Roy? Life on the assembly line ain't for me. I gotta see sumthin' of the world.
And where you wanna go?
I signed up for the air force.
Maybe Germany? Big wide world, here I come...
Watch out!
Oof...!

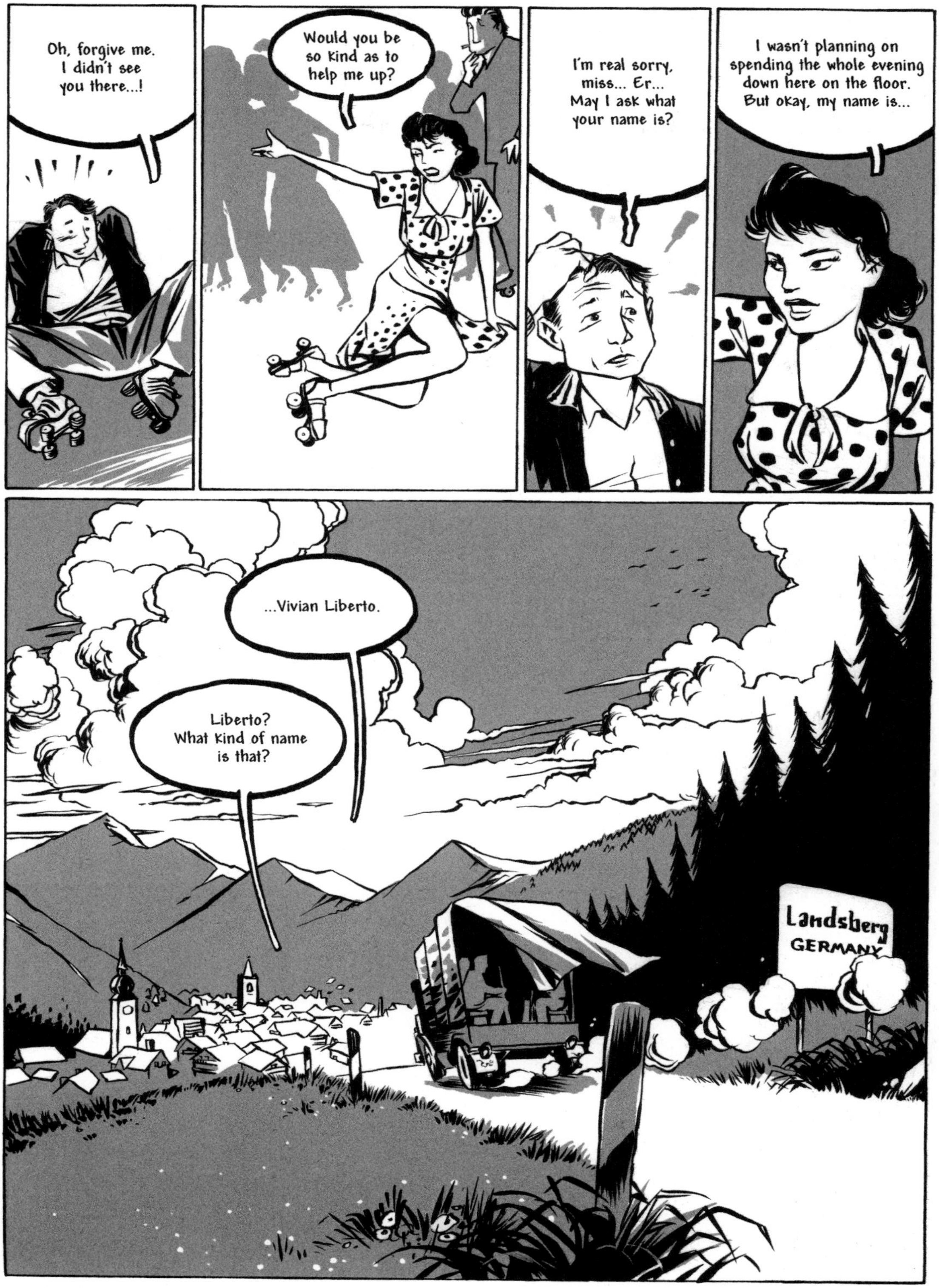
Oh, forgive me. I didn't see you there...!
Would you be so kind as to help me up?
I'm real sorry, miss... Er... May I ask what your name is?
I wasn't planning on spending the whole evening down here on the floor. But okay, my name is...
...Vivian Liberto.
Liberto? What kind of name is that?
Landsberg
GERMANY

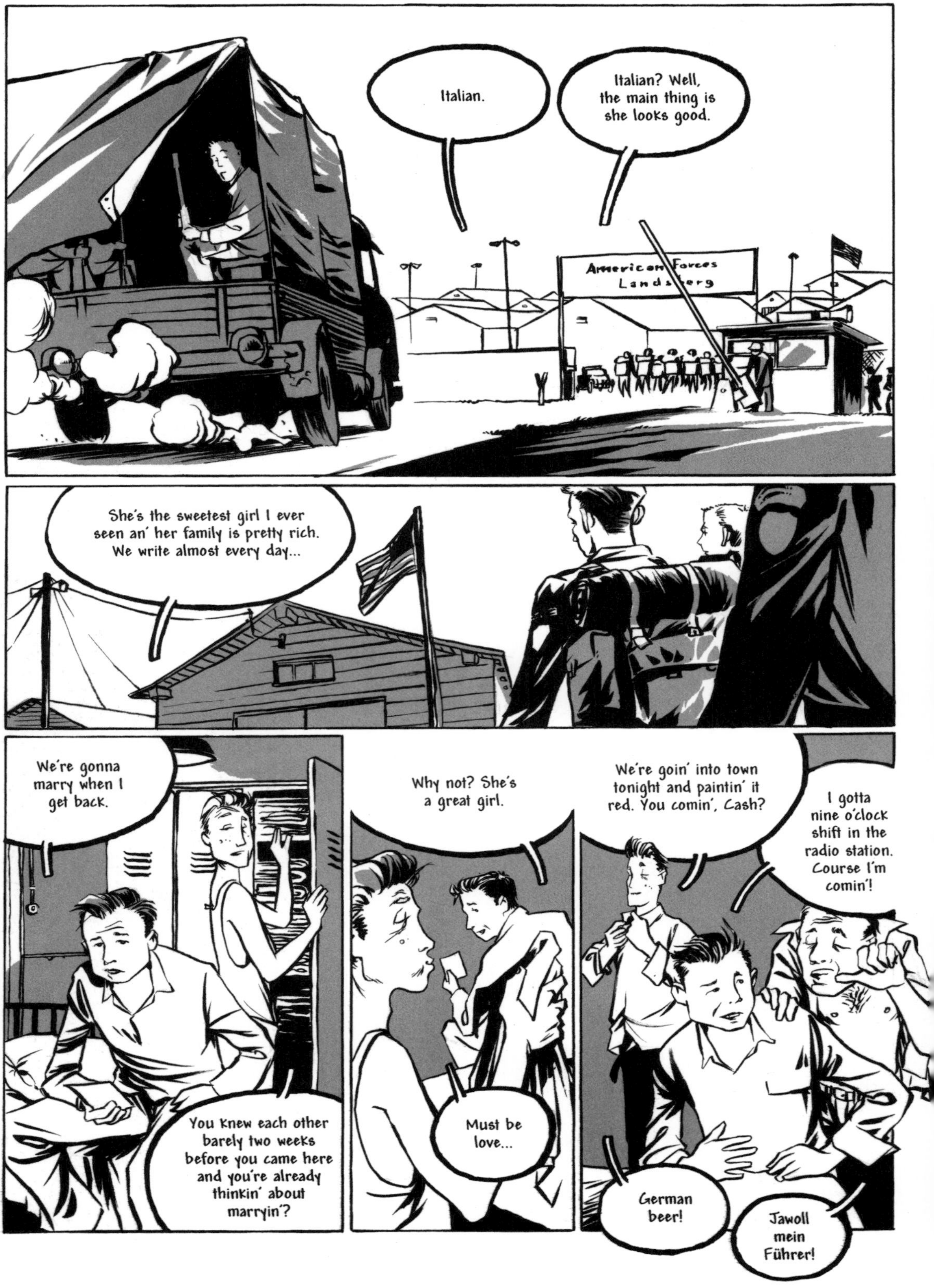
Italian.
Italian? Well, the main thing is she looks good.
American Forces Landsberg
She's the sweetest girl I ever seen an' her family is pretty rich. We write almost every day...
We're gonna marry when I get back.
You knew each other barely two weeks before you came here and you're already thinkin' about marryin'?
Why not? She's a great girl.
Must be love...
We're goin' into town tonight and paintin' it red. You comin', Cash?
I gotta nine o'clock shift in the radio station. Course I'm comin'!
German beer!
Jawoll mein Führer!

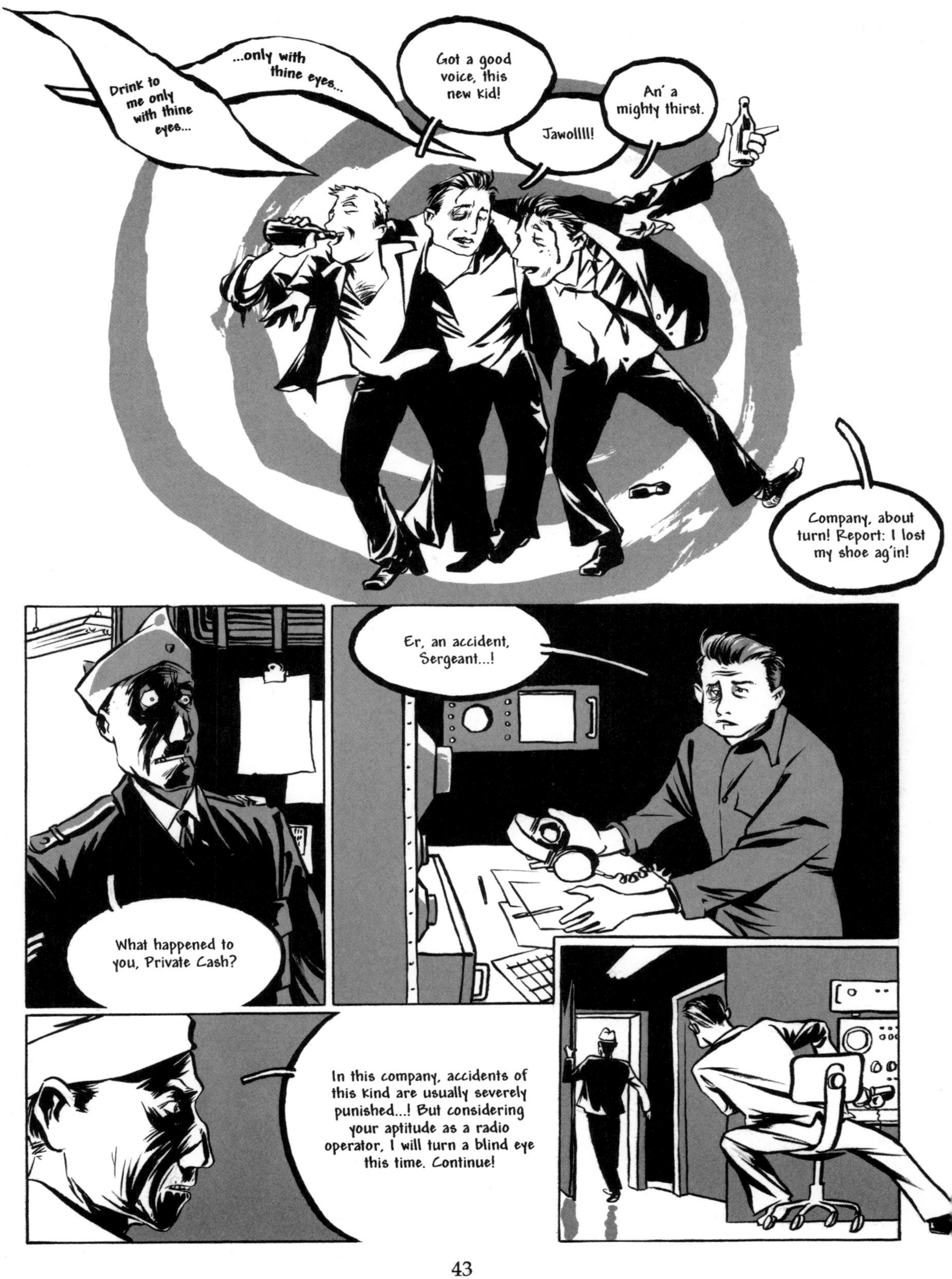
Drink to me only with thine eyes...
...only with thine eyes...
Got a good voice, this new kid!
Jawollll!
An' a mighty thirst.
Company, about turn! Report: I lost my shoe ag'in!
What happened to you, Private Cash?
Er, an accident, Sergeant...!
In this company, accidents of this kind are usually severely punished...! But considering your aptitude as a radio operator, I will turn a blind eye this time. Continue!

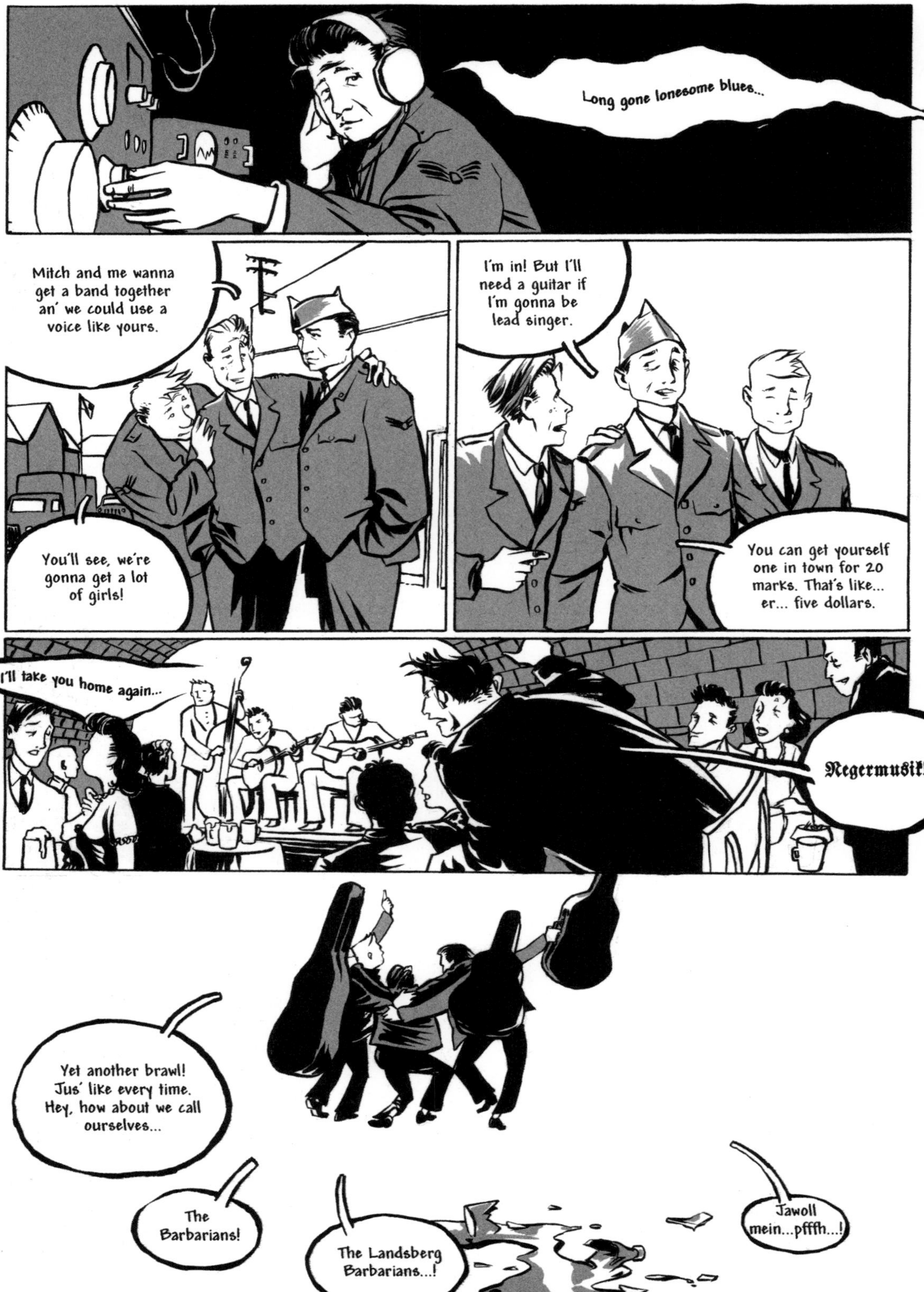

Long gone lonesome blues...
Mitch and me wanna get a band together an' we could use a voice like yours.
You'll see, we're gonna get a lot of girls!
I'm in! But I'll need a guitar if I'm gonna be lead singer.
You can get yourself one in town for 20 marks. That's like... er... five dollars.
I'll take you home again...
Negermusik!!!
Yet another brawl! Jus' like every time. Hey, how about we call ourselves...
The Barbarians!
The Landsberg Barbarians...!
Jawoll mein...pfffh...!

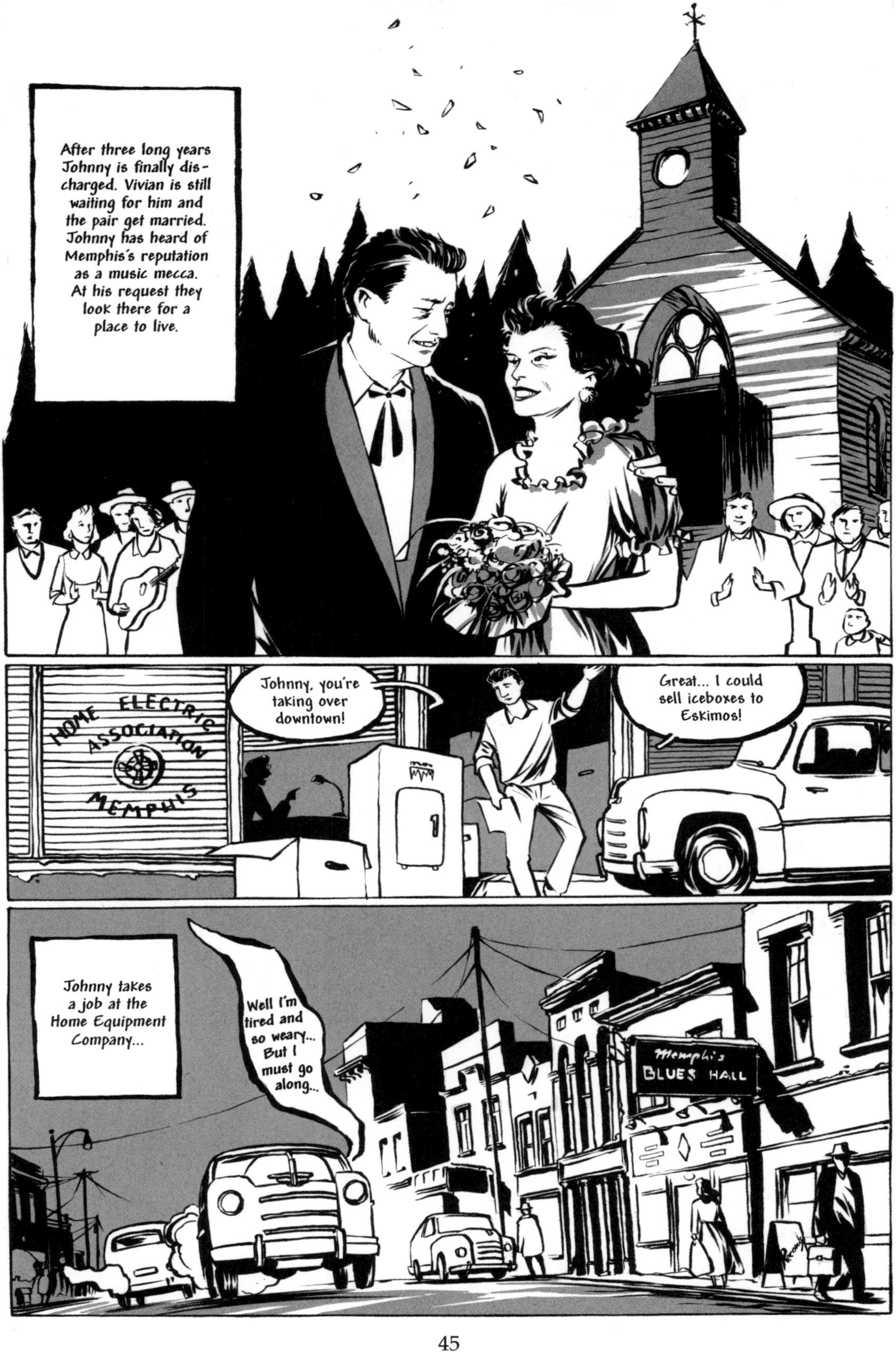
After three long years Johnny is finally discharged. Vivian is still waiting for him and the pair get married. Johnny has heard of Memphis's reputation as a music mecca. At his request they look there for a place to live.
HOME ELECTRIC ASSOCIATION MEMPHIS
Johnny, you're taking over downtown!
Great... I could sell iceboxes to Eskimos!
Johnny takes a job at the Home Equipment Company...
Well I'm tired and so weary... But I must go along...
Memphi's BLUES HALL

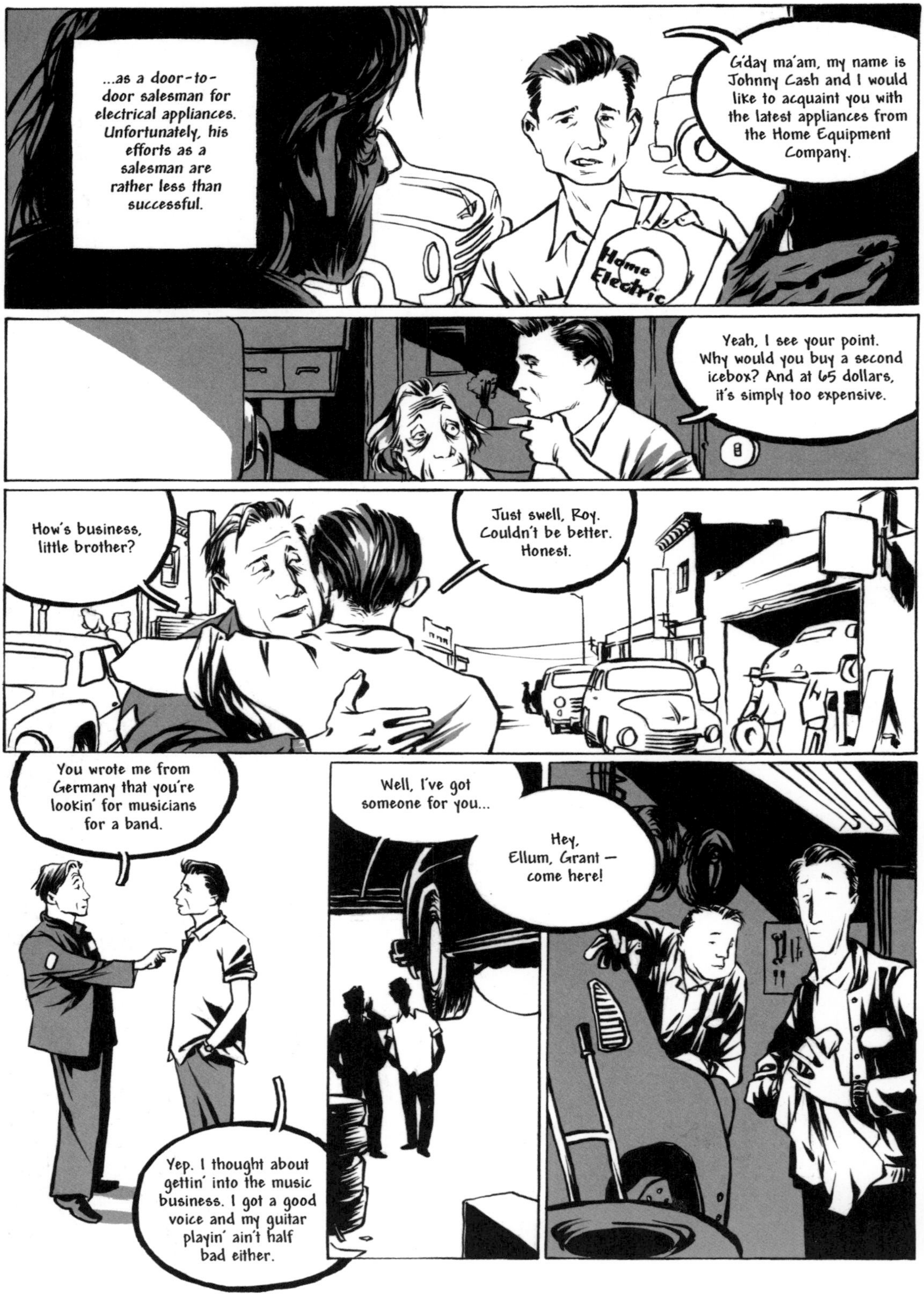

...as a door-to-door salesman for electrical appliances. Unfortunately, his efforts as a salesman are rather less than successful.
G'day ma'am, my name is Johnny Cash and I would like to acquaint you with the latest appliances from the Home Equipment Company.
Home Electric
Yeah, I see your point. Why would you buy a second icebox? And at 65 dollars, it's simply too expensive.
How's business, little brother?
Just swell, Roy. Couldn't be better. Honest.
You wrote me from Germany that you're lookin' for musicians for a band.
Yep. I thought about gettin' into the music business. I got a good voice and my guitar playin' ain't half bad either.
Well, I've got someone for you...
Hey, Ellum, Grant — come here!

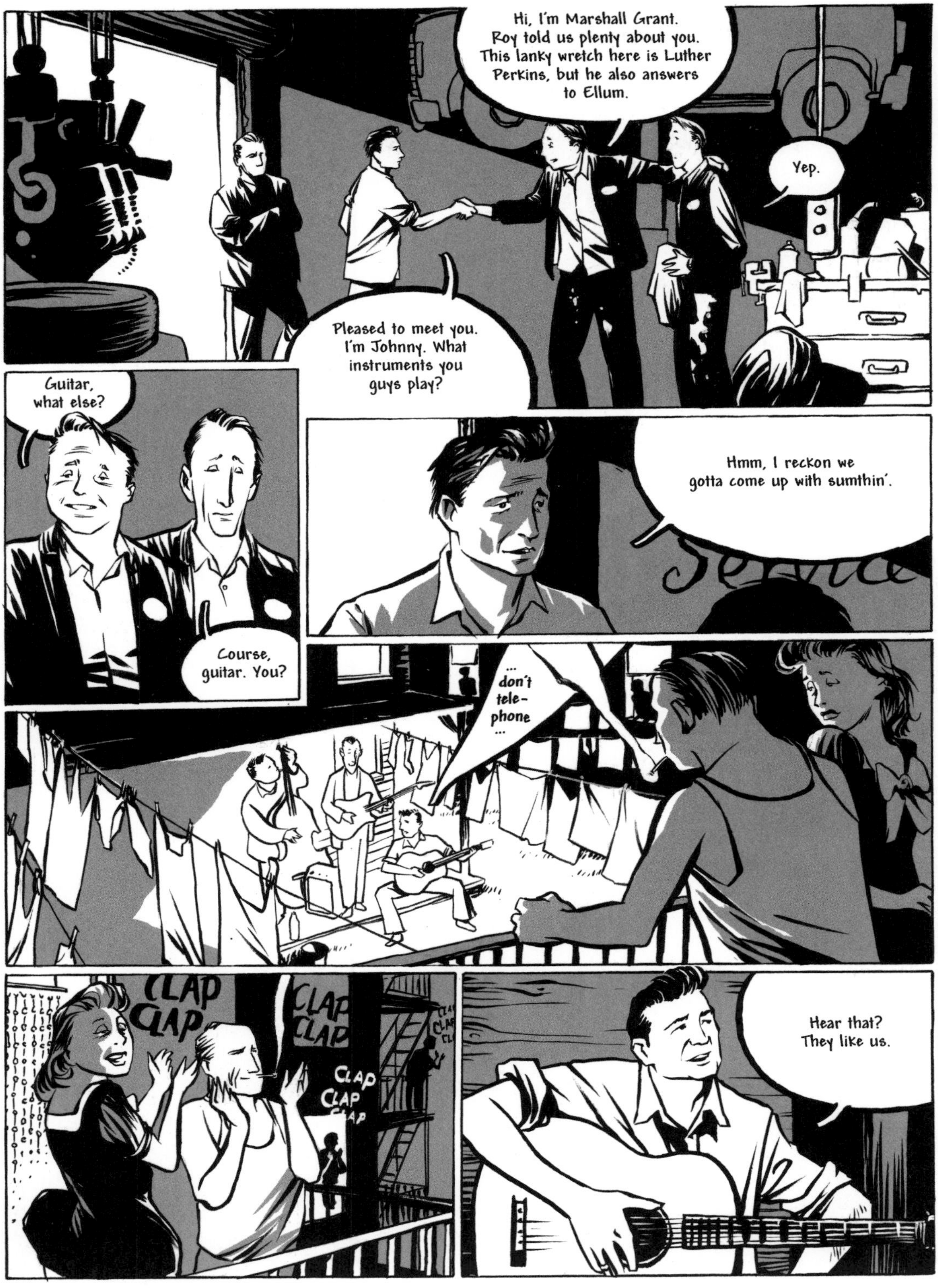
Hi, I'm Marshall Grant. Roy told us plenty about you. This lanky wretch here is Luther Perkins, but he also answers to Ellum.
Yep.
Pleased to meet you. I'm Johnny. What instruments you guys play?
Guitar, what else?
Course, guitar. You?
Hmm, I reckon we gotta come up with sumthin'.
... don't tele- phone ...
CLAP CLAP
CLAP CLAP
CLAP CLAP
Hear that? They like us.

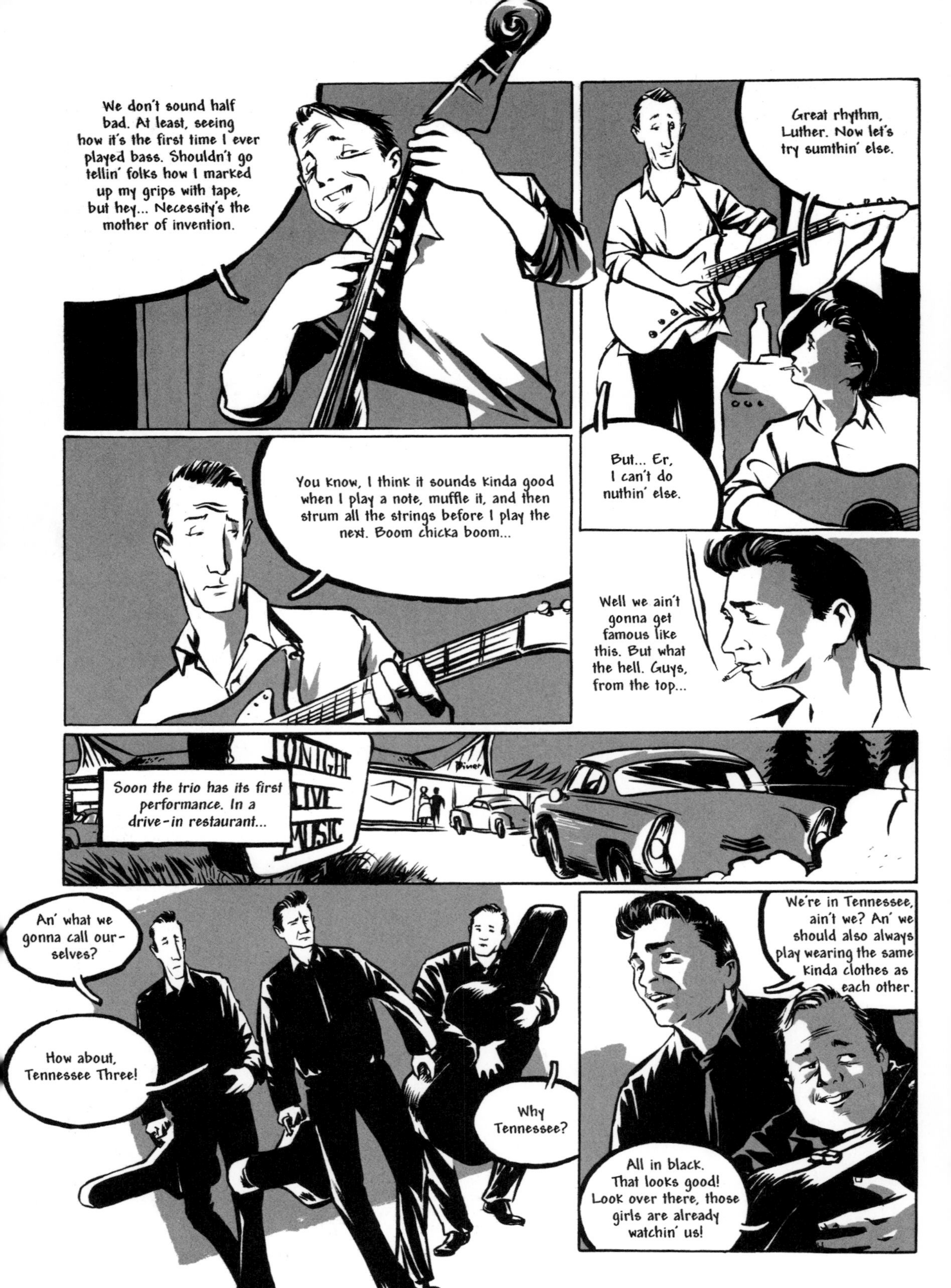
We don't sound half bad. At least, seeing how it's the first time I ever played bass. Shouldn't go tellin' folks how I marked up my grips with tape, but hey... Necessity's the mother of invention.
Great rhythm, Luther. Now let's try sumthin' else.
But... Er, I can't do nuthin' else.
You know, I think it sounds kinda good when I play a note, muffle it, and then strum all the strings before I play the next. Boom chicka boom...
Well we ain't gonna get famous like this. But what the hell. Guys, from the top...
TONIGHT LIVE MUSIC
Diner
Soon the trio has its first performance. In a drive-in restaurant...
An' what we gonna call ourselves?
How about, Tennessee Three!
Why Tennessee?
We're in Tennessee, ain't we? An' we should also always play wearing the same kinda clothes as each other.
All in black. That looks good! Look over there, those girls are already watchin' us!

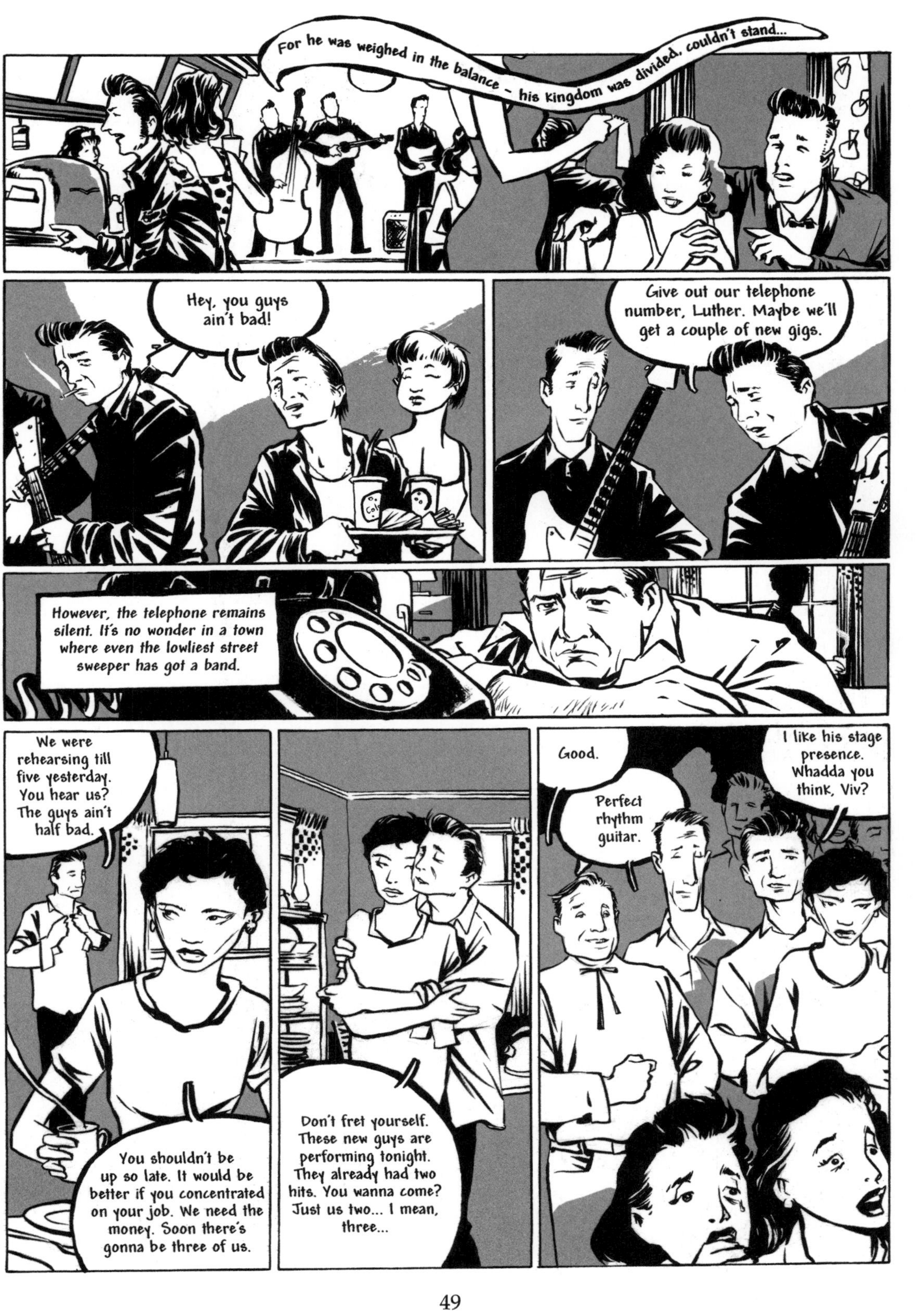
For he was weighed in the balance – his kingdom was divided, couldn't stand...
Hey, you guys ain't bad!
Give out our telephone number, Luther. Maybe we'll get a couple of new gigs.
However, the telephone remains silent. It's no wonder in a town where even the lowliest street sweeper has got a band.
We were rehearsing till five yesterday. You hear us? The guys ain't half bad.
You shouldn't be up so late. It would be better if you concentrated on your job. We need the money. Soon there's gonna be three of us.
Don't fret yourself. These new guys are performing tonight. They already had two hits. You wanna come? Just us two... I mean, three...
Good.
Perfect rhythm guitar.
I like his stage presence. Whadda you think, Viv?

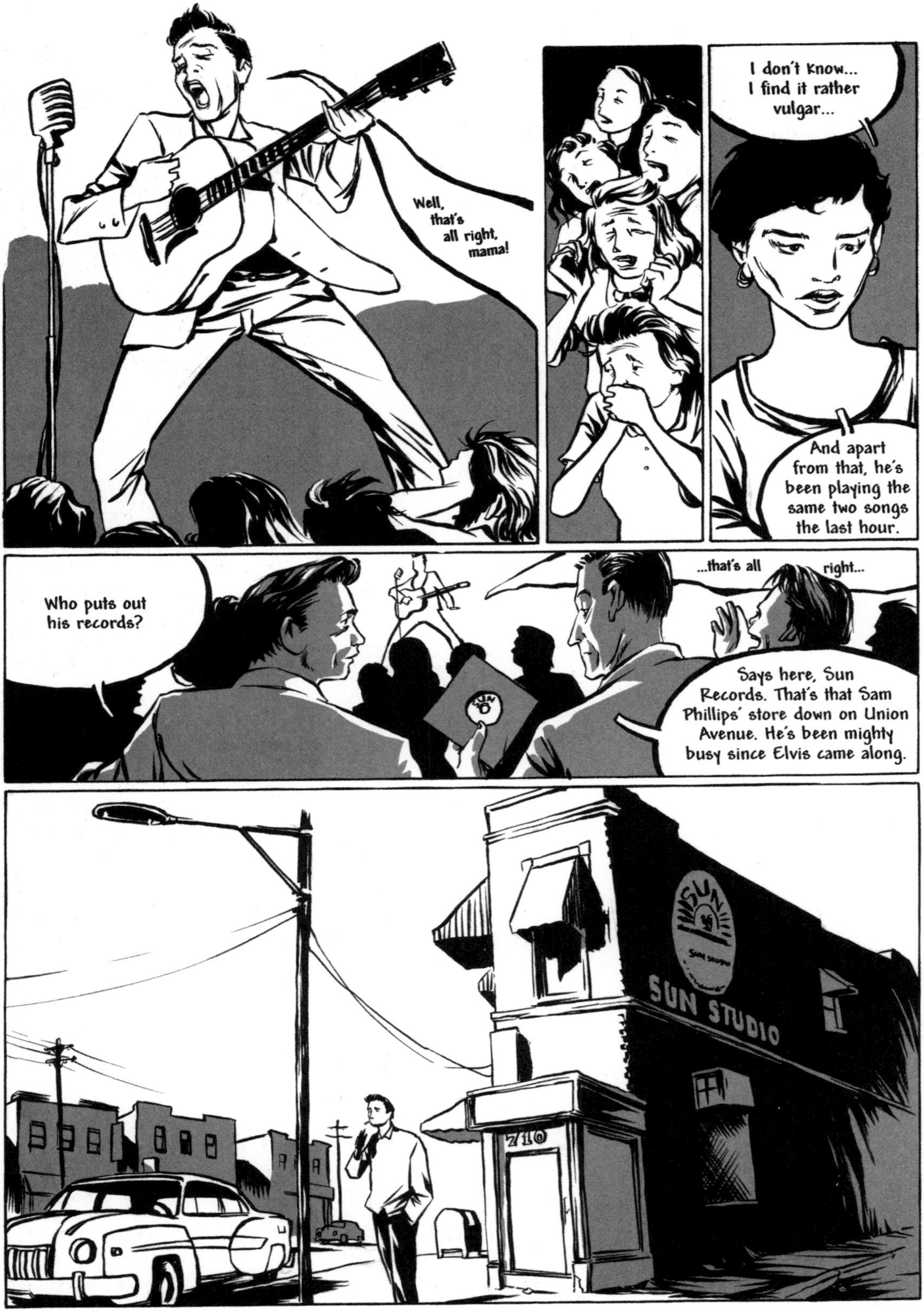
Well, that's all right, mama!
I don't know... I find it rather vulgar...
And apart from that, he's been playing the same two songs the last hour.
Who puts out his records?
...that's all right...
Says here, Sun Records. That's that Sam Phillips' store down on Union Avenue. He's been mighty busy since Elvis came along.
SUN
SUN STUDIO
710

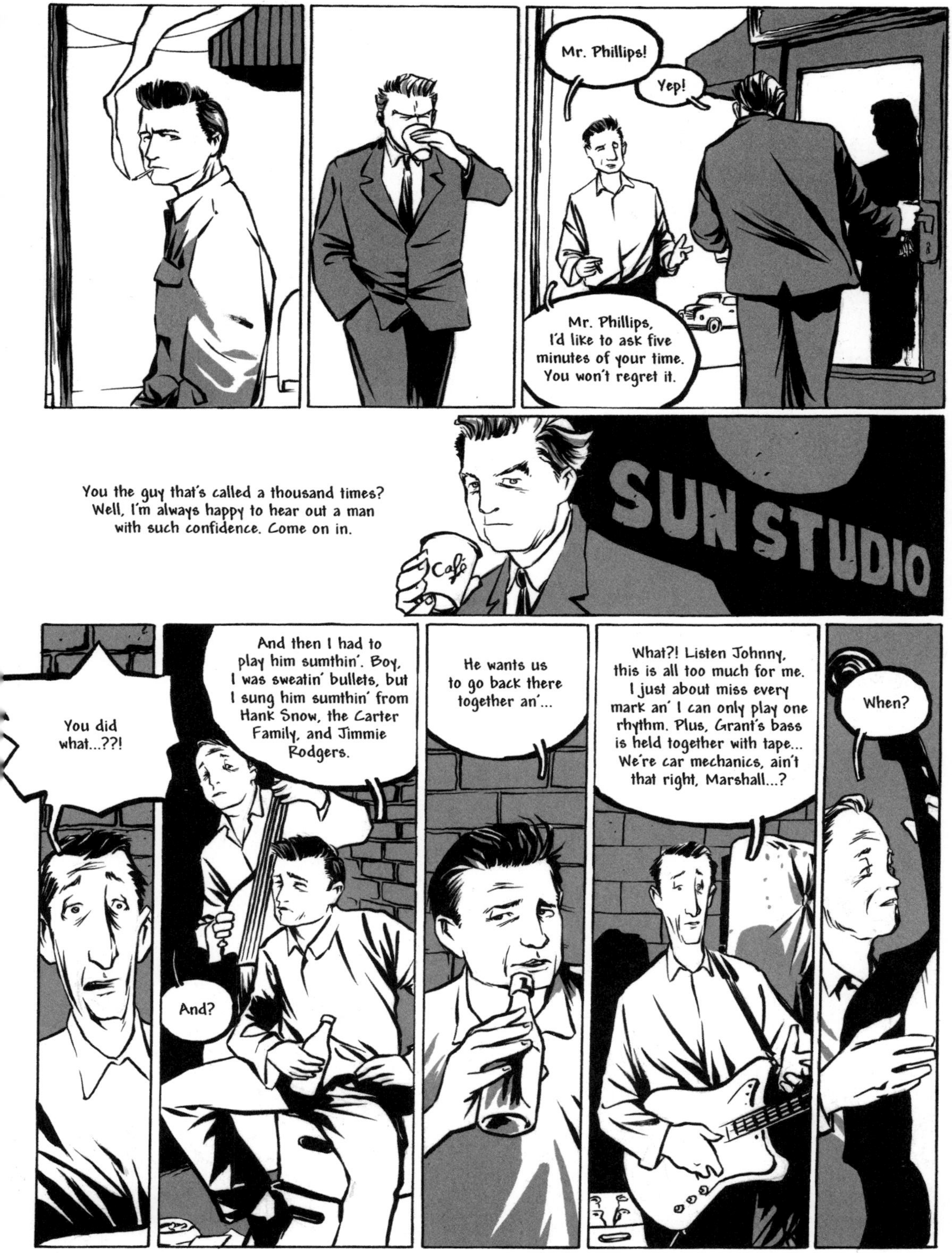
Mr. Phillips!
Yep!
Mr. Phillips, I'd like to ask five minutes of your time. You won't regret it.
You the guy that's called a thousand times? Well, I'm always happy to hear out a man with such confidence. Come on in.
Café
SUN STUDIO
You did what...??!
And then I had to play him sumthin'. Boy, I was sweatin' bullets, but I sung him sumthin' from Hank Snow, the Carter Family, and Jimmie Rodgers.
And?
He wants us to go back there together an'...
What?! Listen Johnny, this is all too much for me. I just about miss every mark an' I can only play one rhythm. Plus, Grant's bass is held together with tape... We're car mechanics, ain't that right, Marshall...?
When?

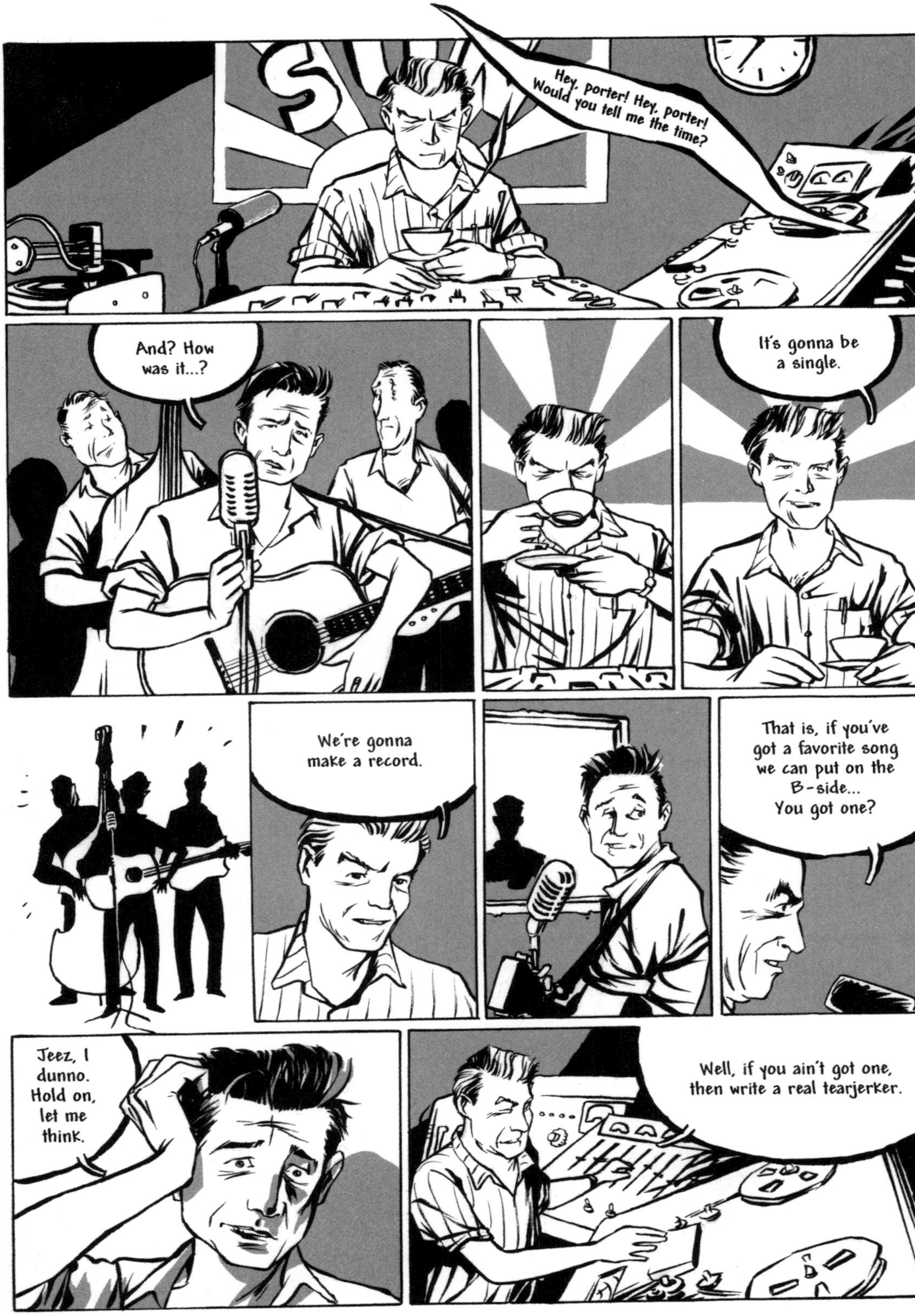

Hey, porter! Hey, porter! Would you tell me the time?
And? How was it...?
It's gonna be a single.
We're gonna make a record.
That is, if you've got a favorite song we can put on the B-side... You got one?
Jeez, I dunno. Hold on, let me think.
Well, if you ain't got one, then write a real tearjerker.

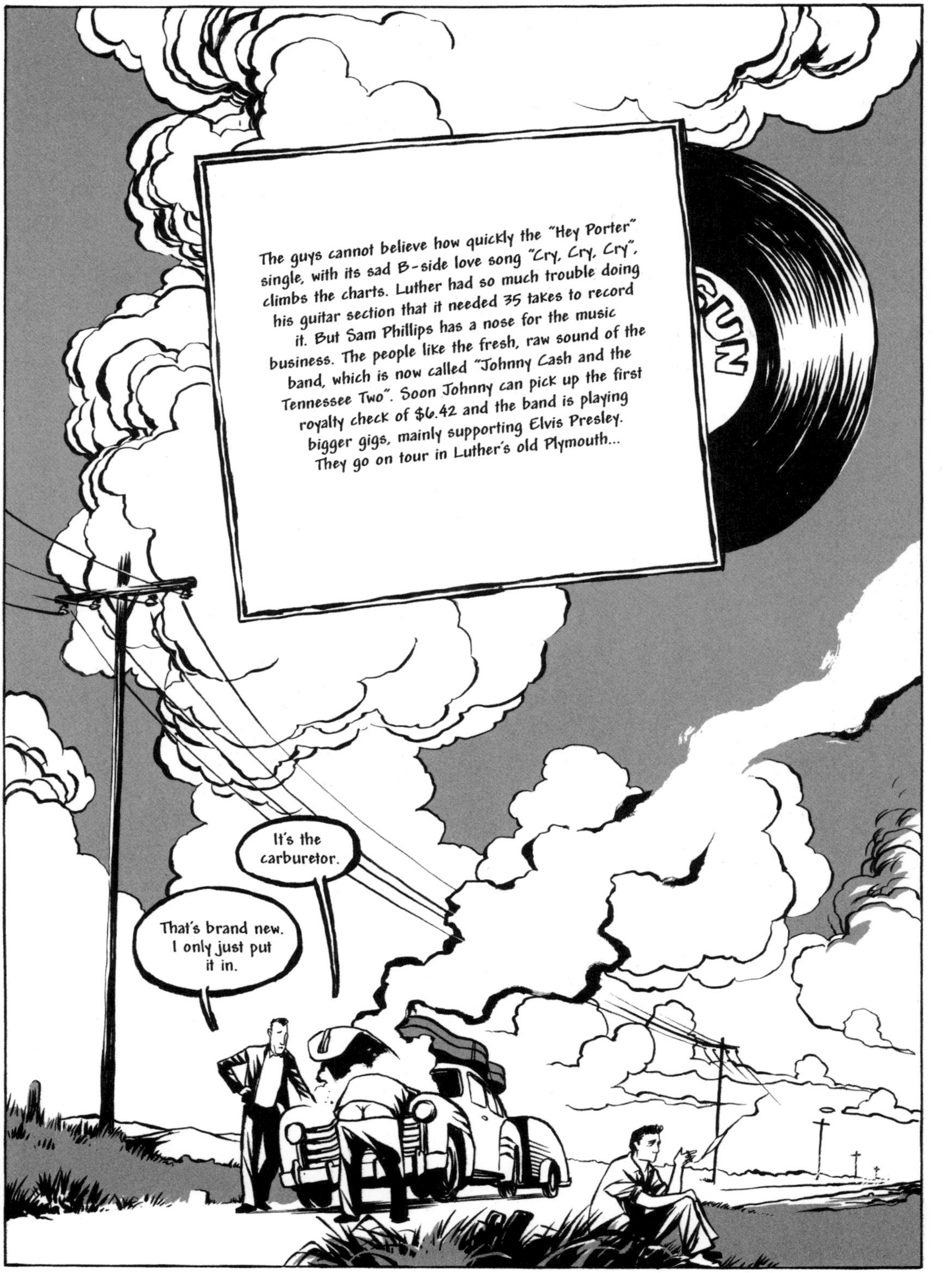
The guys cannot believe how quickly the "Hey Porter" single, with its sad B-side love song "Cry, Cry, Cry", climbs the charts. Luther had so much trouble doing his guitar section that it needed 35 takes to record it. But Sam Phillips has a nose for the music business. The people like the fresh, raw sound of the band, which is now called "Johnny Cash and the Tennessee Two". Soon Johnny can pick up the first royalty check of $6.42 and the band is playing bigger gigs, mainly supporting Elvis Presley. They go on tour in Luther's old Plymouth...
It's the carburetor.
That's brand new. I only just put it in.

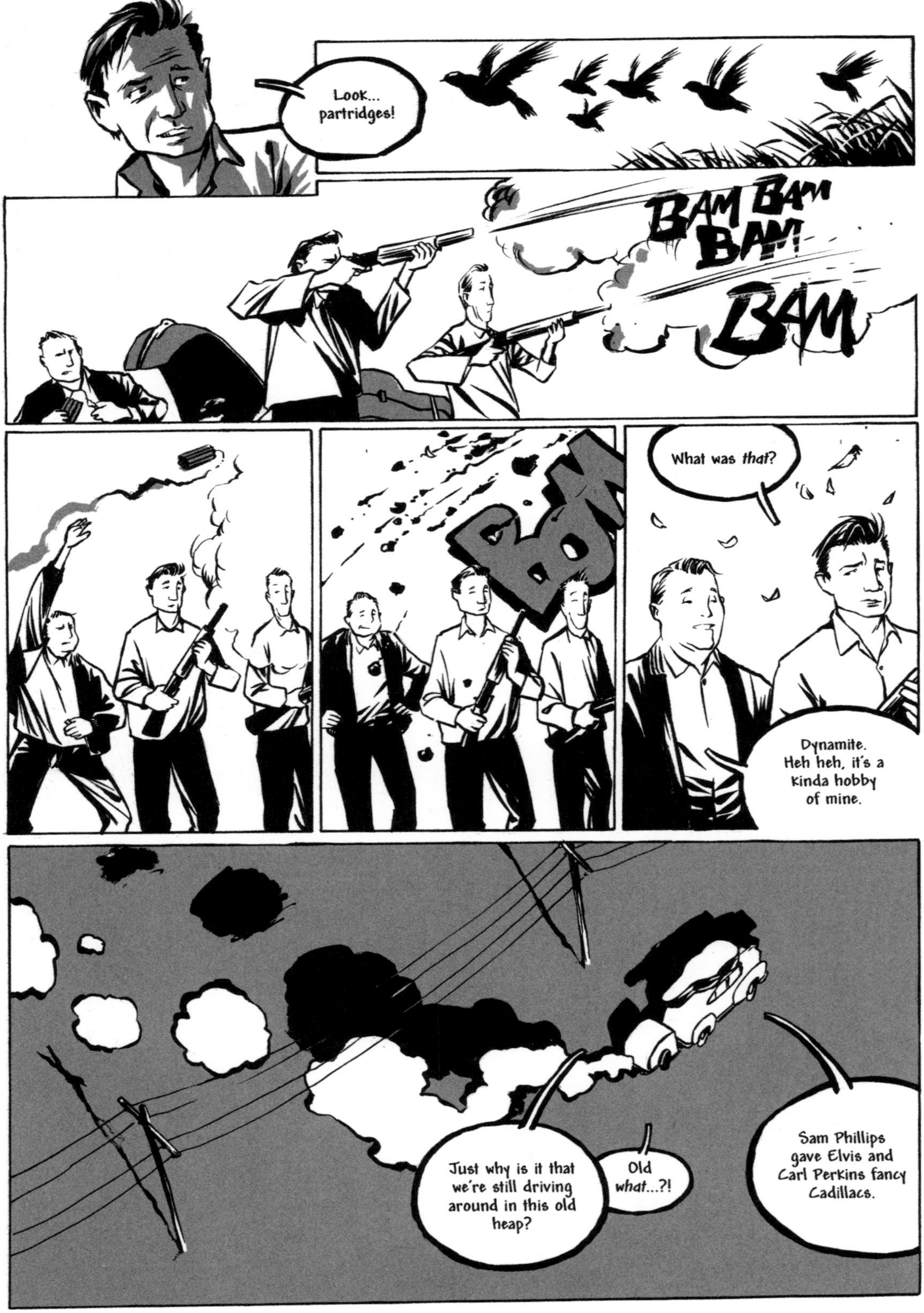
Look... partridges!
BAM BAM BAM
BAM
BOOM
What was *that*?
Dynamite. Heh heh, it's a kinda hobby of mine.
Just why is it that we're still driving around in this old heap?
Old *what*...?!
Sam Phillips gave Elvis and Carl Perkins fancy Cadillacs.

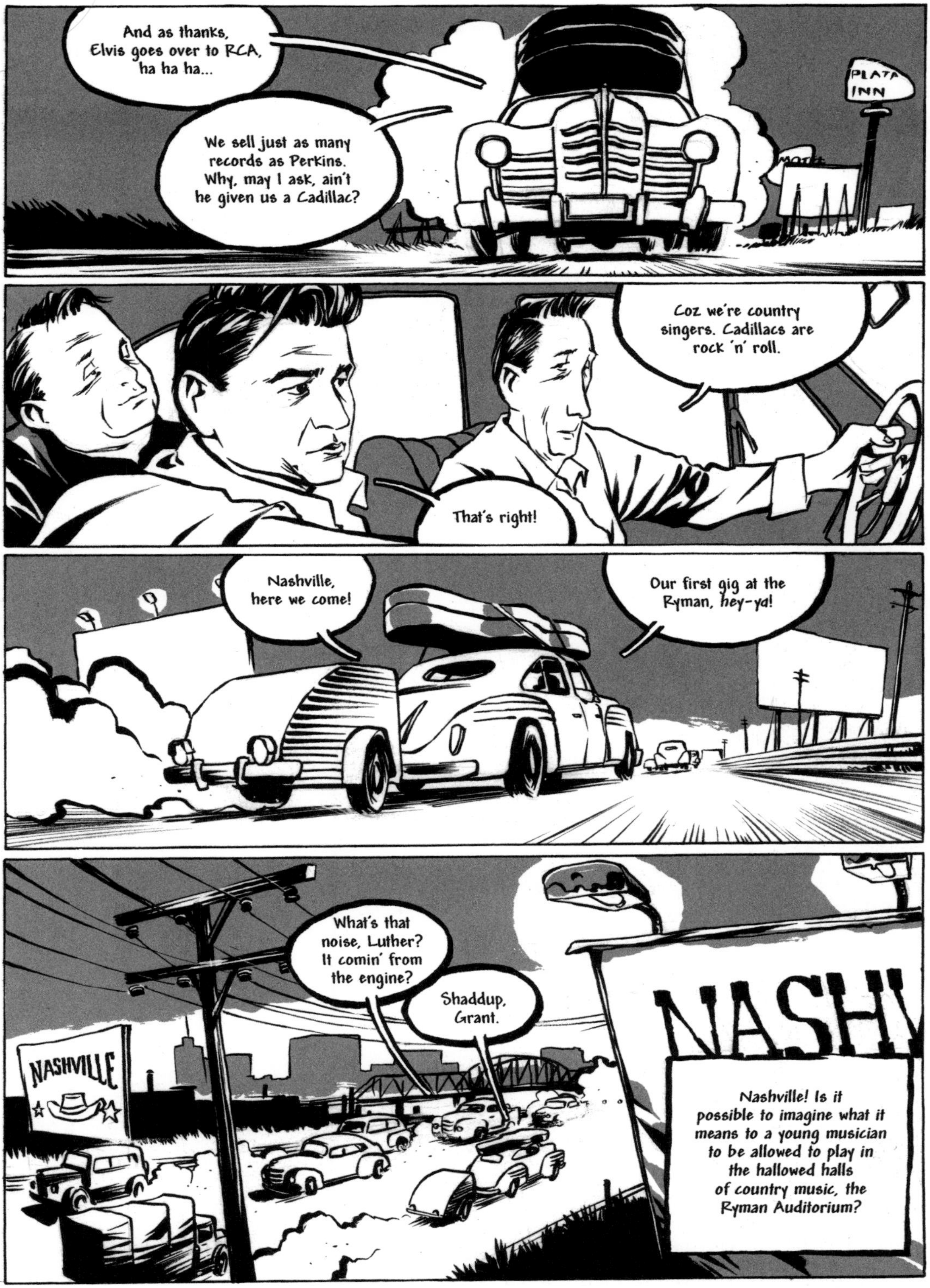
And as thanks, Elvis goes over to RCA, ha ha ha...
We sell just as many records as Perkins. Why, may I ask, ain't he given us a Cadillac?
PLATA INN
Coz we're country singers. Cadillacs are rock 'n' roll.
That's right!
Nashville, here we come!
Our first gig at the Ryman, hey-ya!
What's that noise, Luther? It comin' from the engine?
Shaddup, Grant.
NASHVILLE
NASHV
Nashville! Is it possible to imagine what it means to a young musician to be allowed to play in the hallowed halls of country music, the Ryman Auditorium?

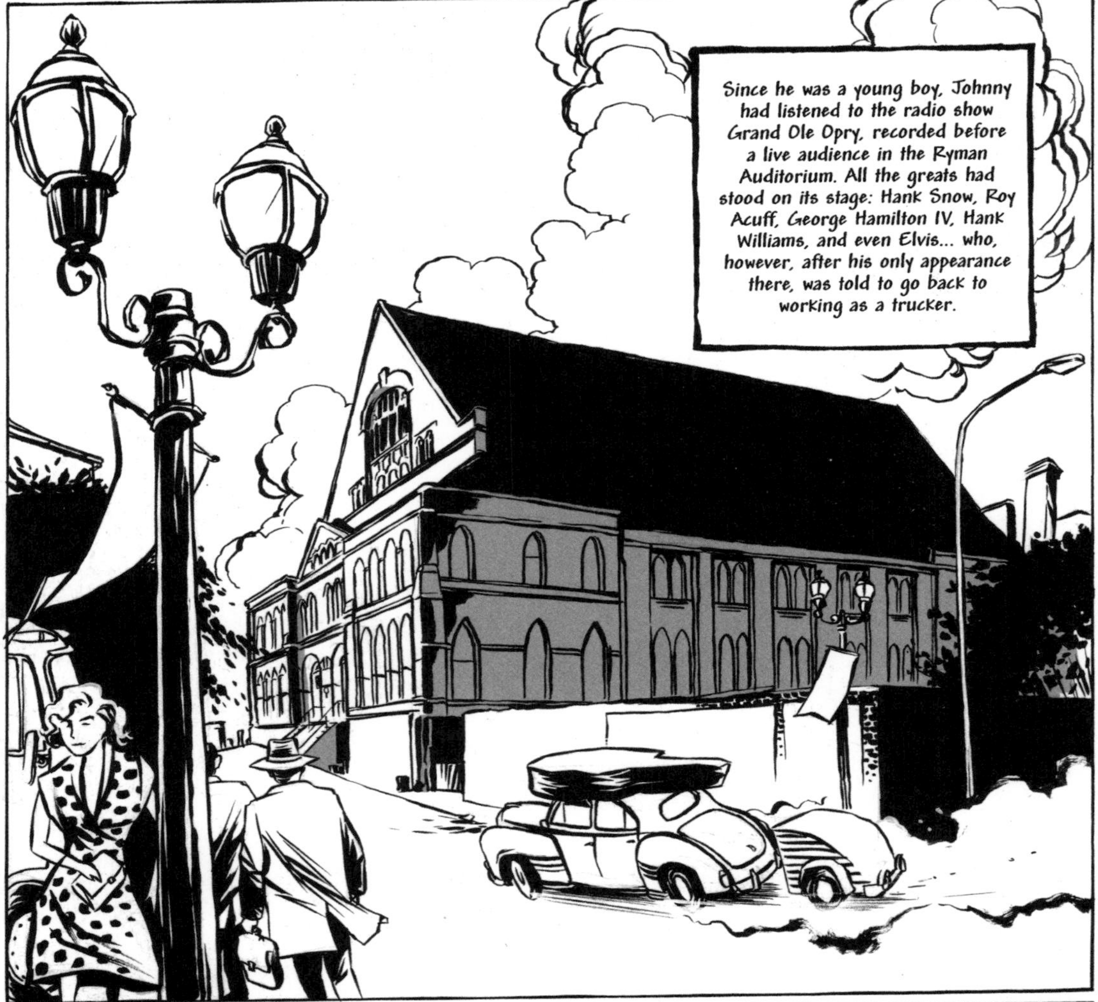
Since he was a young boy, Johnny had listened to the radio show Grand Ole Opry, recorded before a live audience in the Ryman Auditorium. All the greats had stood on its stage: Hank Snow, Roy Acuff, George Hamilton IV, Hank Williams, and even Elvis... who, however, after his only appearance there, was told to go back to working as a trucker.

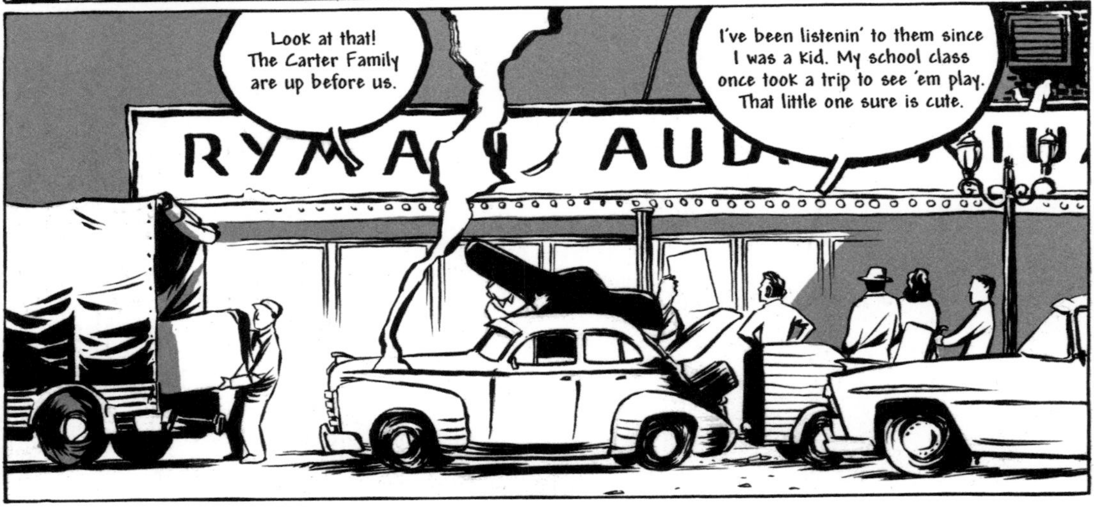
Look at that! The Carter Family are up before us.
I've been listenin' to them since I was a kid. My school class once took a trip to see 'em play. That little one sure is cute.

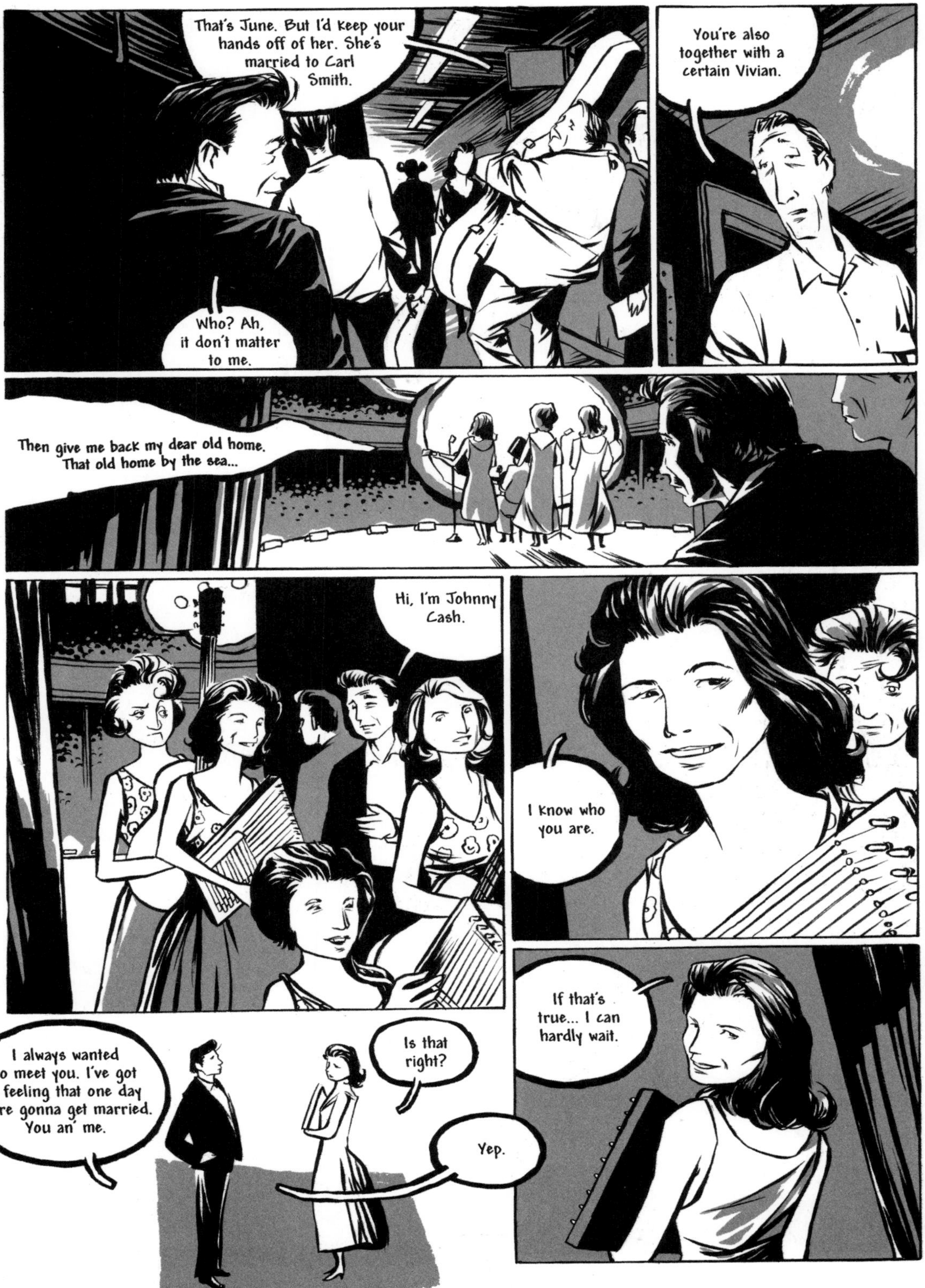
That's June. But I'd keep your hands off of her. She's married to Carl Smith.
Who? Ah, it don't matter to me.
You're also together with a certain Vivian.
Then give me back my dear old home. That old home by the sea...
Hi, I'm Johnny Cash.
I know who you are.
I always wanted to meet you. I've got a feeling that one day we're gonna get married. You an' me.
Is that right?
Yep.
If that's true... I can hardly wait.

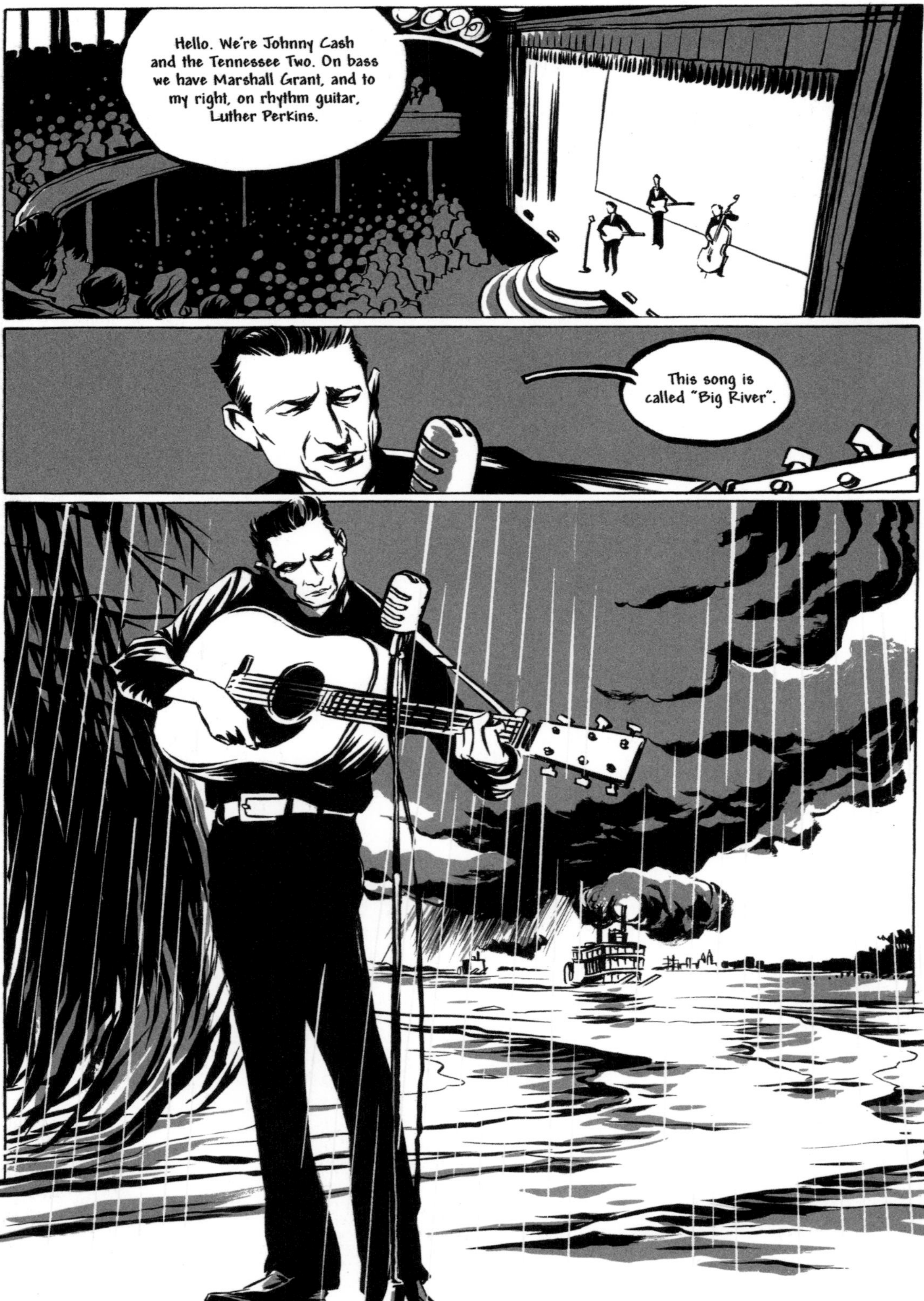
Hello. We're Johnny Cash and the Tennessee Two. On bass we have Marshall Grant, and to my right, on rhythm guitar, Luther Perkins.
This song is called "Big River".

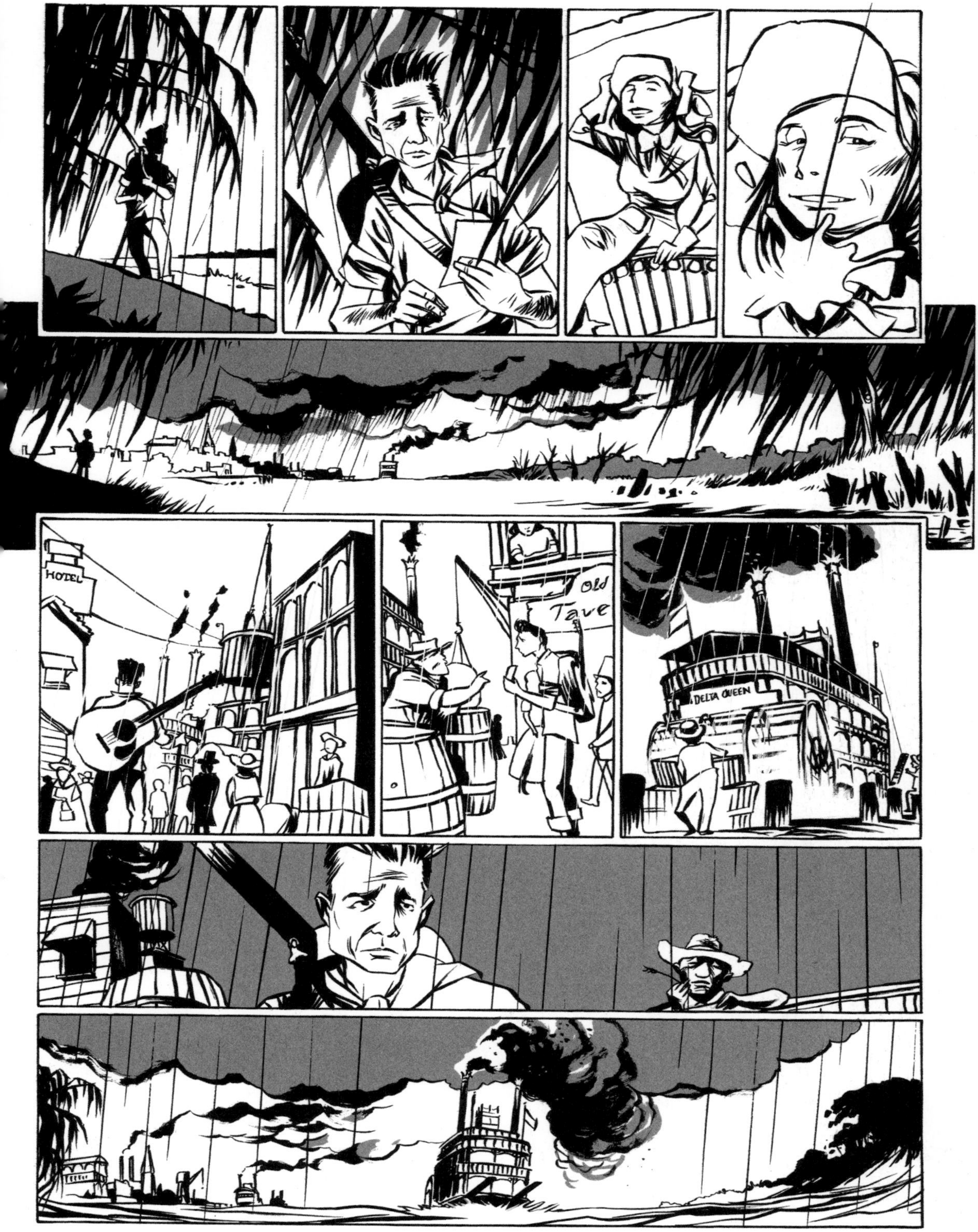
HOTEL
Old
Tave
DELTA QUEEN

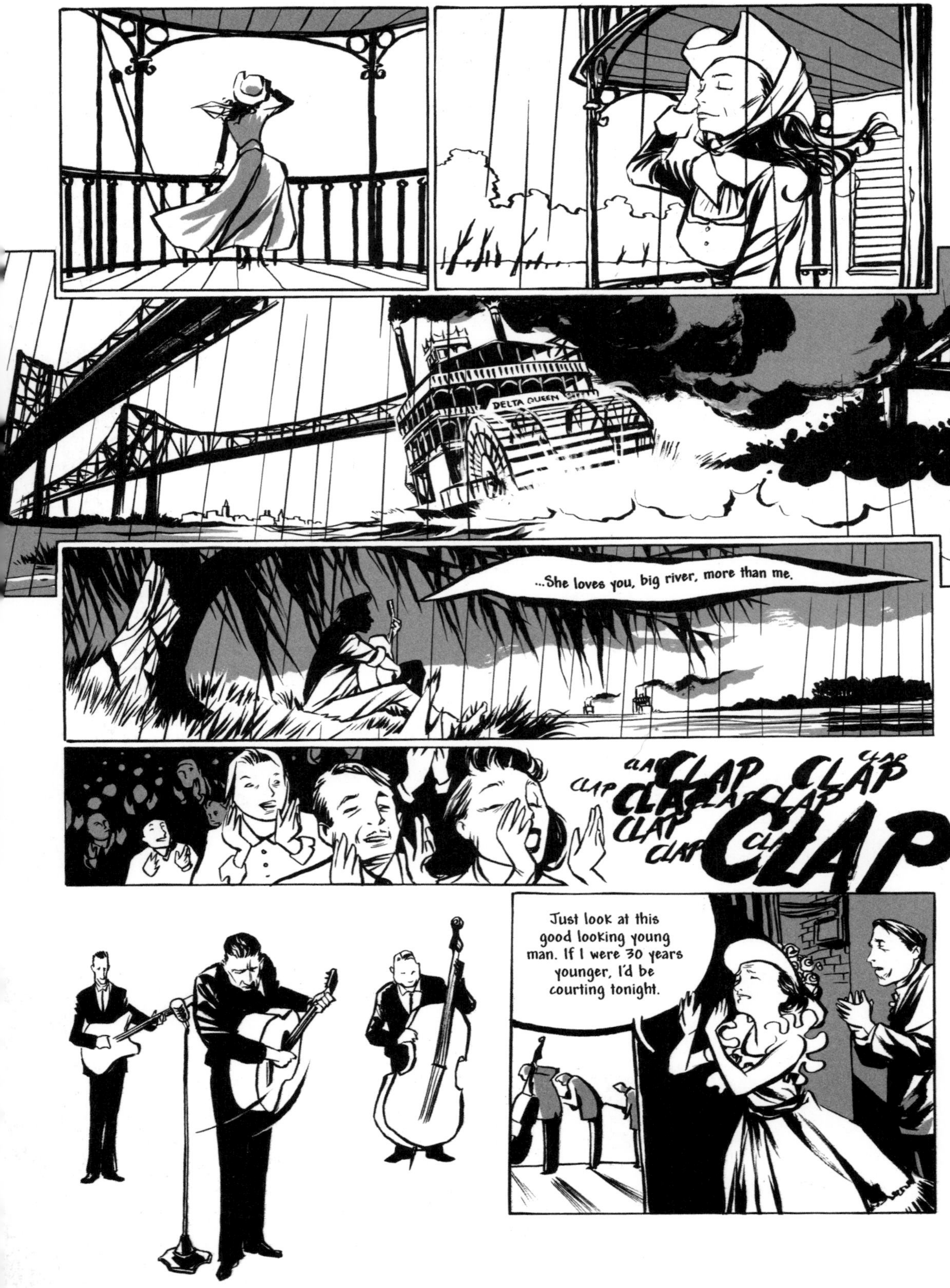
DELTA QUEEN
...She loves you, big river, more than me.
CLAP CLAP CLAP CLAP CLAP CLAP CLAP CLAP CLAP CLAP CLAP CLAP
Just look at this good looking young man. If I were 30 years younger, I'd be courting tonight.

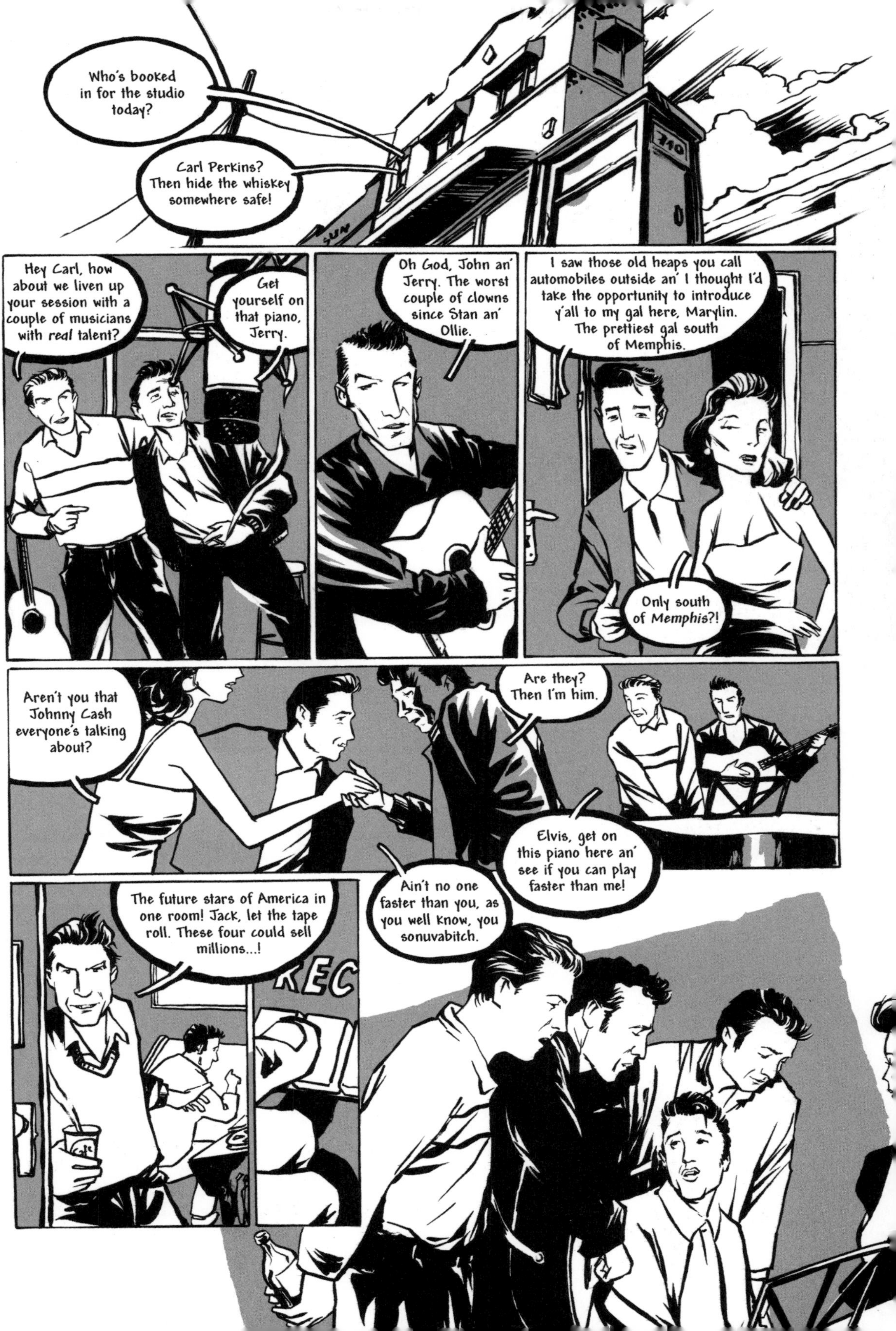

Who's booked in for the studio today?
Carl Perkins? Then hide the whiskey somewhere safe!
Hey Carl, how about we liven up your session with a couple of musicians with *real* talent?
Get yourself on that piano, Jerry.
Oh God, John an' Jerry. The worst couple of clowns since Stan an' Ollie.
I saw those old heaps you call automobiles outside an' I thought I'd take the opportunity to introduce y'all to my gal here, Marylin. The prettiest gal south of Memphis.
Only south of *Memphis*?!
Aren't you that Johnny Cash everyone's talking about?
Are they? Then I'm him.
Elvis, get on this piano here an' see if you can play faster than me!
Ain't no one faster than you, as you well know, you sonuvabitch.
The future stars of America in one room! Jack, let the tape roll. These four could sell millions...!
REC

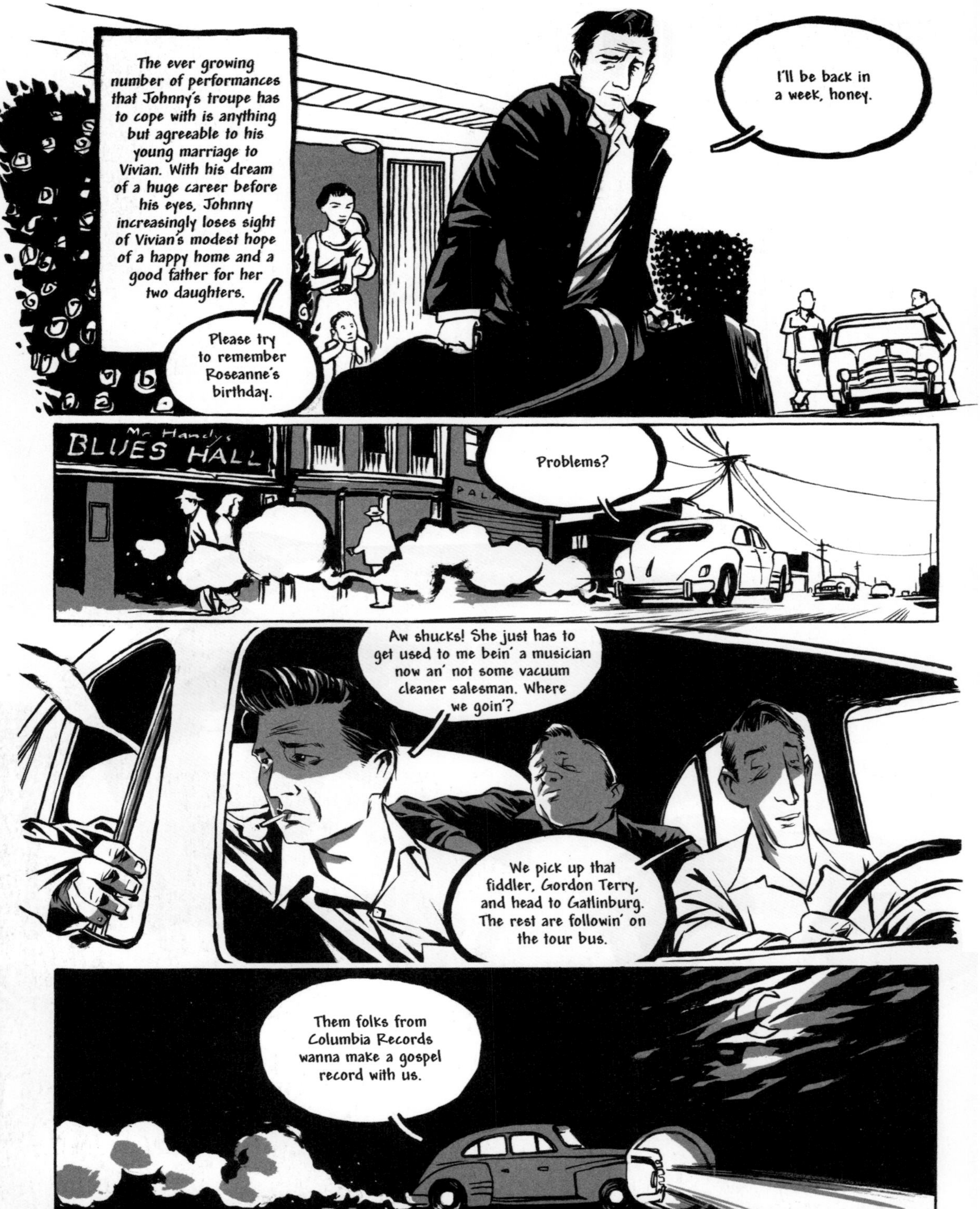
The ever growing number of performances that Johnny's troupe has to cope with is anything but agreeable to his young marriage to Vivian. With his dream of a huge career before his eyes, Johnny increasingly loses sight of Vivian's modest hope of a happy home and a good father for her two daughters.
Please try to remember Roseanne's birthday.
I'll be back in a week, honey.
Mr. Handy's BLUES HALL
Problems?
Aw shucks! She just has to get used to me bein' a musician now an' not some vacuum cleaner salesman. Where we goin'?
We pick up that fiddler, Gordon Terry, and head to Gatlinburg. The rest are followin' on the tour bus.
Them folks from Columbia Records wanna make a gospel record with us.

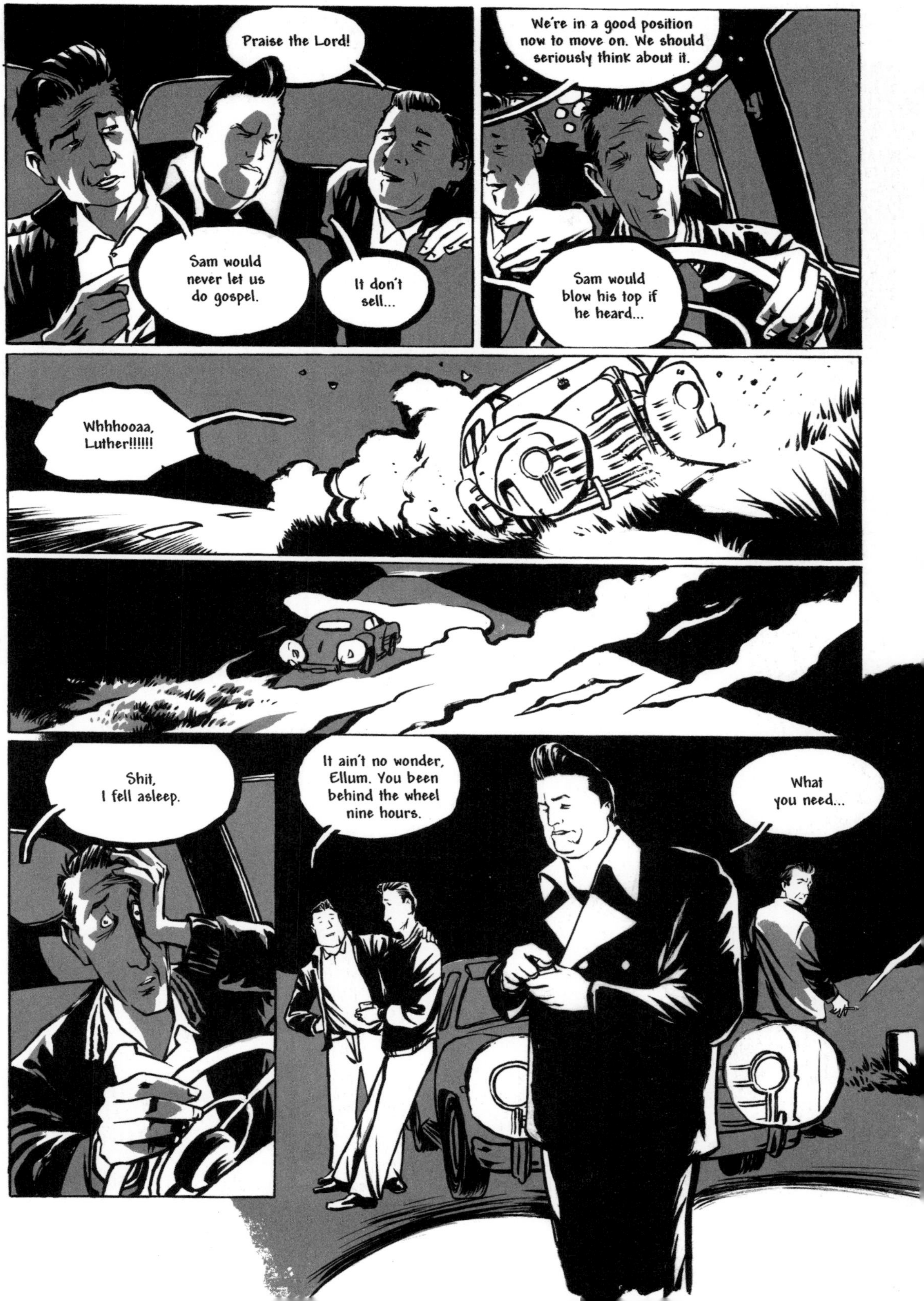
Praise the Lord!
Sam would never let us do gospel.
It don't sell...
We're in a good position now to move on. We should seriously think about it.
Sam would blow his top if he heard...
Whhhooaa, Luther!!!!!!
Shit, I fell asleep.
It ain't no wonder, Ellum. You been behind the wheel nine hours.
What you need...

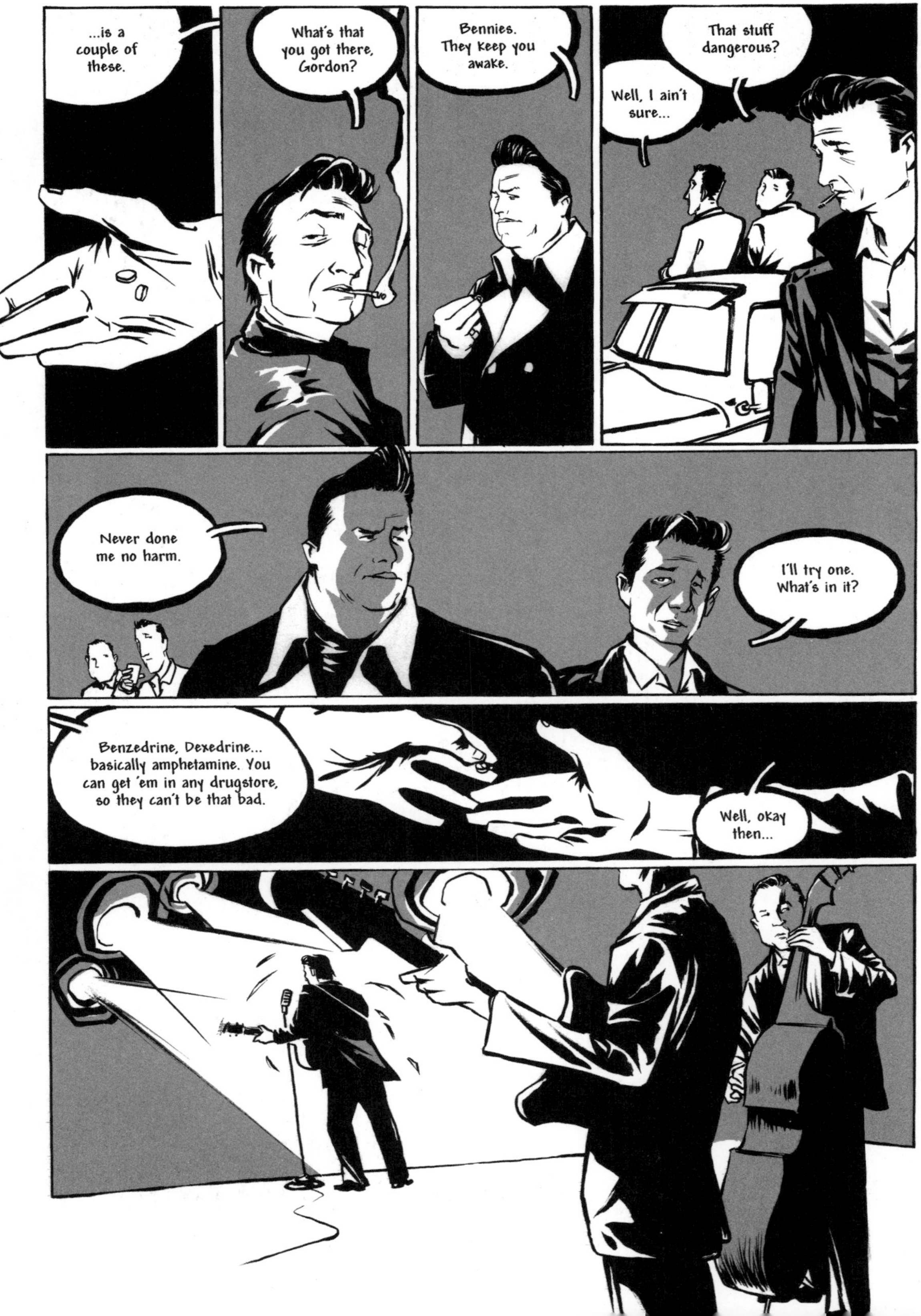
...is a couple of these.
What's that you got there, Gordon?
Bennies. They keep you awake.
That stuff dangerous?
Well, I ain't sure...
Never done me no harm.
I'll try one. What's in it?
Benzedrine, Dexedrine... basically amphetamine. You can get 'em in any drugstore, so they can't be that bad.
Well, okay then...

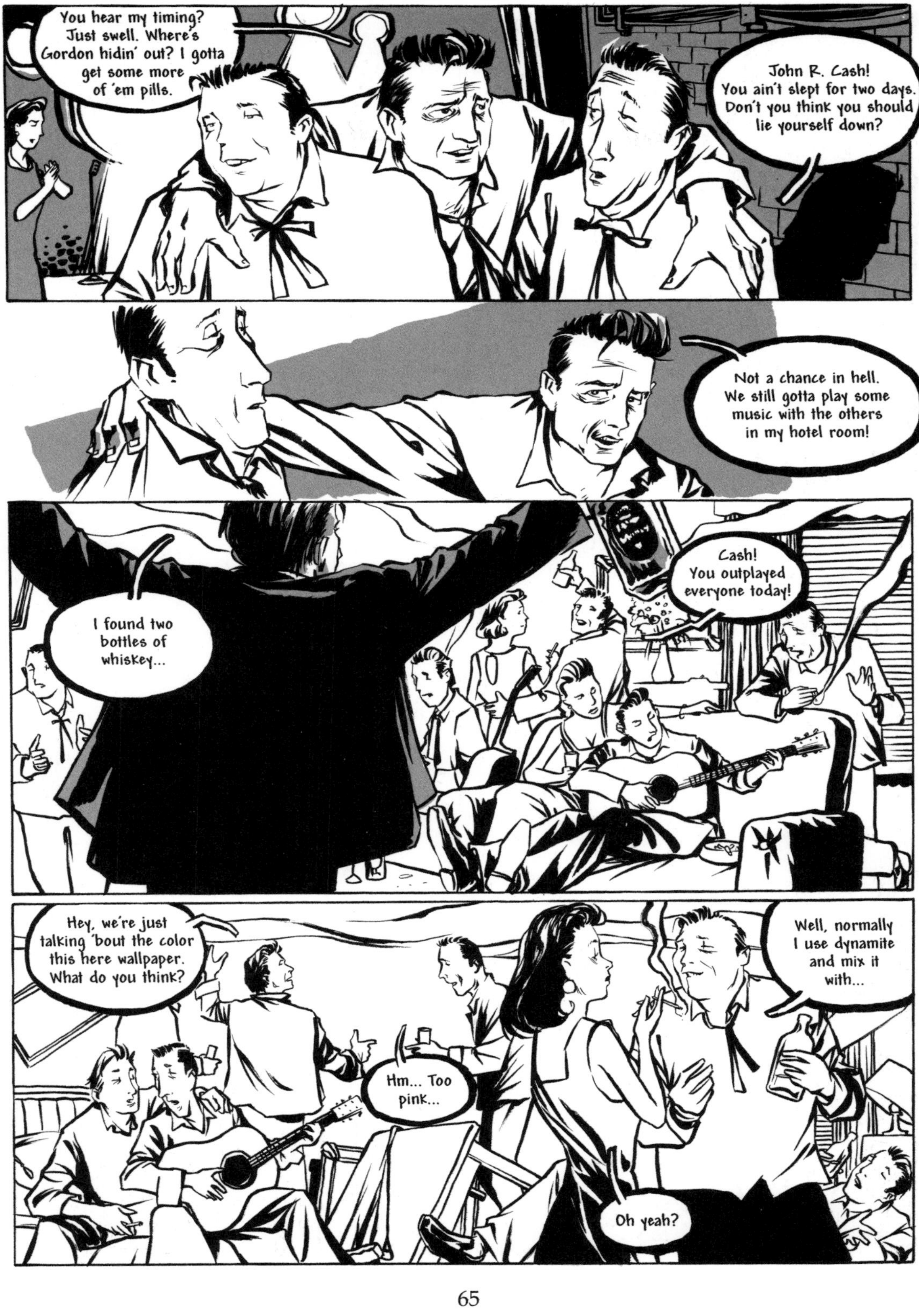
You hear my timing? Just swell. Where's Gordon hidin' out? I gotta get some more of 'em pills.
John R. Cash! You ain't slept for two days. Don't you think you should lie yourself down?
Not a chance in hell. We still gotta play some music with the others in my hotel room!
I found two bottles of whiskey...
Cash! You outplayed everyone today!
Hey, we're just talking 'bout the color this here wallpaper. What do you think?
Hm... Too pink...
Well, normally I use dynamite and mix it with...
Oh yeah?

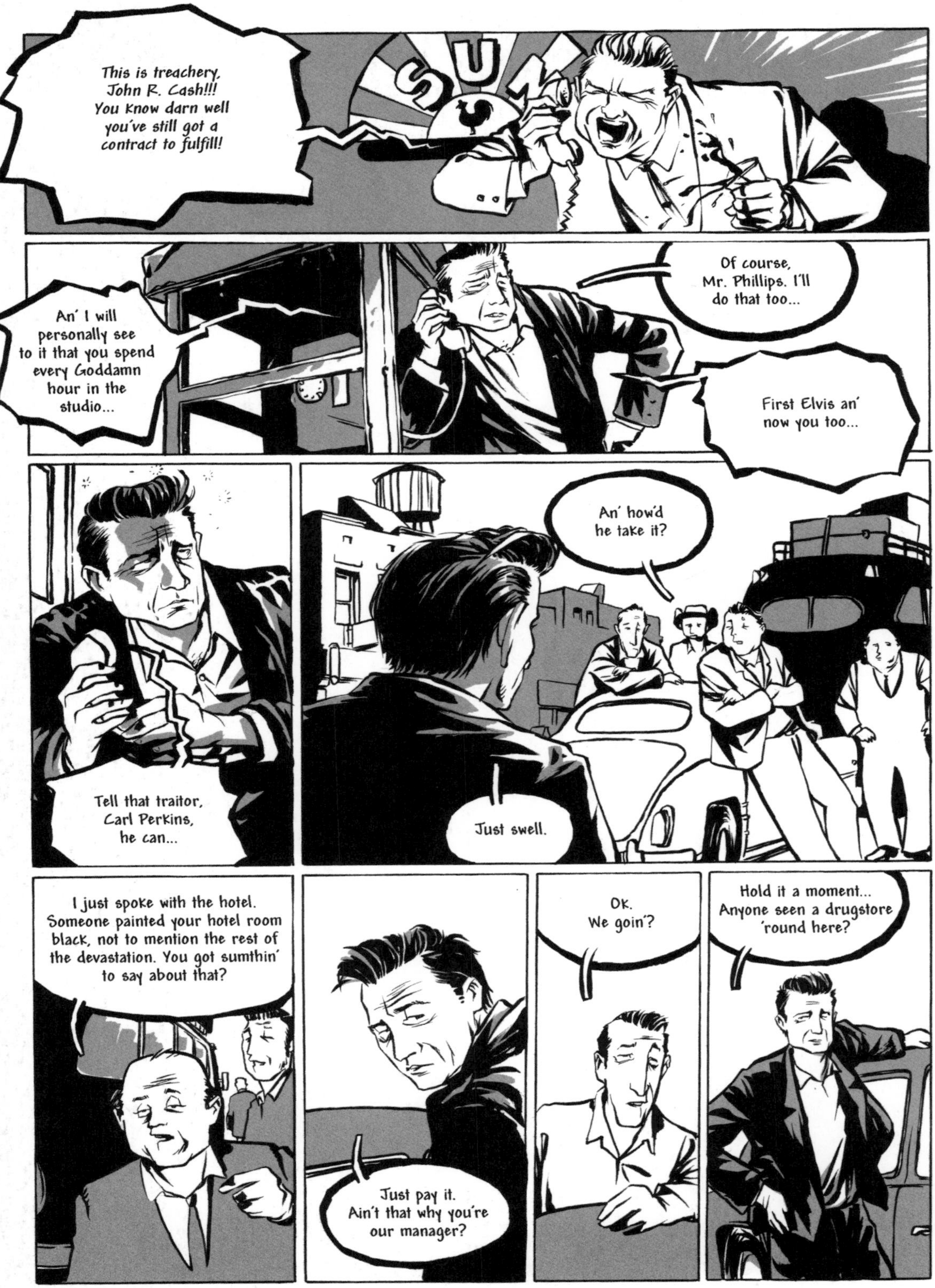

SUN
This is treachery, John R. Cash!!! You know darn well you've still got a contract to fulfill!
An' I will personally see to it that you spend every Goddamn hour in the studio...
Of course, Mr. Phillips. I'll do that too...
First Elvis an' now you too...
Tell that traitor, Carl Perkins, he can...
An' how'd he take it?
Just swell.
I just spoke with the hotel. Someone painted your hotel room black, not to mention the rest of the devastation. You got sumthin' to say about that?
Just pay it. Ain't that why you're our manager?
Ok. We goin'?
Hold it a moment... Anyone seen a drugstore 'round here?

CHAPTER 2
1957-1967

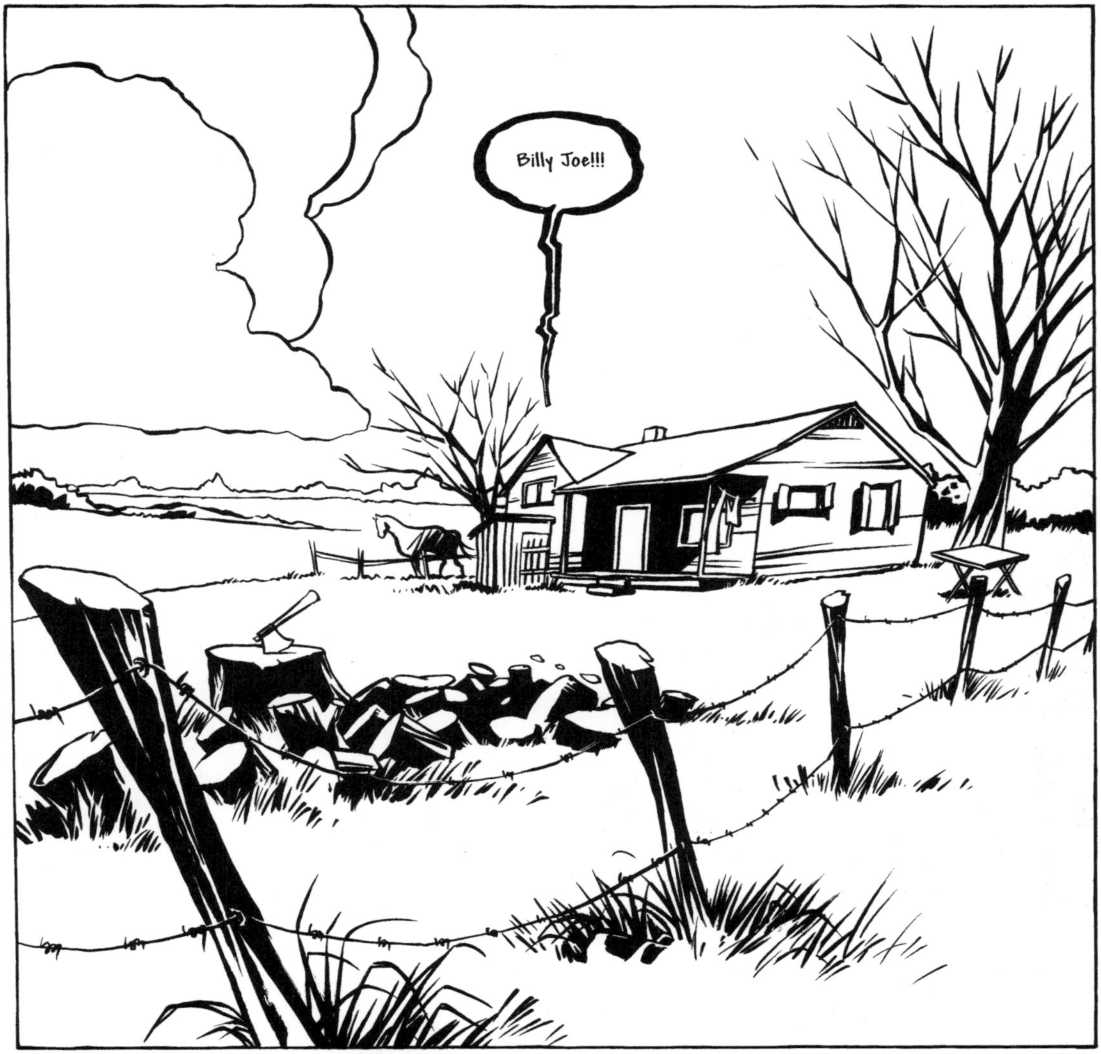
Billy Joe!!!

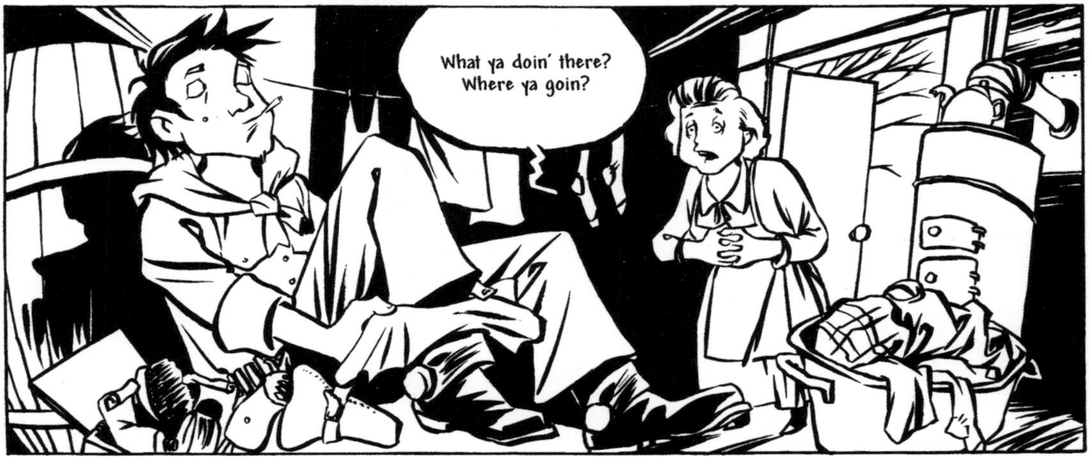
What ya doin' there?
Where ya goin?

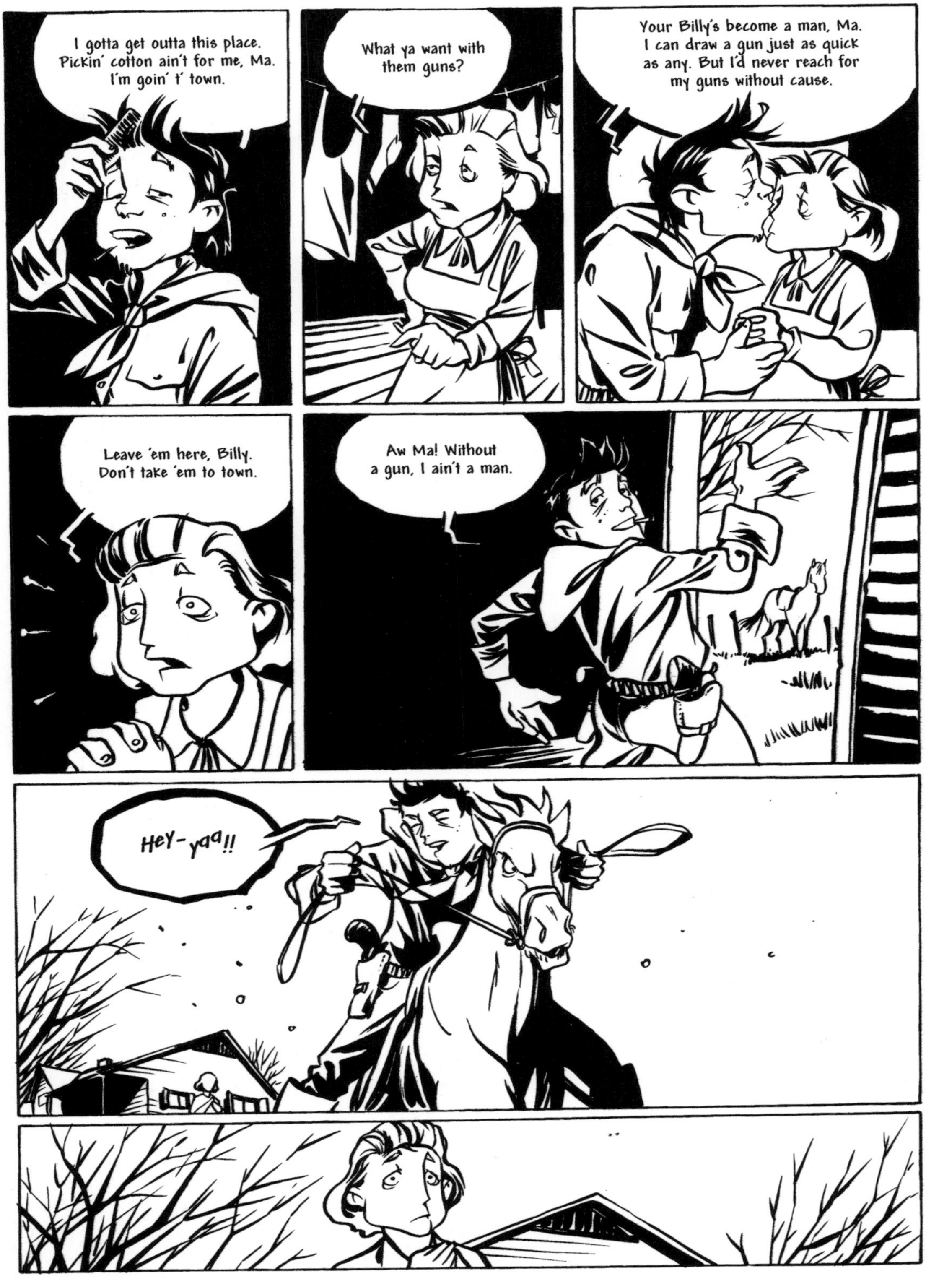
I gotta get outta this place. Pickin' cotton ain't for me, Ma. I'm goin' t' town.
What ya want with them guns?
Your Billy's become a man, Ma. I can draw a gun just as quick as any. But I'd never reach for my guns without cause.
Leave 'em here, Billy. Don't take 'em to town.
Aw Ma! Without a gun, I ain't a man.
Hey-yaa!!

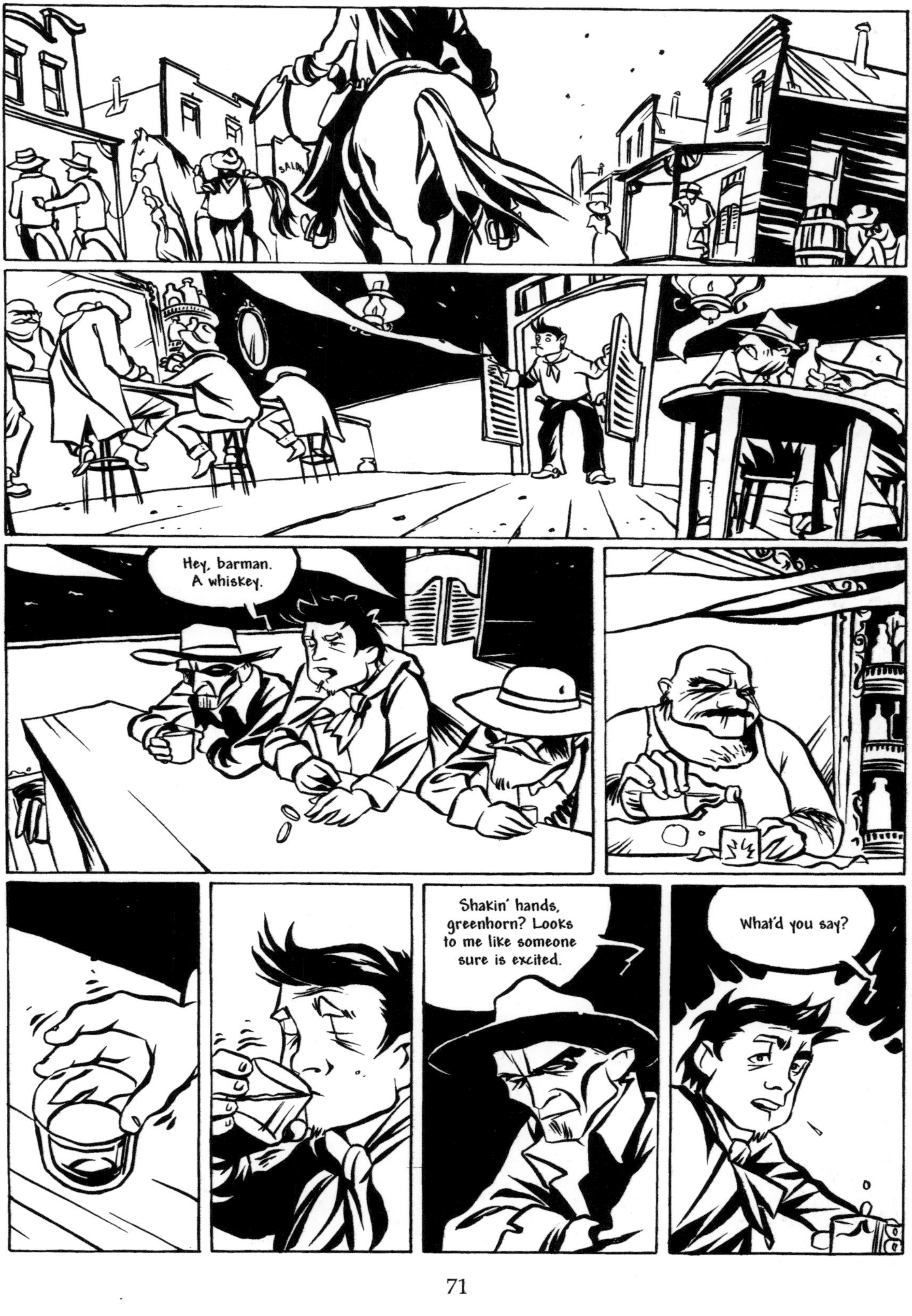
SALOON
Hey, barman.
A whiskey.
Shakin' hands, greenhorn? Looks to me like someone sure is excited.
What'd you say?

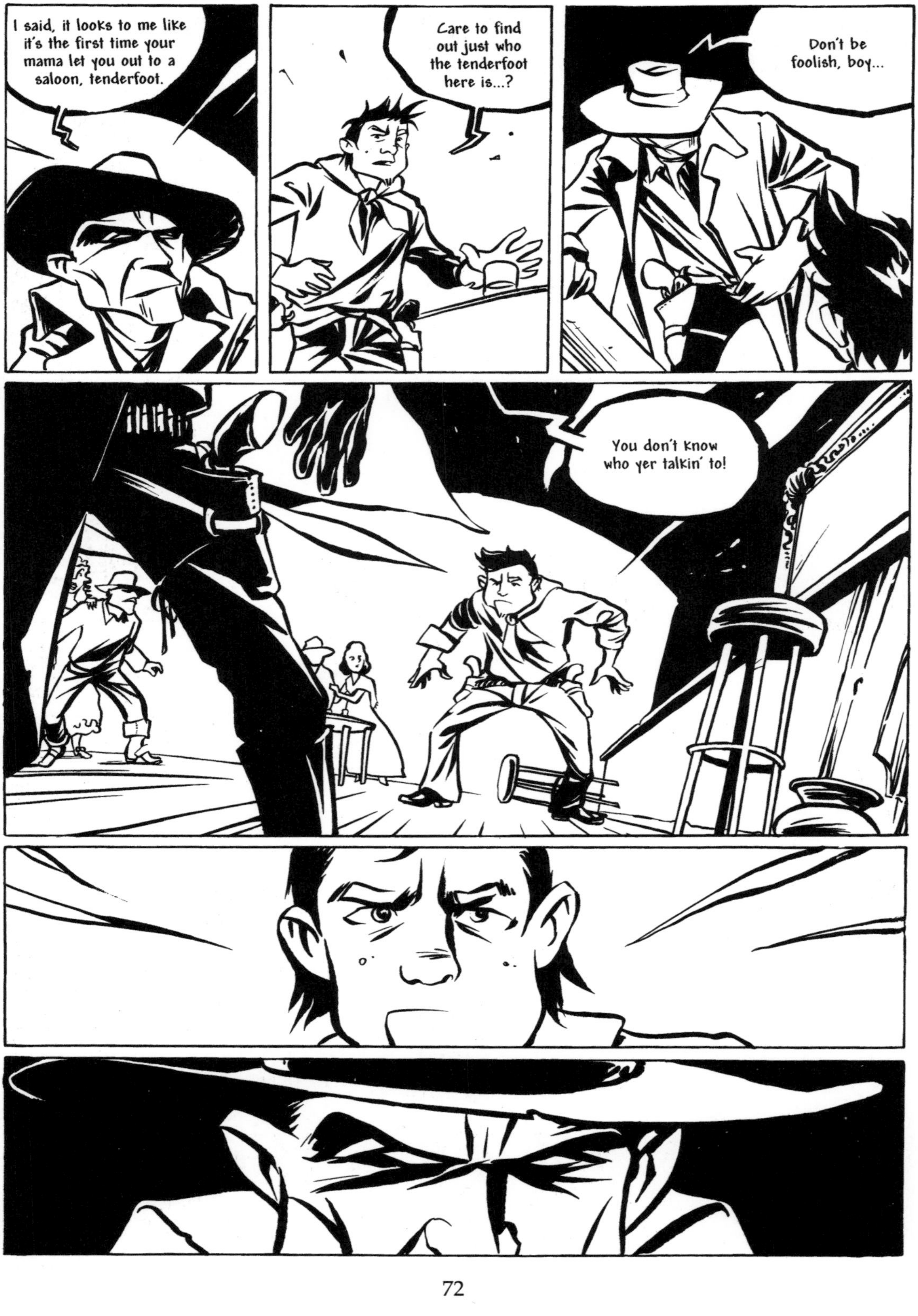
I said, it looks to me like it's the first time your mama let you out to a saloon, tenderfoot.
Care to find out just who the tenderfoot here is...?
Don't be foolish, boy...
You don't know who yer talkin' to!

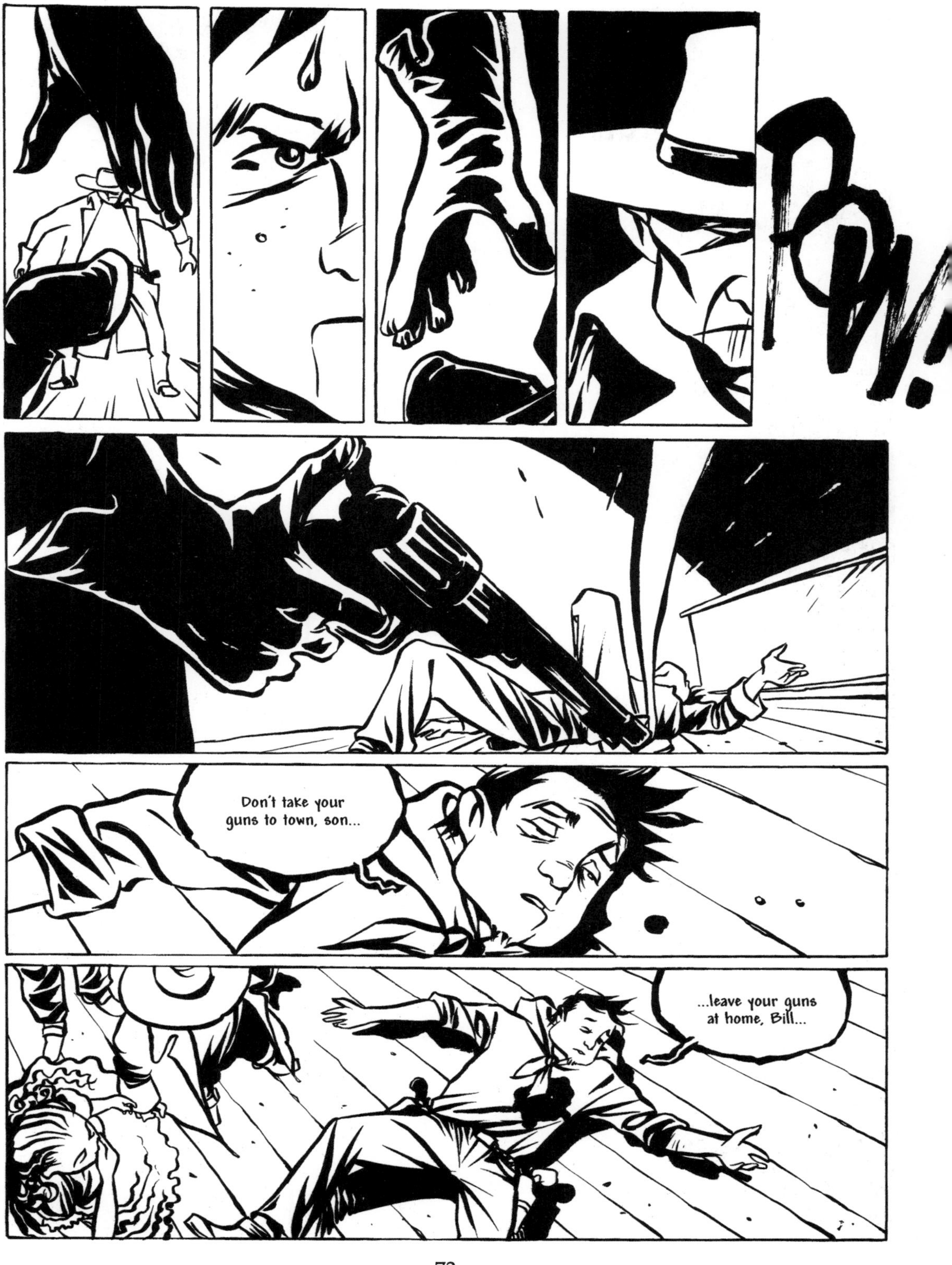
POW!!
Don't take your guns to town, son...
...leave your guns at home, Bill...

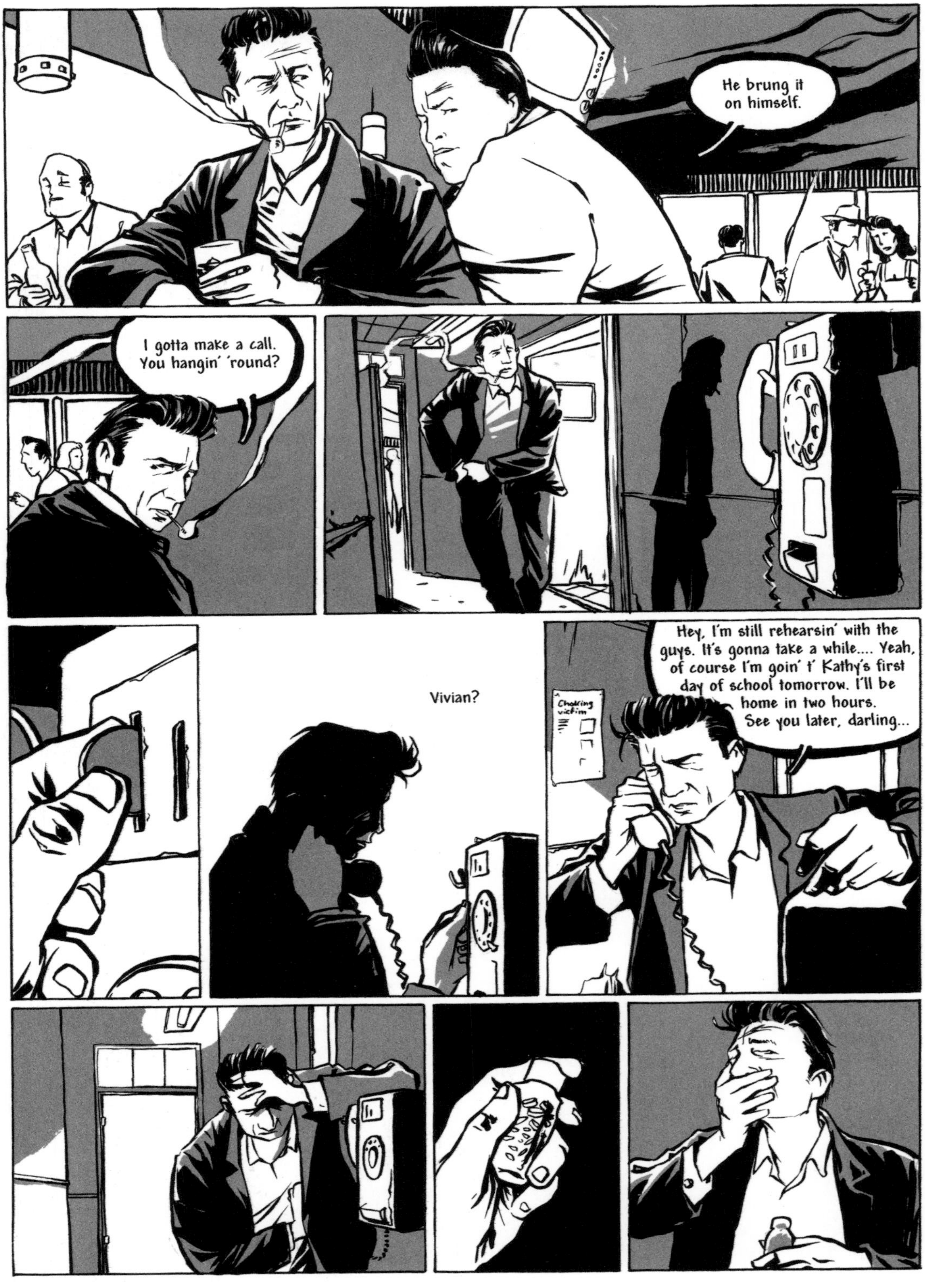
He brung it on himself.
I gotta make a call. You hangin' 'round?
Vivian?
Choking victim
Hey, I'm still rehearsin' with the guys. It's gonna take a while.... Yeah, of course I'm goin' t' Kathy's first day of school tomorrow. I'll be home in two hours. See you later, darling...

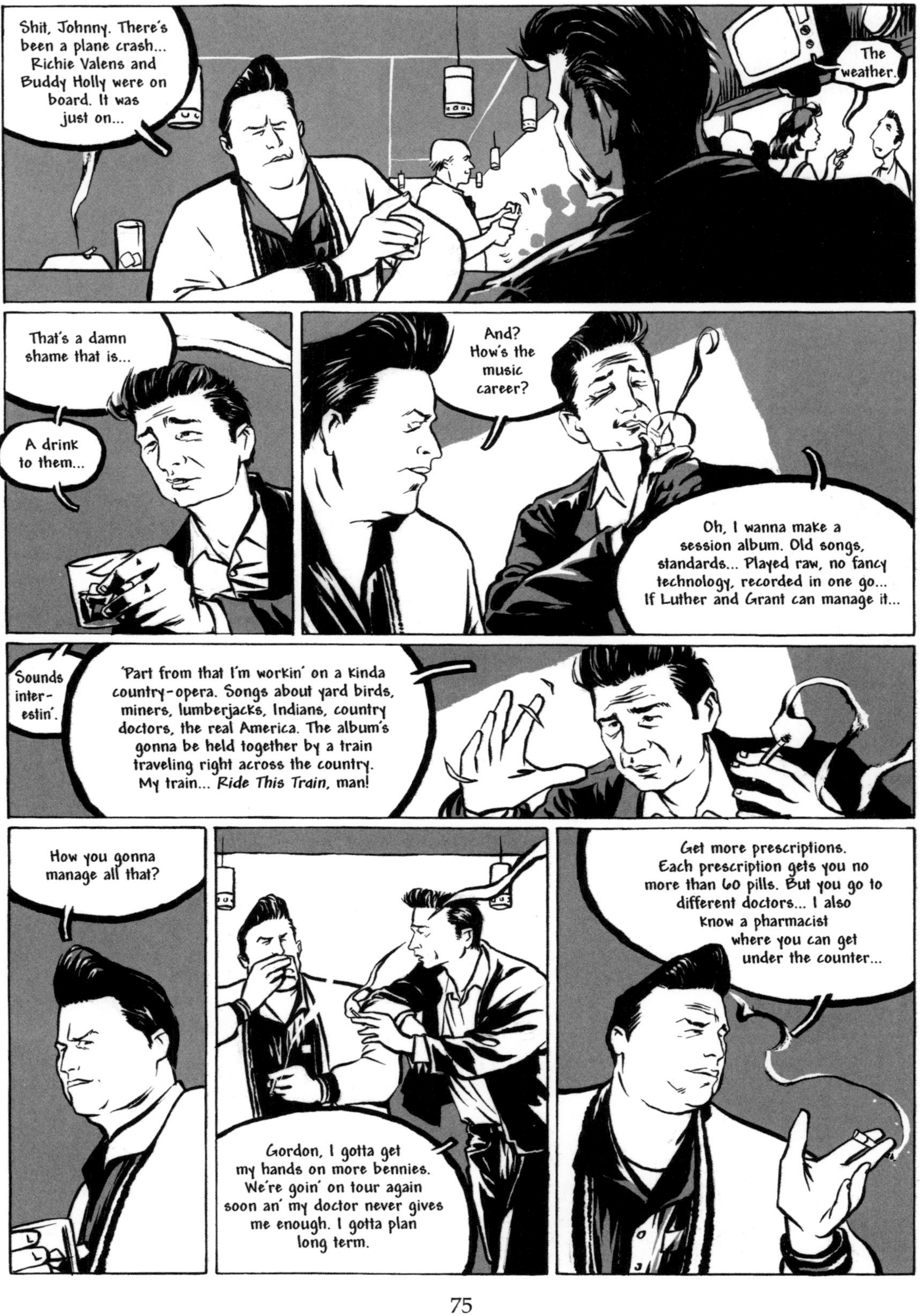
Shit, Johnny. There's been a plane crash... Richie Valens and Buddy Holly were on board. It was just on...
The weather.
That's a damn shame that is...
A drink to them...
And? How's the music career?
Oh, I wanna make a session album. Old songs, standards... Played raw, no fancy technology, recorded in one go... If Luther and Grant can manage it...
Sounds inter-estin'.
'Part from that I'm workin' on a kinda country-opera. Songs about yard birds, miners, lumberjacks, Indians, country doctors, the real America. The album's gonna be held together by a train traveling right across the country. My train... *Ride This Train*, man!
How you gonna manage all that?
Gordon, I gotta get my hands on more bennies. We're goin' on tour again soon an' my doctor never gives me enough. I gotta plan long term.
Get more prescriptions. Each prescription gets you no more than 60 pills. But you go to different doctors... I also know a pharmacist where you can get under the counter...

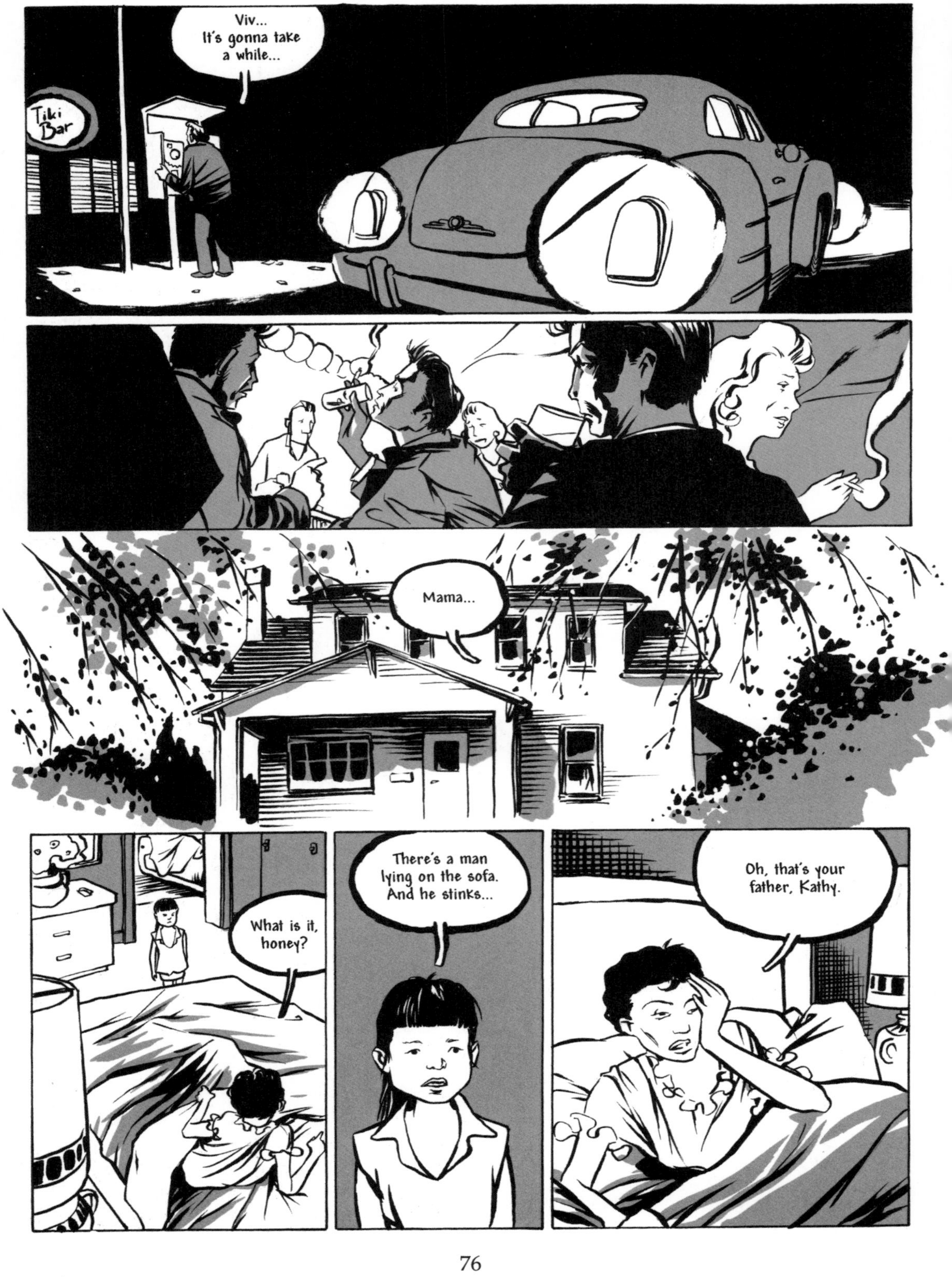
Viv...
It's gonna take
a while...
Tiki
Bar
Mama...
What is it,
honey?
There's a man
lying on the sofa.
And he stinks...
Oh, that's your
father, Kathy.

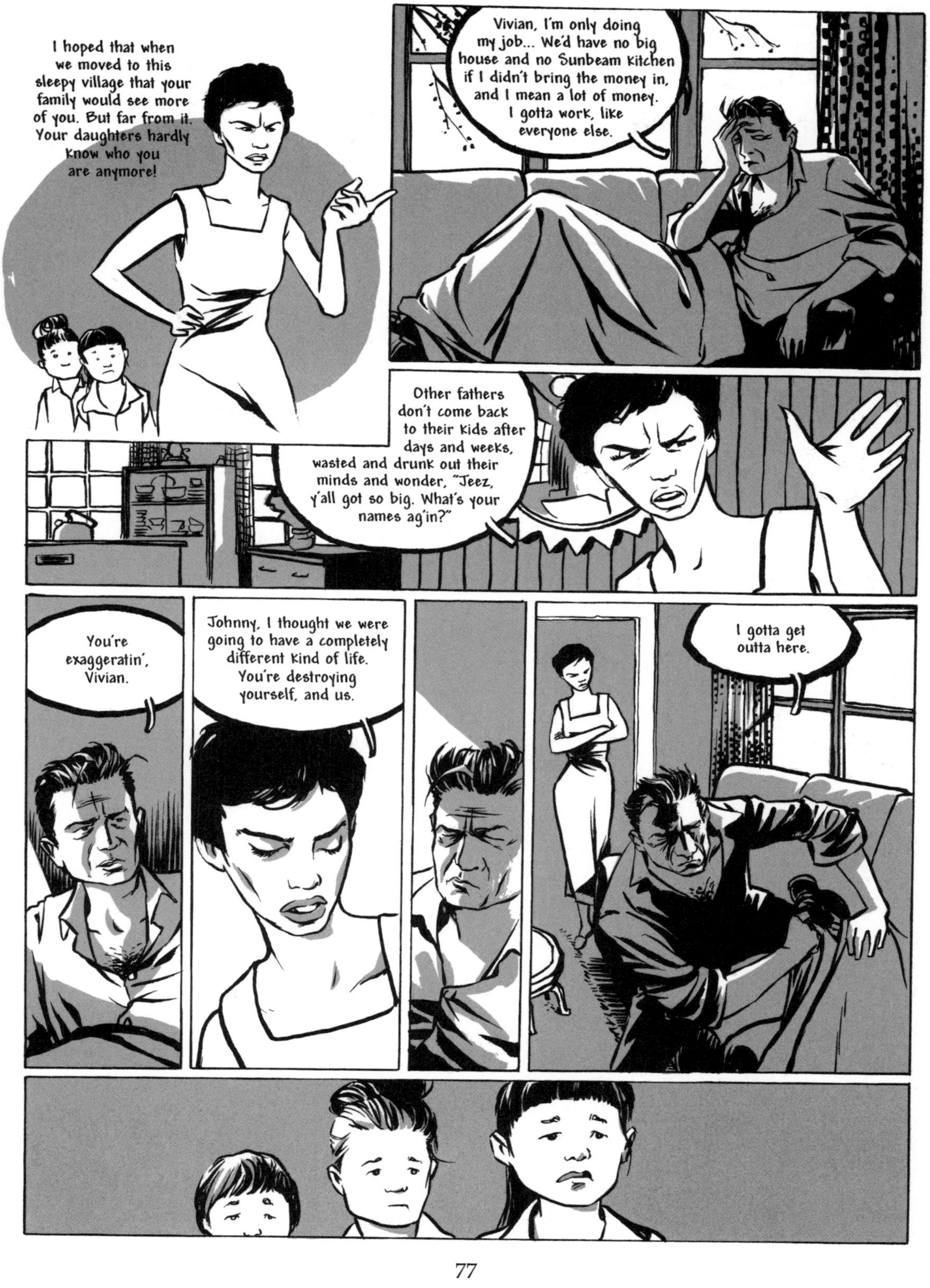
I hoped that when we moved to this sleepy village that your family would see more of you. But far from it. Your daughters hardly know who you are anymore!
Vivian, I'm only doing my job... We'd have no big house and no Sunbeam kitchen if I didn't bring the money in, and I mean a lot of money. I gotta work, like everyone else.
Other fathers don't come back to their kids after days and weeks, wasted and drunk out their minds and wonder, "Jeez, y'all got so big. What's your names ag'in?"
You're exaggeratin', Vivian.
Johnny, I thought we were going to have a completely different kind of life. You're destroying yourself, and us.
I gotta get outta here.

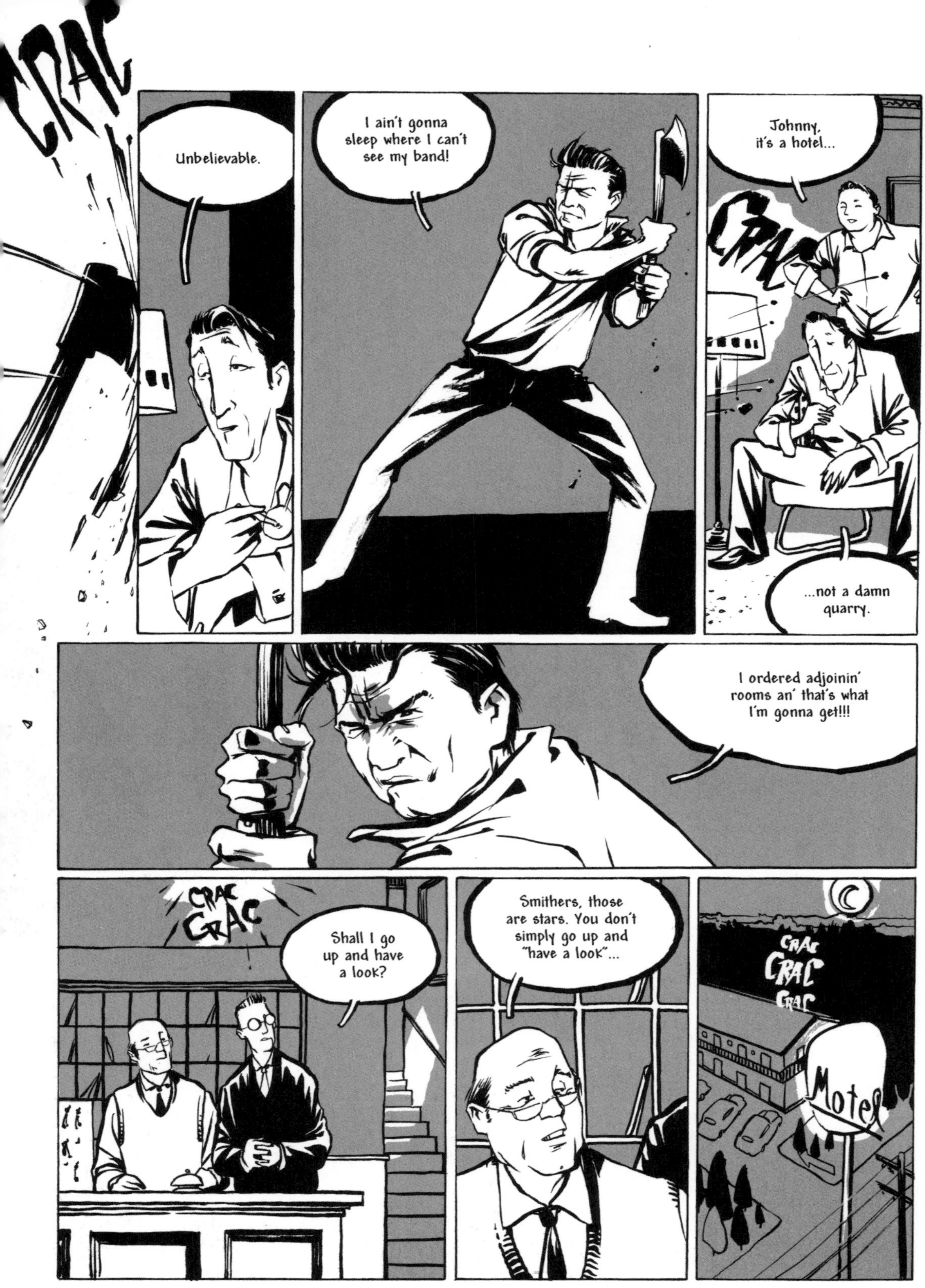
CRAC
Unbelievable.
I ain't gonna sleep where I can't see my band!
Johnny, it's a hotel...
CRAC
...not a damn quarry.
I ordered adjoinin' rooms an' that's what I'm gonna get!!!
CRAC
CRAC
Shall I go up and have a look?
Smithers, those are stars. You don't simply go up and "have a look"...
CRAC
CRAC
CRAC
Motel

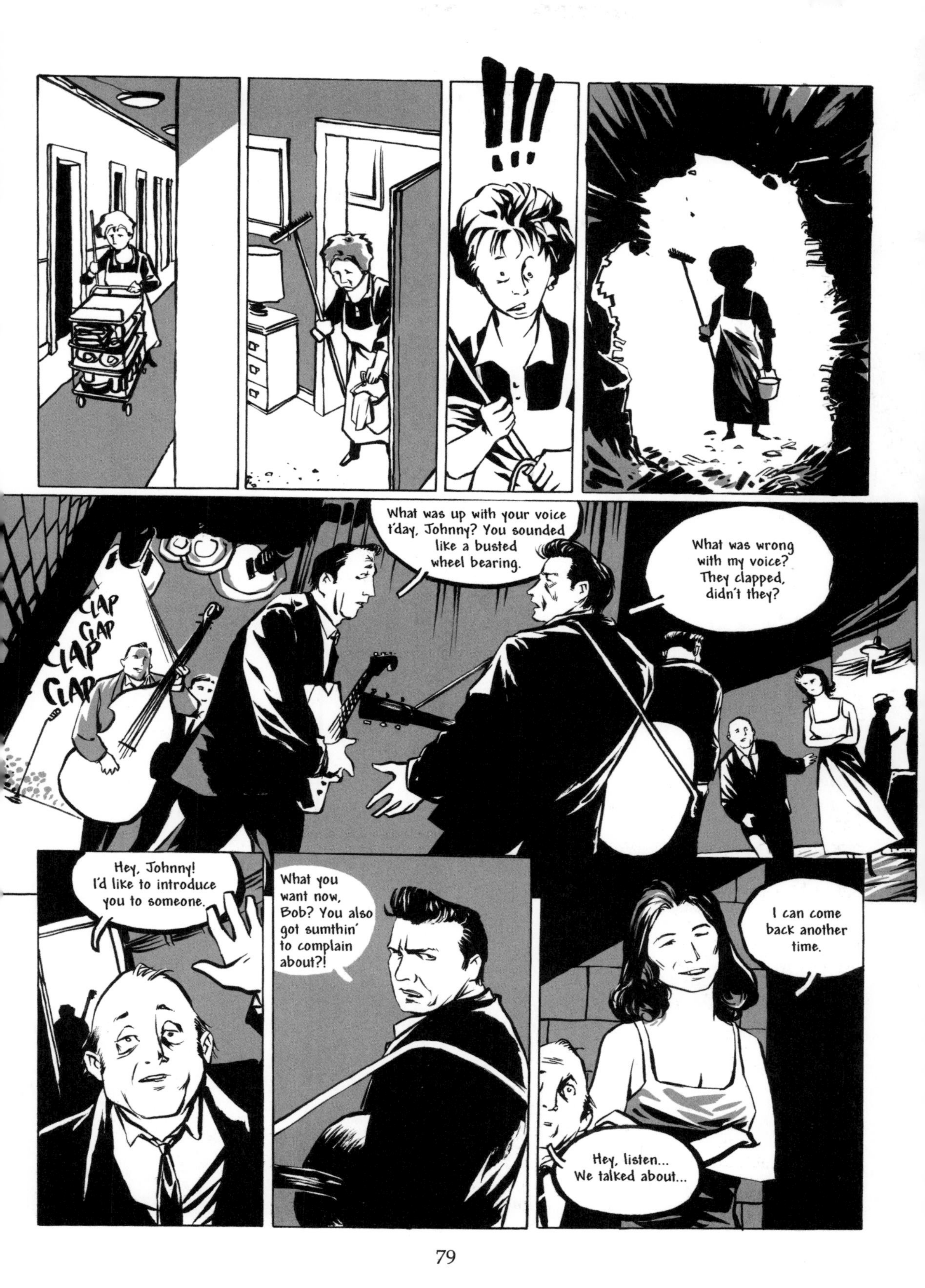

CLAP
CLAP
CLAP
CLAP
What was up with your voice t'day, Johnny? You sounded like a busted wheel bearing.
What was wrong with my voice? They clapped, didn't they?
Hey, Johnny! I'd like to introduce you to someone.
What you want now, Bob? You also got sumthin' to complain about?!
I can come back another time.
Hey, listen... We talked about...

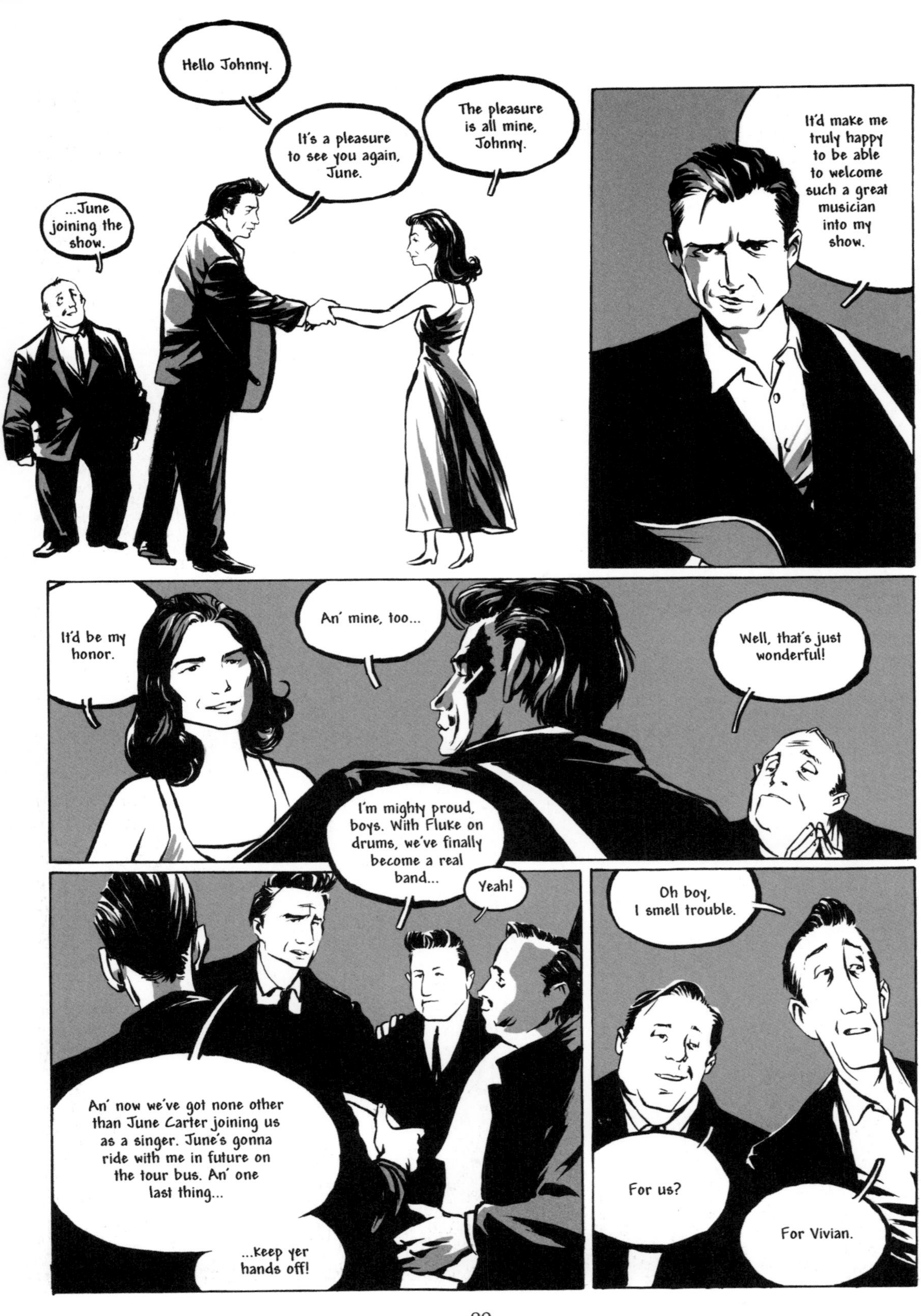
...June joining the show.
Hello Johnny.
It's a pleasure to see you again, June.
The pleasure is all mine, Johnny.
It'd make me truly happy to be able to welcome such a great musician into my show.
It'd be my honor.
An' mine, too...
Well, that's just wonderful!
I'm mighty proud, boys. With Fluke on drums, we've finally become a real band...
Yeah!
An' now we've got none other than June Carter joining us as a singer. June's gonna ride with me in future on the tour bus. An' one last thing...
...keep yer hands off!
Oh boy, I smell trouble.
For us?
For Vivian.

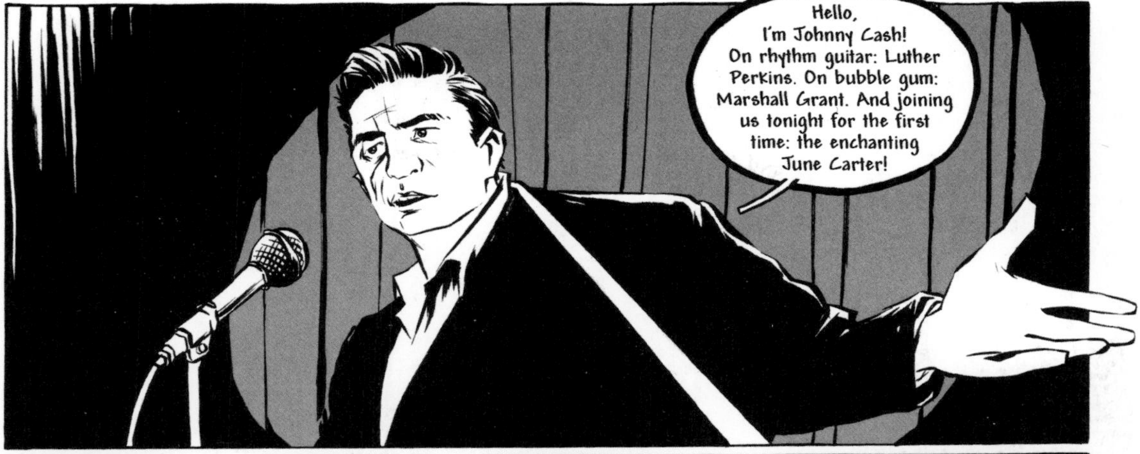
Hello, I'm Johnny Cash! On rhythm guitar: Luther Perkins. On bubble gum: Marshall Grant. And joining us tonight for the first time: the enchanting June Carter!

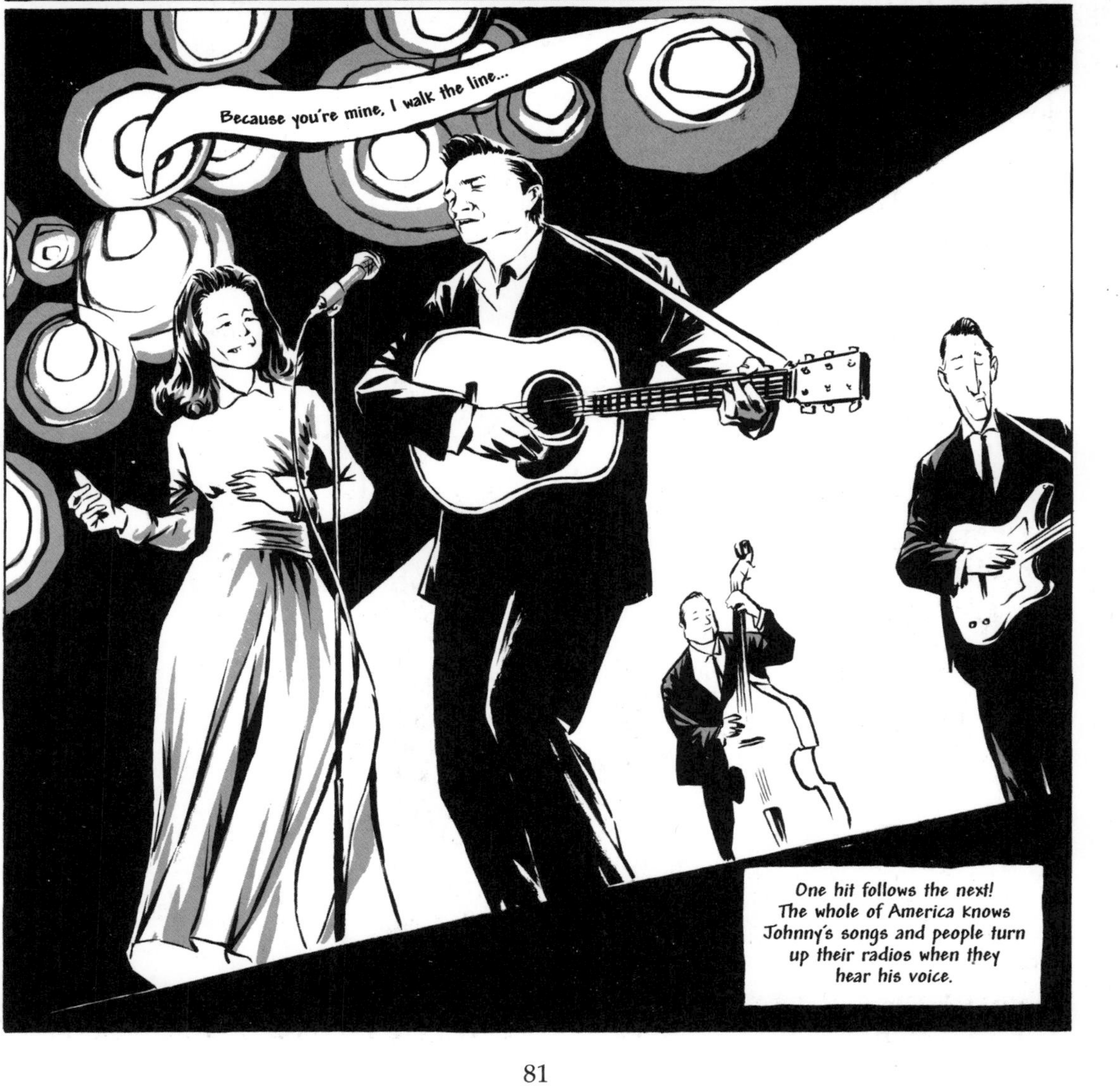
Because you're mine, I walk the line...
One hit follows the next! The whole of America knows Johnny's songs and people turn up their radios when they hear his voice.

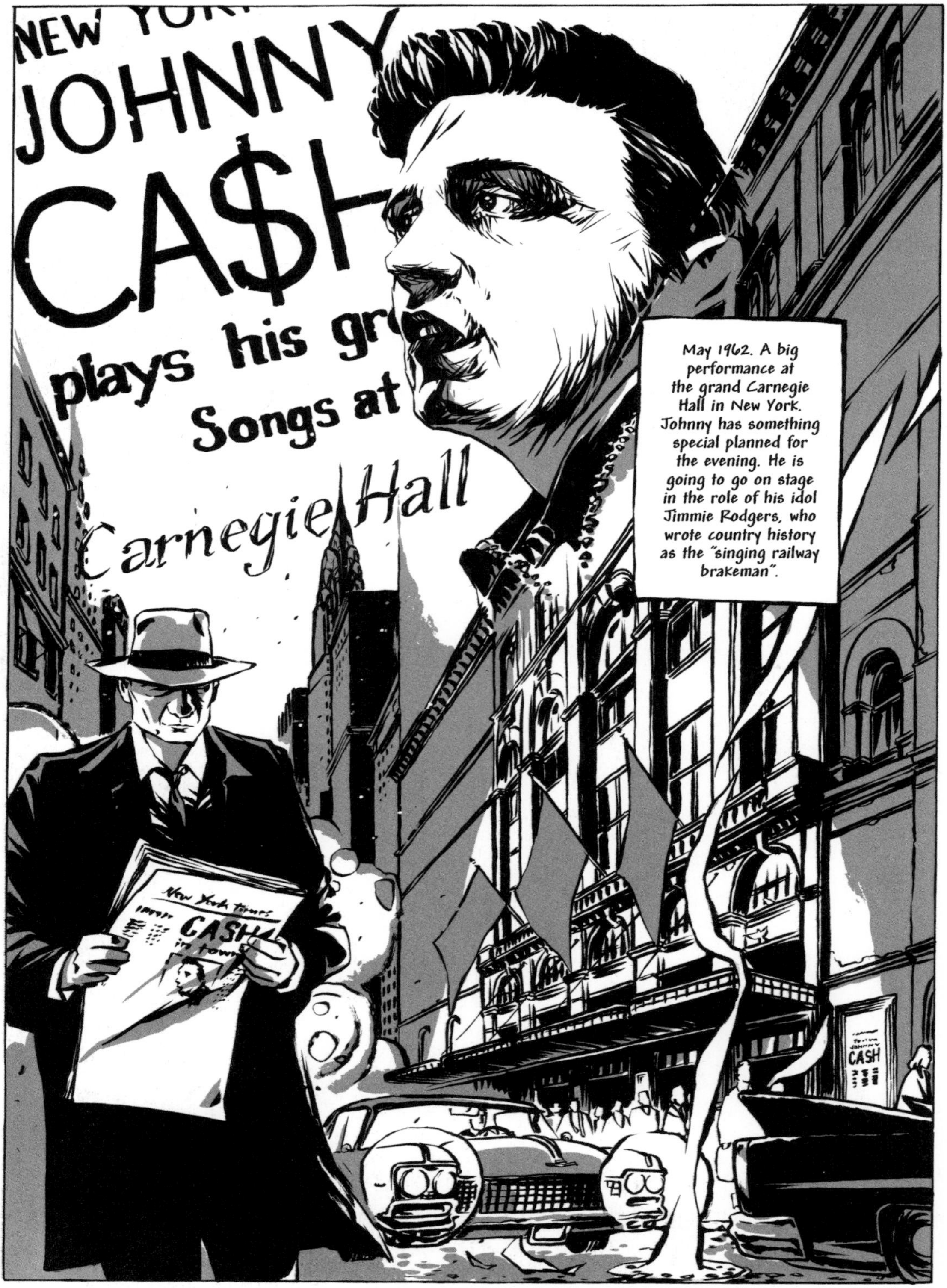
NEW YOR
JOHNNY
CA$H
plays his gr
Songs at
Carnegie Hall
May 1962. A big performance at the grand Carnegie Hall in New York. Johnny has something special planned for the evening. He is going to go on stage in the role of his idol Jimmie Rodgers, who wrote country history as the "singing railway brakeman".
New York Times
CASH
CASH

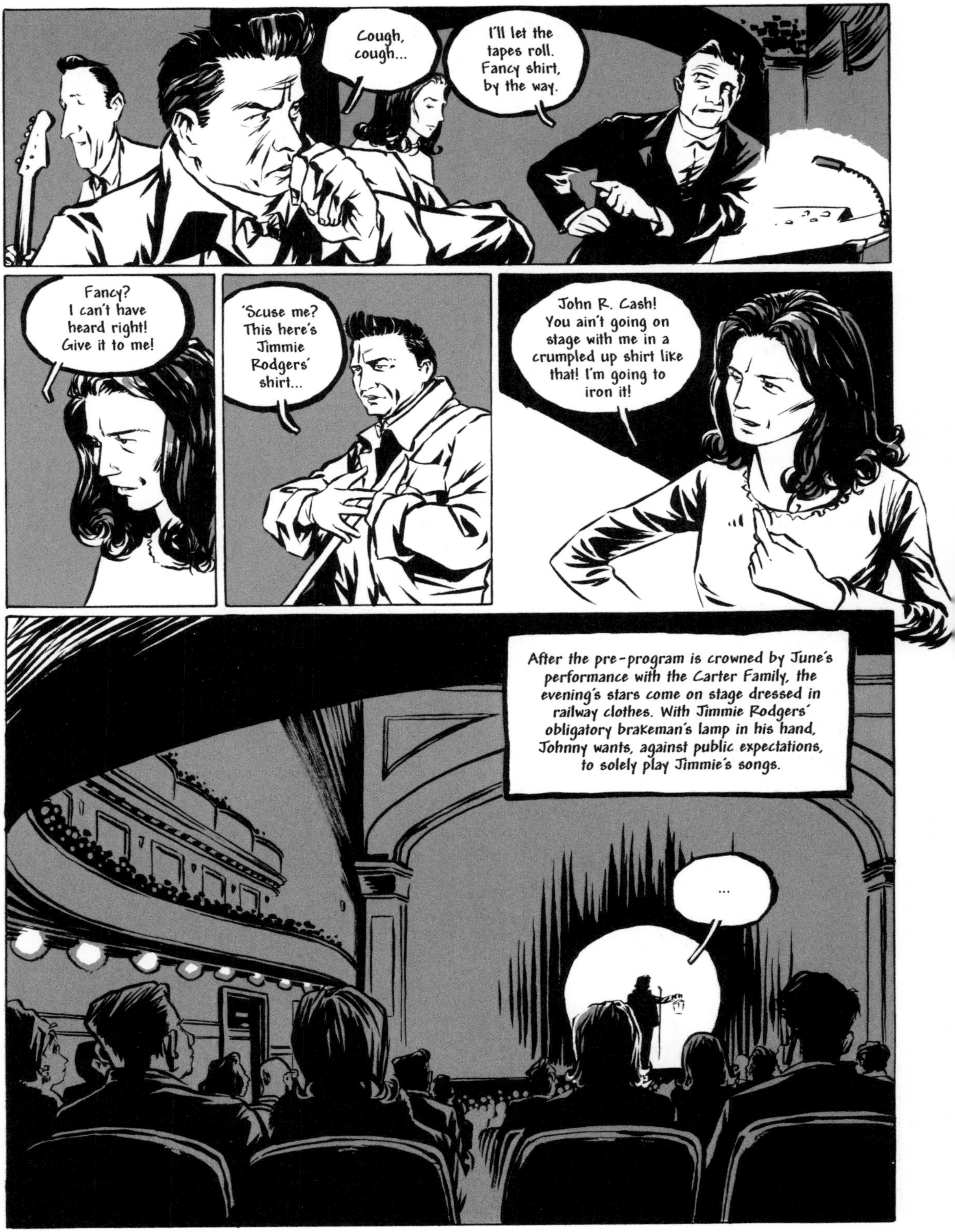
Cough, cough...
I'll let the tapes roll. Fancy shirt, by the way.
Fancy? I can't have heard right! Give it to me!
'Scuse me? This here's Jimmie Rodgers' shirt...
John R. Cash! You ain't going on stage with me in a crumpled up shirt like that! I'm going to iron it!
After the pre-program is crowned by June's performance with the Carter Family, the evening's stars come on stage dressed in railway clothes. With Jimmie Rodgers' obligatory brakeman's lamp in his hand, Johnny wants, against public expectations, to solely play Jimmie's songs.
...

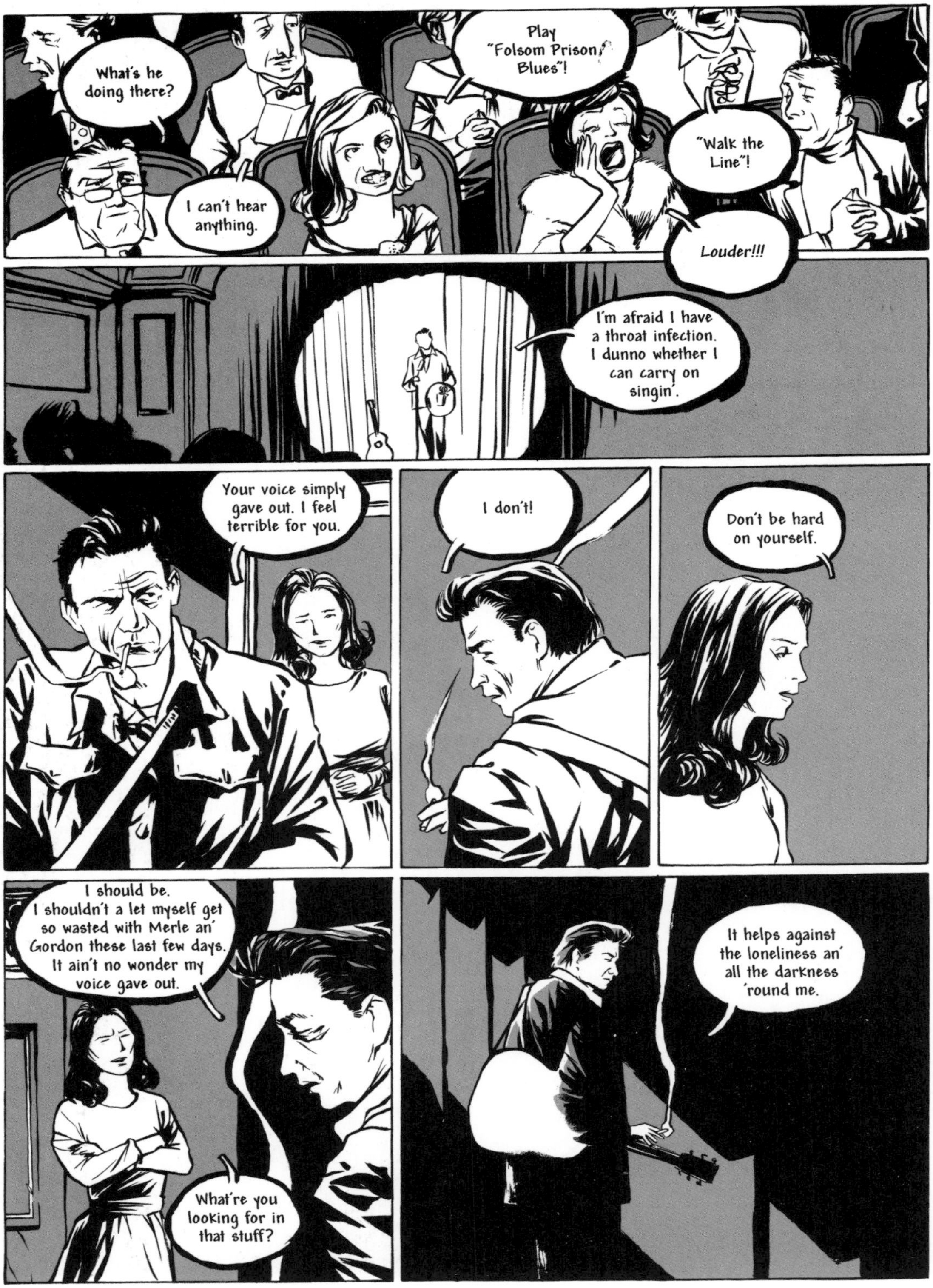
What's he doing there?
I can't hear anything.
Play "Folsom Prison Blues"!
"Walk the Line"!
Louder!!!
I'm afraid I have a throat infection. I dunno whether I can carry on singin'.
Your voice simply gave out. I feel terrible for you.
I don't!
Don't be hard on yourself.
I should be. I shouldn't a let myself get so wasted with Merle an' Gordon these last few days. It ain't no wonder my voice gave out.
What're you looking for in that stuff?
It helps against the loneliness an' all the darkness 'round me.

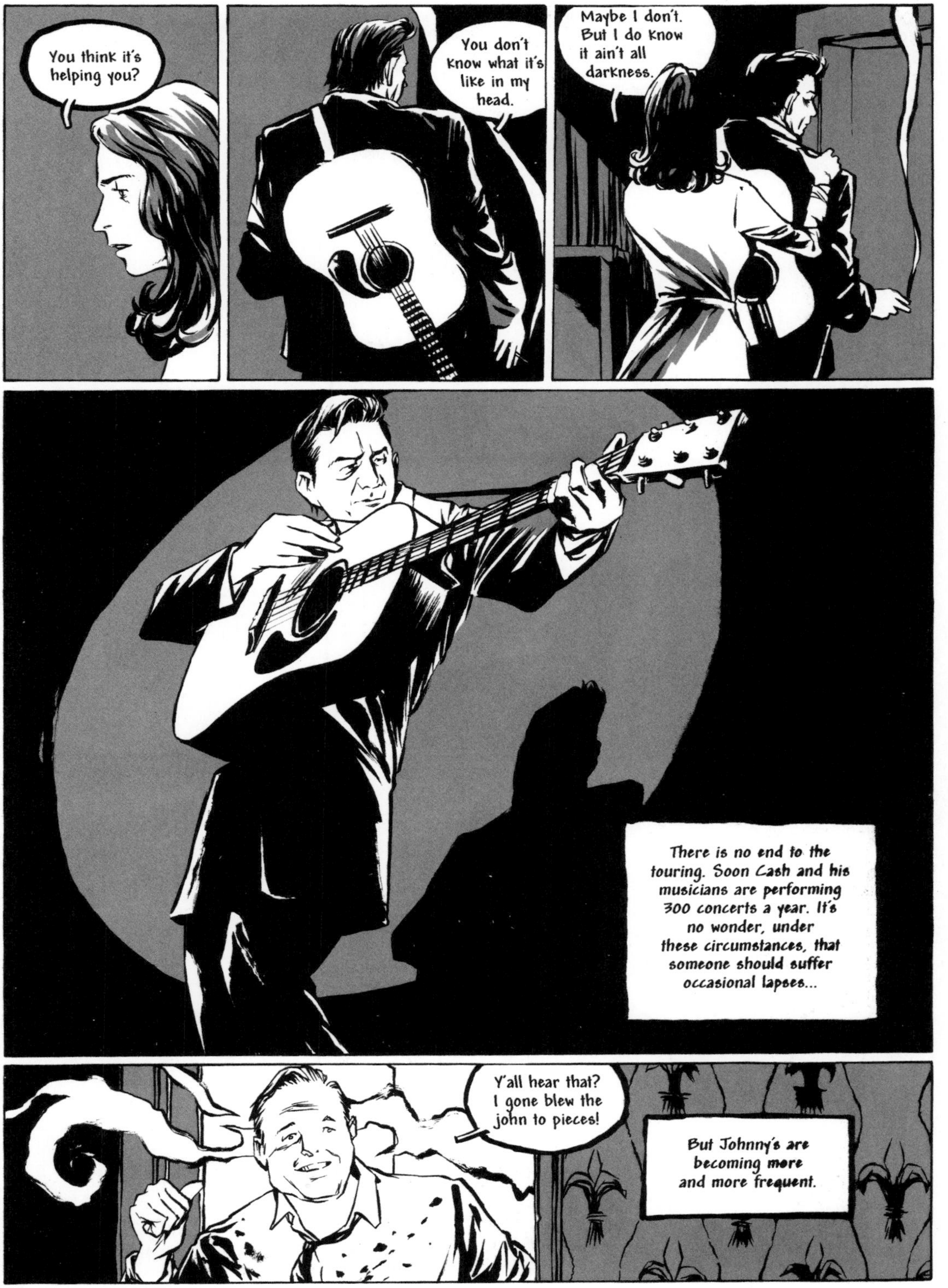
You think it's helping you?
You don't know what it's like in my head.
Maybe I don't. But I do know it ain't all darkness.
There is no end to the touring. Soon Cash and his musicians are performing 300 concerts a year. It's no wonder, under these circumstances, that someone should suffer occasional lapses...
Y'all hear that? I gone blew the john to pieces!
But Johnny's are becoming more and more frequent.

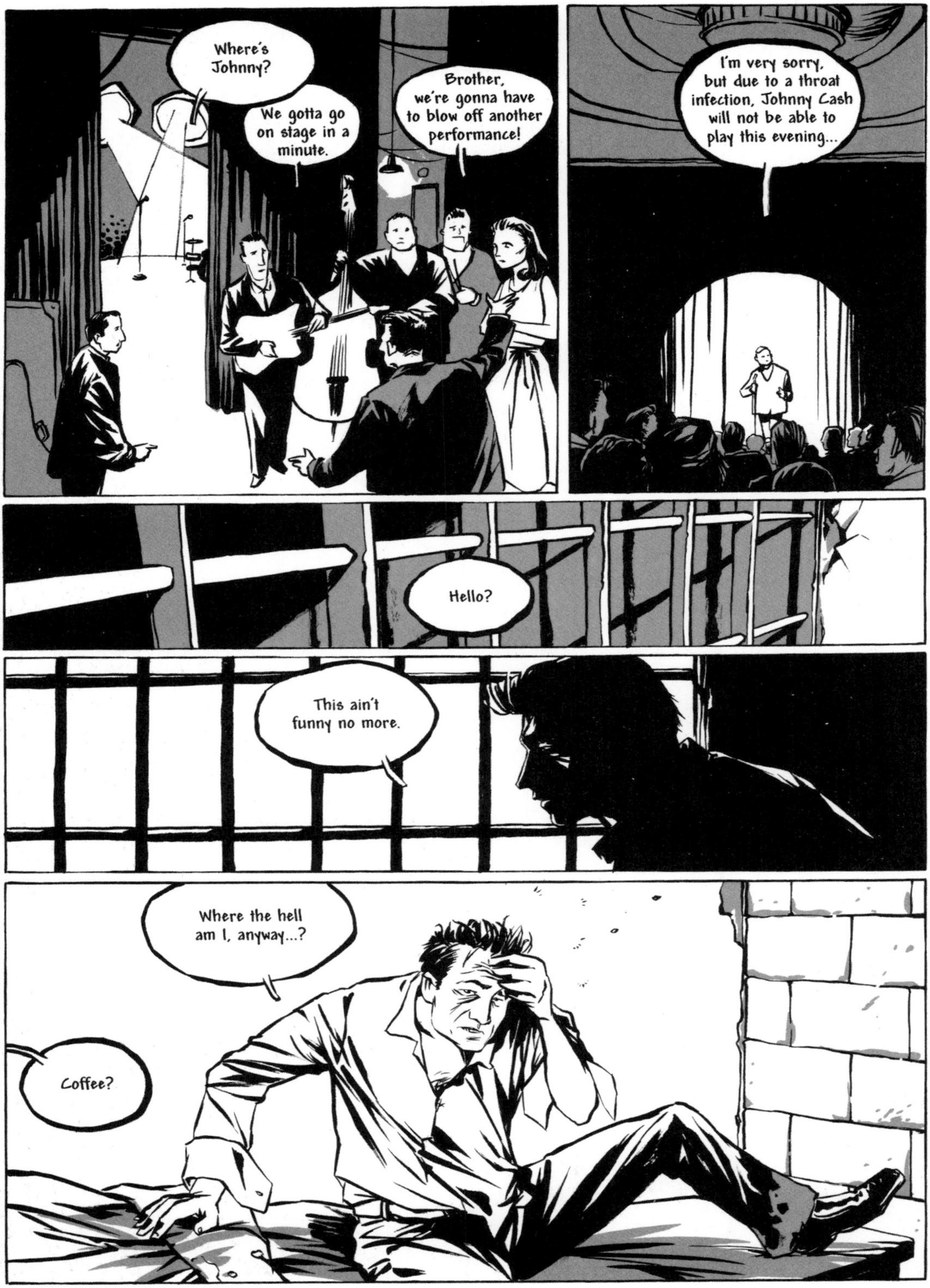
Where's Johnny?
We gotta go on stage in a minute.
Brother, we're gonna have to blow off another performance!
I'm very sorry, but due to a throat infection, Johnny Cash will not be able to play this evening...
Hello?
This ain't funny no more.
Where the hell am I, anyway...?
Coffee?

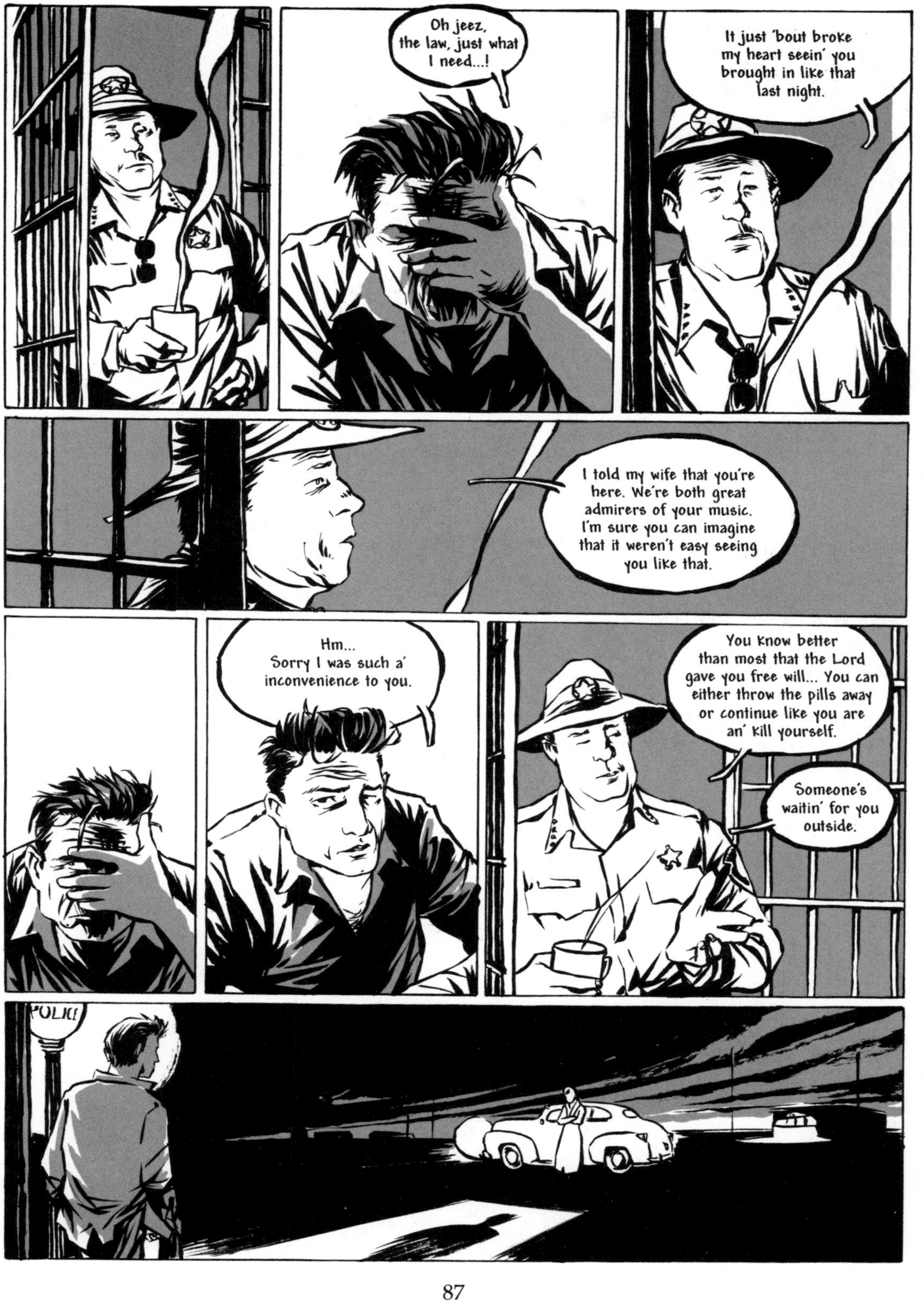
Oh jeez, the law, just what I need...!
It just 'bout broke my heart seein' you brought in like that last night.
I told my wife that you're here. We're both great admirers of your music. I'm sure you can imagine that it weren't easy seeing you like that.
Hm... Sorry I was such a' inconvenience to you.
You know better than most that the Lord gave you free will... You can either throw the pills away or continue like you are an' kill yourself.
Someone's waitin' for you outside.
POLICE

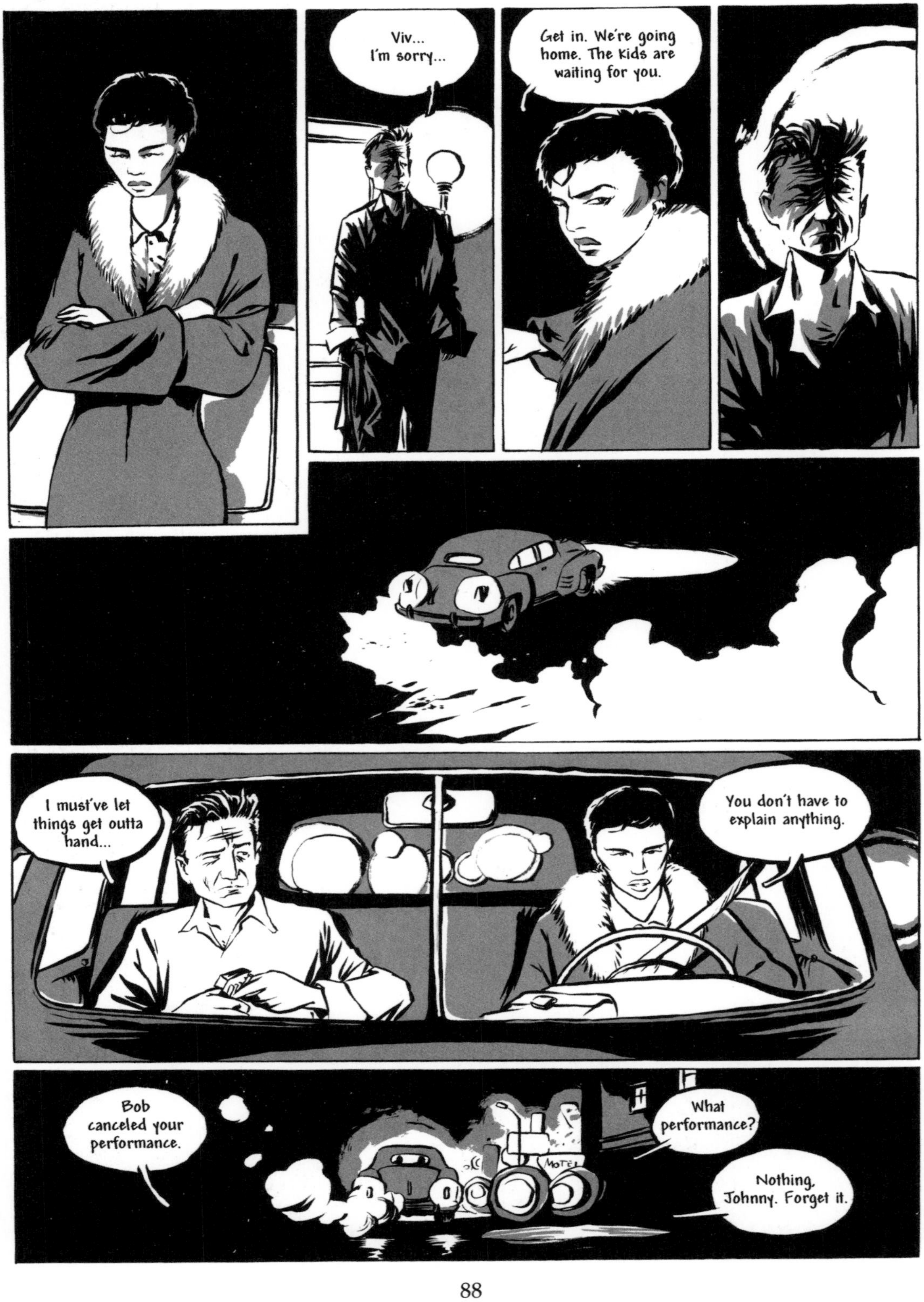
Viv...
I'm sorry...
Get in. We're going home. The kids are waiting for you.
I must've let things get outta hand...
You don't have to explain anything.
Bob canceled your performance.
What performance?
Nothing, Johnny. Forget it.
MOTEL

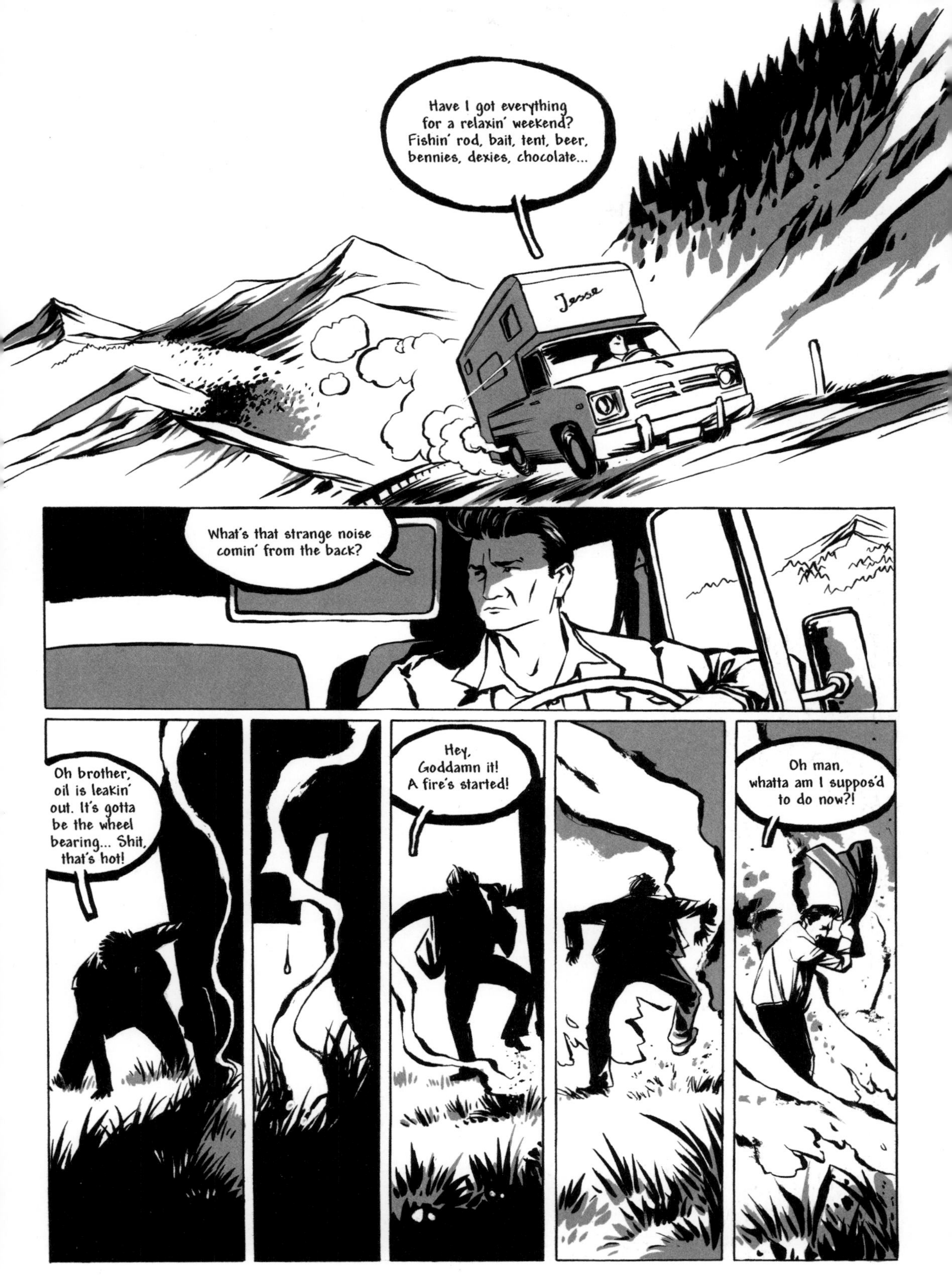

Have I got everything for a relaxin' weekend? Fishin' rod, bait, tent, beer, bennies, dexies, chocolate...
Jesse
What's that strange noise comin' from the back?
Oh brother, oil is leakin' out. It's gotta be the wheel bearing... Shit, that's hot!
Hey, Goddamn it! A fire's started!
Oh man, whatta am I suppos'd to do now?!

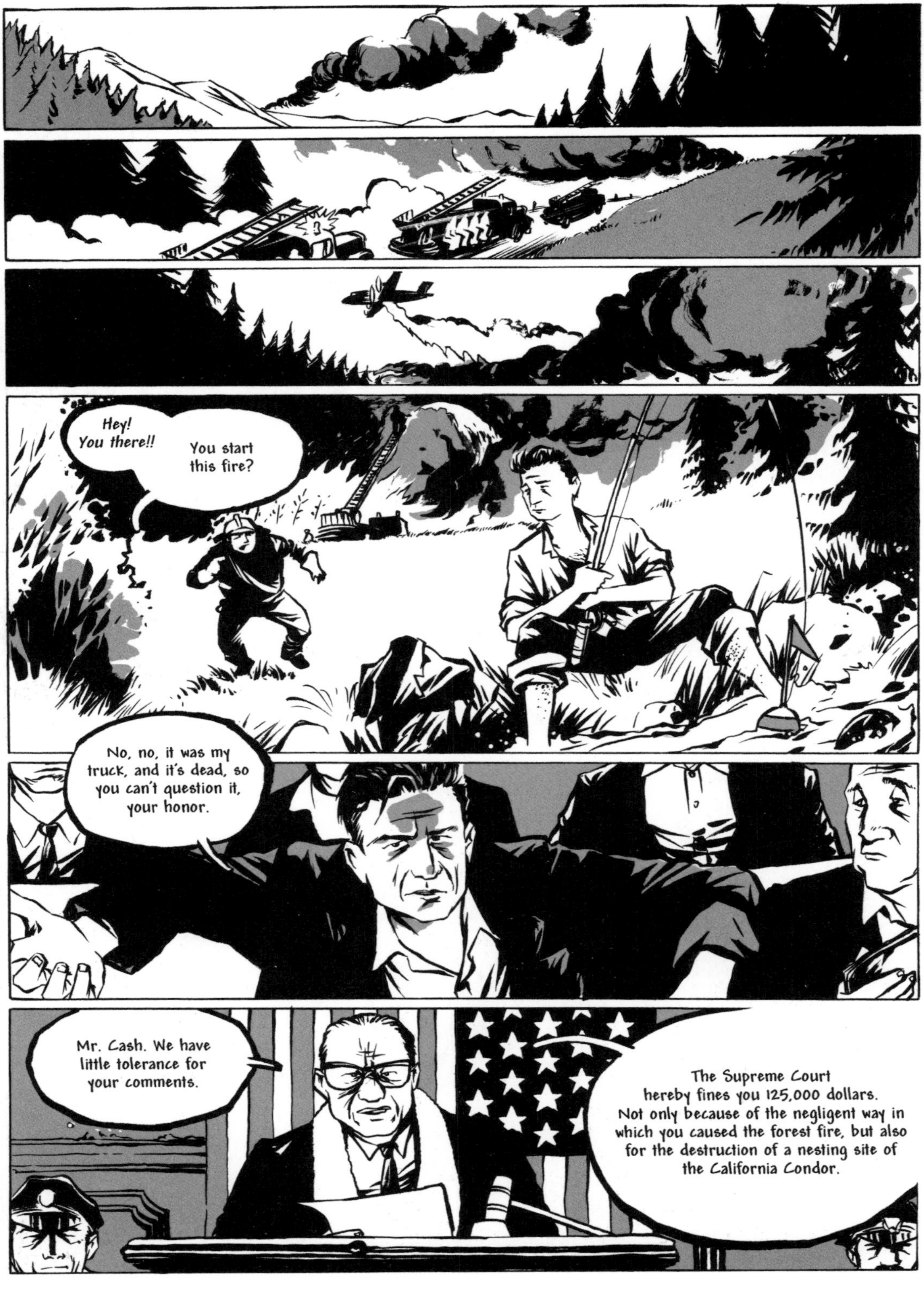
Hey! You there!!
You start this fire?
No, no, it was my truck, and it's dead, so you can't question it, your honor.
Mr. Cash. We have little tolerance for your comments.
The Supreme Court hereby fines you 125,000 dollars. Not only because of the negligent way in which you caused the forest fire, but also for the destruction of a nesting site of the California Condor.

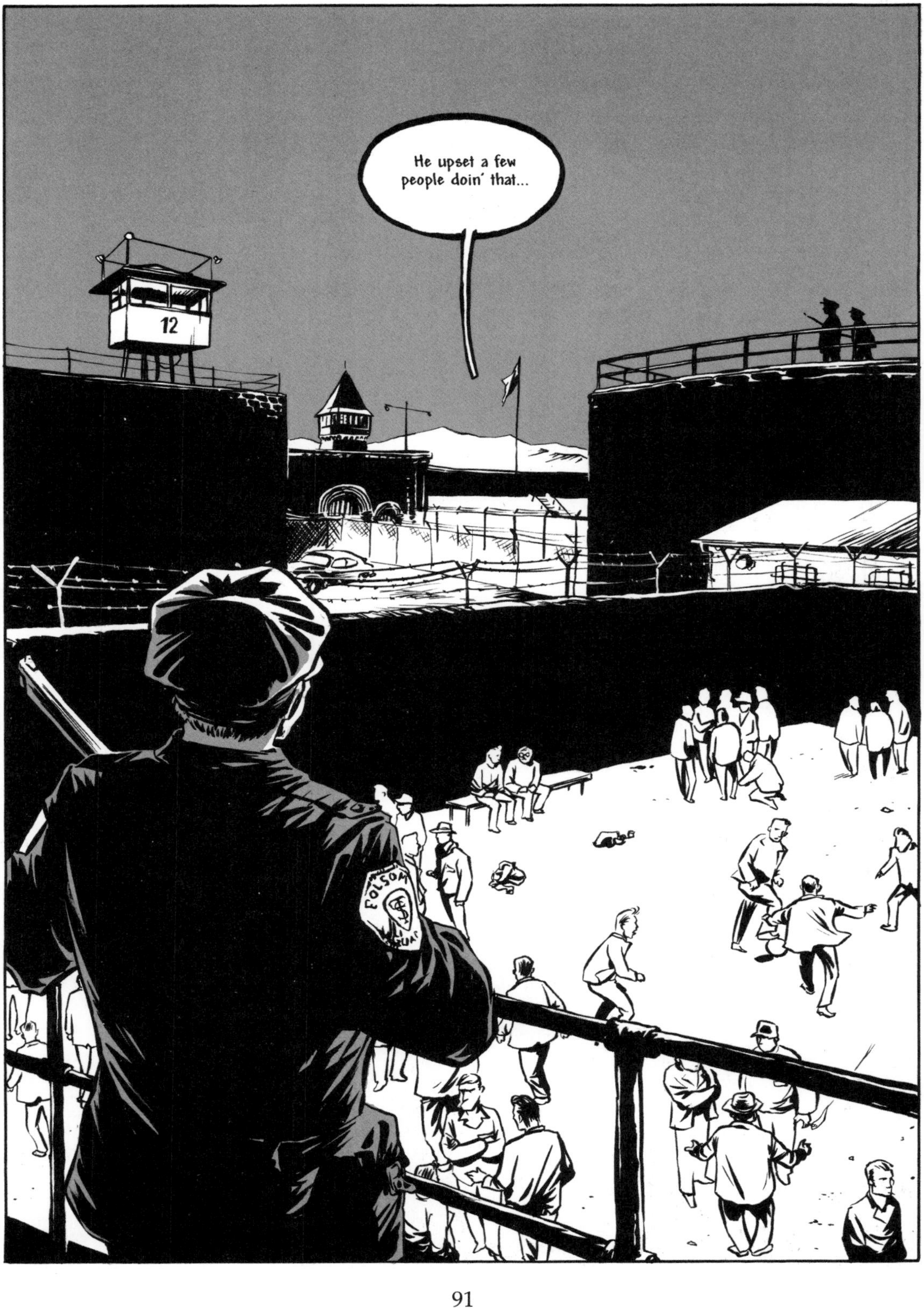
He upset a few people doin' that...
12
FOLSOM

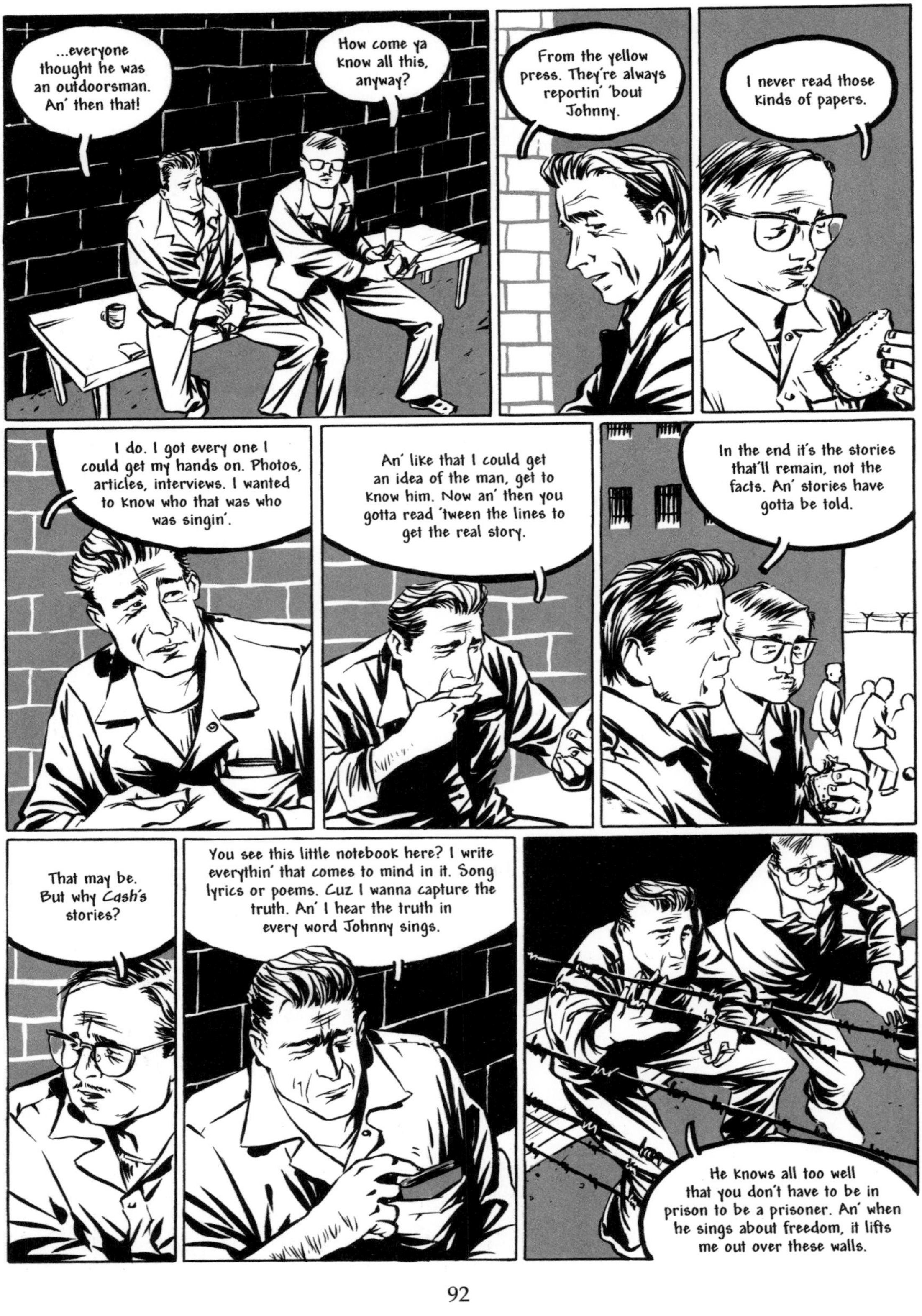
...everyone thought he was an outdoorsman. An' then that!
How come ya know all this, anyway?
From the yellow press. They're always reportin' 'bout Johnny.
I never read those kinds of papers.
I do. I got every one I could get my hands on. Photos, articles, interviews. I wanted to know who that was who was singin'.
An' like that I could get an idea of the man, get to know him. Now an' then you gotta read 'tween the lines to get the real story.
In the end it's the stories that'll remain, not the facts. An' stories have gotta be told.
That may be. But why *Cash's* stories?
You see this little notebook here? I write everythin' that comes to mind in it. Song lyrics or poems. Cuz I wanna capture the truth. An' I hear the truth in every word Johnny sings.
He knows all too well that you don't have to be in prison to be a prisoner. An' when he sings about freedom, it lifts me out over these walls.

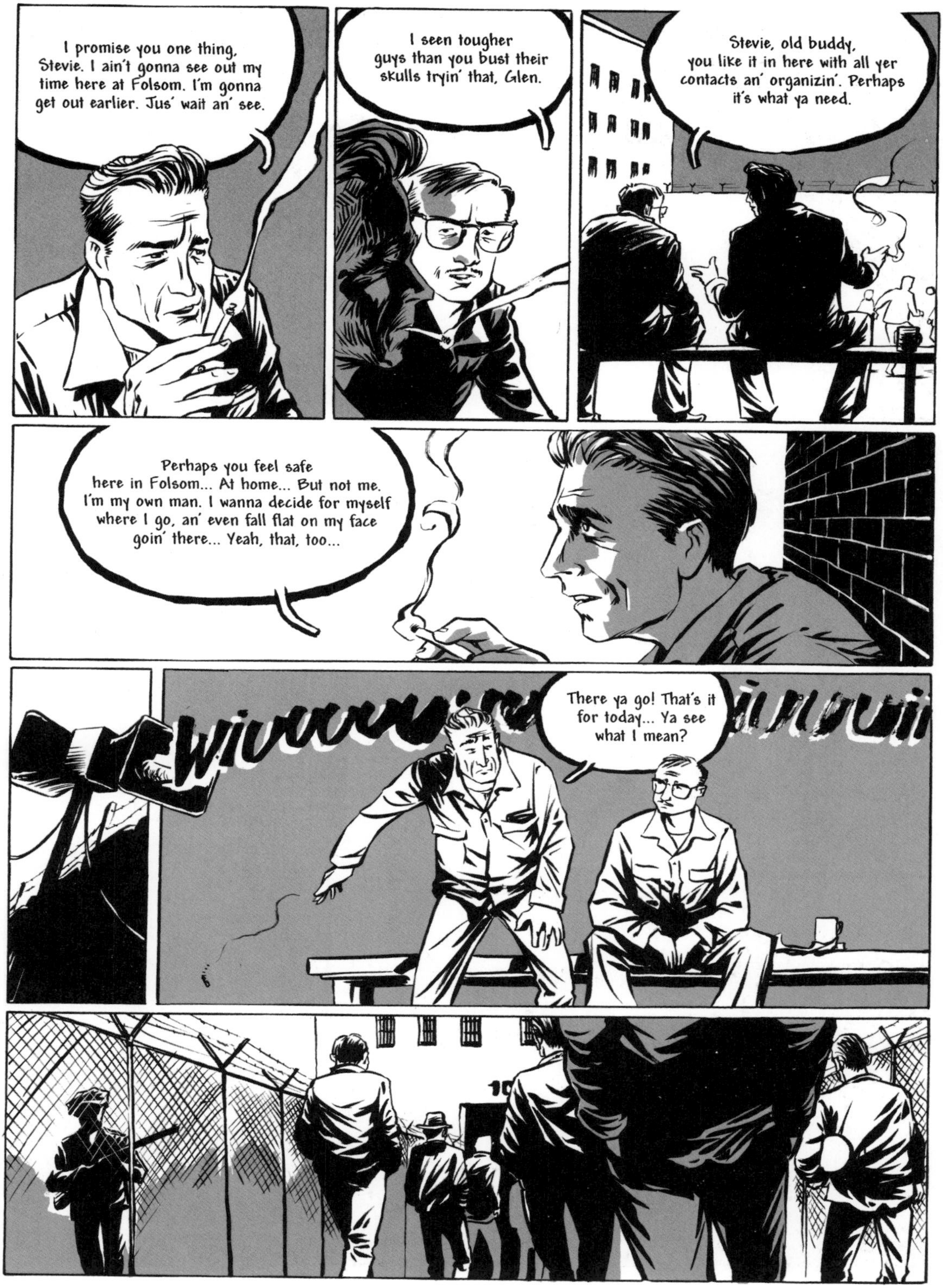
I promise you one thing, Stevie. I ain't gonna see out my time here at Folsom. I'm gonna get out earlier. Jus' wait an' see.
I seen tougher guys than you bust their skulls tryin' that, Glen.
Stevie, old buddy, you like it in here with all yer contacts an' organizin'. Perhaps it's what ya need.
Perhaps you feel safe here in Folsom... At home... But not me. I'm my own man. I wanna decide for myself where I go, an' even fall flat on my face goin' there... Yeah, that, too...
WIIIIIIIIIIIIIII
There ya go! That's it for today... Ya see what I mean?

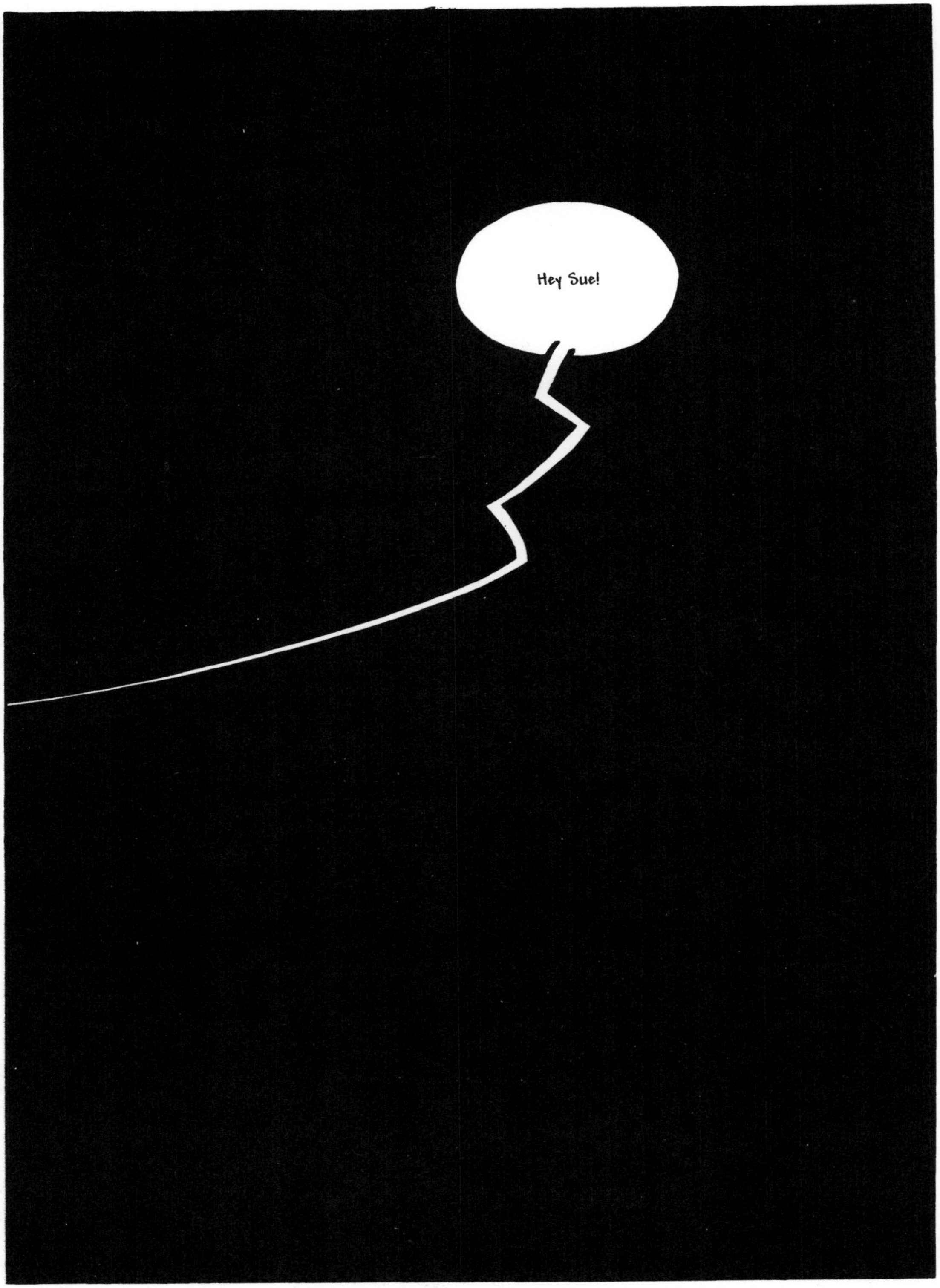
Hey Sue!

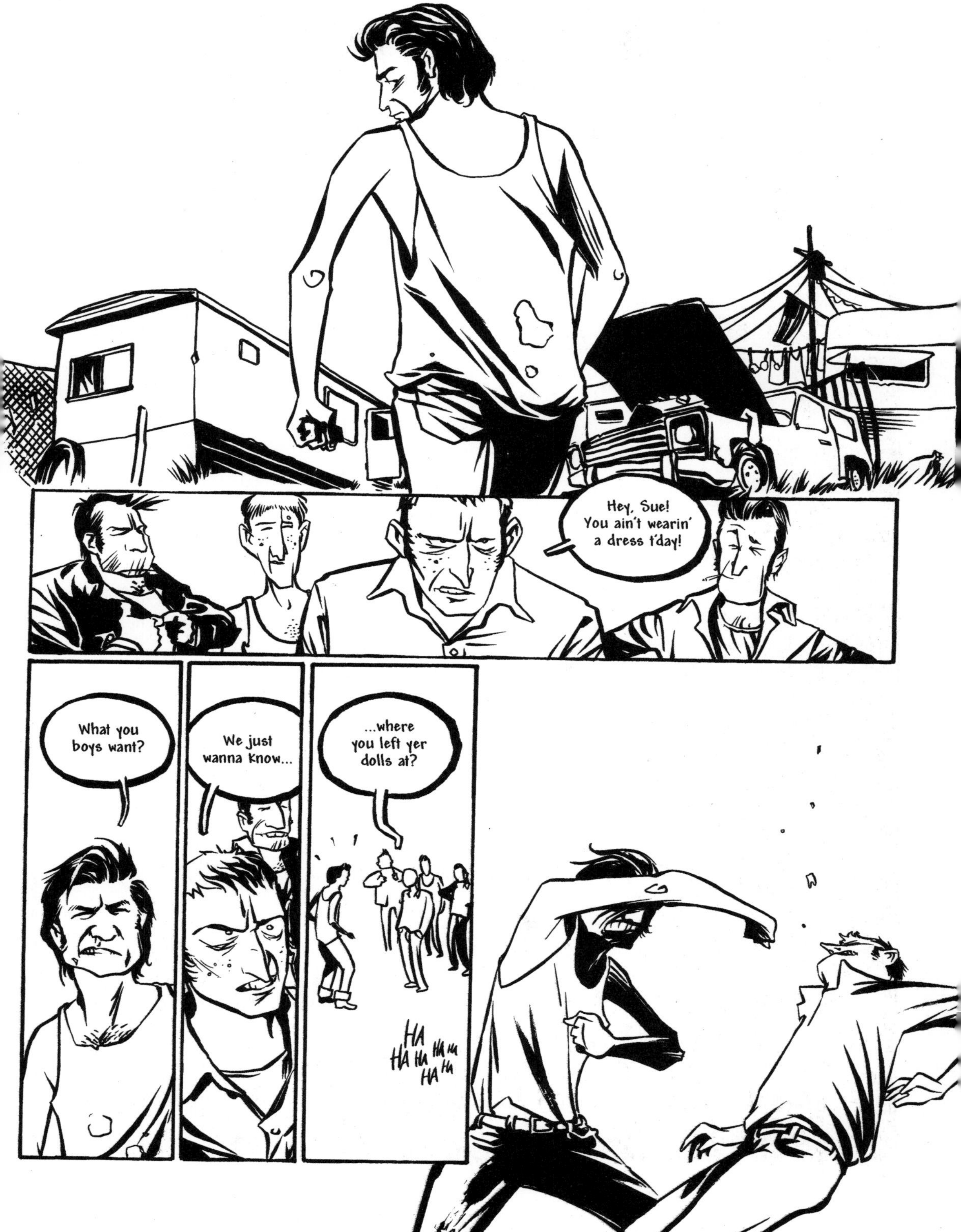

Hey, Sue! You ain't wearin' a dress t'day!
What you boys want?
We just wanna know...
...where you left yer dolls at?
HA HA HA HA HA HA HA HA

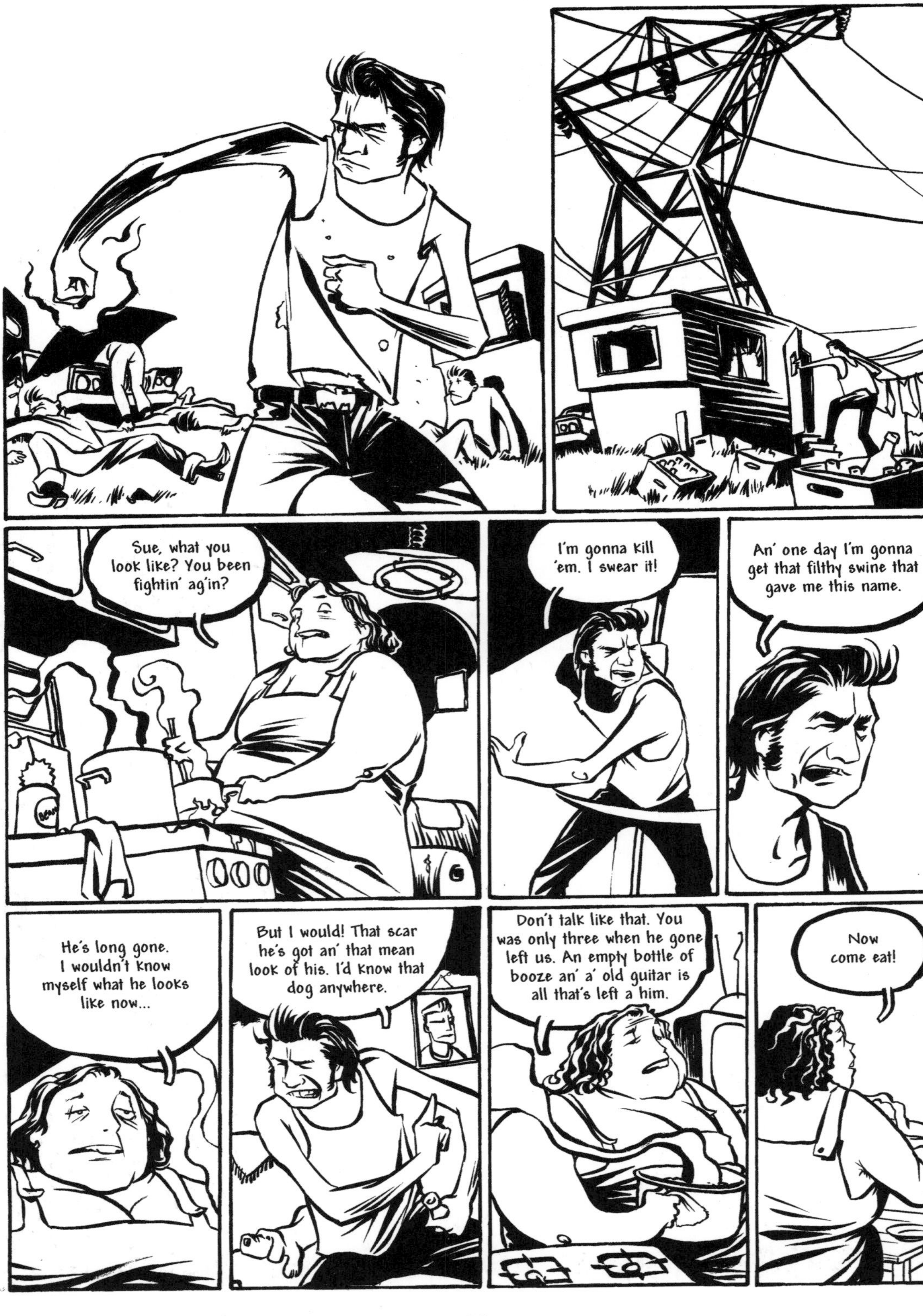
Sue, what you look like? You been fightin' ag'in?
I'm gonna kill 'em. I swear it!
An' one day I'm gonna get that filthy swine that gave me this name.
He's long gone. I wouldn't know myself what he looks like now...
But I would! That scar he's got an' that mean look of his. I'd know that dog anywhere.
Don't talk like that. You was only three when he gone left us. An empty bottle of booze an' a' old guitar is all that's left a him.
Now come eat!

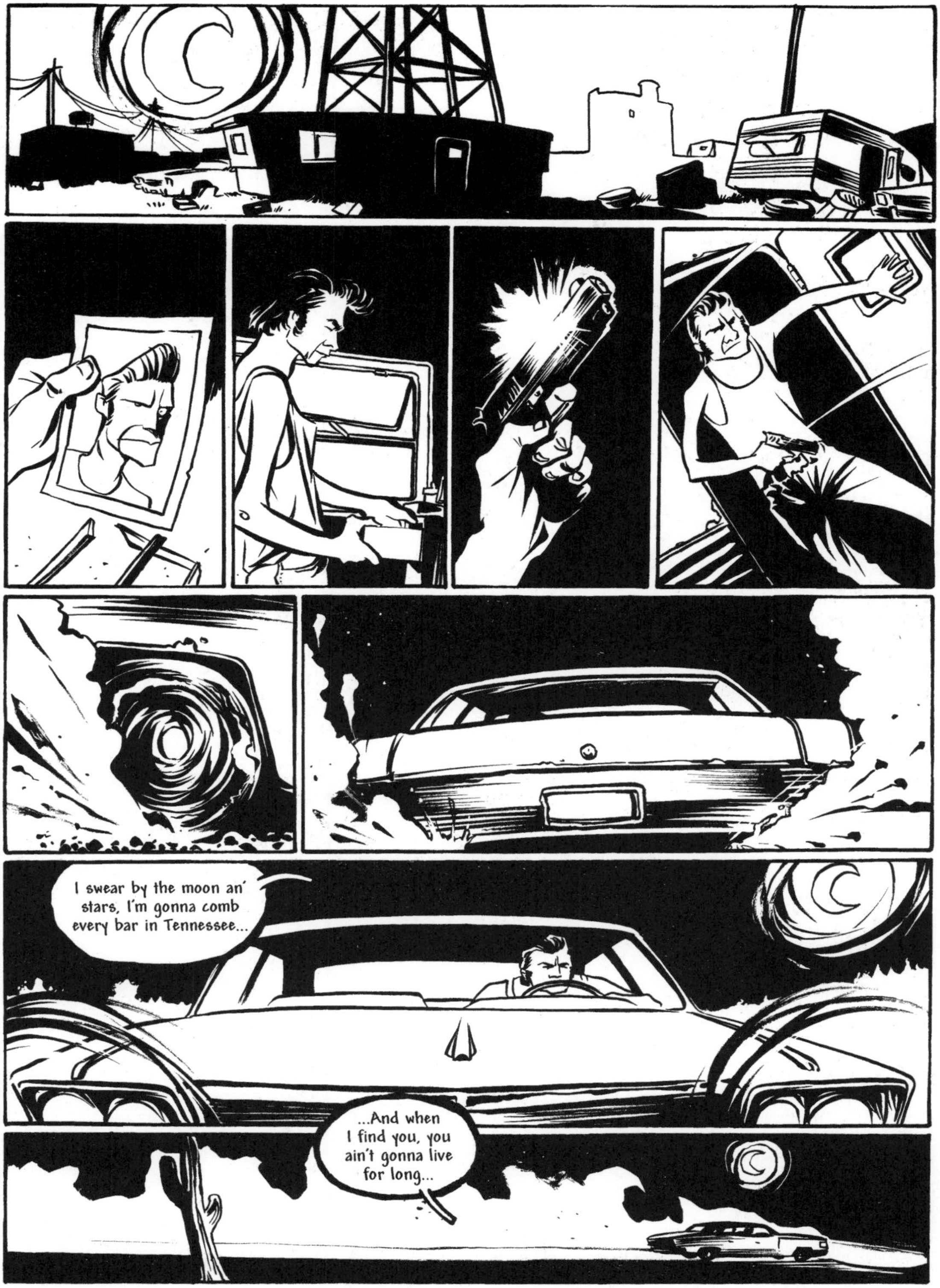
I swear by the moon an' stars, I'm gonna comb every bar in Tennessee...
...And when I find you, you ain't gonna live for long...

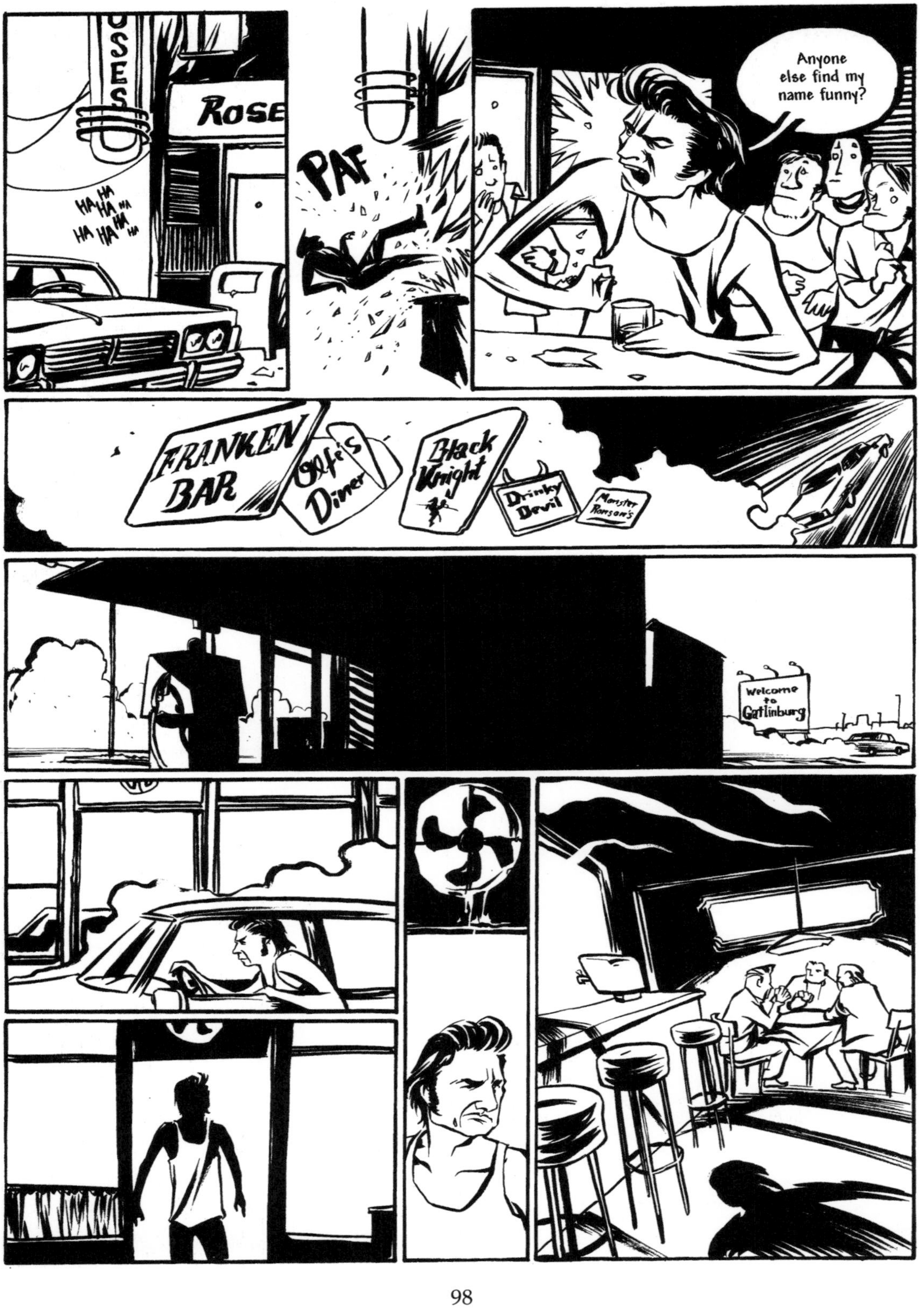
ROSES
ROSE
HA HA HA HA HA HA HA HA HA HA
PAF
Anyone else find my name funny?
FRANKEN BAR
Olfe's Diner
Black Knight
Drinky Devil
Monster Ronson's
Welcome to Gatlinburg

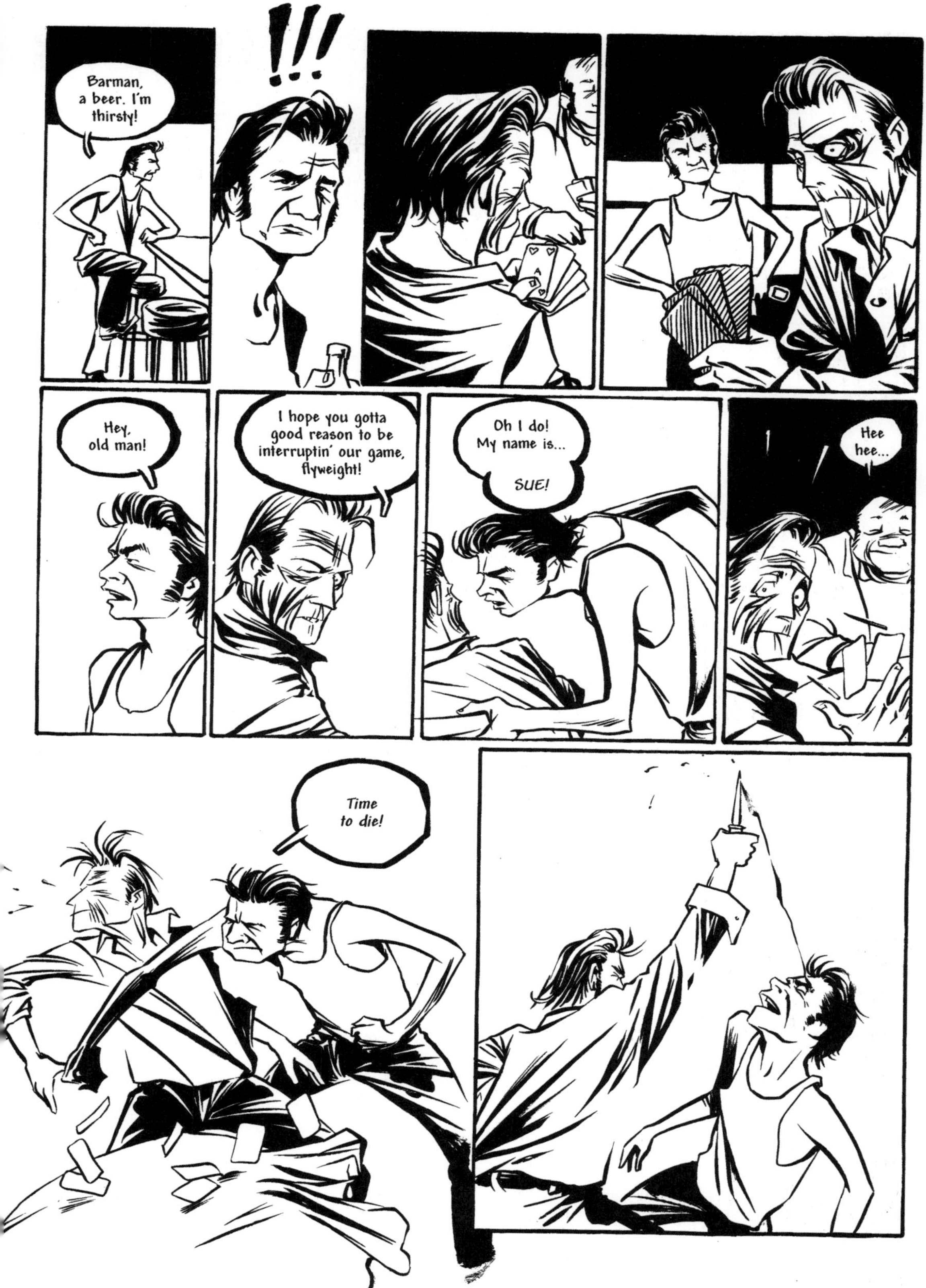
Barman, a beer. I'm thirsty!
!!!
Hey, old man!
I hope you gotta good reason to be interruptin' our game, flyweight!
Oh I do! My name is...
SUE!
Hee hee...
Time to die!

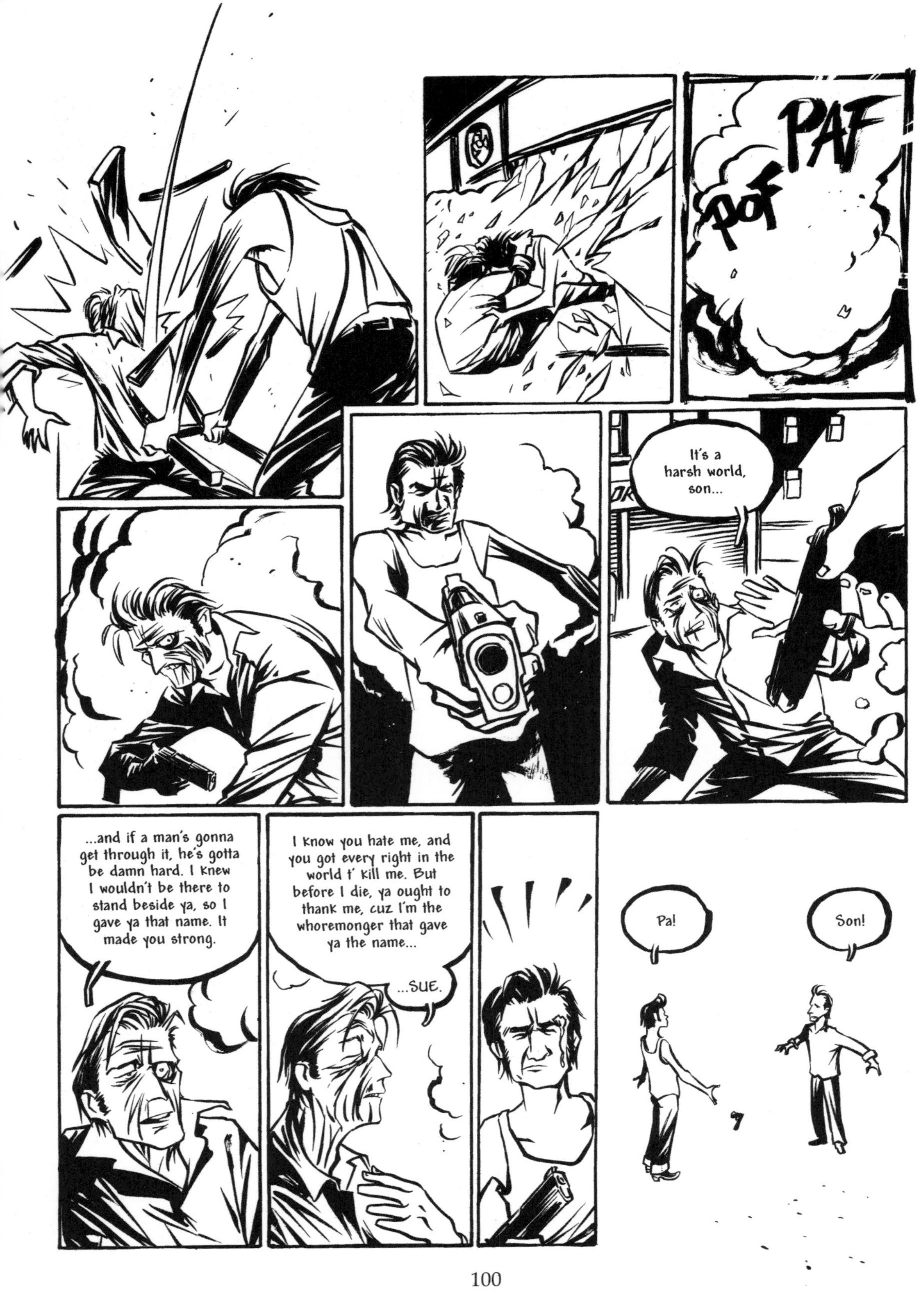
PAF
POF
It's a harsh world, son...
...and if a man's gonna get through it, he's gotta be damn hard. I knew I wouldn't be there to stand beside ya, so I gave ya that name. It made you strong.
I know you hate me, and you got every right in the world t' kill me. But before I die, ya ought to thank me, cuz I'm the whoremonger that gave ya the name...
...SUE.
Pa!
Son!

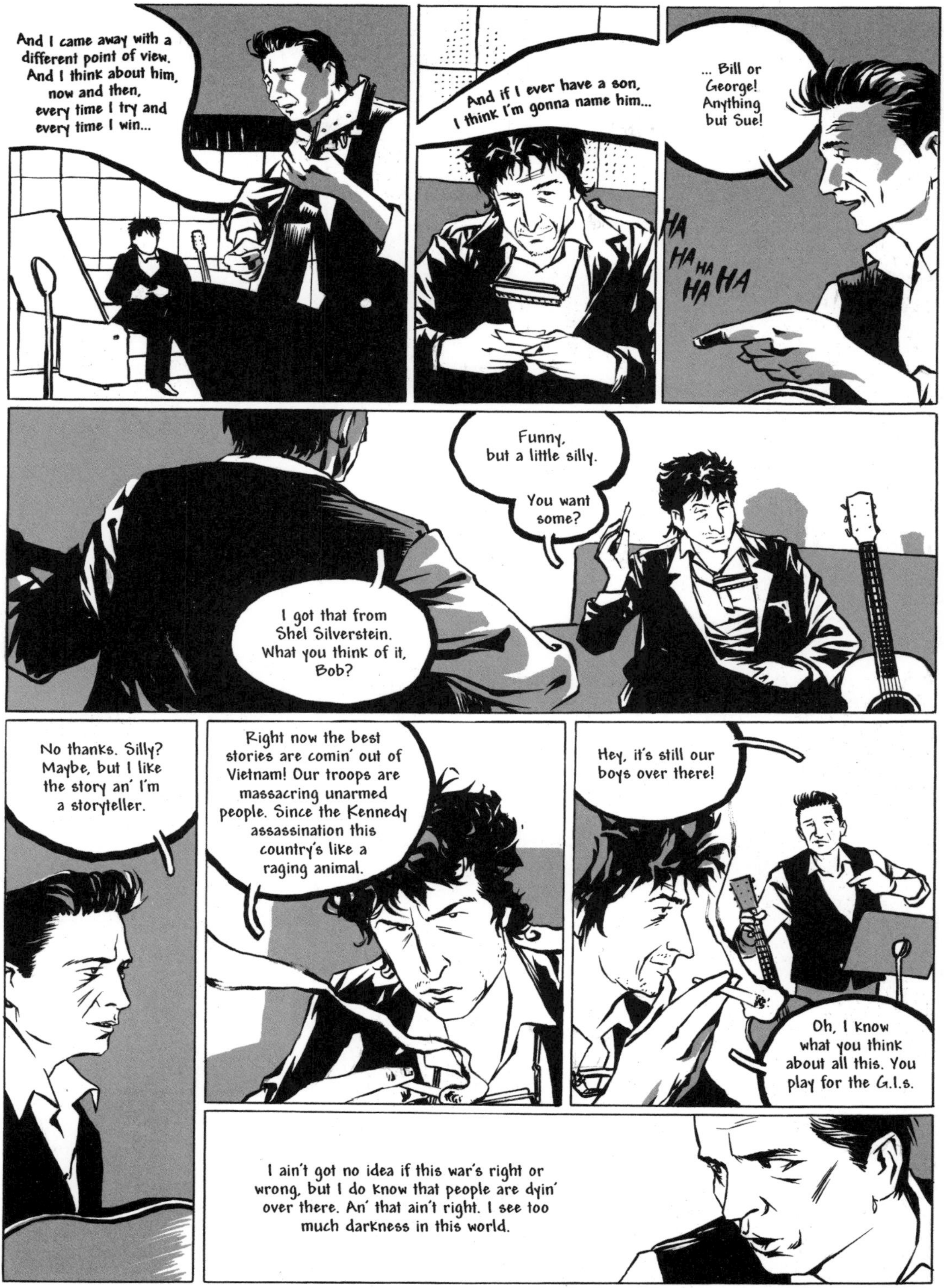
And I came away with a different point of view. And I think about him, now and then, every time I try and every time I win...
And if I ever have a son, I think I'm gonna name him...
... Bill or George! Anything but Sue!
HA HA HA HA HA HA
Funny, but a little silly.
You want some?
I got that from Shel Silverstein. What you think of it, Bob?
No thanks. Silly? Maybe, but I like the story an' I'm a storyteller.
Right now the best stories are comin' out of Vietnam! Our troops are massacring unarmed people. Since the Kennedy assassination this country's like a raging animal.
Hey, it's still our boys over there!
Oh, I know what you think about all this. You play for the G.I.s.
I ain't got no idea if this war's right or wrong, but I do know that people are dyin' over there. An' that ain't right. I see too much darkness in this world.

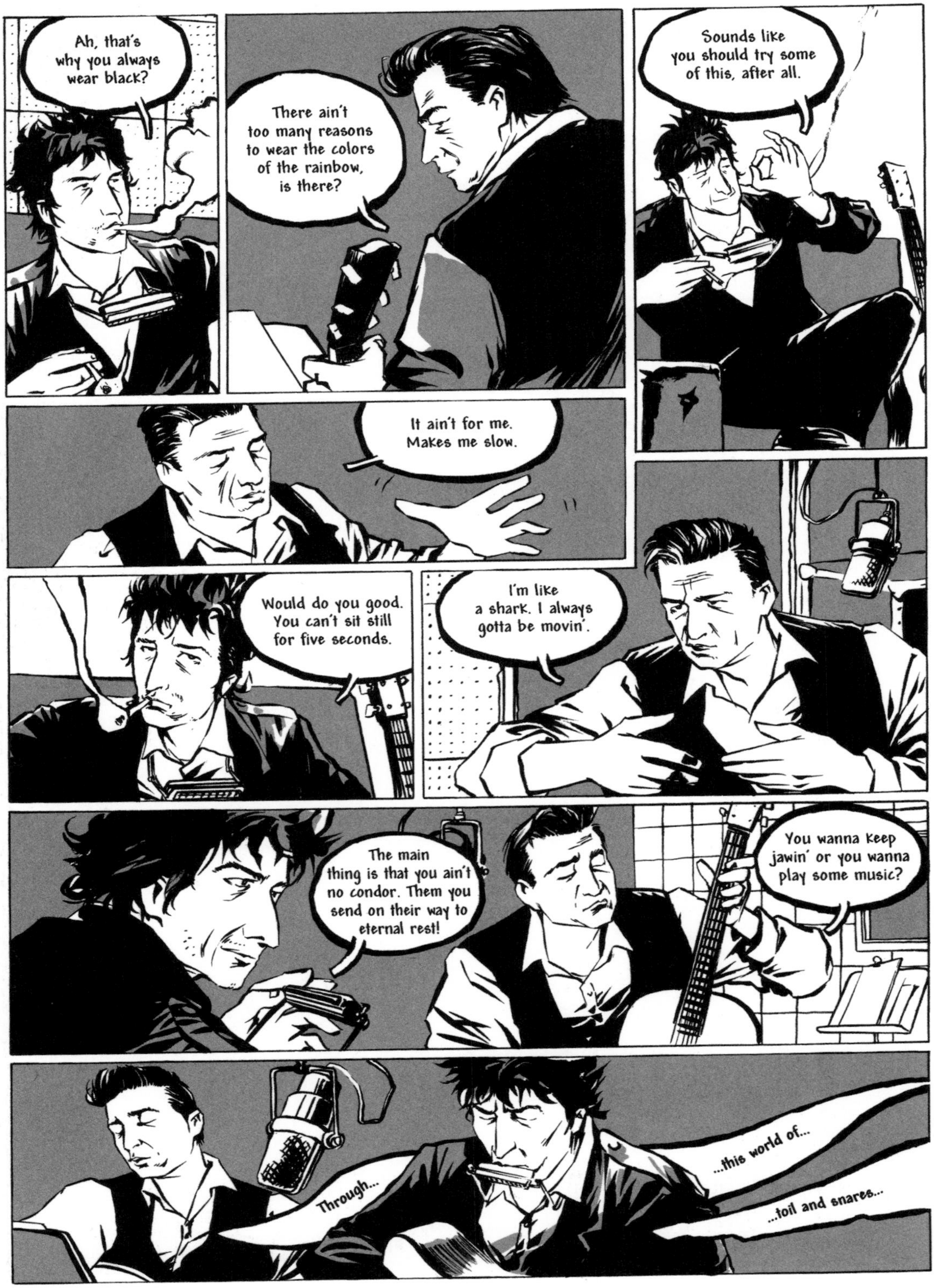
Ah, that's why you always wear black?
There ain't too many reasons to wear the colors of the rainbow, is there?
Sounds like you should try some of this, after all.
It ain't for me. Makes me slow.
Would do you good. You can't sit still for five seconds.
I'm like a shark. I always gotta be movin'.
The main thing is that you ain't no condor. Them you send on their way to eternal rest!
You wanna keep jawin' or you wanna play some music?
Through...
...this world of...
...toil and snares...

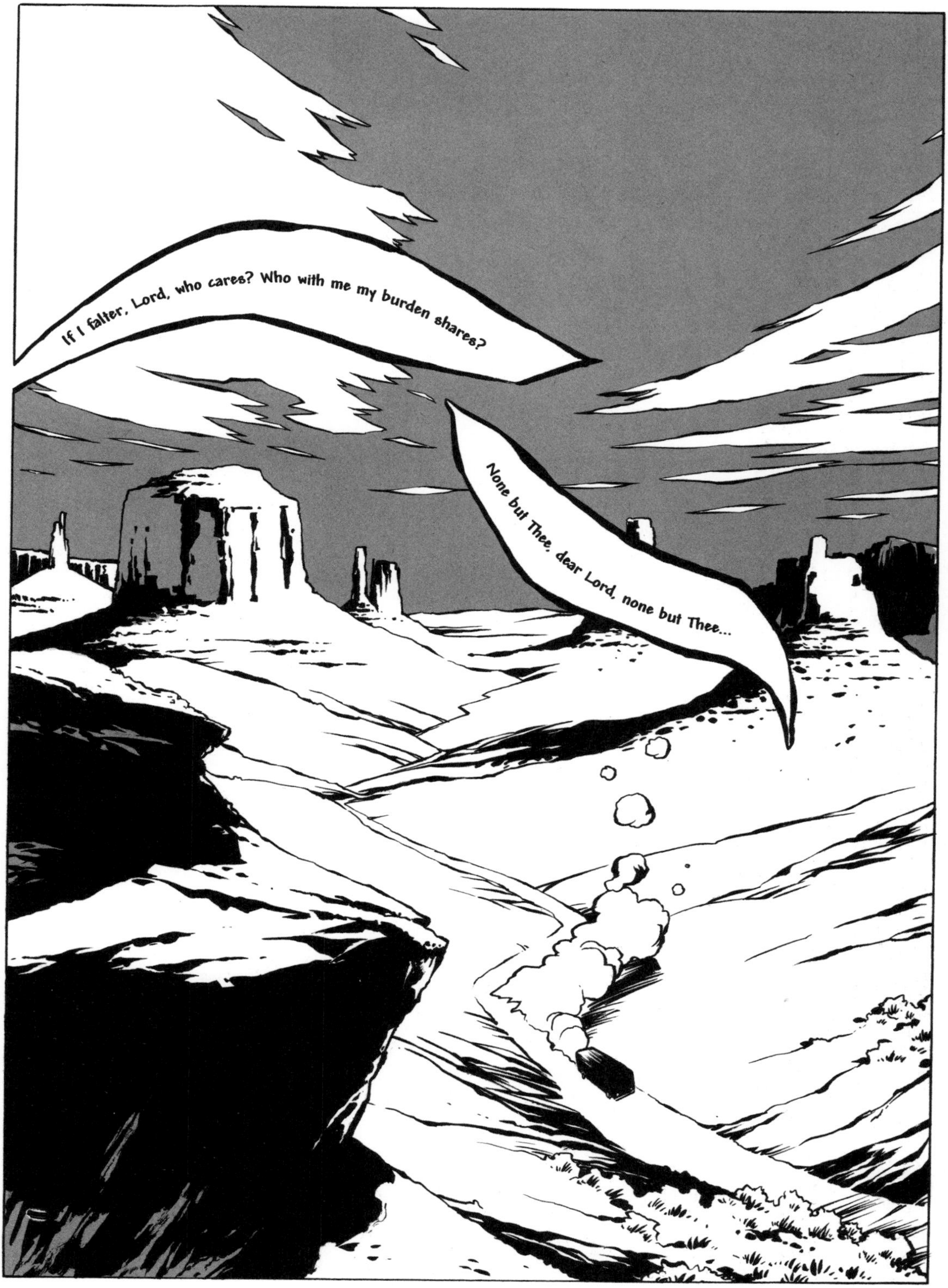
If I falter, Lord, who cares? Who with me my burden shares?
None but Thee, dear Lord, none but Thee...

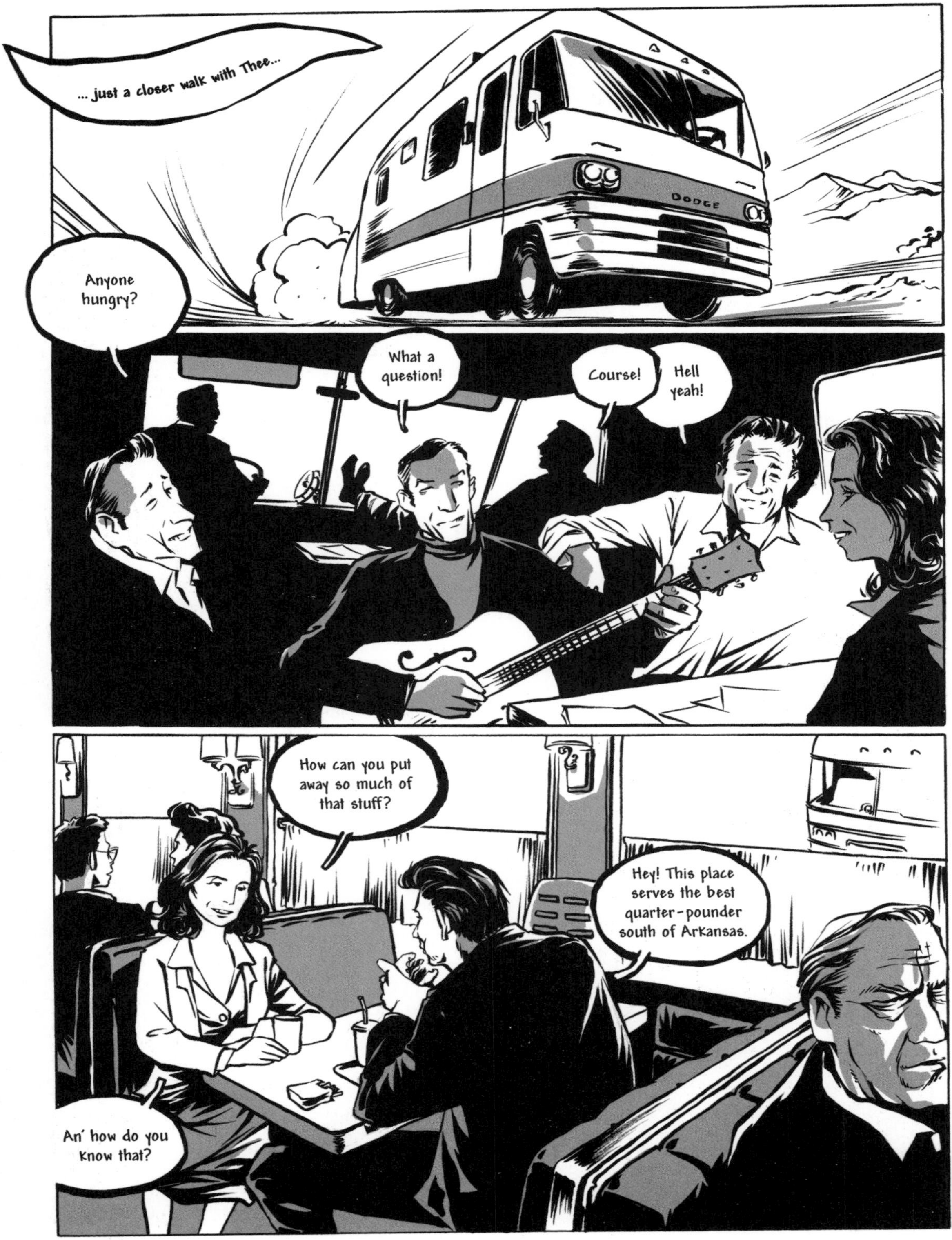
... just a closer walk with Thee...
DODGE
Anyone hungry?
What a question!
Course!
Hell yeah!
How can you put away so much of that stuff?
Hey! This place serves the best quarter-pounder south of Arkansas.
An' how do you know that?

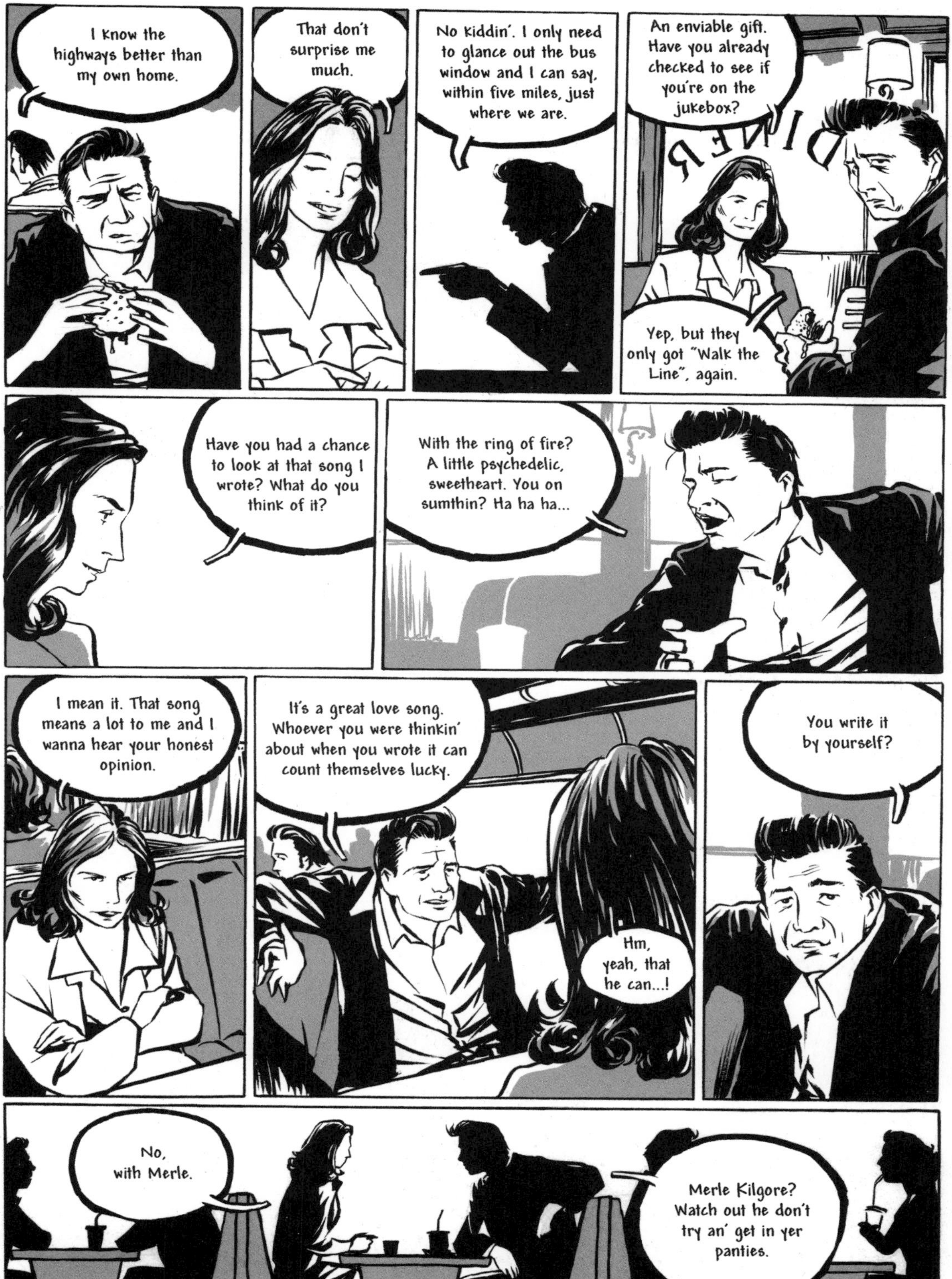
I know the highways better than my own home.
That don't surprise me much.
No kiddin'. I only need to glance out the bus window and I can say, within five miles, just where we are.
An enviable gift. Have you already checked to see if you're on the jukebox?
DINER
Yep, but they only got "Walk the Line", again.
Have you had a chance to look at that song I wrote? What do you think of it?
With the ring of fire? A little psychedelic, sweetheart. You on sumthin? Ha ha ha...
I mean it. That song means a lot to me and I wanna hear your honest opinion.
It's a great love song. Whoever you were thinkin' about when you wrote it can count themselves lucky.
Hm, yeah, that he can...!
You write it by yourself?
No, with Merle.
Merle Kilgore? Watch out he don't try an' get in yer panties.

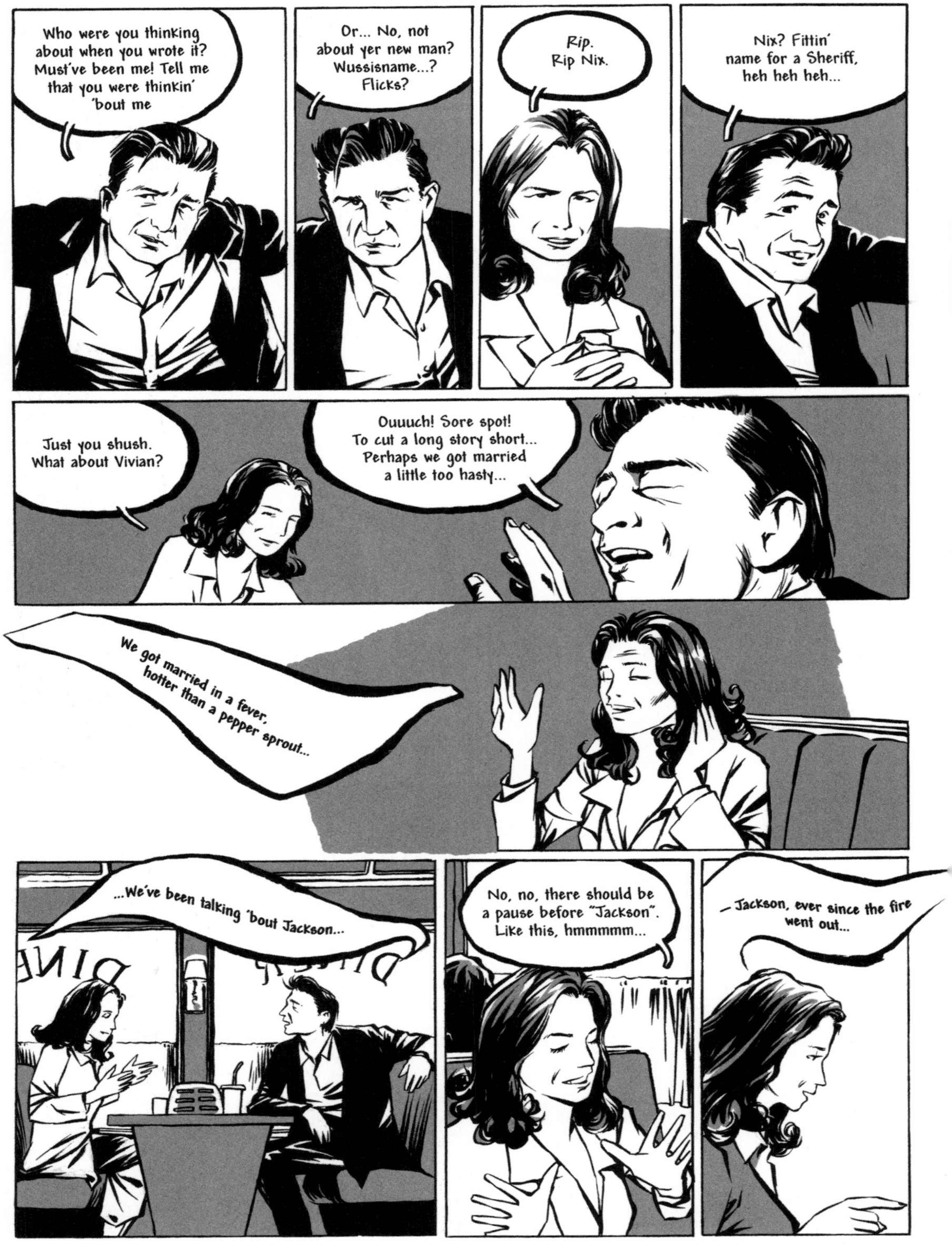
Who were you thinking about when you wrote it? Must've been me! Tell me that you were thinkin' 'bout me
Or... No, not about yer new man? Wussisname...? Flicks?
Rip. Rip Nix.
Nix? Fittin' name for a Sheriff, heh heh heh...
Just you shush. What about Vivian?
Ouuuch! Sore spot! To cut a long story short... Perhaps we got married a little too hasty...
We got married in a fever, hotter than a pepper sprout...
...We've been talking 'bout Jackson...
No, no, there should be a pause before "Jackson". Like this, hmmmmm...
– Jackson, ever since the fire went out...

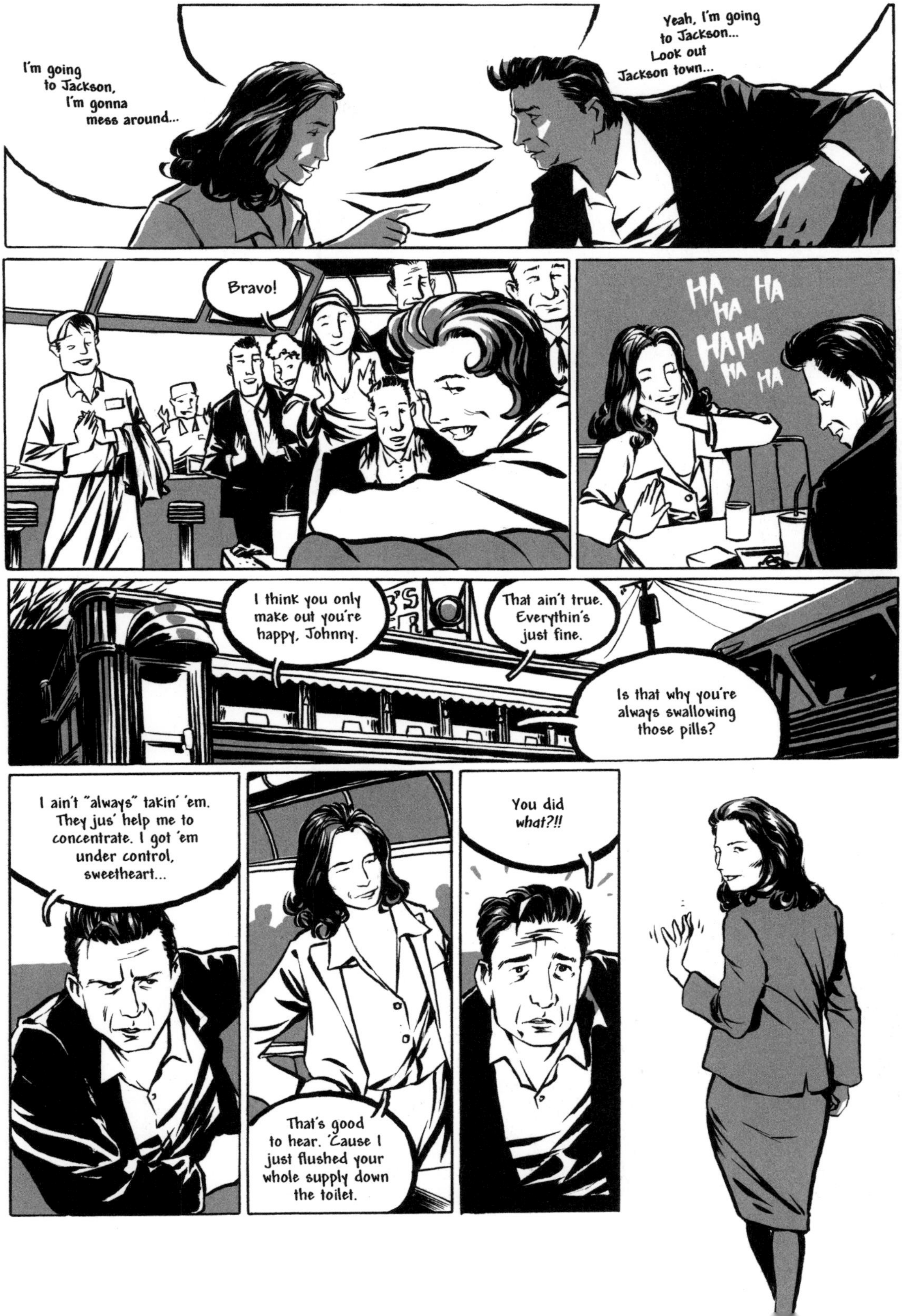
I'm going to Jackson, I'm gonna mess around...
Yeah, I'm going to Jackson... Look out Jackson town...
Bravo!
HA HA HA HAHA HA HA
I think you only make out you're happy, Johnny.
That ain't true. Everythin's just fine.
Is that why you're always swallowing those pills?
I ain't "always" takin' 'em. They jus' help me to concentrate. I got 'em under control, sweetheart...
That's good to hear. 'Cause I just flushed your whole supply down the toilet.
You did *what?!!*

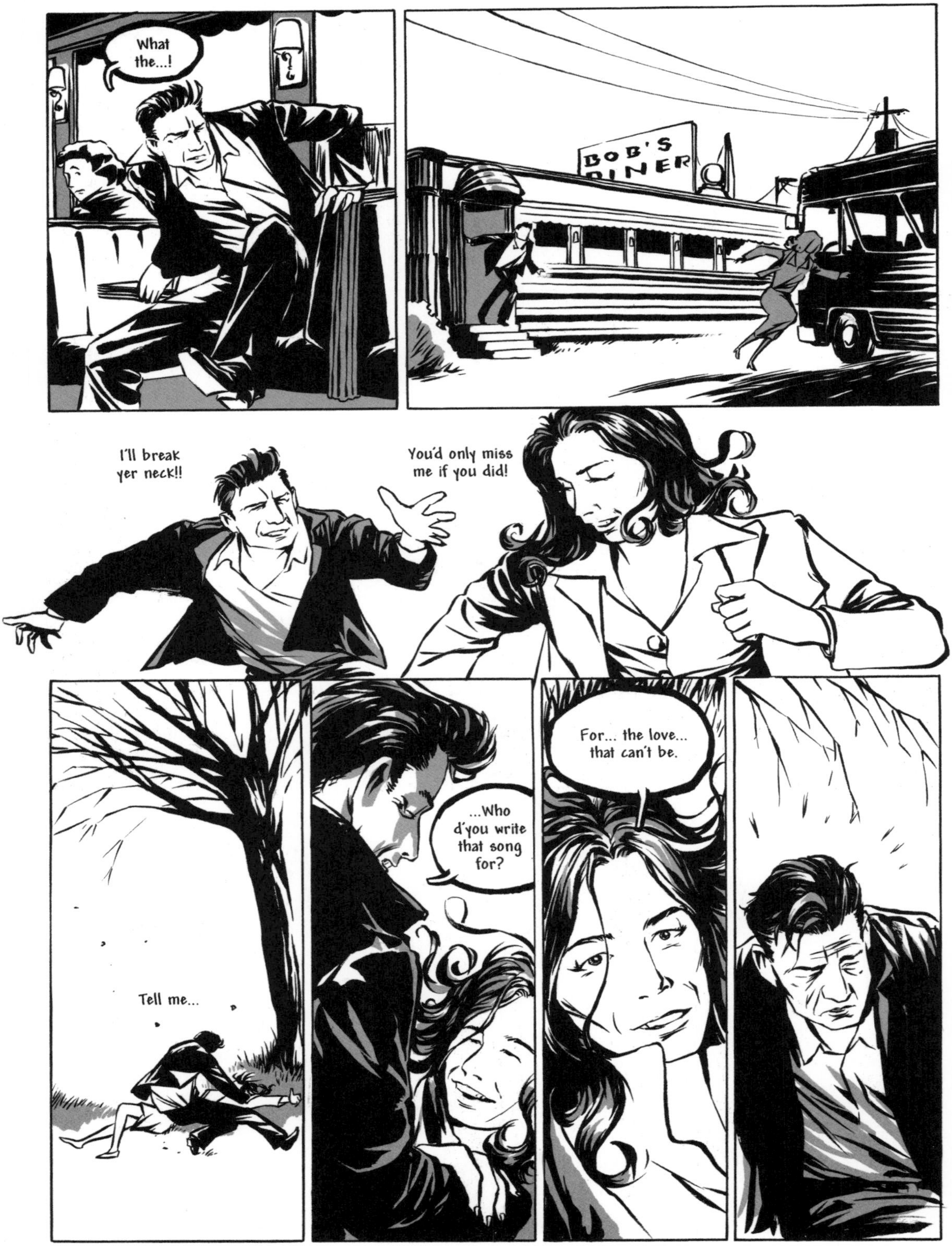
What the...!
BOB'S DINER
I'll break yer neck!!
You'd only miss me if you did!
Tell me...
...Who d'you write that song for?
For... the love... that can't be.

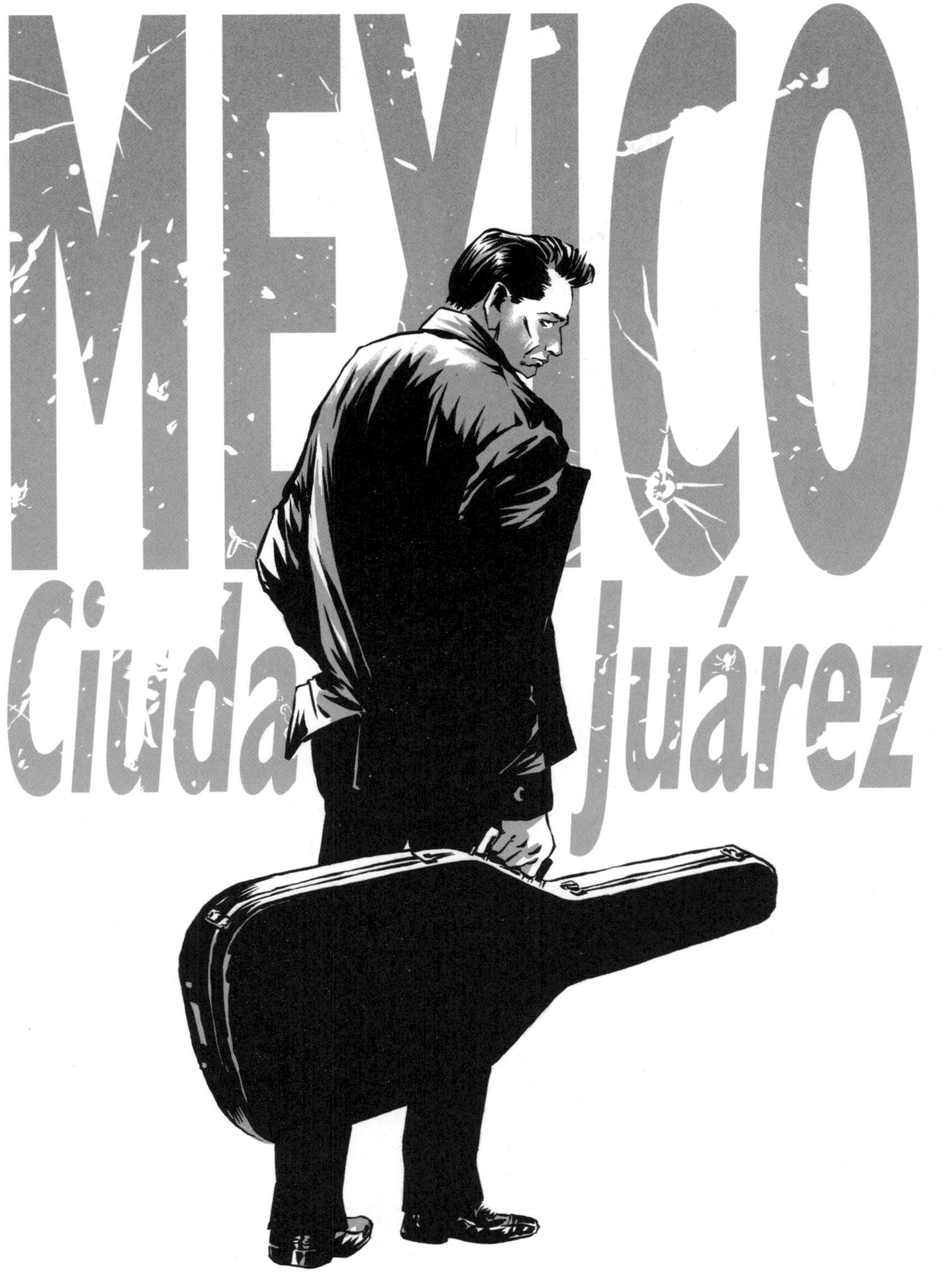

MEXICO
Ciuda
Juárez

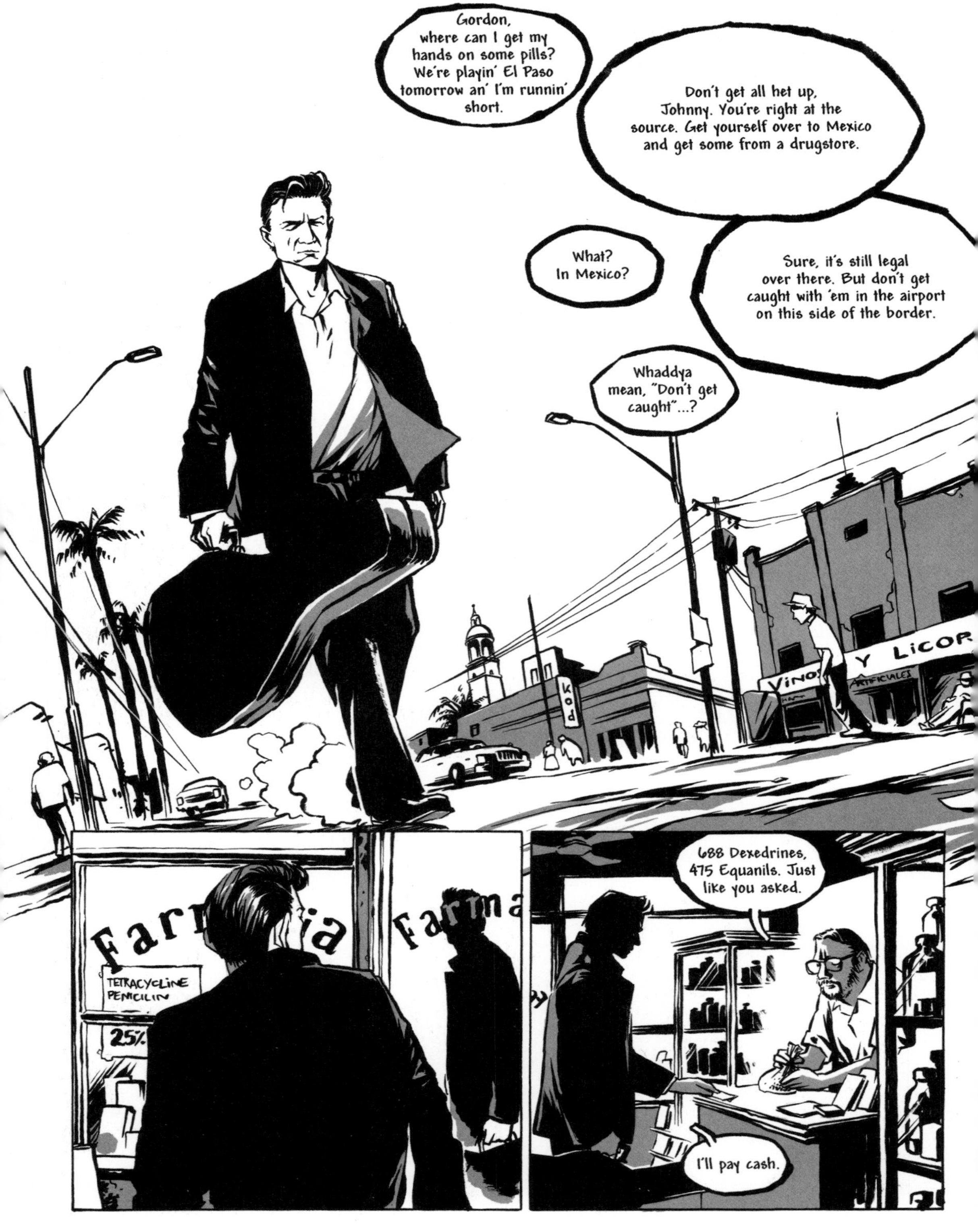
Gordon, where can I get my hands on some pills? We're playin' El Paso tomorrow an' I'm runnin' short.
Don't get all het up, Johnny. You're right at the source. Get yourself over to Mexico and get some from a drugstore.
What? In Mexico?
Sure, it's still legal over there. But don't get caught with 'em in the airport on this side of the border.
Whaddya mean, "Don't get caught"...?
Y LICOR
Farma
Farma
TETRACYCLINE PENICILIN
25%
688 Dexedrines, 475 Equanils. Just like you asked.
I'll pay cash.

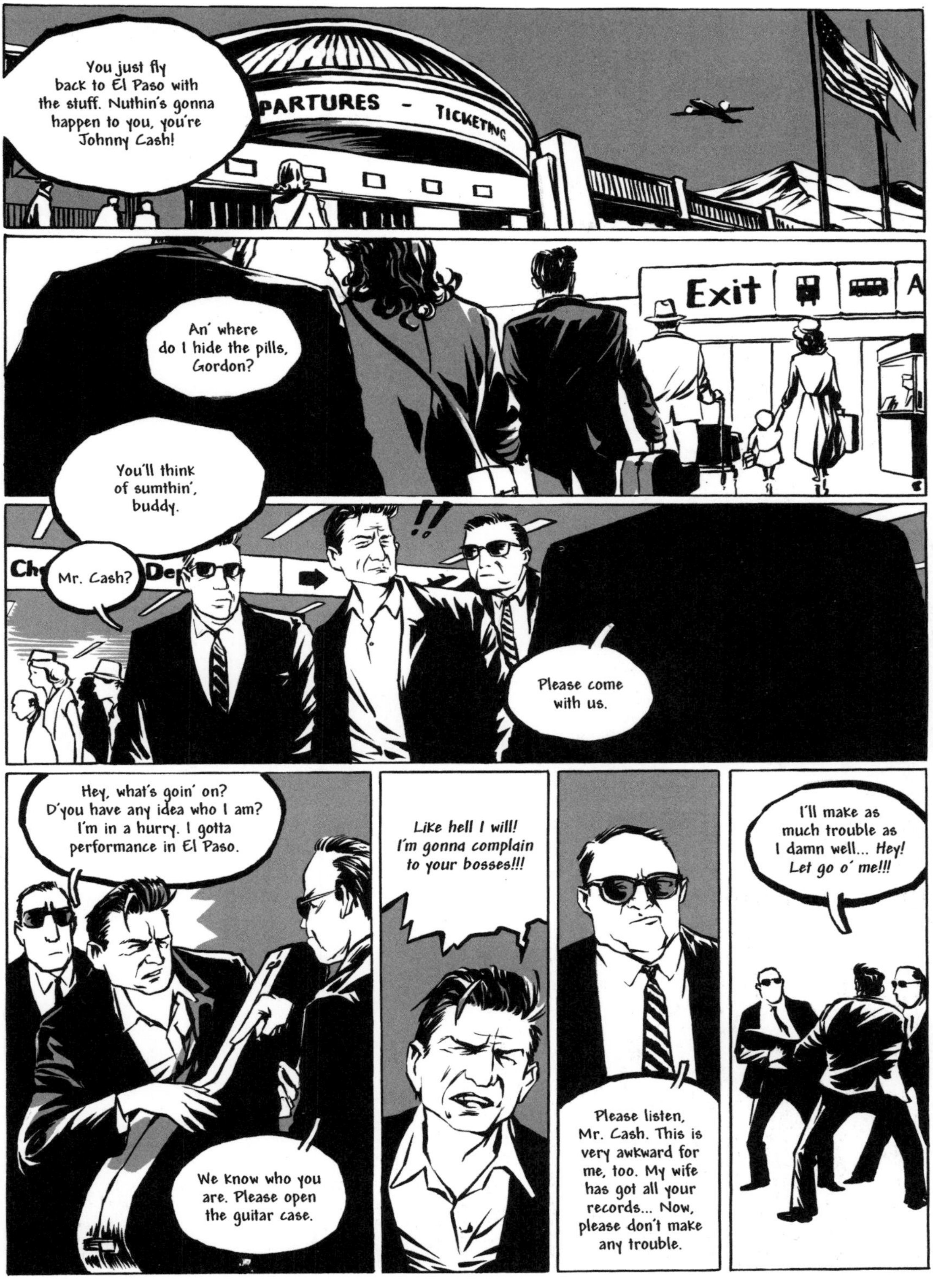
You just fly back to El Paso with the stuff. Nuthin's gonna happen to you, you're Johnny Cash!
PARTURES - TICKETING
An' where do I hide the pills, Gordon?
Exit
You'll think of sumthin', buddy.
Mr. Cash?
!!
Please come with us.
Hey, what's goin' on? D'you have any idea who I am? I'm in a hurry. I gotta performance in El Paso.
We know who you are. Please open the guitar case.
Like hell I will! I'm gonna complain to your bosses!!!
Please listen, Mr. Cash. This is very awkward for me, too. My wife has got all your records... Now, please don't make any trouble.
I'll make as much trouble as I damn well... Hey! Let go o' me!!!

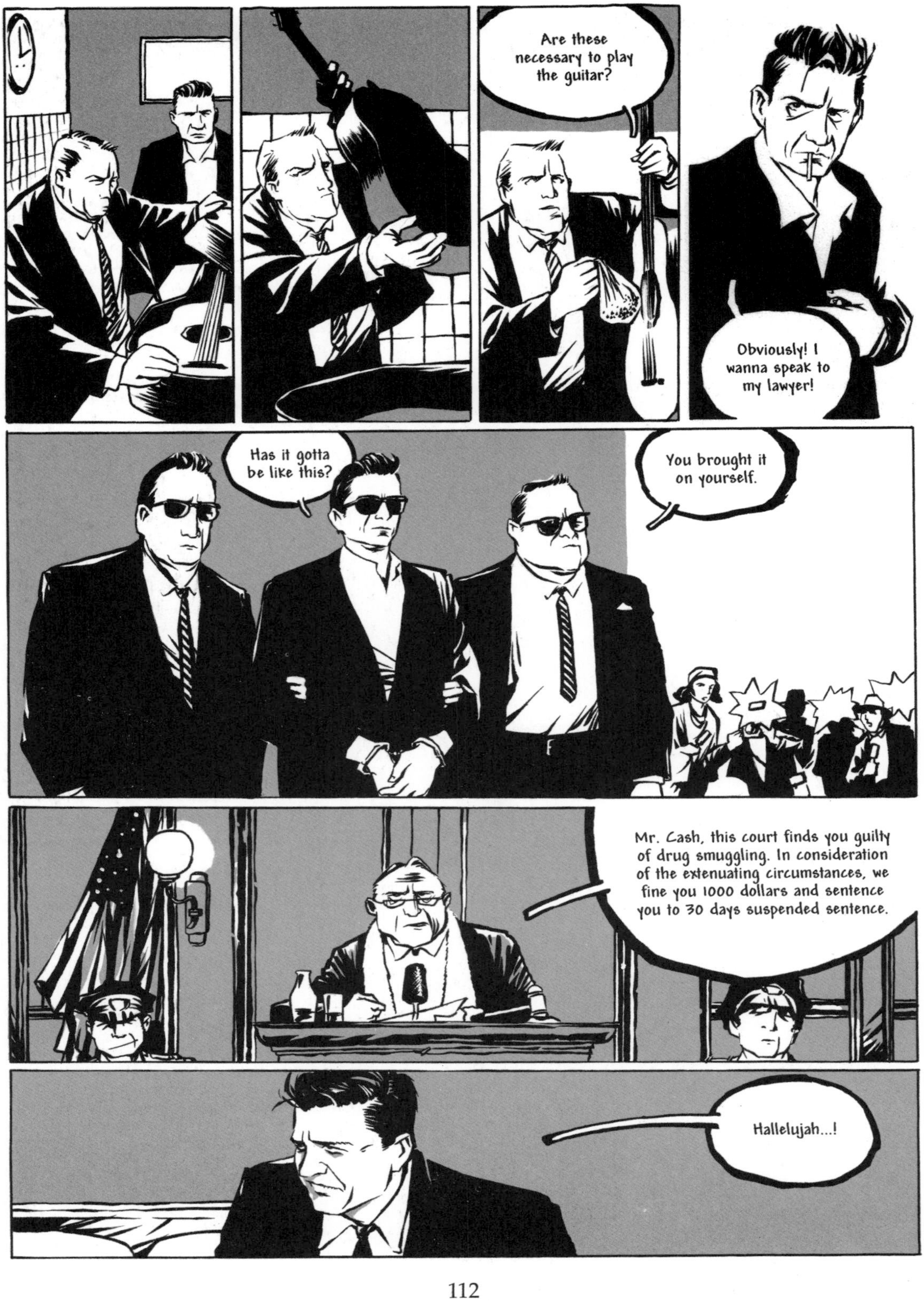
Are these necessary to play the guitar?
Obviously! I wanna speak to my lawyer!
Has it gotta be like this?
You brought it on yourself.
Mr. Cash, this court finds you guilty of drug smuggling. In consideration of the extenuating circumstances, we fine you 1000 dollars and sentence you to 30 days suspended sentence.
Hallelujah...!

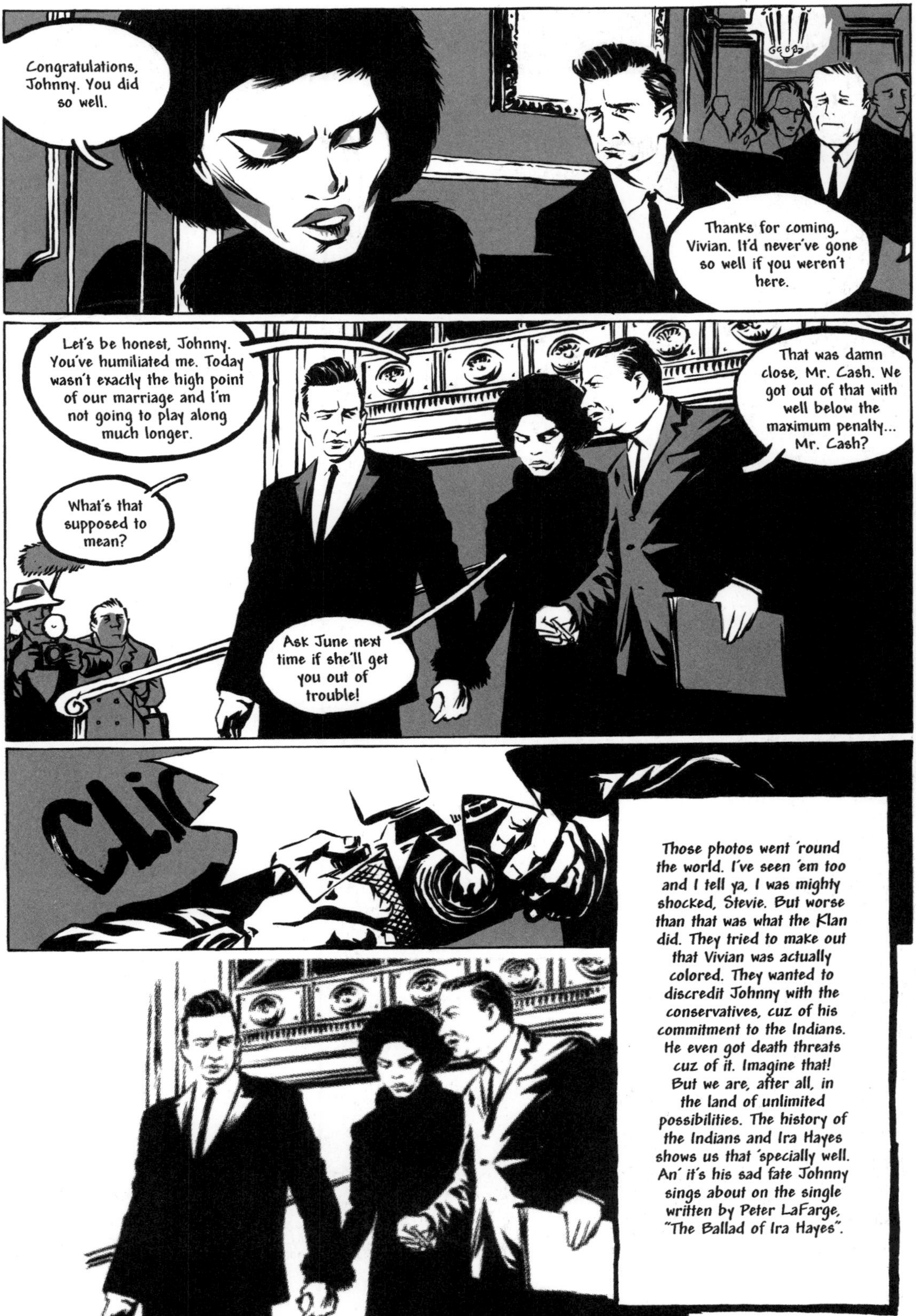
Congratulations, Johnny. You did so well.
Thanks for coming, Vivian. It'd never've gone so well if you weren't here.
Let's be honest, Johnny. You've humiliated me. Today wasn't exactly the high point of our marriage and I'm not going to play along much longer.
That was damn close, Mr. Cash. We got out of that with well below the maximum penalty... Mr. Cash?
What's that supposed to mean?
Ask June next time if she'll get you out of trouble!
CLIC
Those photos went 'round the world. I've seen 'em too and I tell ya, I was mighty shocked, Stevie. But worse than that was what the Klan did. They tried to make out that Vivian was actually colored. They wanted to discredit Johnny with the conservatives, cuz of his commitment to the Indians. He even got death threats cuz of it. Imagine that! But we are, after all, in the land of unlimited possibilities. The history of the Indians and Ira Hayes shows us that 'specially well. An' it's his sad fate Johnny sings about on the single written by Peter LaFarge, "The Ballad of Ira Hayes".

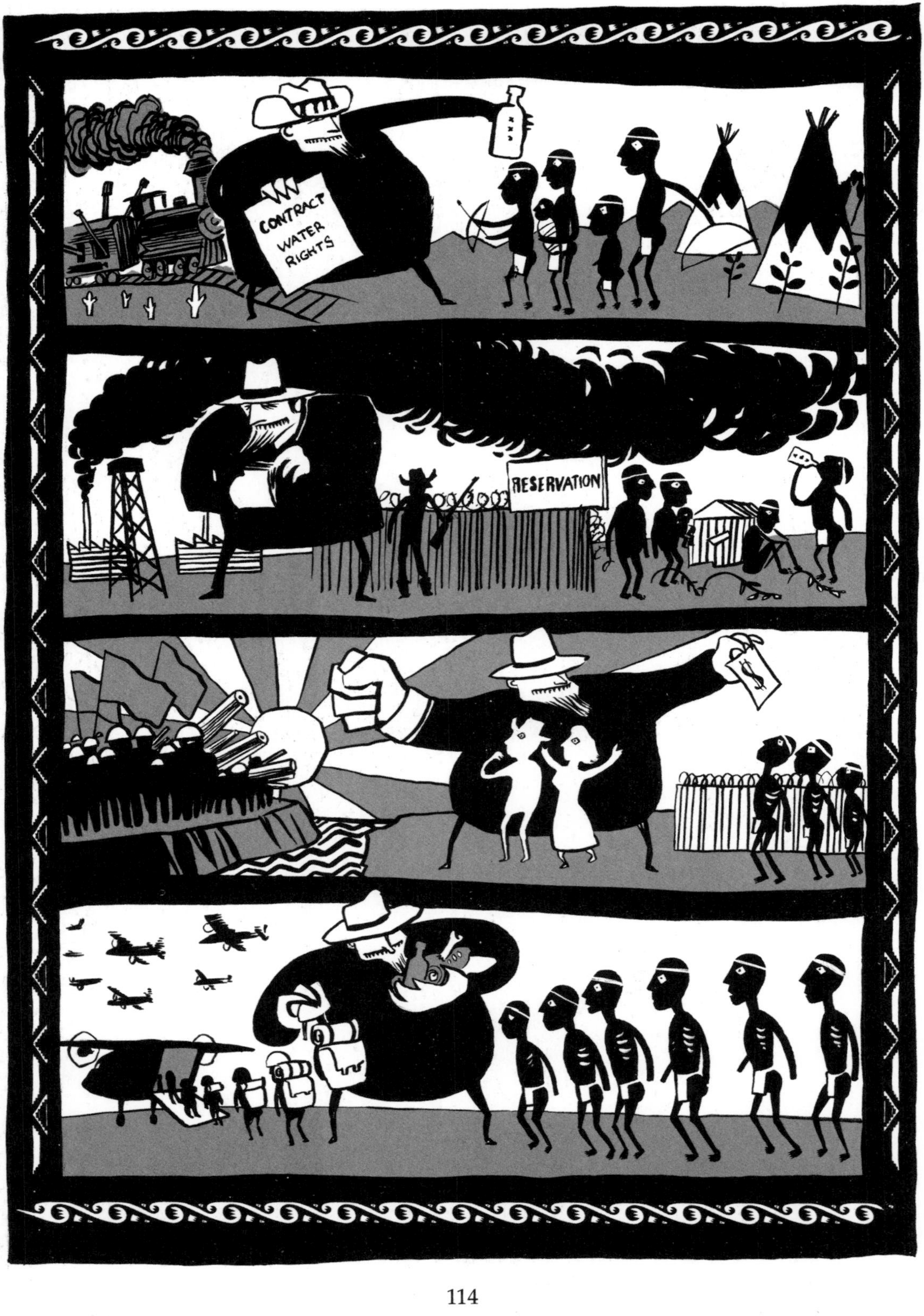
CONTRACT
WATER
RIGHTS
RESERVATION

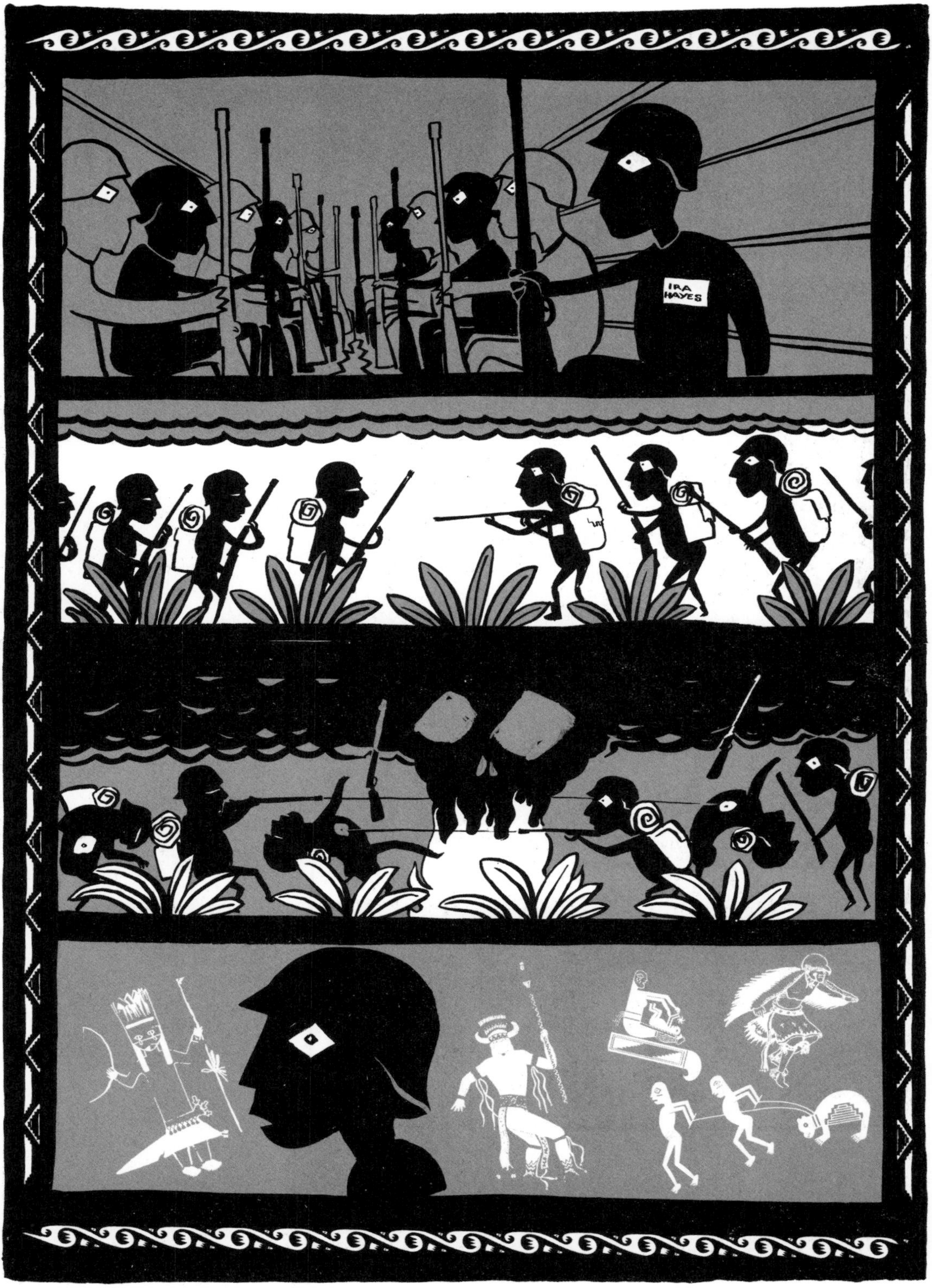
IRA
HAYES

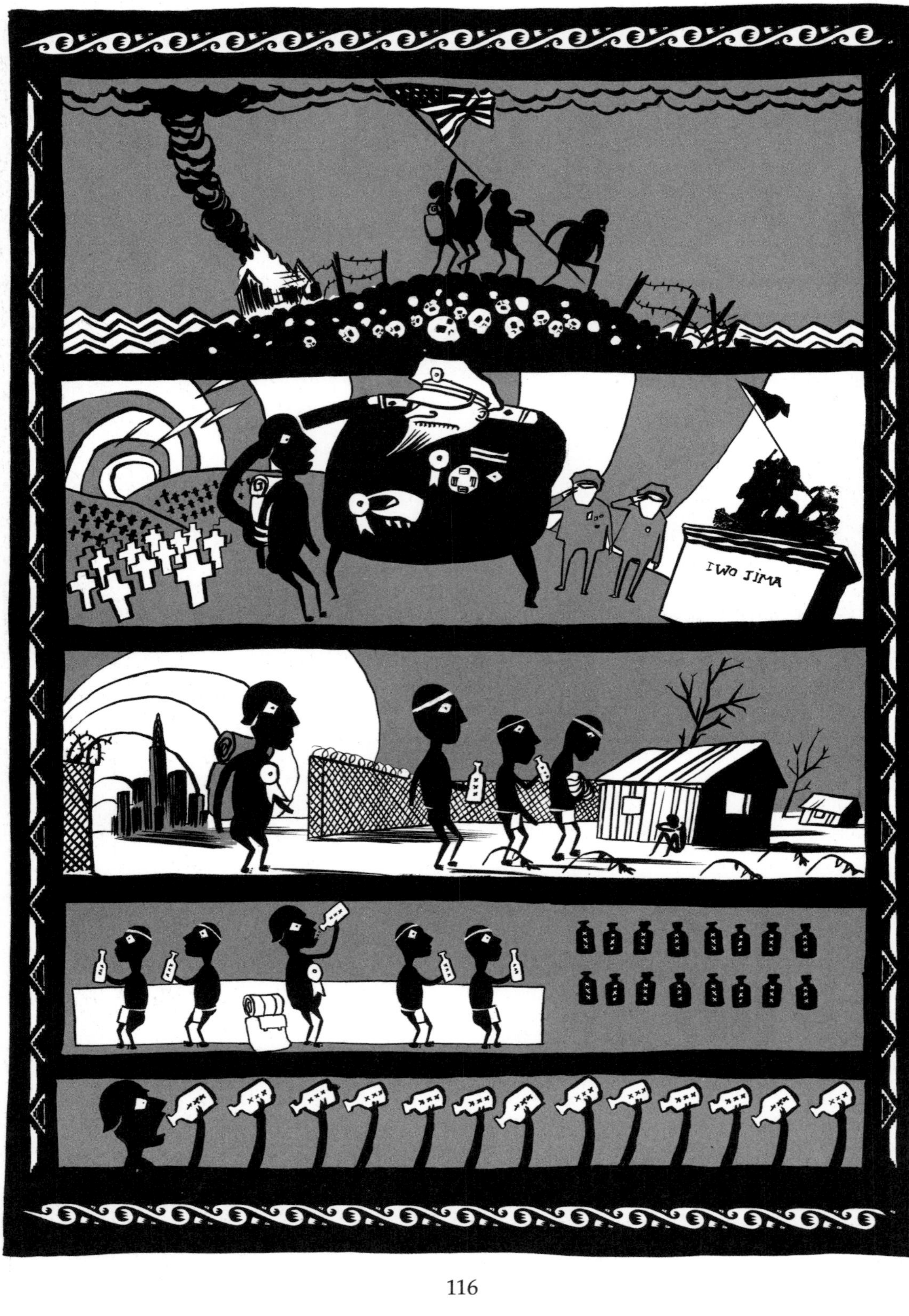
IWO JIMA

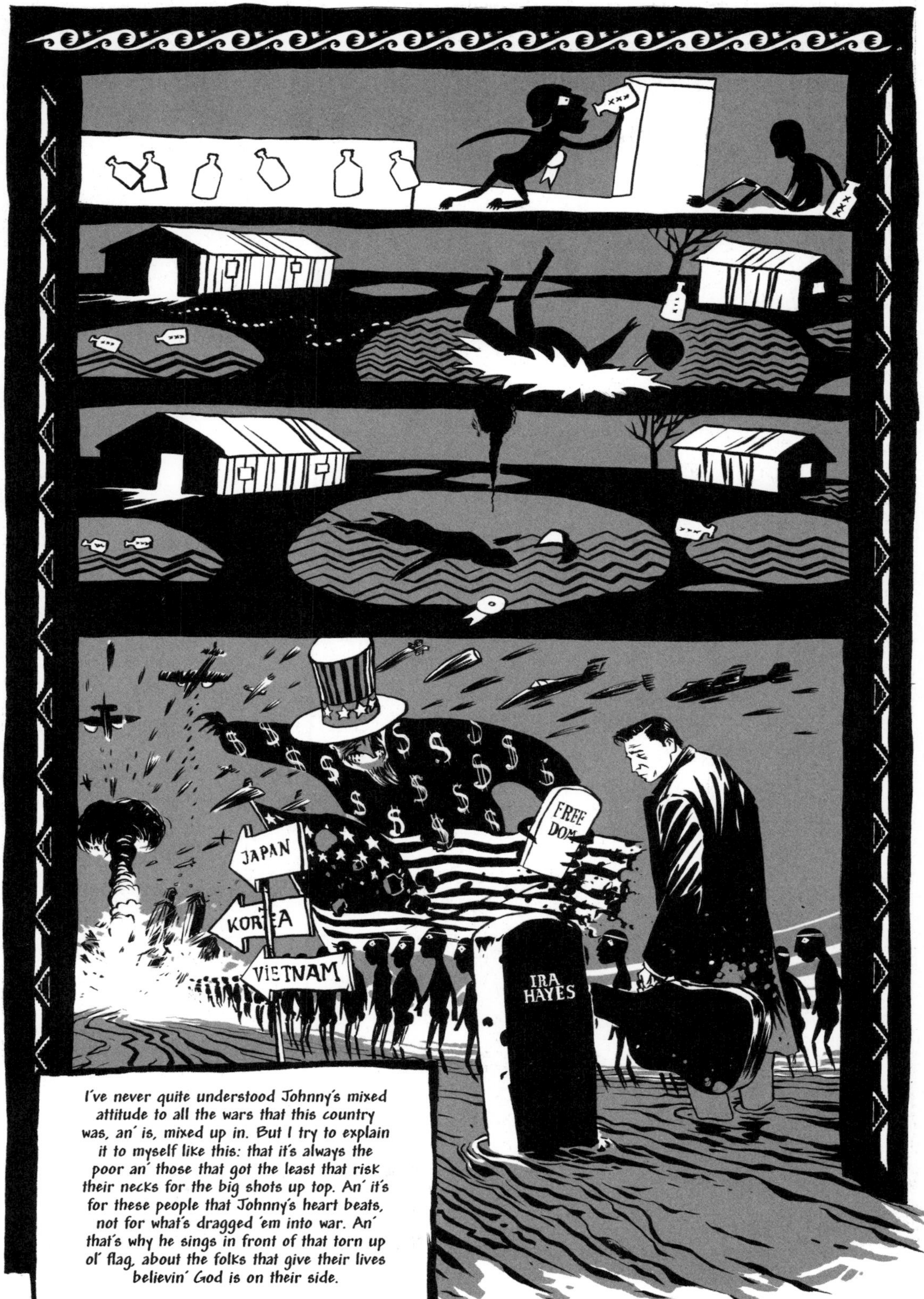
FREE DOM
JAPAN
KOREA
VIETNAM
IRA HAYES
I've never quite understood Johnny's mixed attitude to all the wars that this country was, an' is, mixed up in. But I try to explain it to myself like this: that it's always the poor an' those that got the least that risk their necks for the big shots up top. An' it's for these people that Johnny's heart beats, not for what's dragged 'em into war. An' that's why he sings in front of that torn up ol' flag, about the folks that give their lives believin' God is on their side.

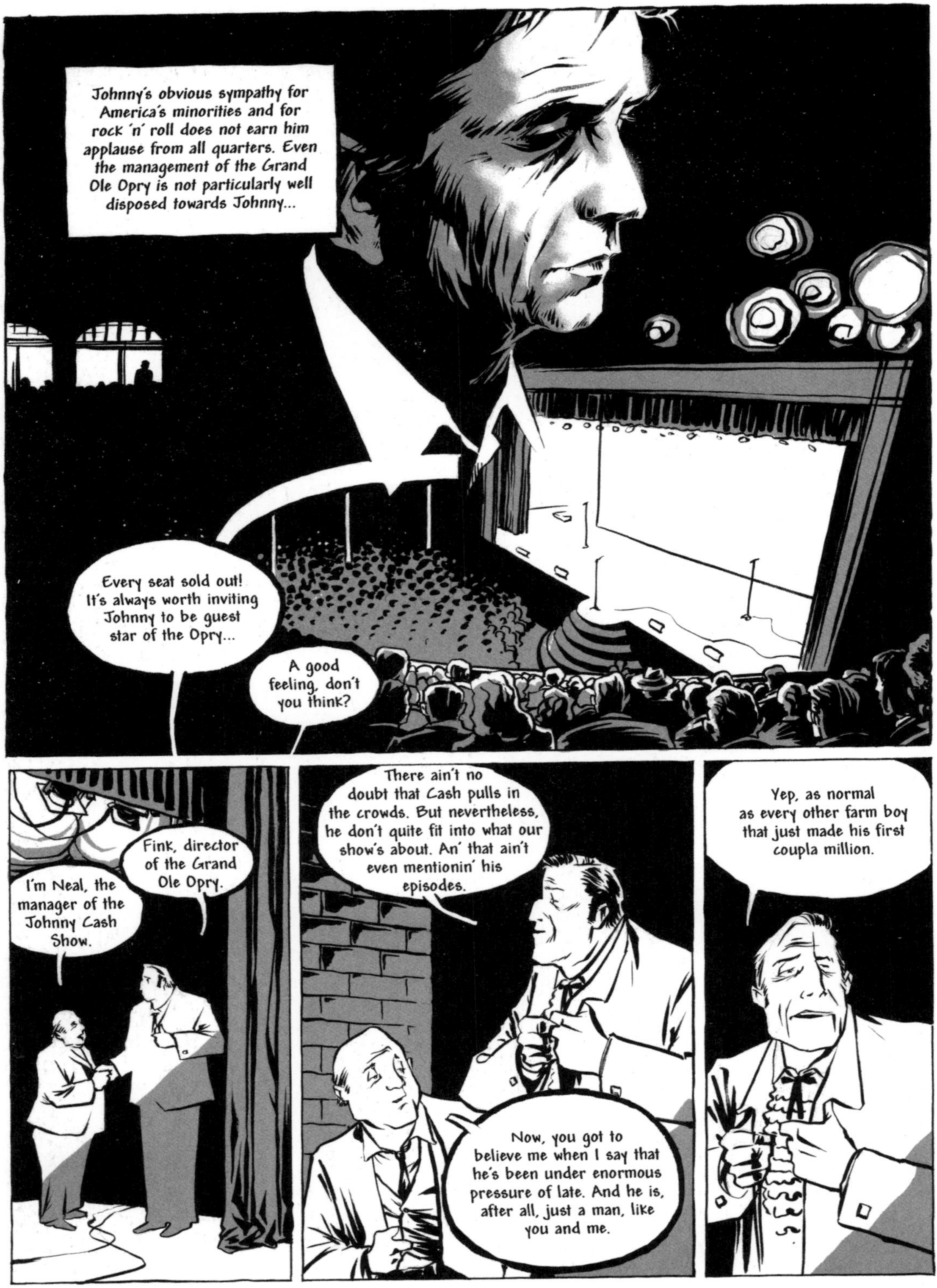
Johnny's obvious sympathy for America's minorities and for rock 'n' roll does not earn him applause from all quarters. Even the management of the Grand Ole Opry is not particularly well disposed towards Johnny...
Every seat sold out! It's always worth inviting Johnny to be guest star of the Opry...
A good feeling, don't you think?
I'm Neal, the manager of the Johnny Cash Show.
Fink, director of the Grand Ole Opry.
There ain't no doubt that Cash pulls in the crowds. But nevertheless, he don't quite fit into what our show's about. An' that ain't even mentionin' his episodes.
Now, you got to believe me when I say that he's been under enormous pressure of late. And he is, after all, just a man, like you and me.
Yep, as normal as every other farm boy that just made his first coupla million.

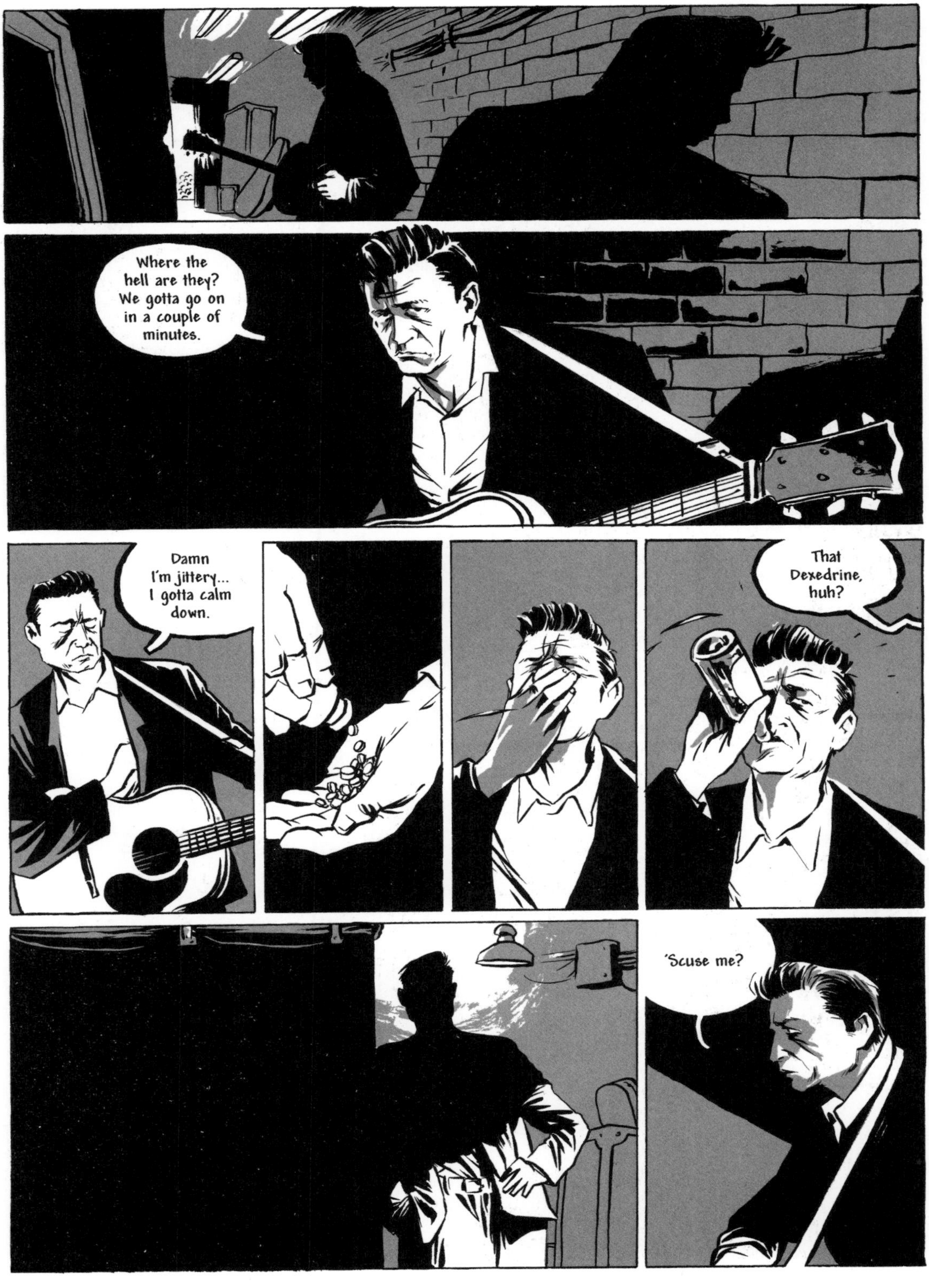
Where the hell are they? We gotta go on in a couple of minutes.
Damn I'm jittery... I gotta calm down.
That Dexedrine, huh?
'Scuse me?

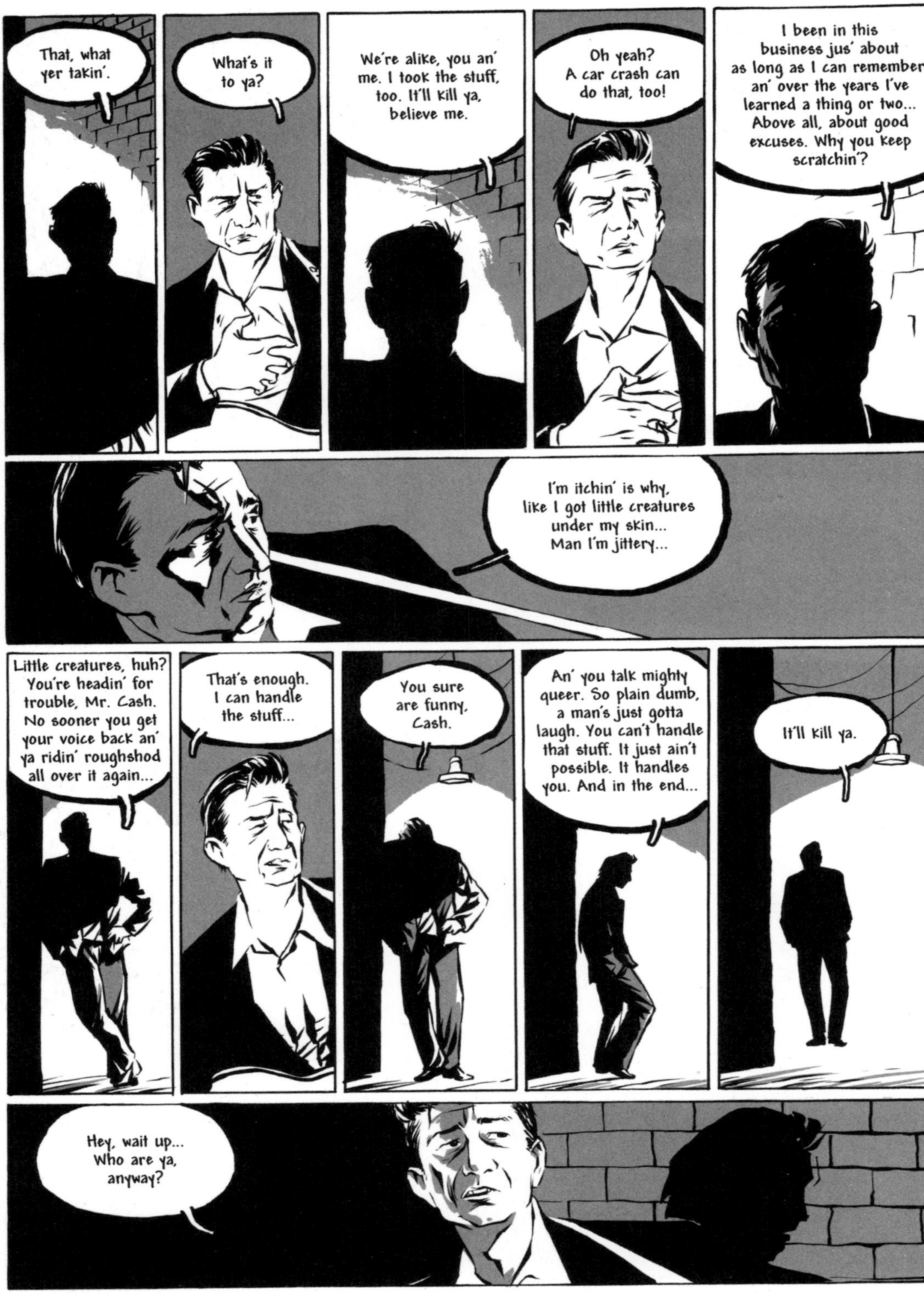

That, what yer takin'.
What's it to ya?
We're alike, you an' me. I took the stuff, too. It'll kill ya, believe me.
Oh yeah? A car crash can do that, too!
I been in this business jus' about as long as I can remember, an' over the years I've learned a thing or two... Above all, about good excuses. Why you keep scratchin'?
I'm itchin' is why, like I got little creatures under my skin... Man I'm jittery...
Little creatures, huh? You're headin' for trouble, Mr. Cash. No sooner you get your voice back an' ya ridin' roughshod all over it again...
That's enough. I can handle the stuff...
You sure are funny, Cash.
An' you talk mighty queer. So plain dumb, a man's just gotta laugh. You can't handle that stuff. It just ain't possible. It handles you. And in the end...
It'll kill ya.
Hey, wait up... Who are ya, anyway?

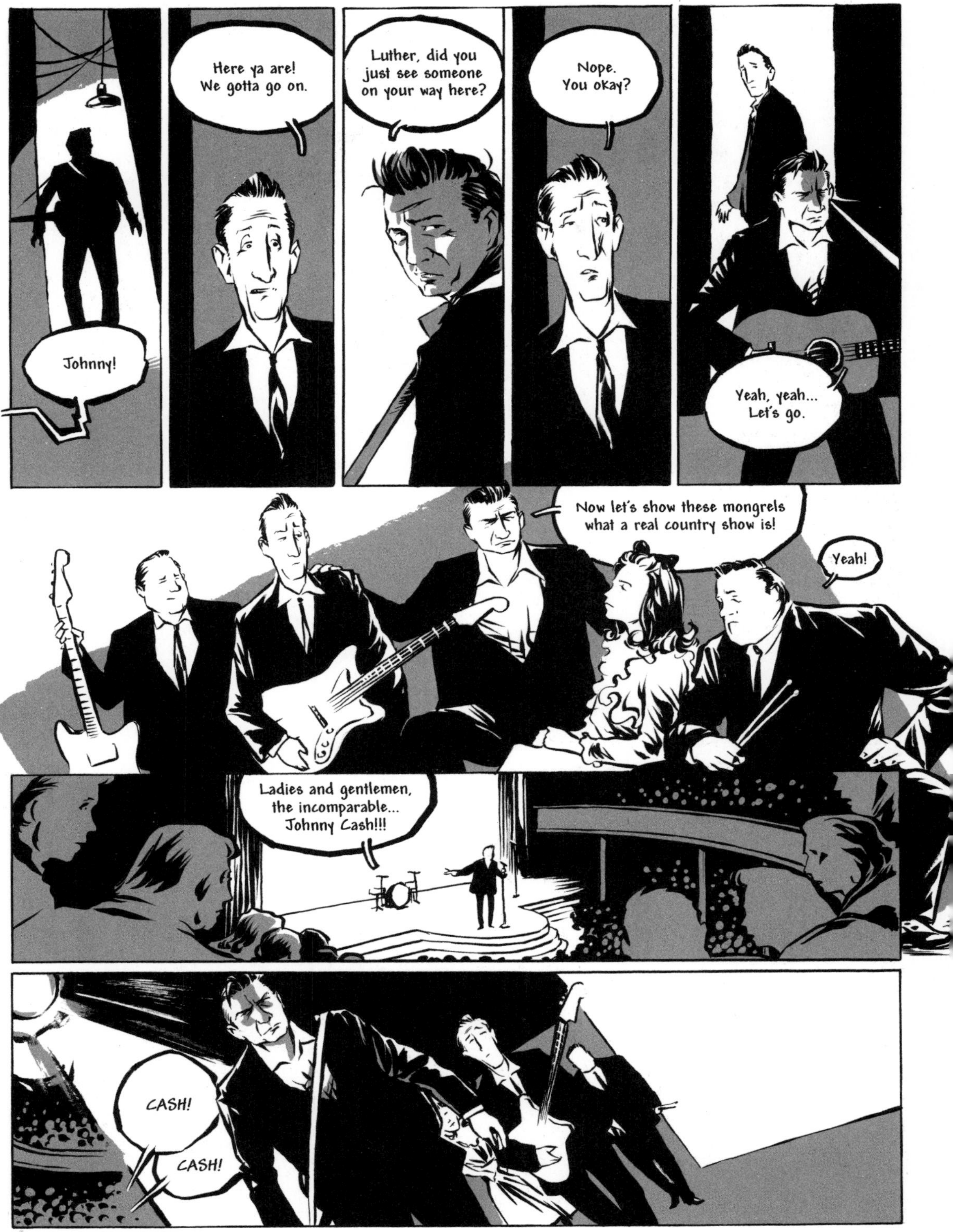
Johnny!
Here ya are! We gotta go on.
Luther, did you just see someone on your way here?
Nope. You okay?
Yeah, yeah... Let's go.
Now let's show these mongrels what a real country show is!
Yeah!
Ladies and gentlemen, the incomparable... Johnny Cash!!!
CASH!
CASH!

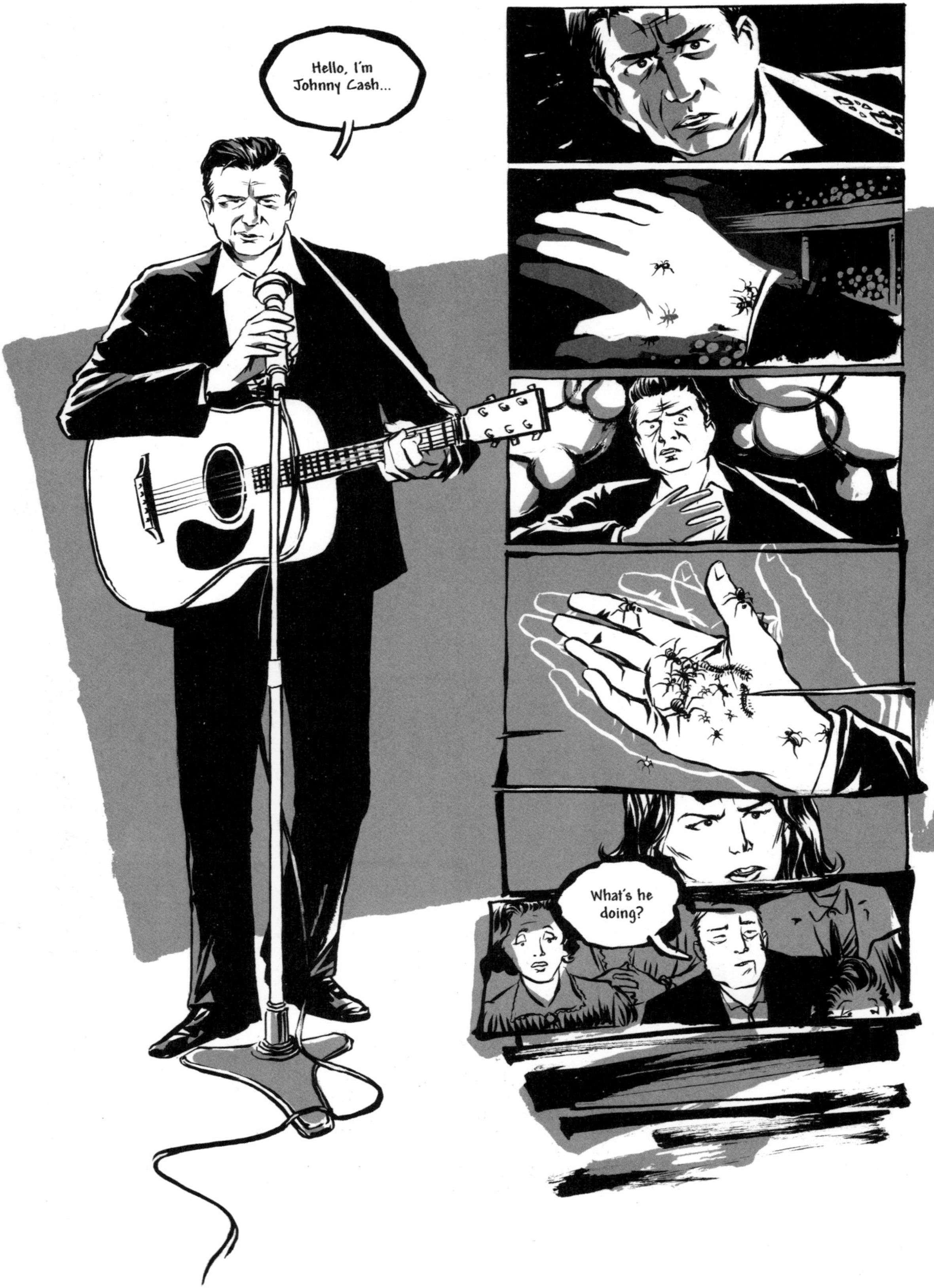
Hello, I'm Johnny Cash...
What's he doing?

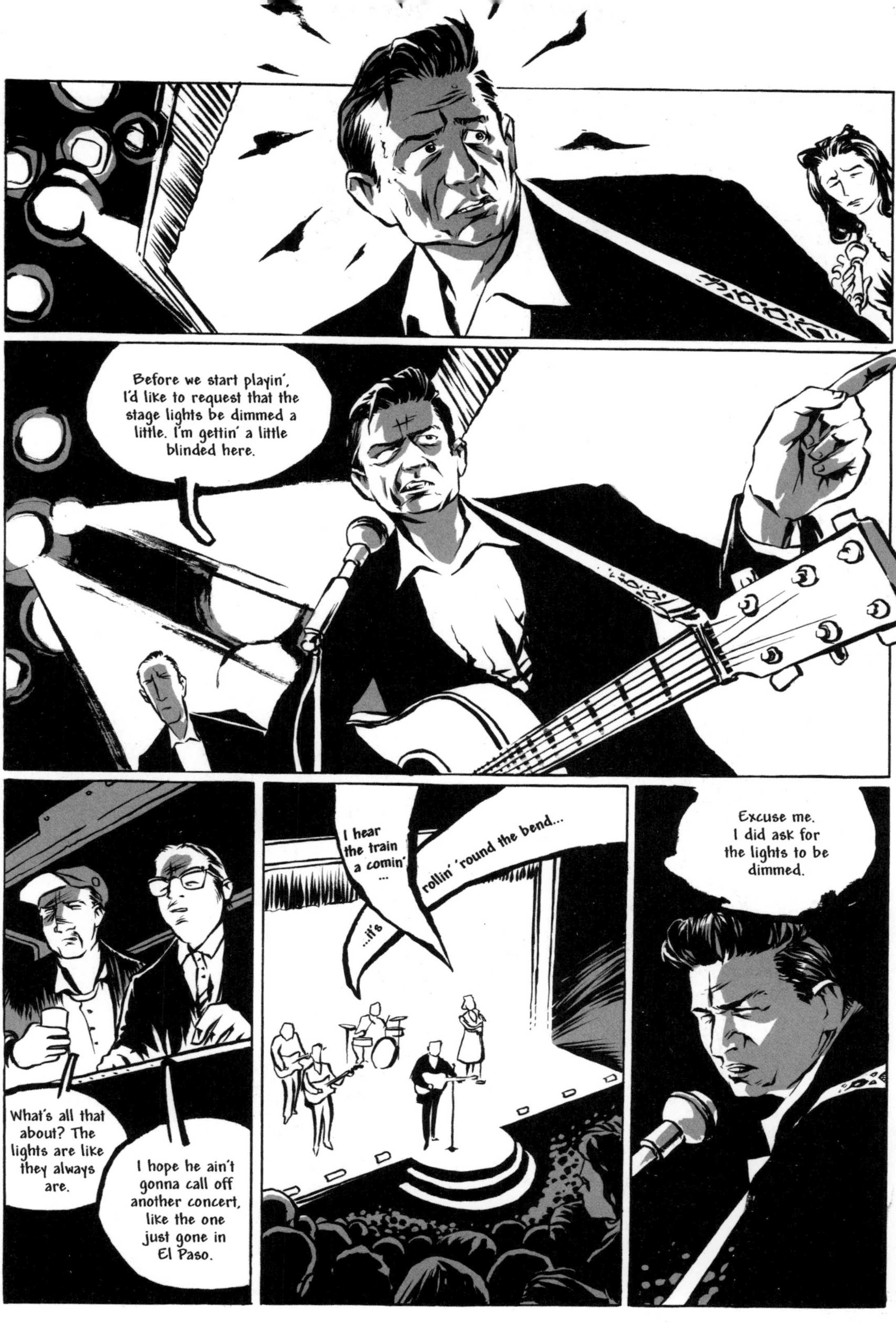
Before we start playin', I'd like to request that the stage lights be dimmed a little. I'm gettin' a little blinded here.
What's all that about? The lights are like they always are.
I hope he ain't gonna call off another concert, like the one just gone in El Paso.
I hear the train a comin' ...
rollin' 'round the bend...
...it's
Excuse me. I did ask for the lights to be dimmed.

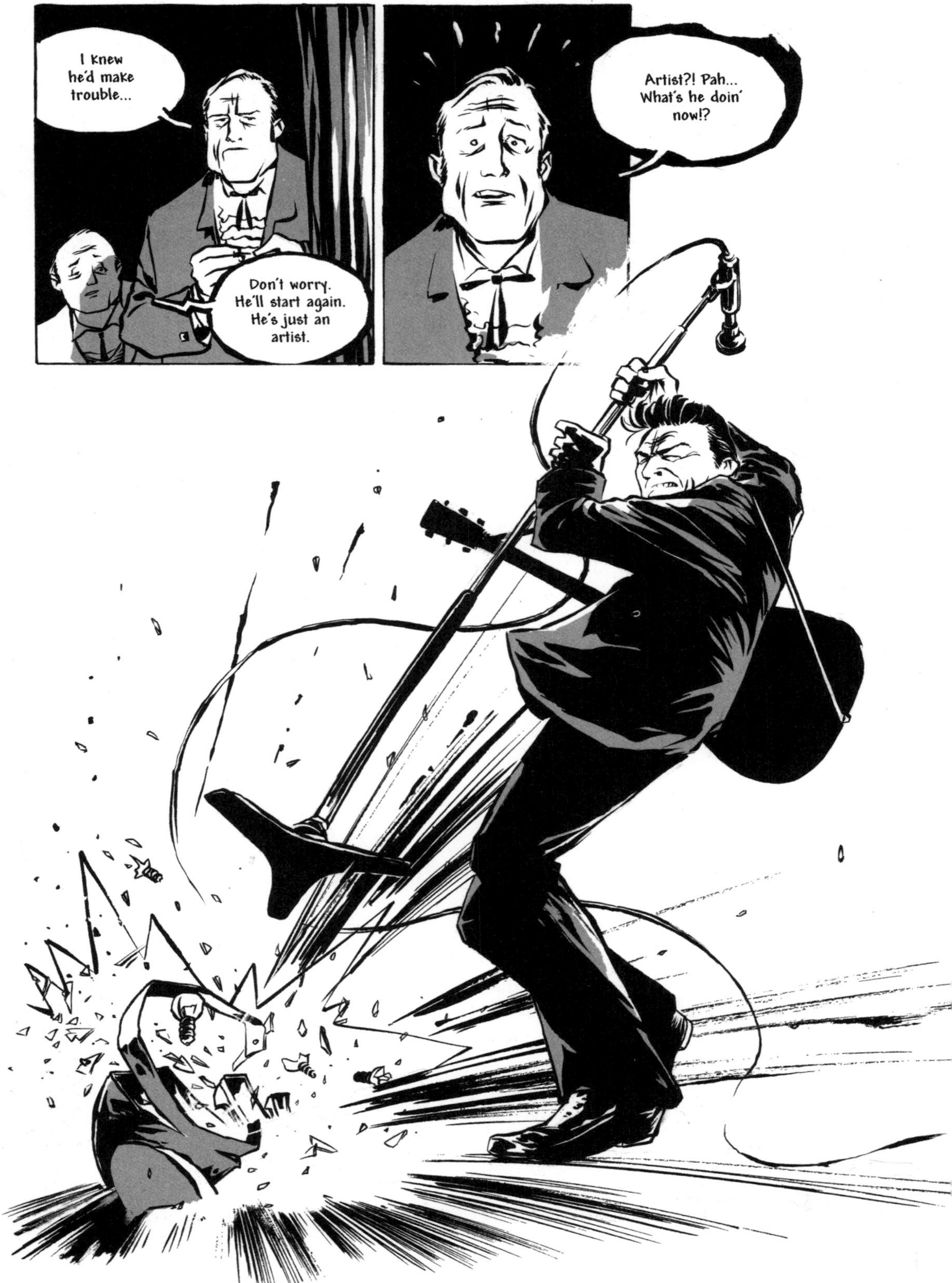
I knew he'd make trouble...
Don't worry. He'll start again. He's just an artist.
Artist?! Pah... What's he doin' now!?

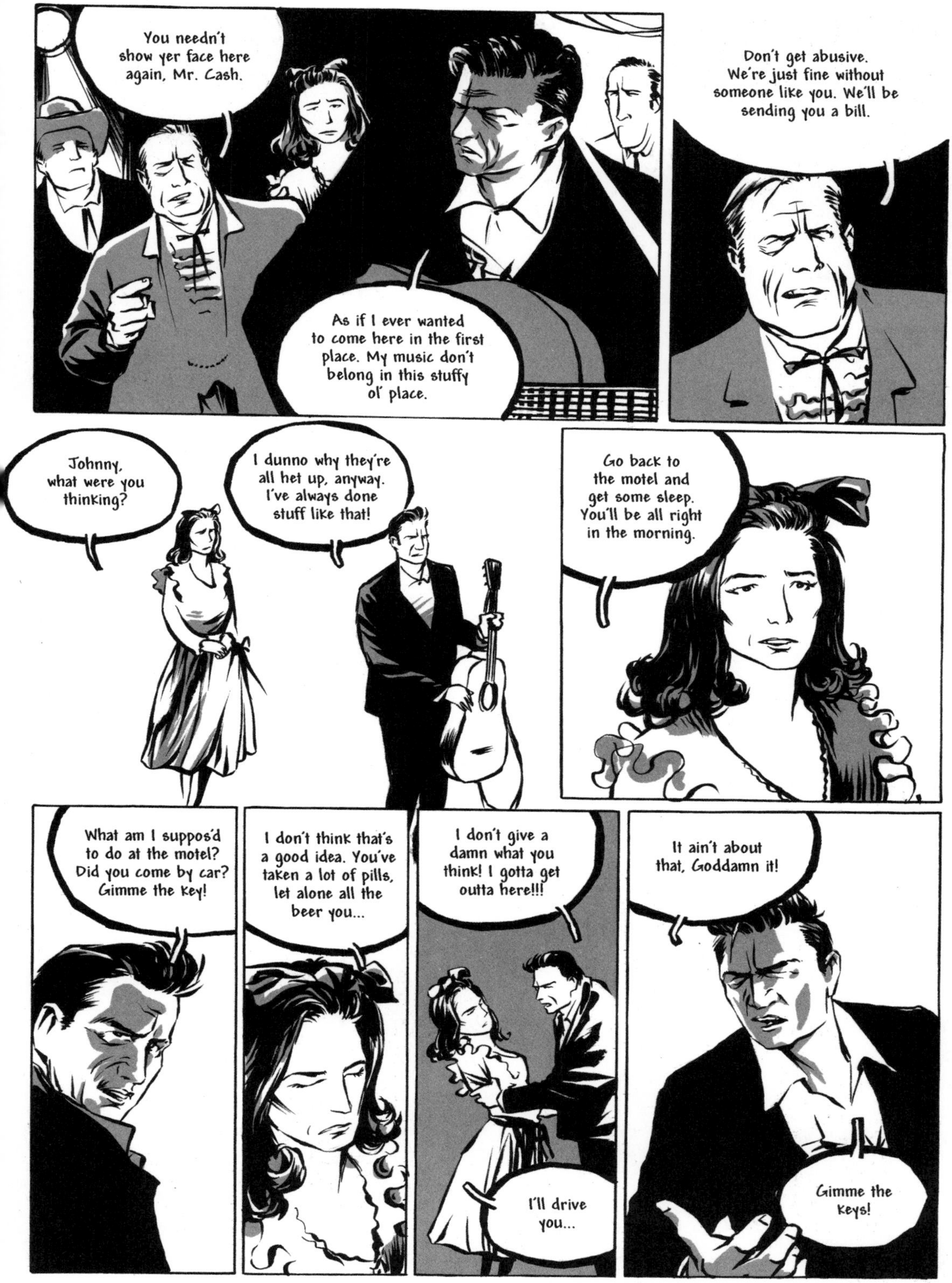
You needn't show yer face here again, Mr. Cash.
As if I ever wanted to come here in the first place. My music don't belong in this stuffy ol' place.
Don't get abusive. We're just fine without someone like you. We'll be sending you a bill.
Johnny, what were you thinking?
I dunno why they're all het up, anyway. I've always done stuff like that!
Go back to the motel and get some sleep. You'll be all right in the morning.
What am I suppos'd to do at the motel? Did you come by car? Gimme the key!
I don't think that's a good idea. You've taken a lot of pills, let alone all the beer you...
I don't give a damn what you think! I gotta get outta here!!!
I'll drive you...
It ain't about that, Goddamn it!
Gimme the keys!

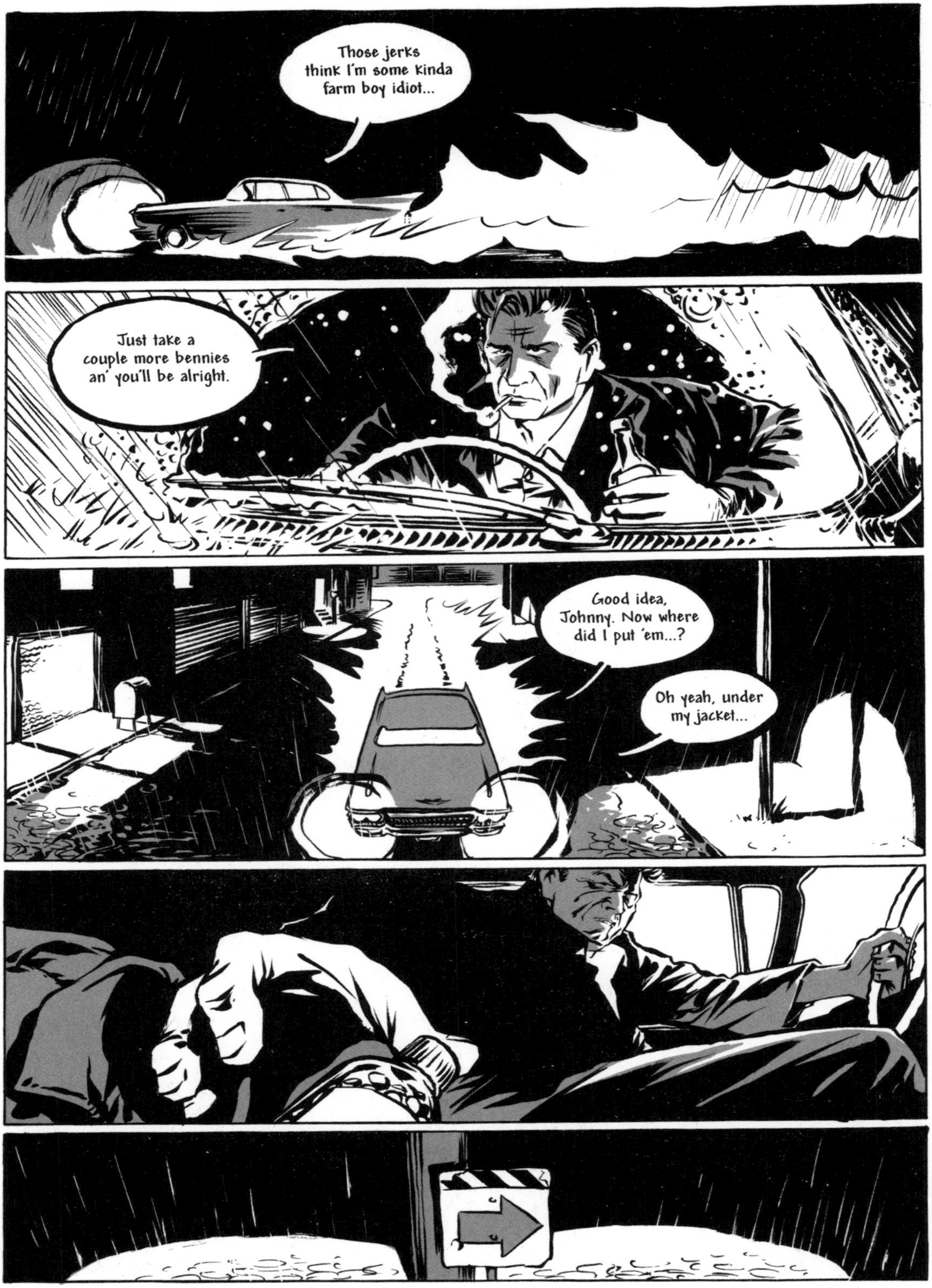
Those jerks think I'm some kinda farm boy idiot...
Just take a couple more bennies an' you'll be alright.
Good idea, Johnny. Now where did I put 'em...?
Oh yeah, under my jacket...

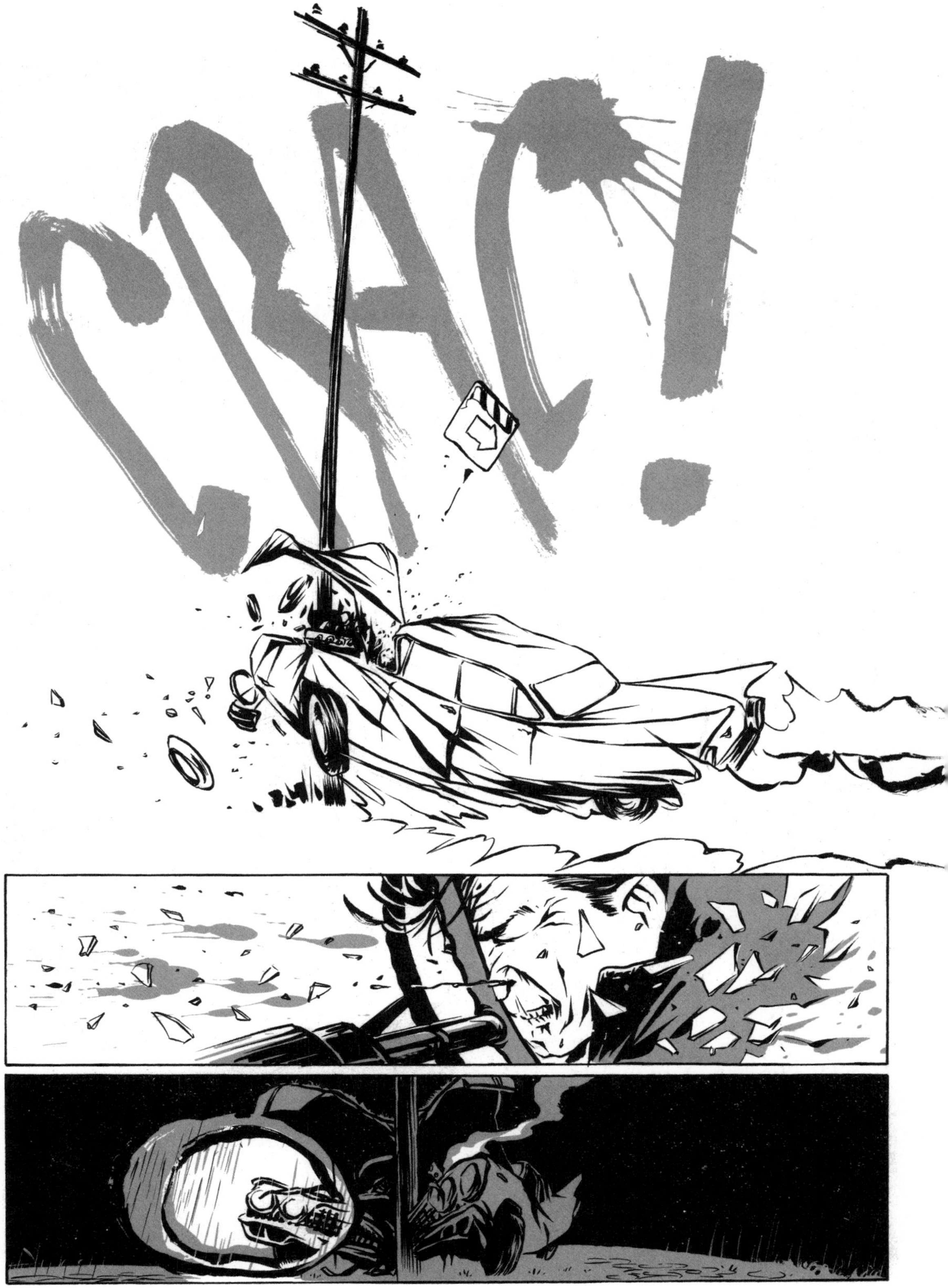
CRAC!

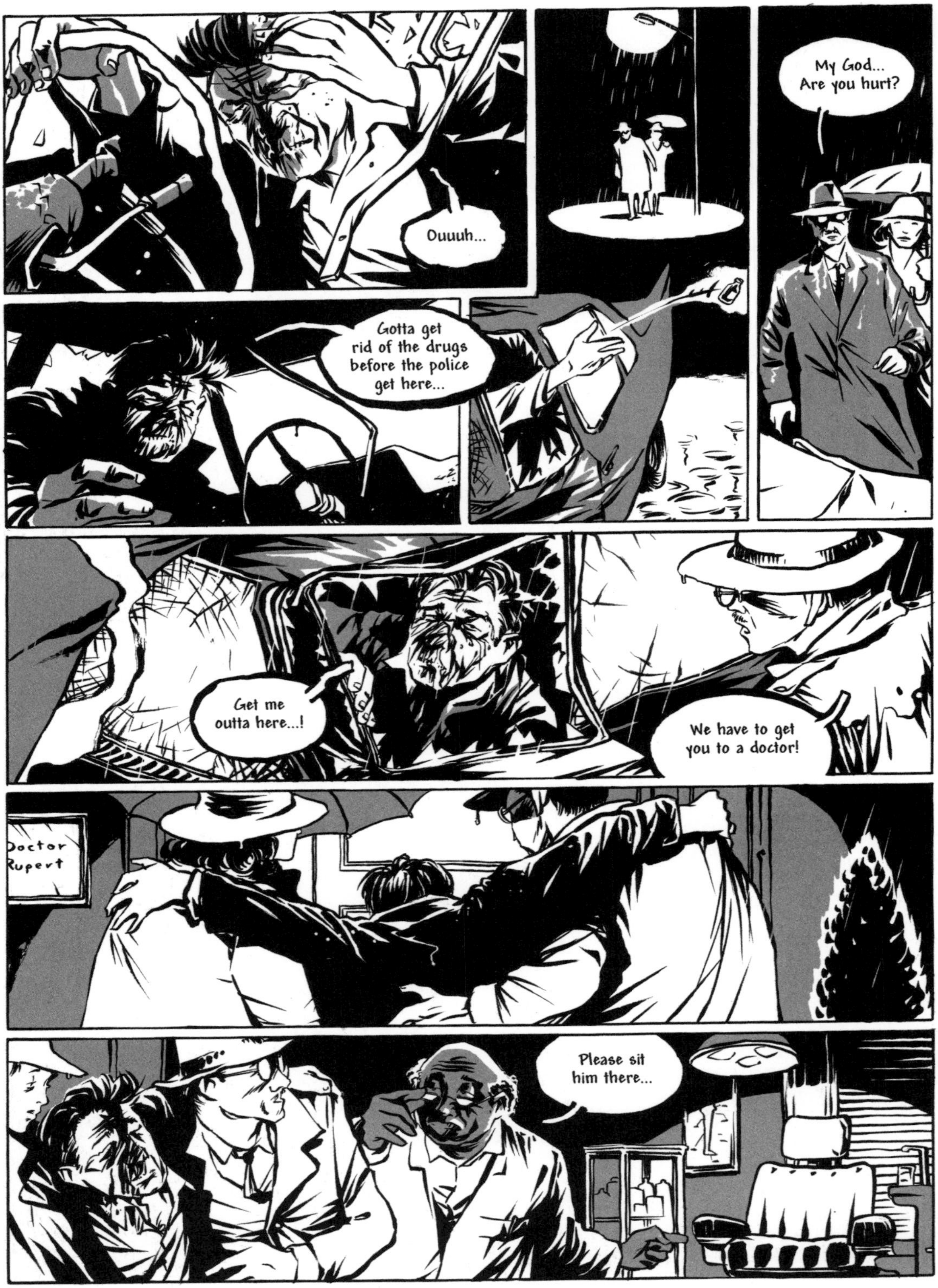
Ouuuh...
My God... Are you hurt?
Gotta get rid of the drugs before the police get here...
Get me outta here...!
We have to get you to a doctor!
Doctor Rupert
Please sit him there...

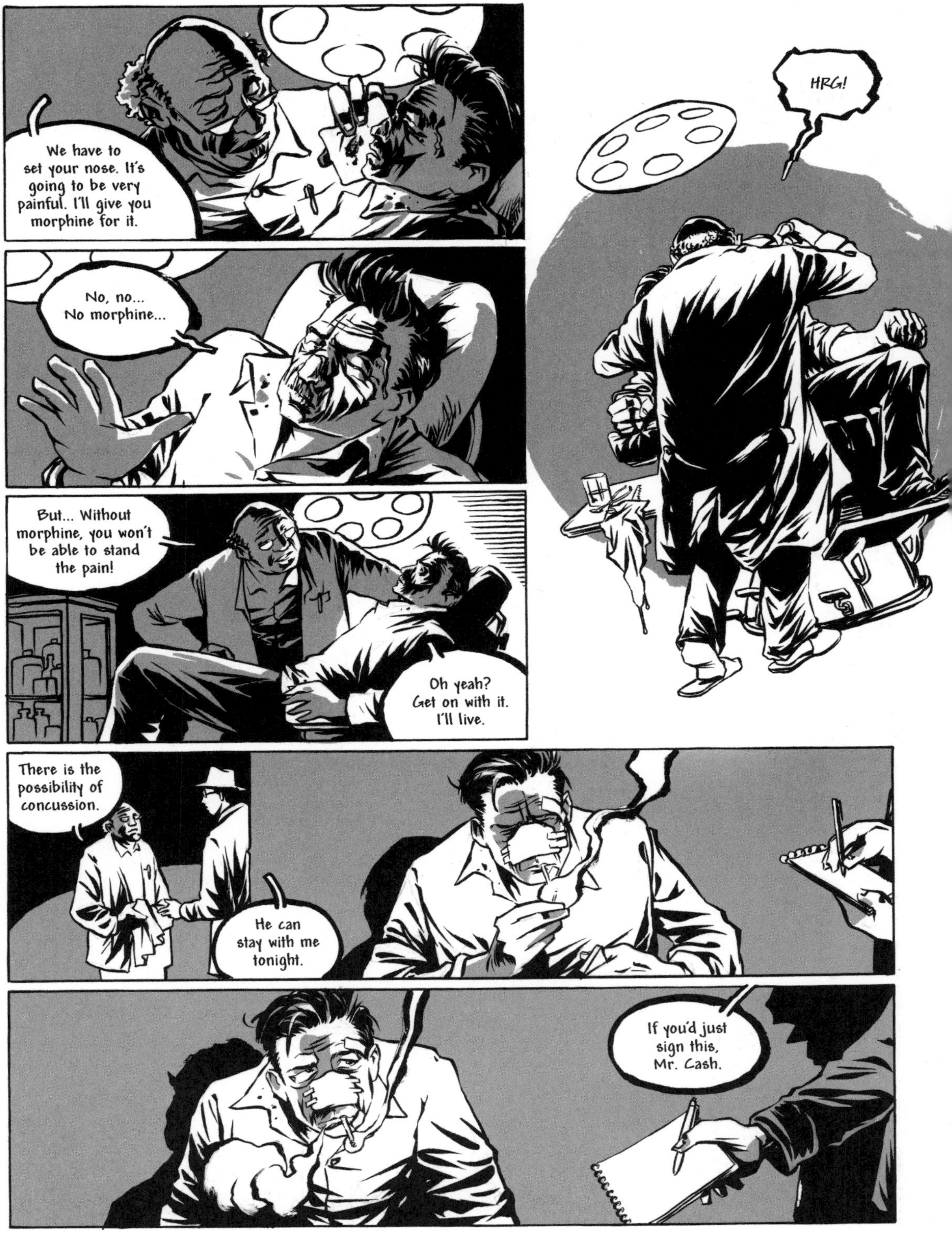
We have to set your nose. It's going to be very painful. I'll give you morphine for it.
No, no... No morphine...
But... Without morphine, you won't be able to stand the pain!
Oh yeah? Get on with it. I'll live.
HRG!
There is the possibility of concussion.
He can stay with me tonight.
If you'd just sign this, Mr. Cash.

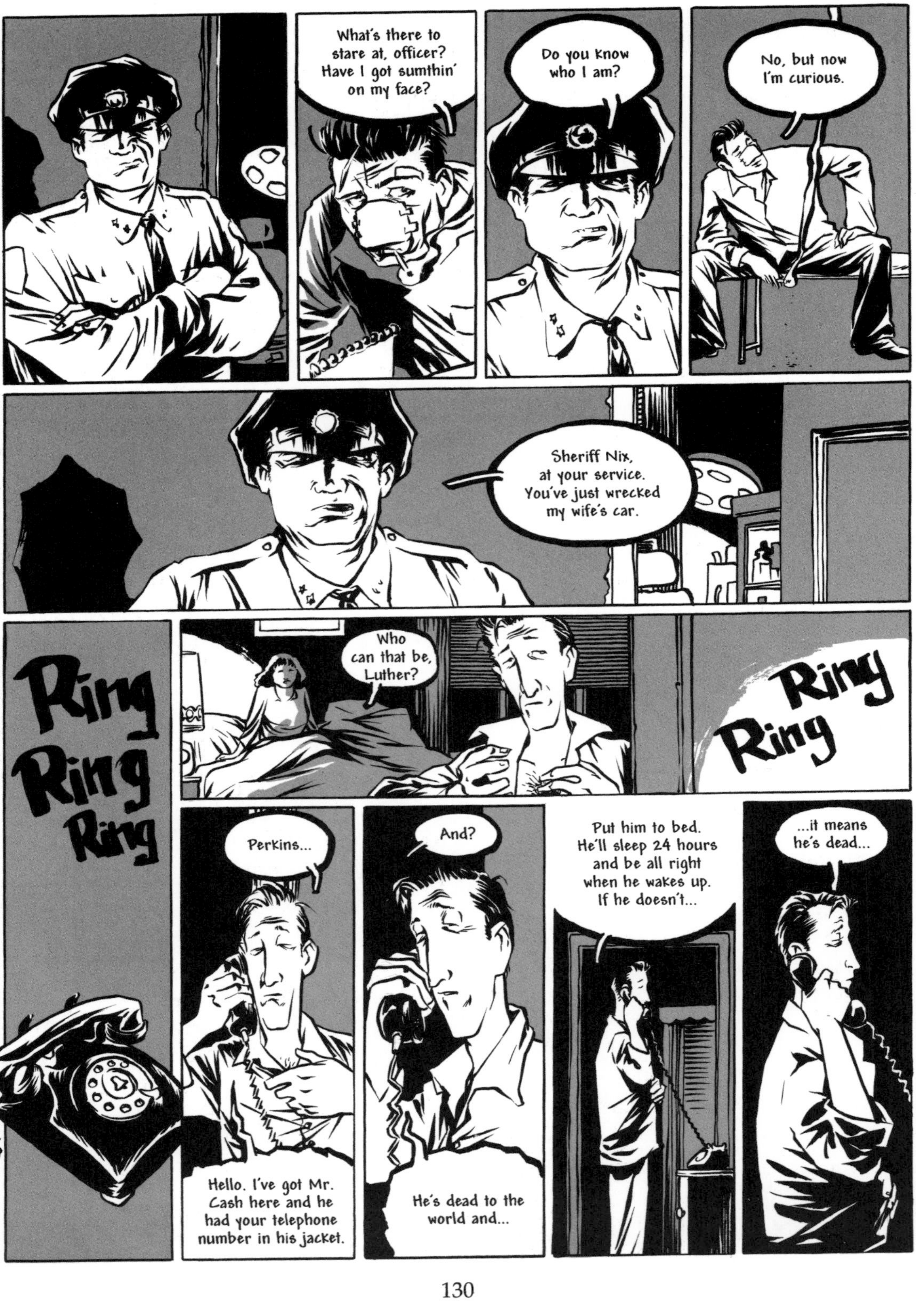

What's there to stare at, officer? Have I got sumthin' on my face?
Do you know who I am?
No, but now I'm curious.
Sheriff Nix, at your service. You've just wrecked my wife's car.
Ring Ring Ring
Who can that be, Luther?
Ring Ring
Perkins...
Hello. I've got Mr. Cash here and he had your telephone number in his jacket.
And?
He's dead to the world and...
Put him to bed. He'll sleep 24 hours and be all right when he wakes up. If he doesn't...
...it means he's dead...

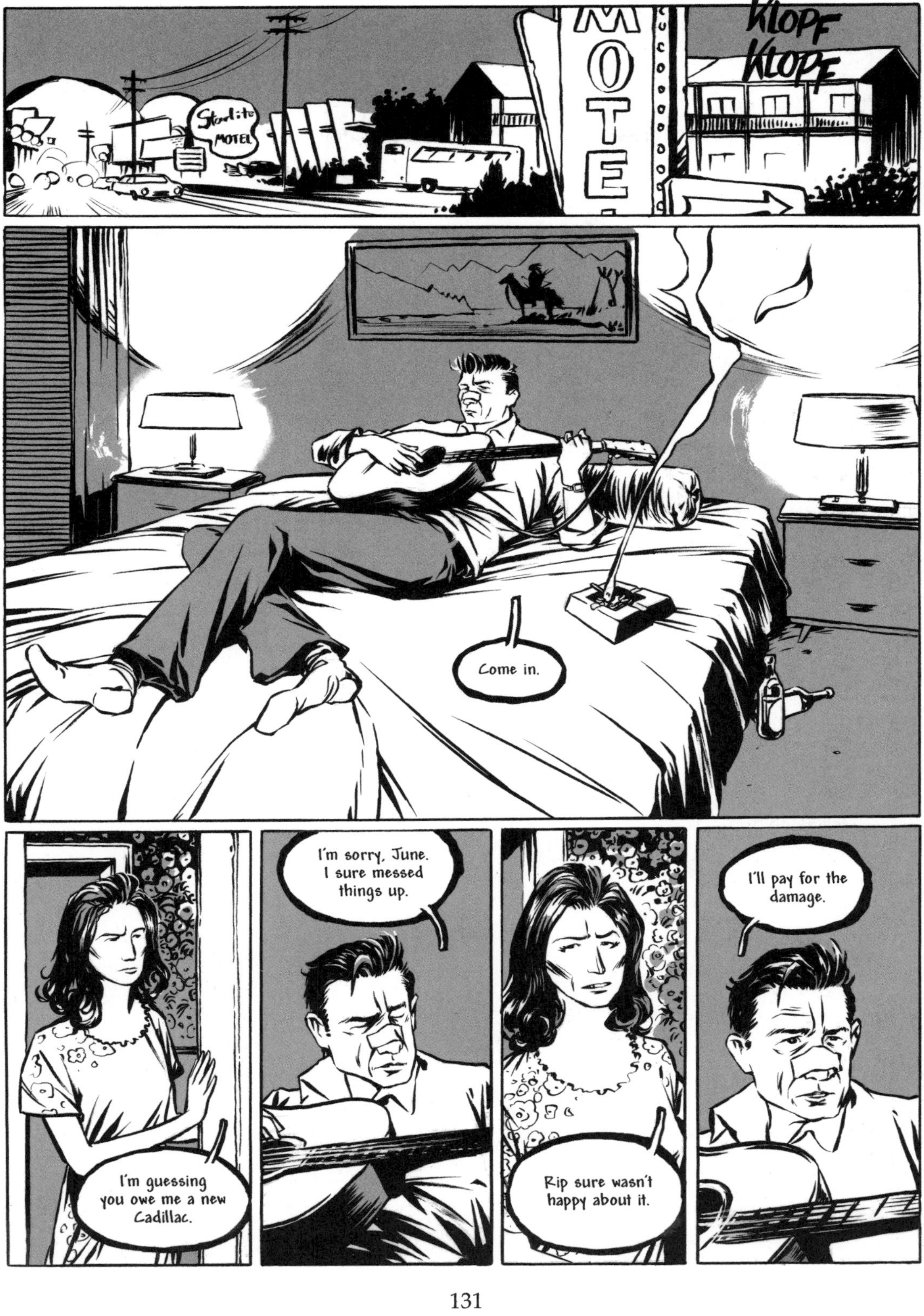
Starlite MOTEL
MOTEL
KLOPF KLOPF
Come in.
I'm guessing you owe me a new Cadillac.
I'm sorry, June. I sure messed things up.
Rip sure wasn't happy about it.
I'll pay for the damage.

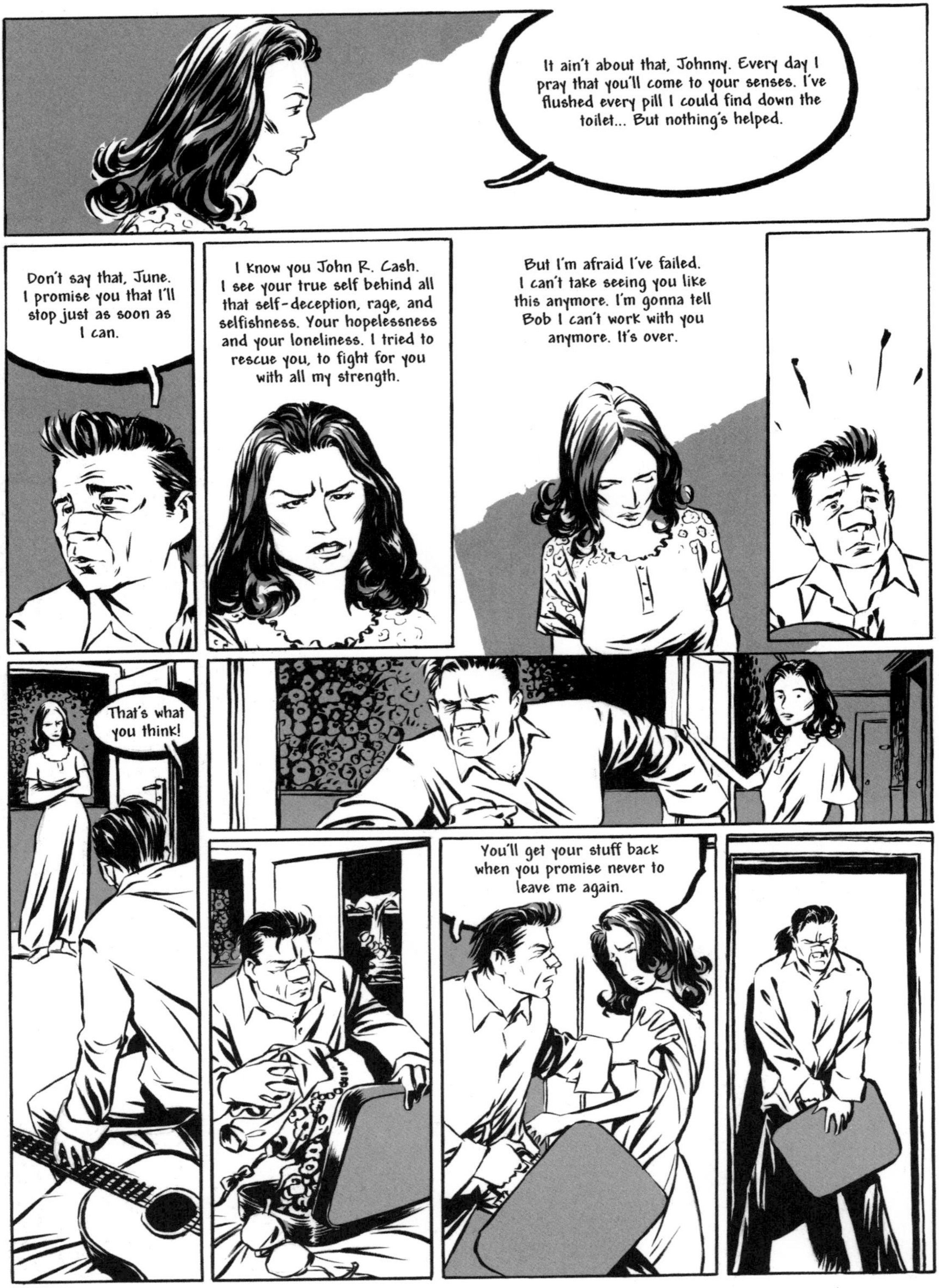
It ain't about that, Johnny. Every day I pray that you'll come to your senses. I've flushed every pill I could find down the toilet... But nothing's helped.
Don't say that, June. I promise you that I'll stop just as soon as I can.
I know you John R. Cash. I see your true self behind all that self-deception, rage, and selfishness. Your hopelessness and your loneliness. I tried to rescue you, to fight for you with all my strength.
But I'm afraid I've failed. I can't take seeing you like this anymore. I'm gonna tell Bob I can't work with you anymore. It's over.
That's what you think!
You'll get your stuff back when you promise never to leave me again.

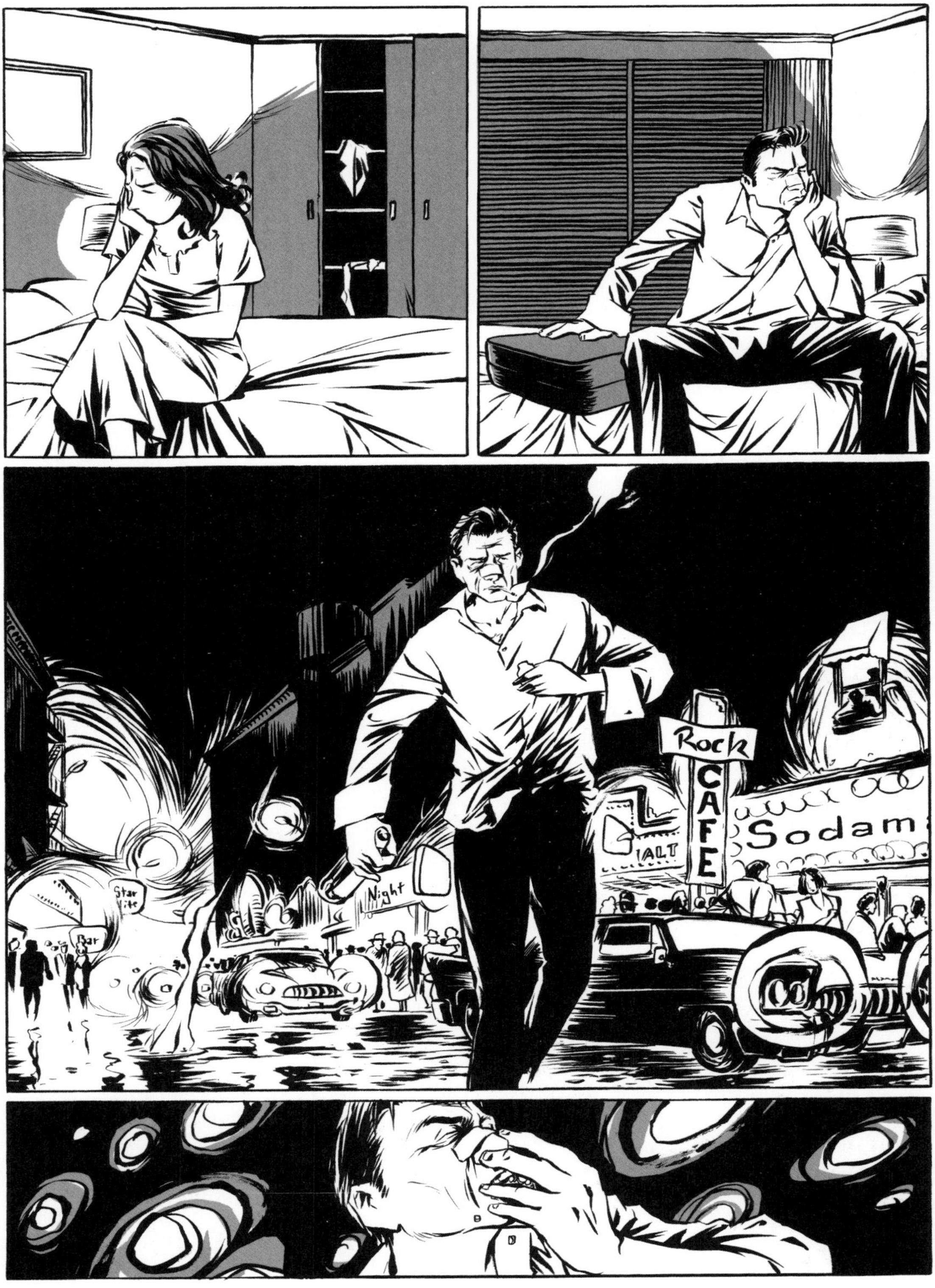
Rock
CAFE
Sodam
Night
Bar

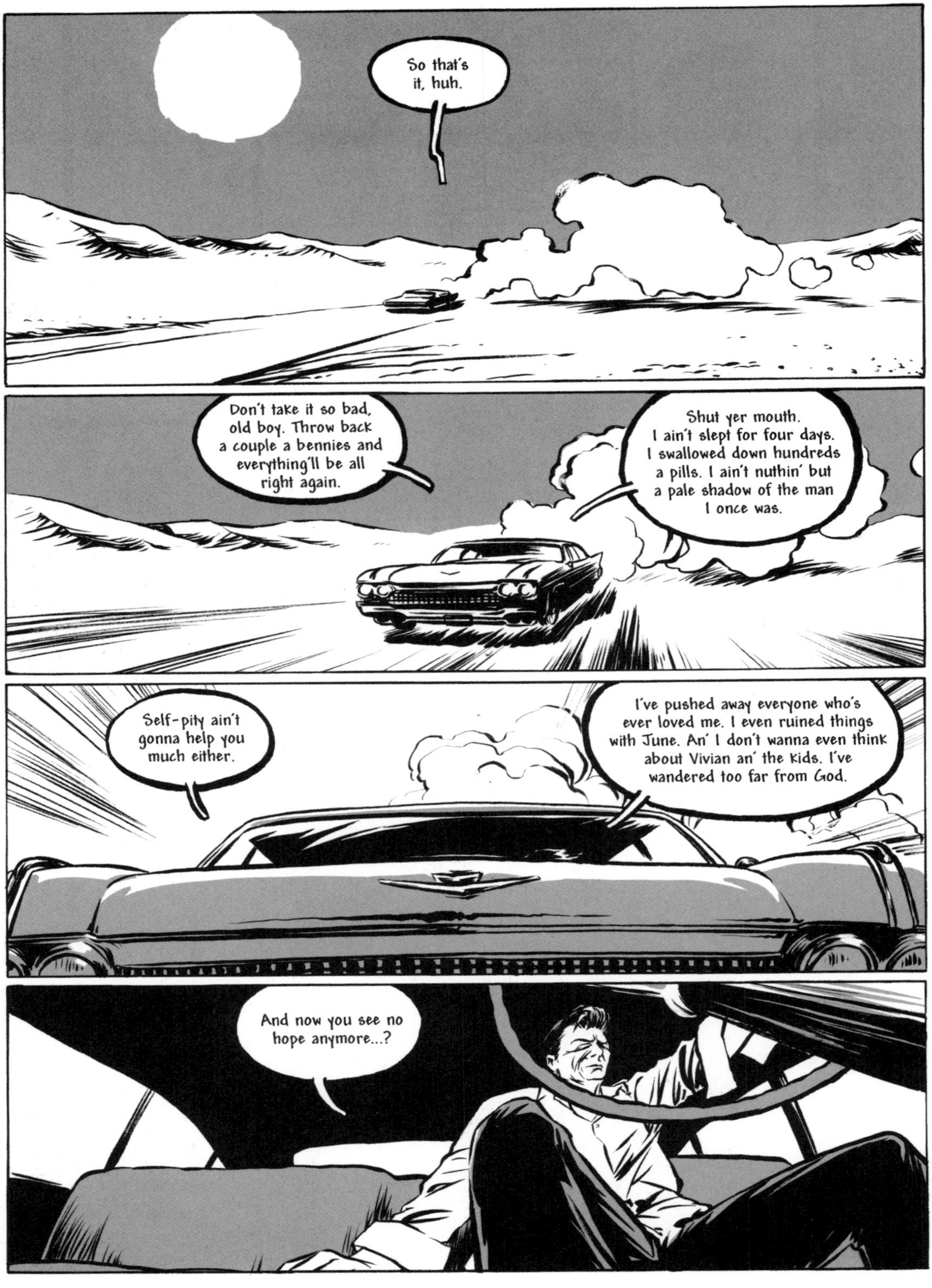
So that's it, huh.
Don't take it so bad, old boy. Throw back a couple a bennies and everything'll be all right again.
Shut yer mouth. I ain't slept for four days. I swallowed down hundreds a pills. I ain't nuthin' but a pale shadow of the man I once was.
Self-pity ain't gonna help you much either.
I've pushed away everyone who's ever loved me. I even ruined things with June. An' I don't wanna even think about Vivian an' the kids. I've wandered too far from God.
And now you see no hope anymore...?

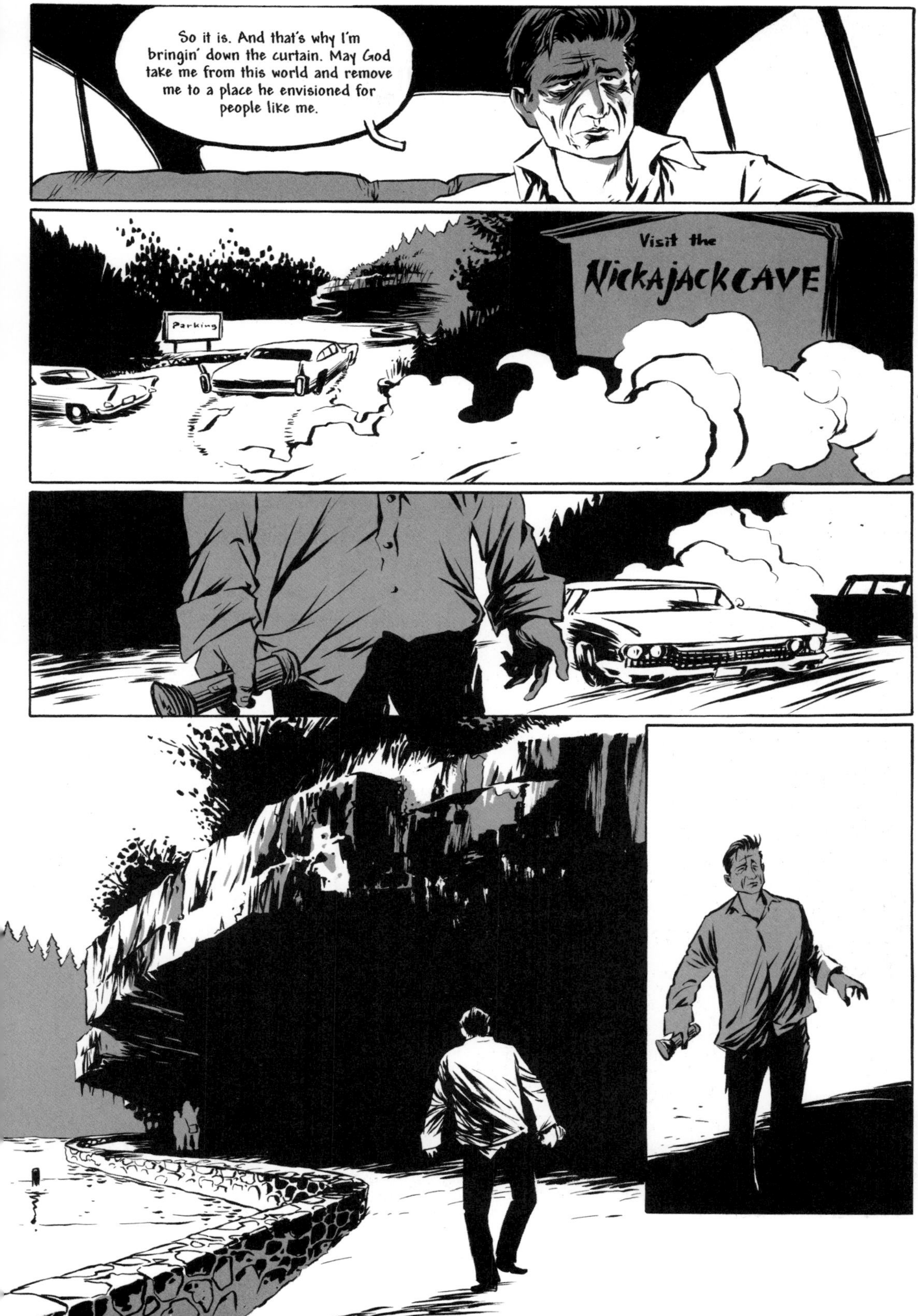
So it is. And that's why I'm bringin' down the curtain. May God take me from this world and remove me to a place he envisioned for people like me.
Visit the NICKAJACK CAVE
Parking

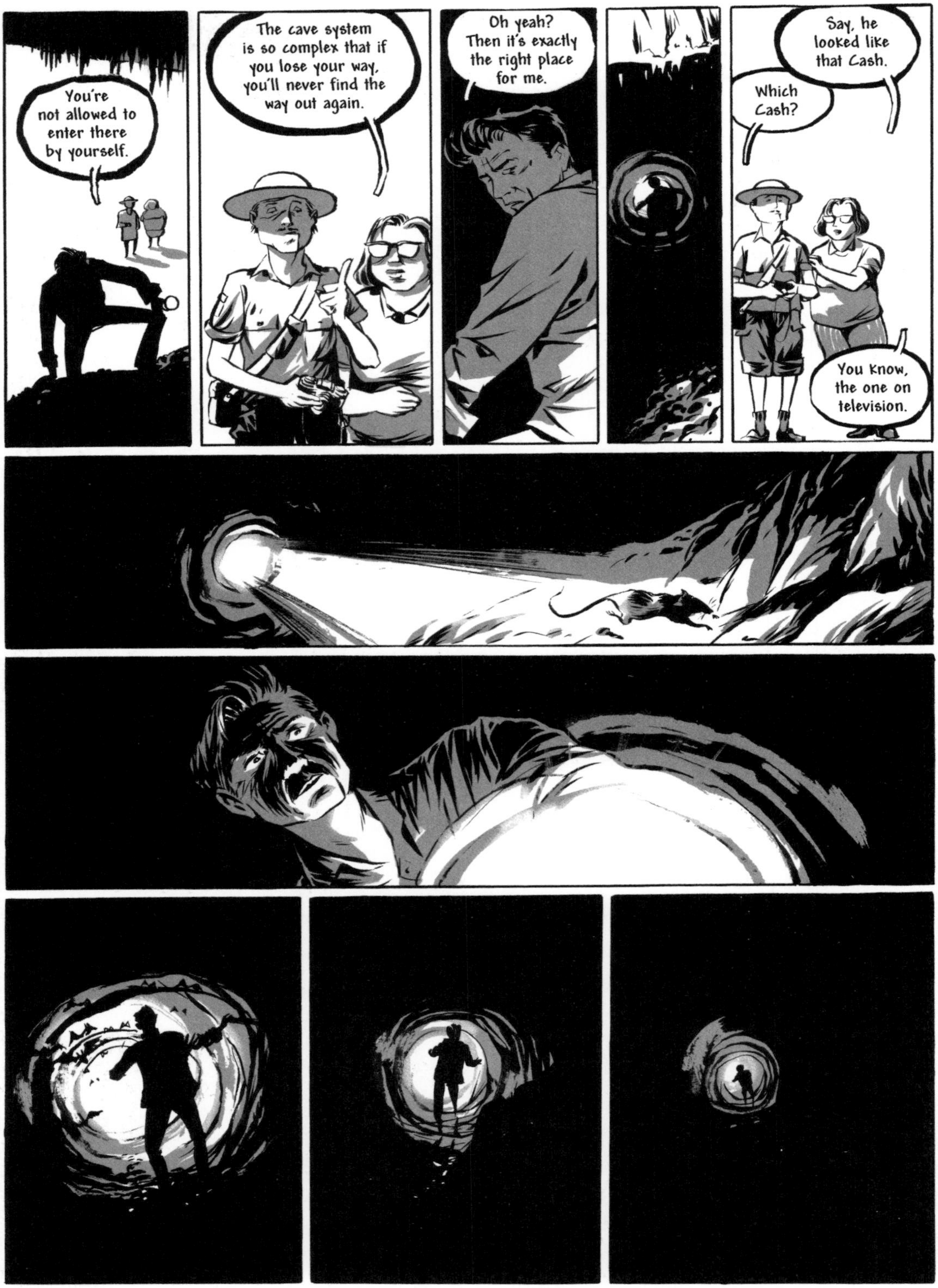
You're not allowed to enter there by yourself.
The cave system is so complex that if you lose your way, you'll never find the way out again.
Oh yeah? Then it's exactly the right place for me.
Say, he looked like that Cash.
Which Cash?
You know, the one on television.

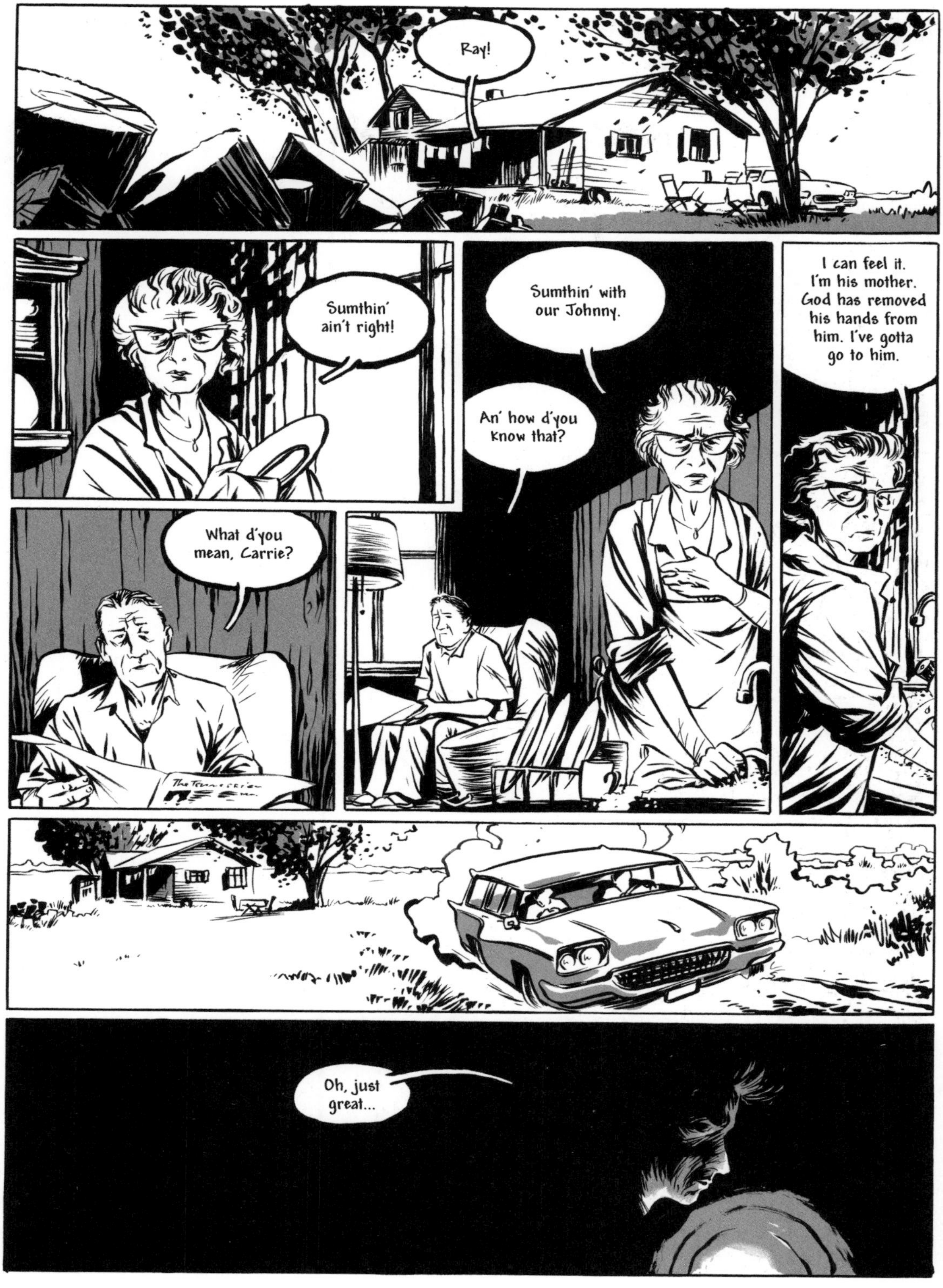
Ray!
Sumthin' ain't right!
Sumthin' with our Johnny.
An' how d'you know that?
I can feel it. I'm his mother. God has removed his hands from him. I've gotta go to him.
What d'you mean, Carrie?
Oh, just great...

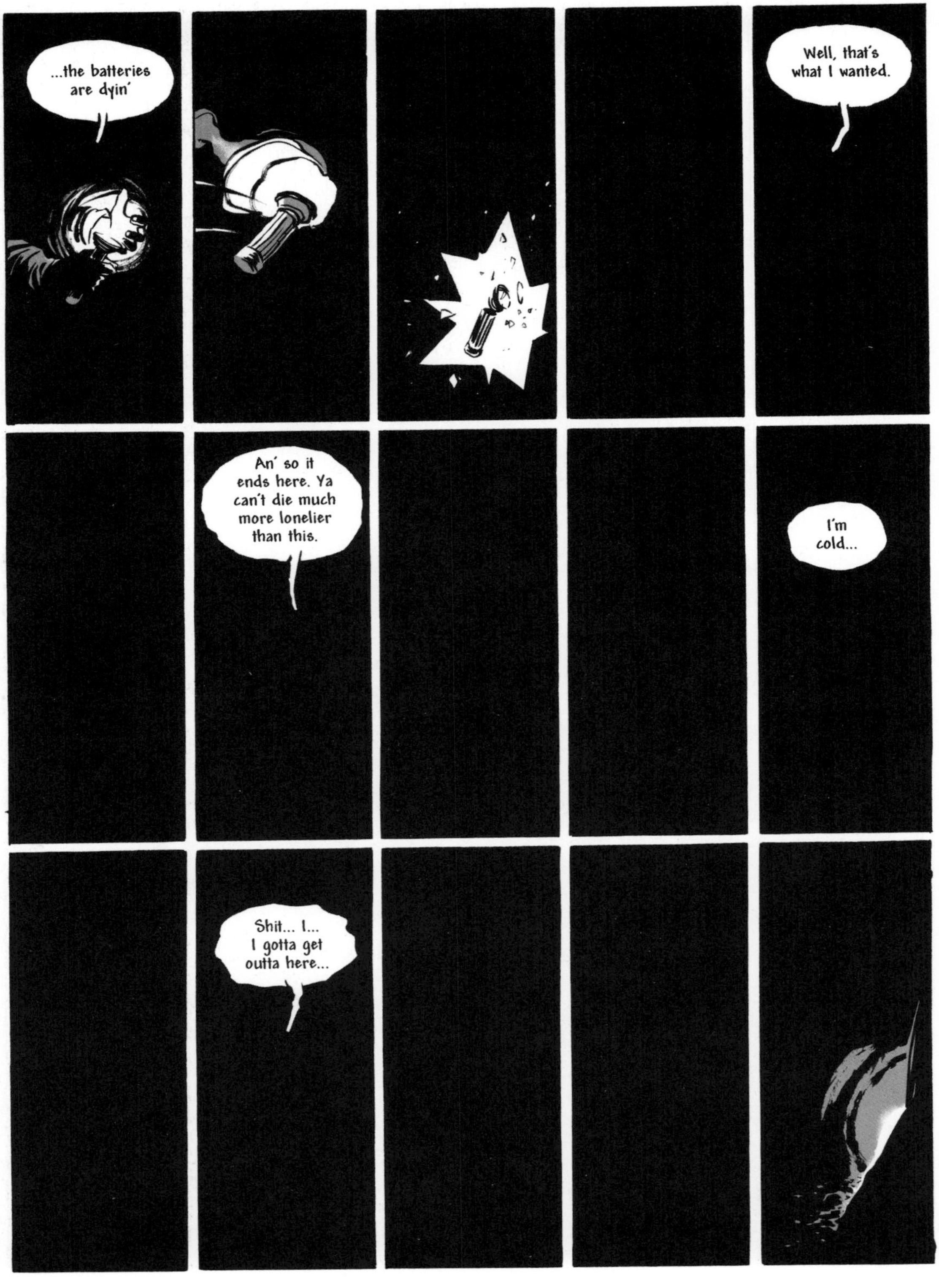
...the batteries are dyin'
Well, that's what I wanted.
An' so it ends here. Ya can't die much more lonelier than this.
I'm cold...
Shit... I... I gotta get outta here...

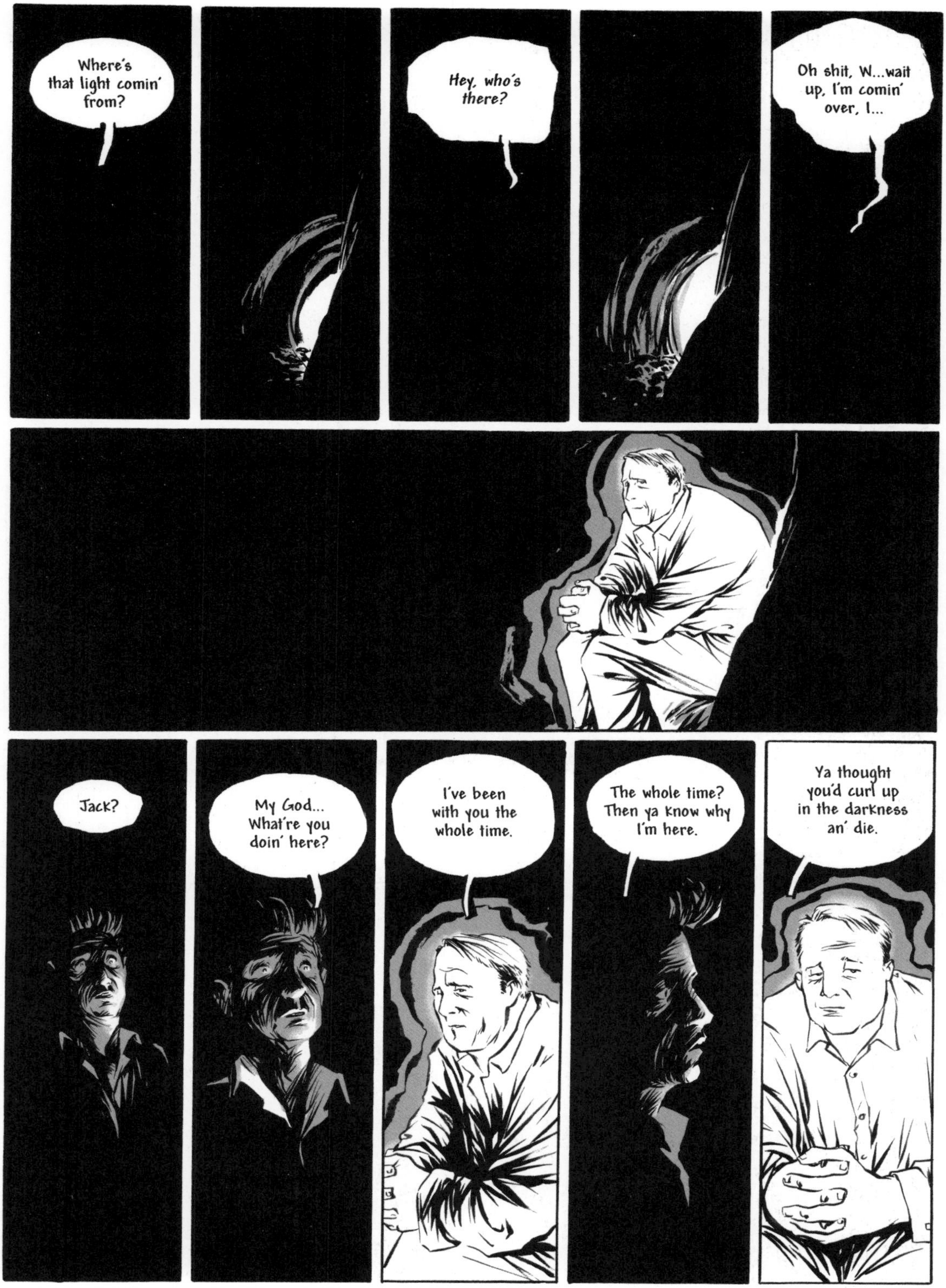
Where's that light comin' from?
Hey, who's there?
Oh shit, W...wait up, I'm comin' over, I...
Jack?
My God... What're you doin' here?
I've been with you the whole time.
The whole time? Then ya know why I'm here.
Ya thought you'd curl up in the darkness an' die.

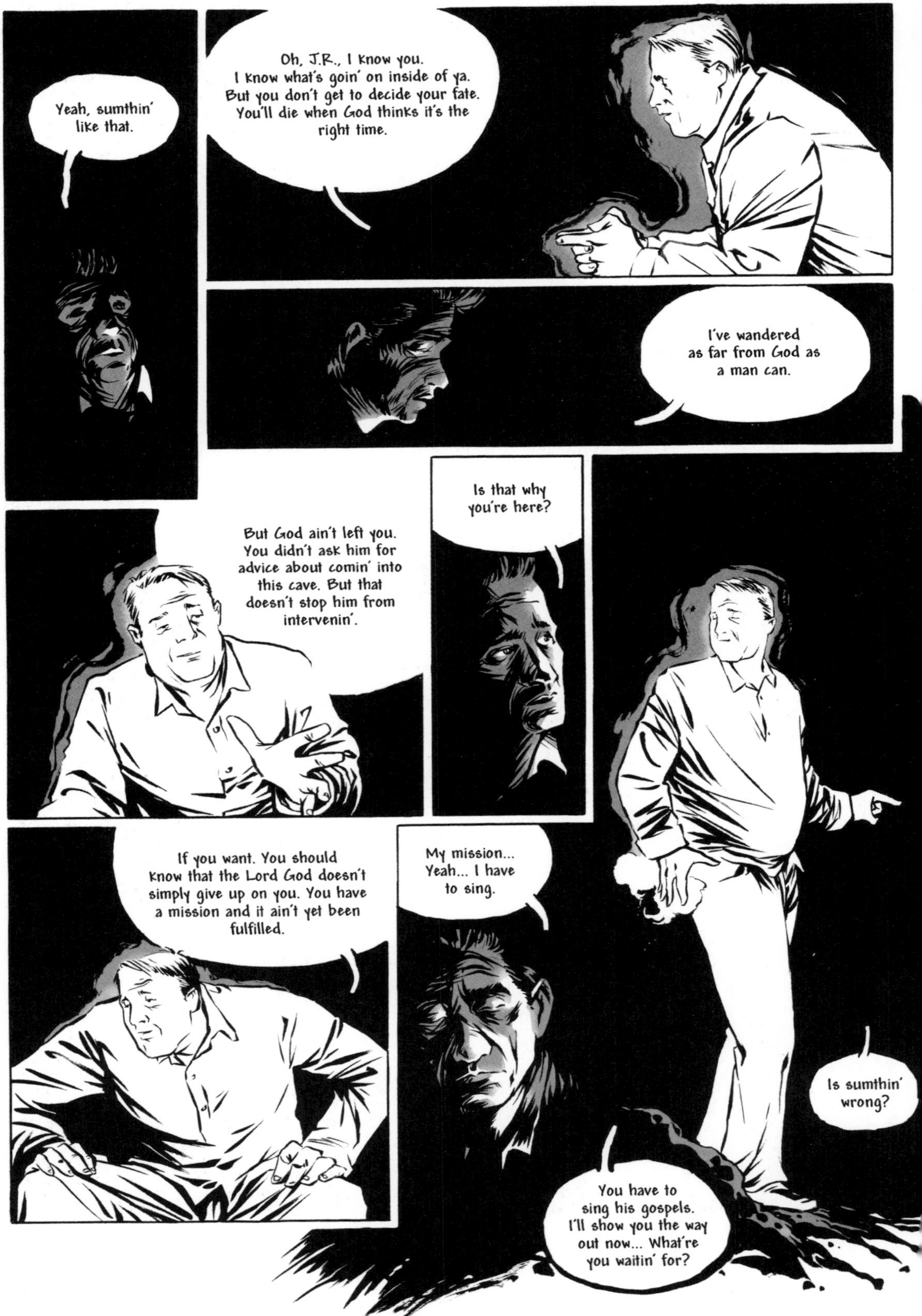
Yeah, sumthin' like that.
Oh, J.R., I know you. I know what's goin' on inside of ya. But you don't get to decide your fate. You'll die when God thinks it's the right time.
I've wandered as far from God as a man can.
But God ain't left you. You didn't ask him for advice about comin' into this cave. But that doesn't stop him from intervenin'.
Is that why you're here?
If you want. You should know that the Lord God doesn't simply give up on you. You have a mission and it ain't yet been fulfilled.
My mission... Yeah... I have to sing.
Is sumthin' wrong?
You have to sing his gospels. I'll show you the way out now... What're you waitin' for?

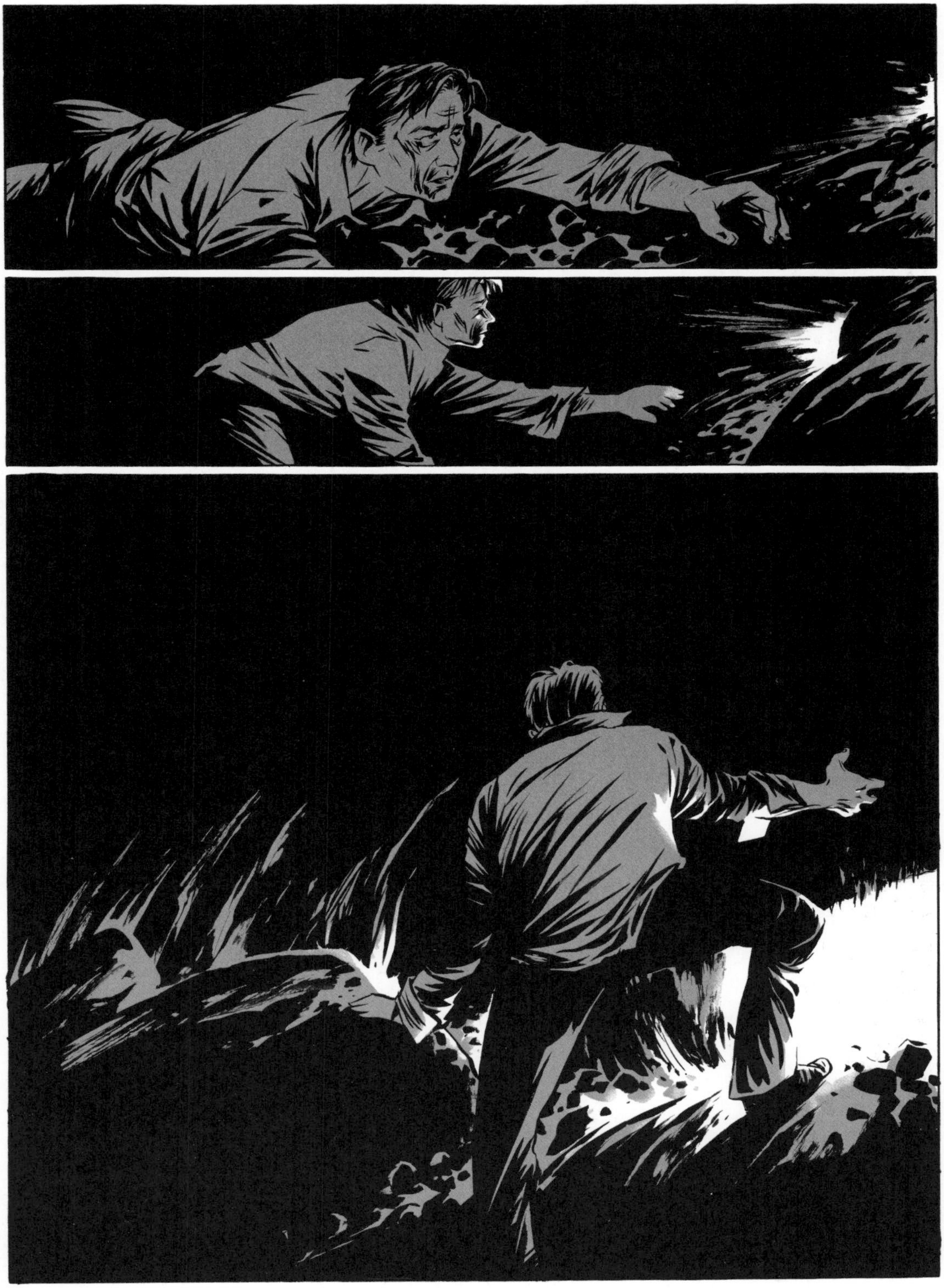

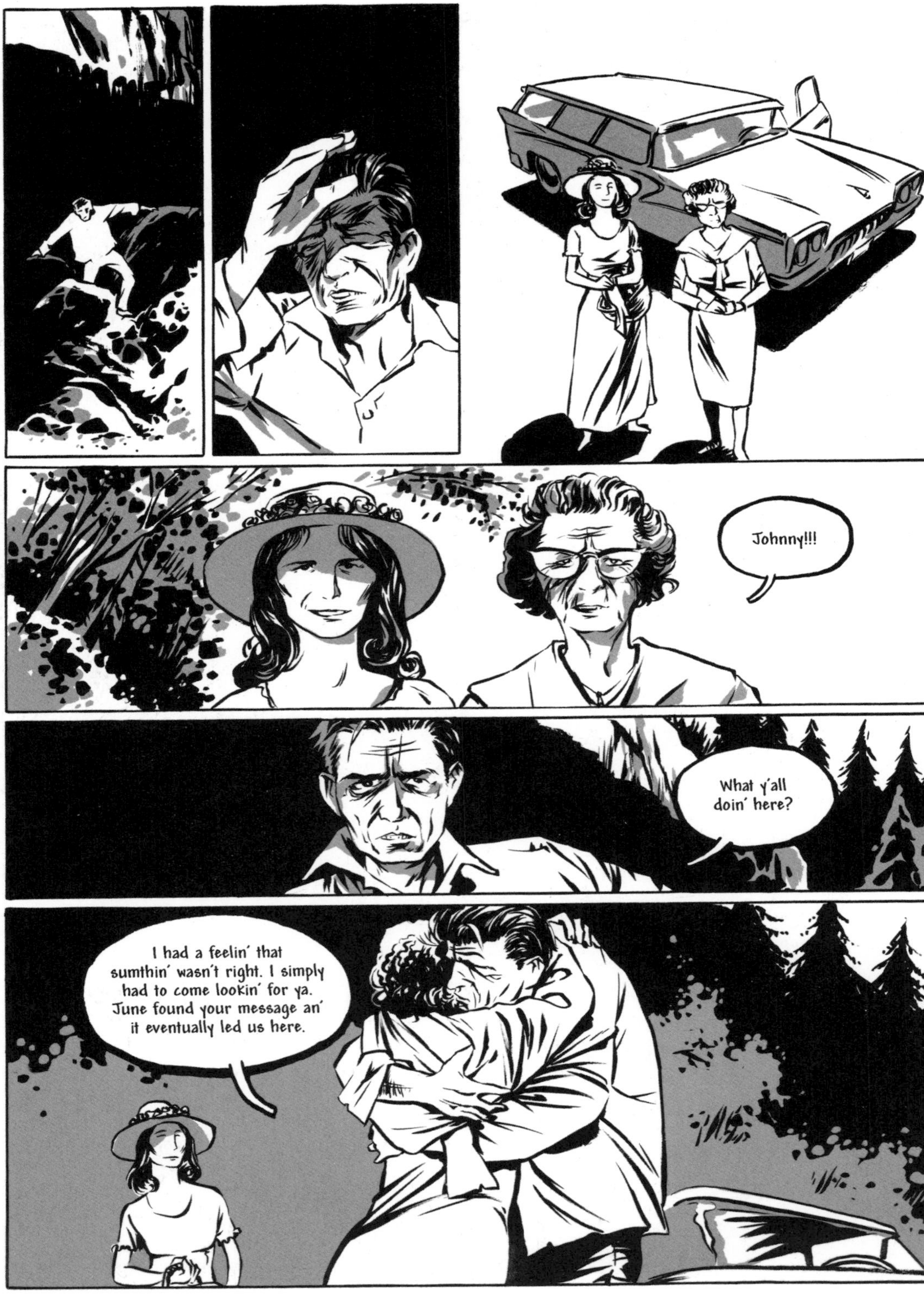
Johnny!!!
What y'all doin' here?
I had a feelin' that sumthin' wasn't right. I simply had to come lookin' for ya. June found your message an' it eventually led us here.

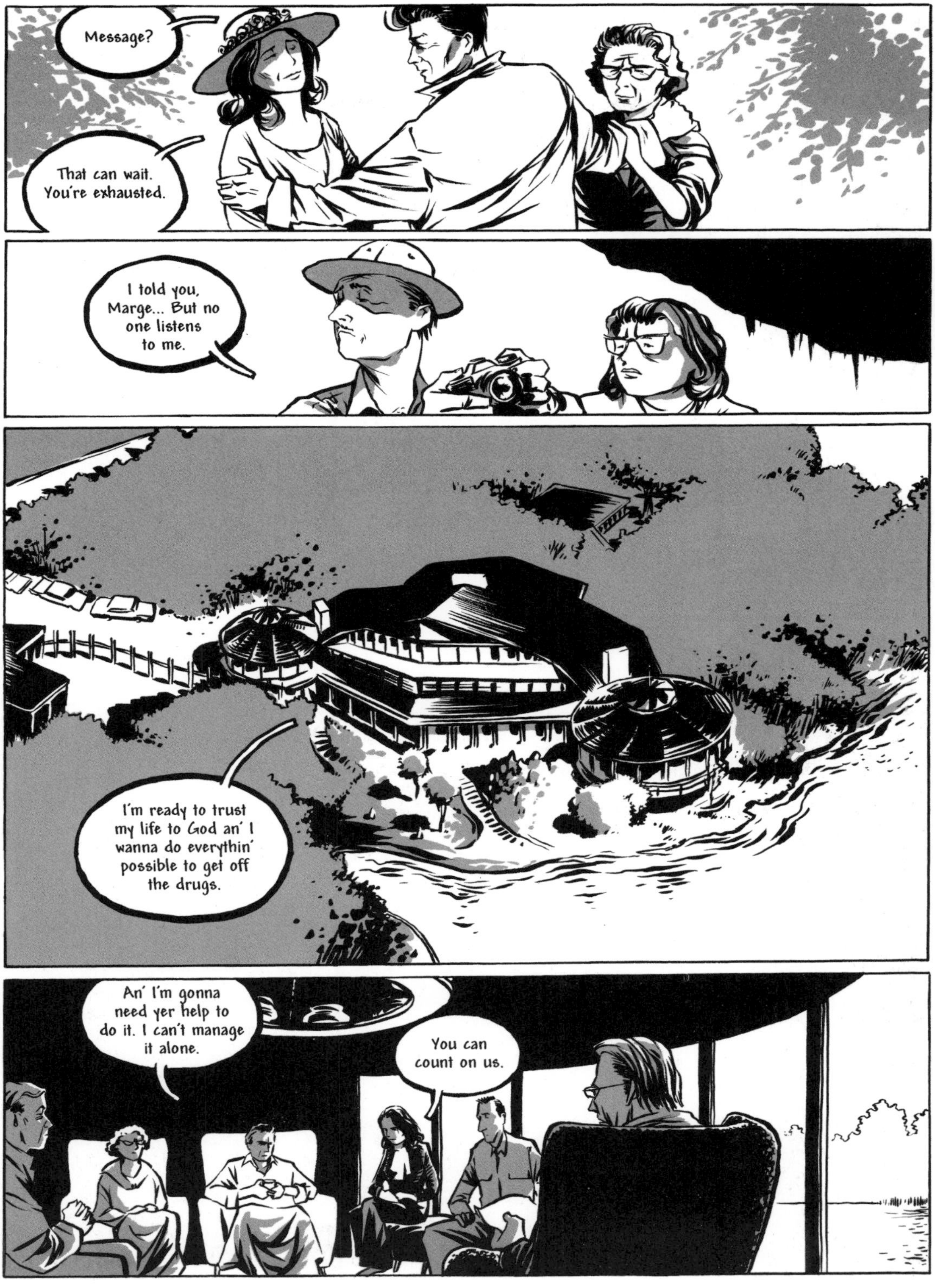
Message?
That can wait. You're exhausted.
I told you, Marge... But no one listens to me.
I'm ready to trust my life to God an' I wanna do everythin' possible to get off the drugs.
An' I'm gonna need yer help to do it. I can't manage it alone.
You can count on us.

The withdrawals aren't gonna be easy. We have to completely shield him here at home in Hendersonville... Especially from people, particularly friends, who he took drugs with or who sold him drugs.

That can be my job. I'm good at that.

The best thing would be for you to stay in your room. I'll check up on you regularly.

Thank you, Dr. Winston. May the Lord lend us strength.

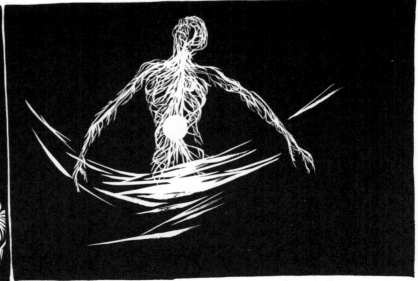

144

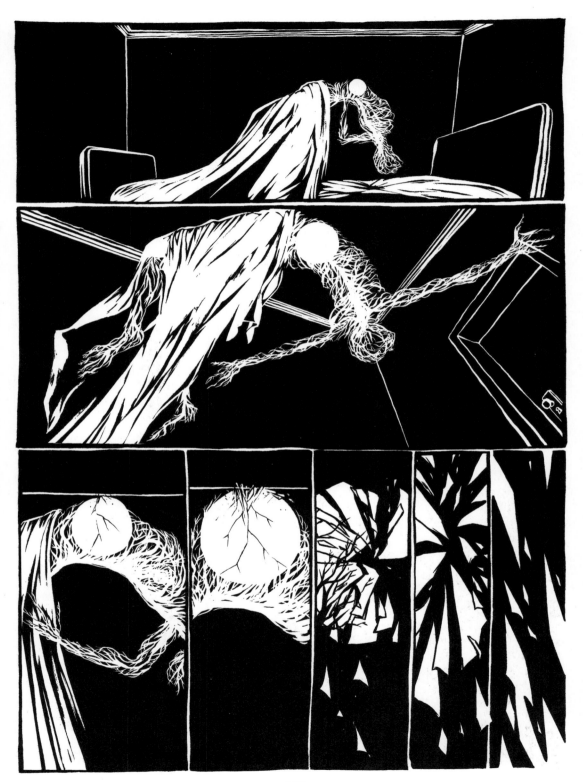

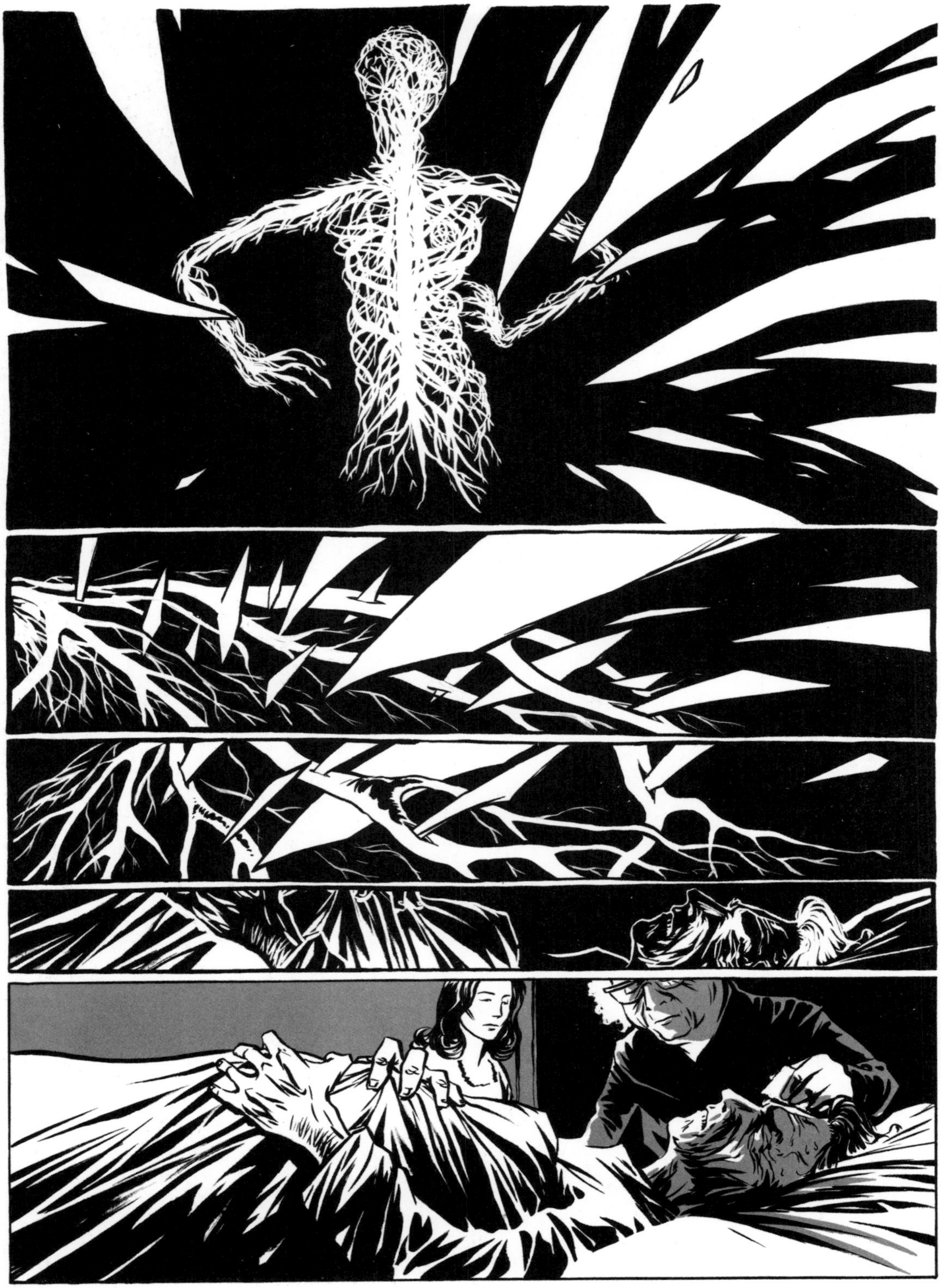

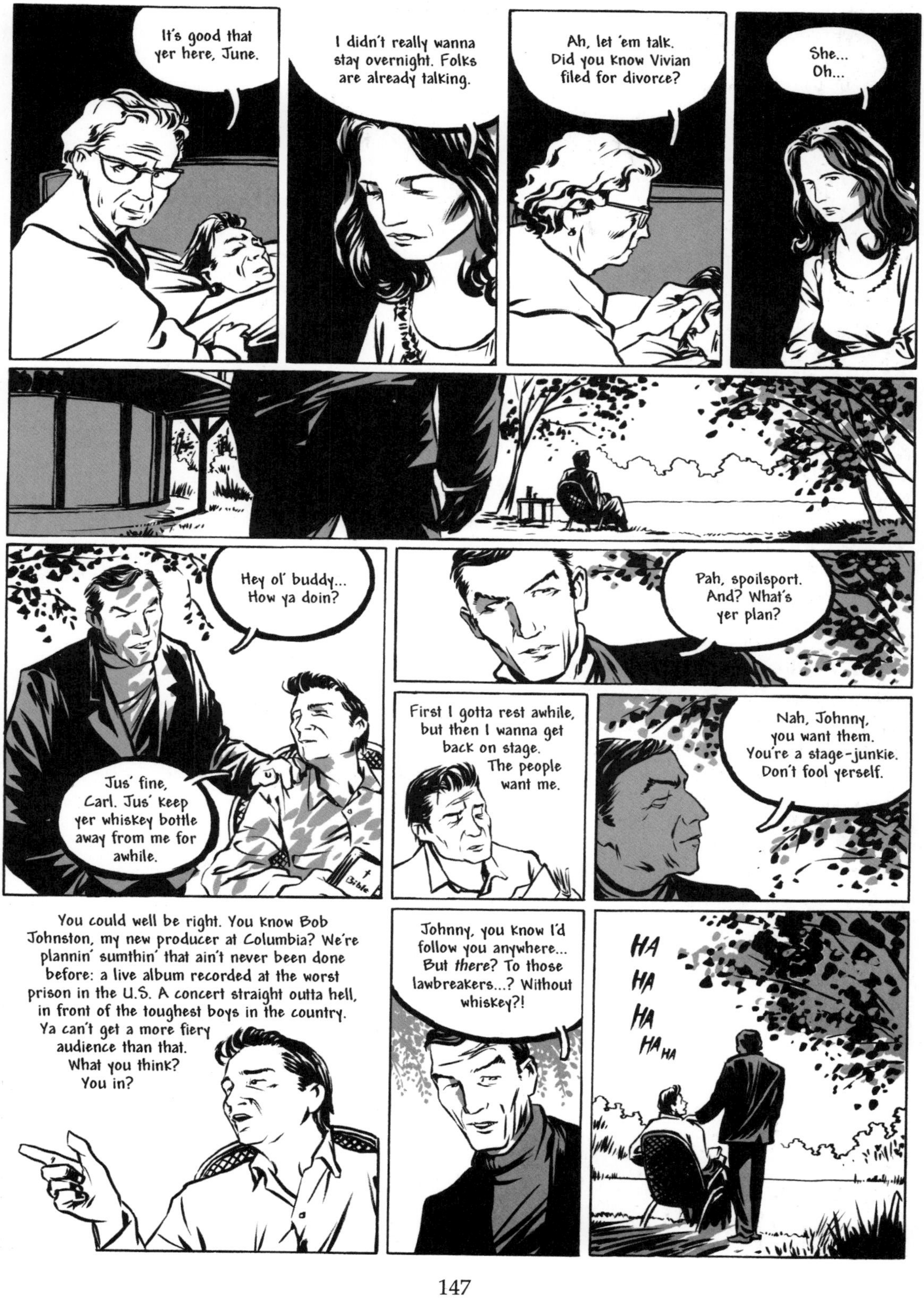
It's good that yer here, June.
I didn't really wanna stay overnight. Folks are already talking.
Ah, let 'em talk. Did you know Vivian filed for divorce?
She... Oh...
Hey ol' buddy... How ya doin?
Jus' fine, Carl. Jus' keep yer whiskey bottle away from me for awhile.
Bible
Pah, spoilsport. And? What's yer plan?
First I gotta rest awhile, but then I wanna get back on stage. The people want me.
Nah, Johnny, you want them. You're a stage-junkie. Don't fool yerself.
You could well be right. You know Bob Johnston, my new producer at Columbia? We're plannin' sumthin' that ain't never been done before: a live album recorded at the worst prison in the U.S. A concert straight outta hell, in front of the toughest boys in the country. Ya can't get a more fiery audience than that. What you think? You in?
Johnny, you know I'd follow you anywhere... But *there*? To those lawbreakers...? Without whiskey?!
HA HA HA HA HA

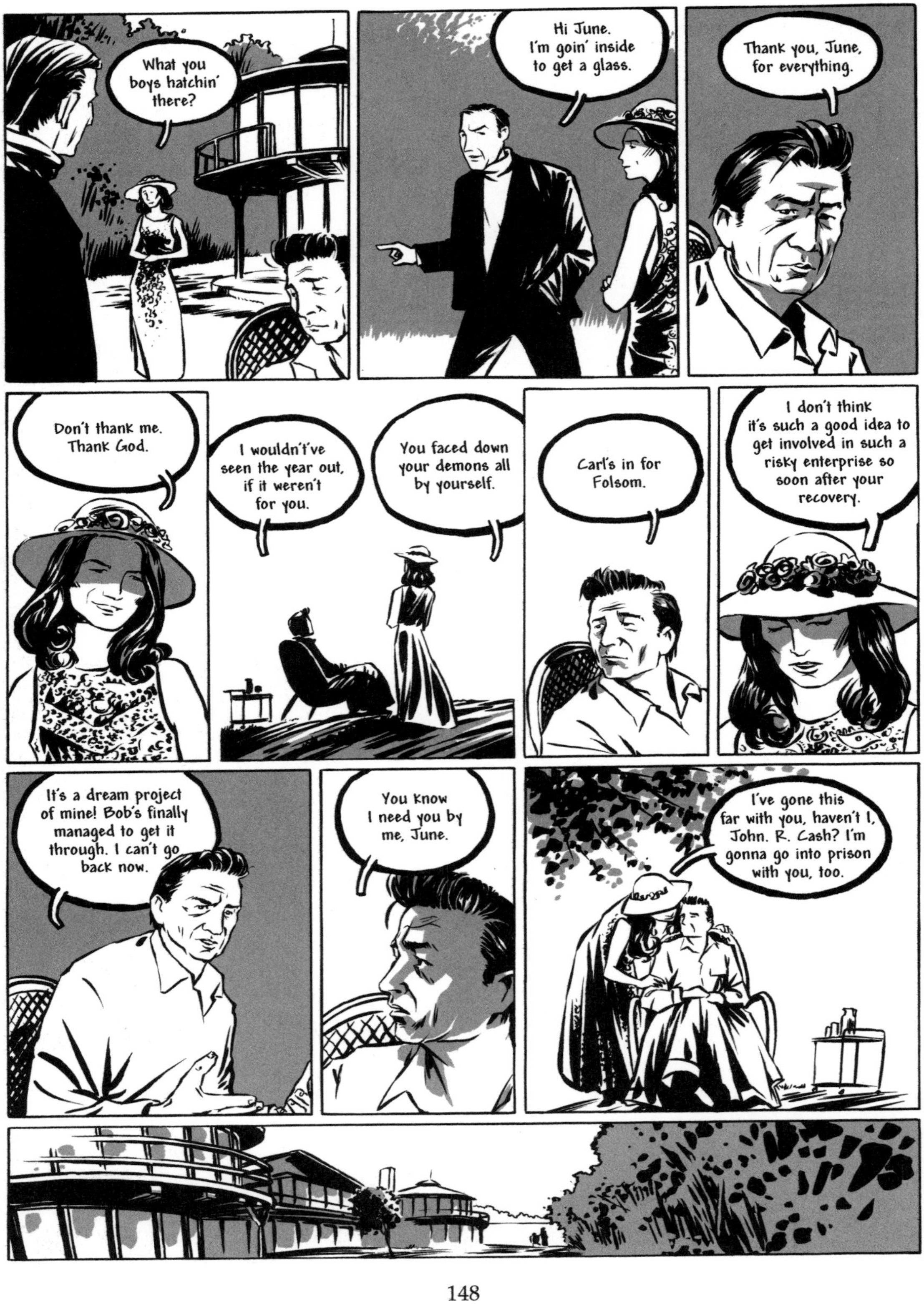
What you boys hatchin' there?
Hi June. I'm goin' inside to get a glass.
Thank you, June, for everything.
Don't thank me. Thank God.
I wouldn't've seen the year out, if it weren't for you.
You faced down your demons all by yourself.
Carl's in for Folsom.
I don't think it's such a good idea to get involved in such a risky enterprise so soon after your recovery.
It's a dream project of mine! Bob's finally managed to get it through. I can't go back now.
You know I need you by me, June.
I've gone this far with you, haven't I, John. R. Cash? I'm gonna go into prison with you, too.

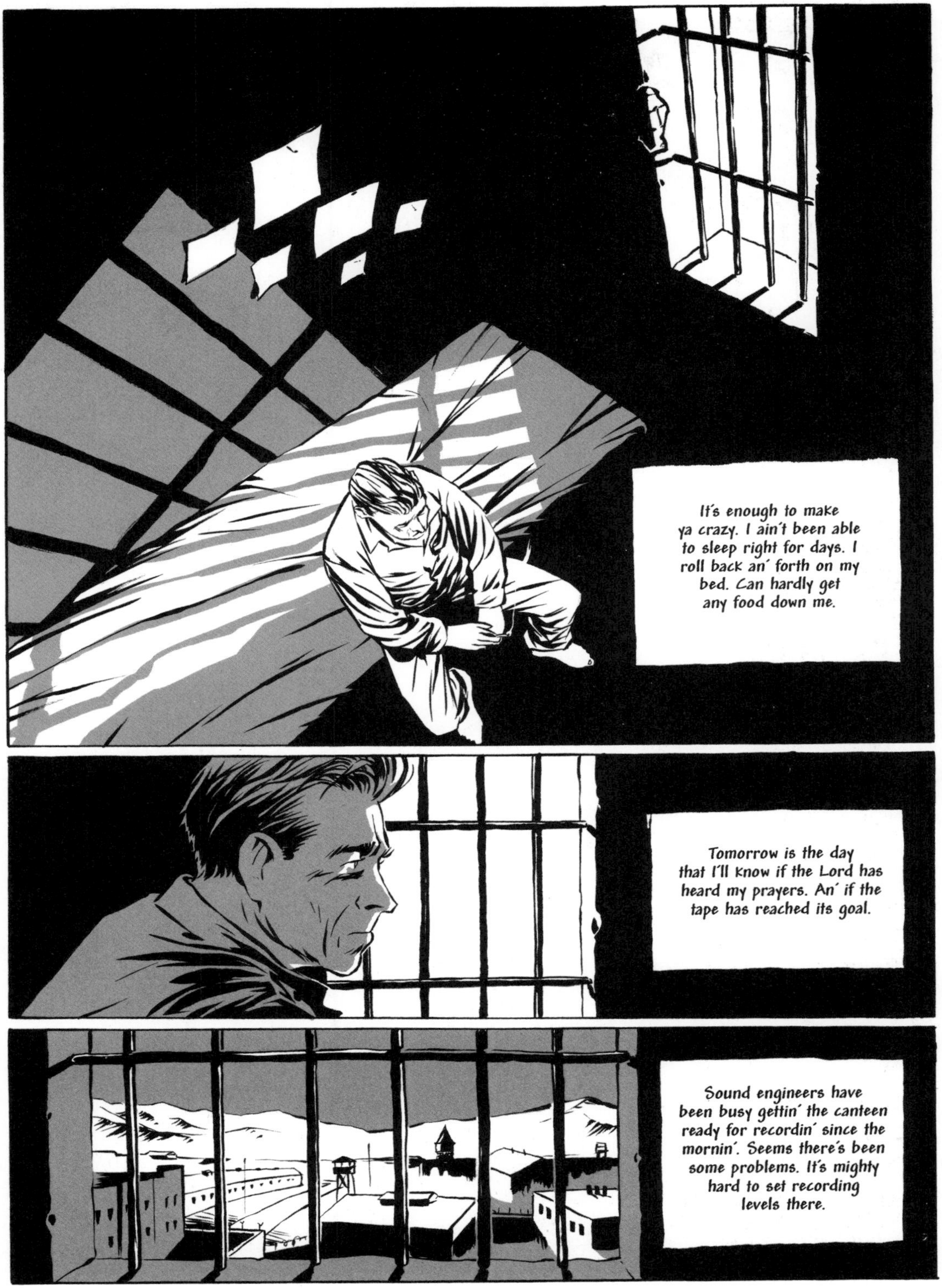
It's enough to make ya crazy. I ain't been able to sleep right for days. I roll back an' forth on my bed. Can hardly get any food down me.
Tomorrow is the day that I'll know if the Lord has heard my prayers. An' if the tape has reached its goal.
Sound engineers have been busy gettin' the canteen ready for recordin' since the mornin'. Seems there's been some problems. It's mighty hard to set recording levels there.

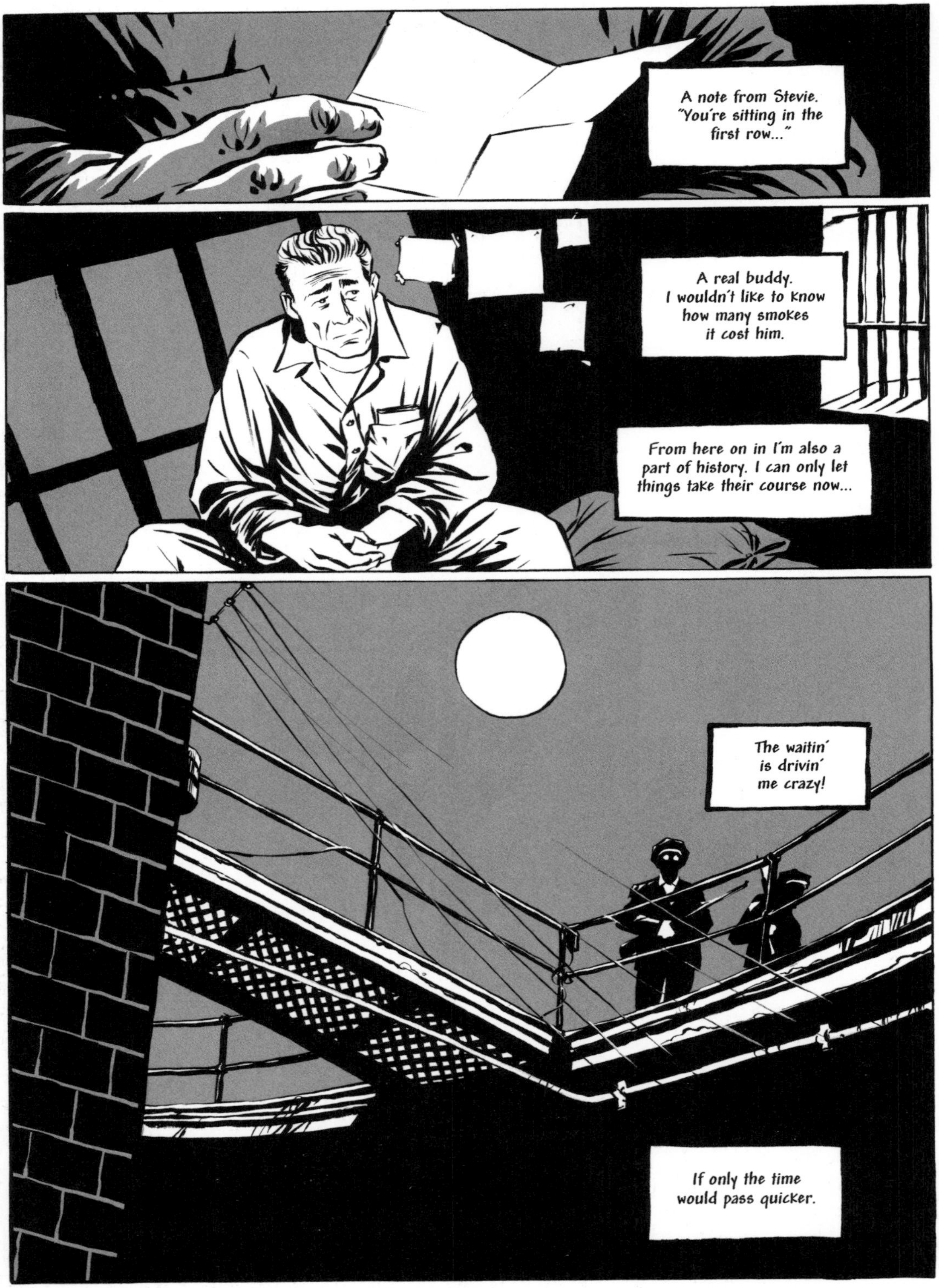
A note from Stevie. "You're sitting in the first row..."
A real buddy. I wouldn't like to know how many smokes it cost him.
From here on in I'm also a part of history. I can only let things take their course now...
The waitin' is drivin' me crazy!
If only the time would pass quicker.

CHAPTER 3
January 1968

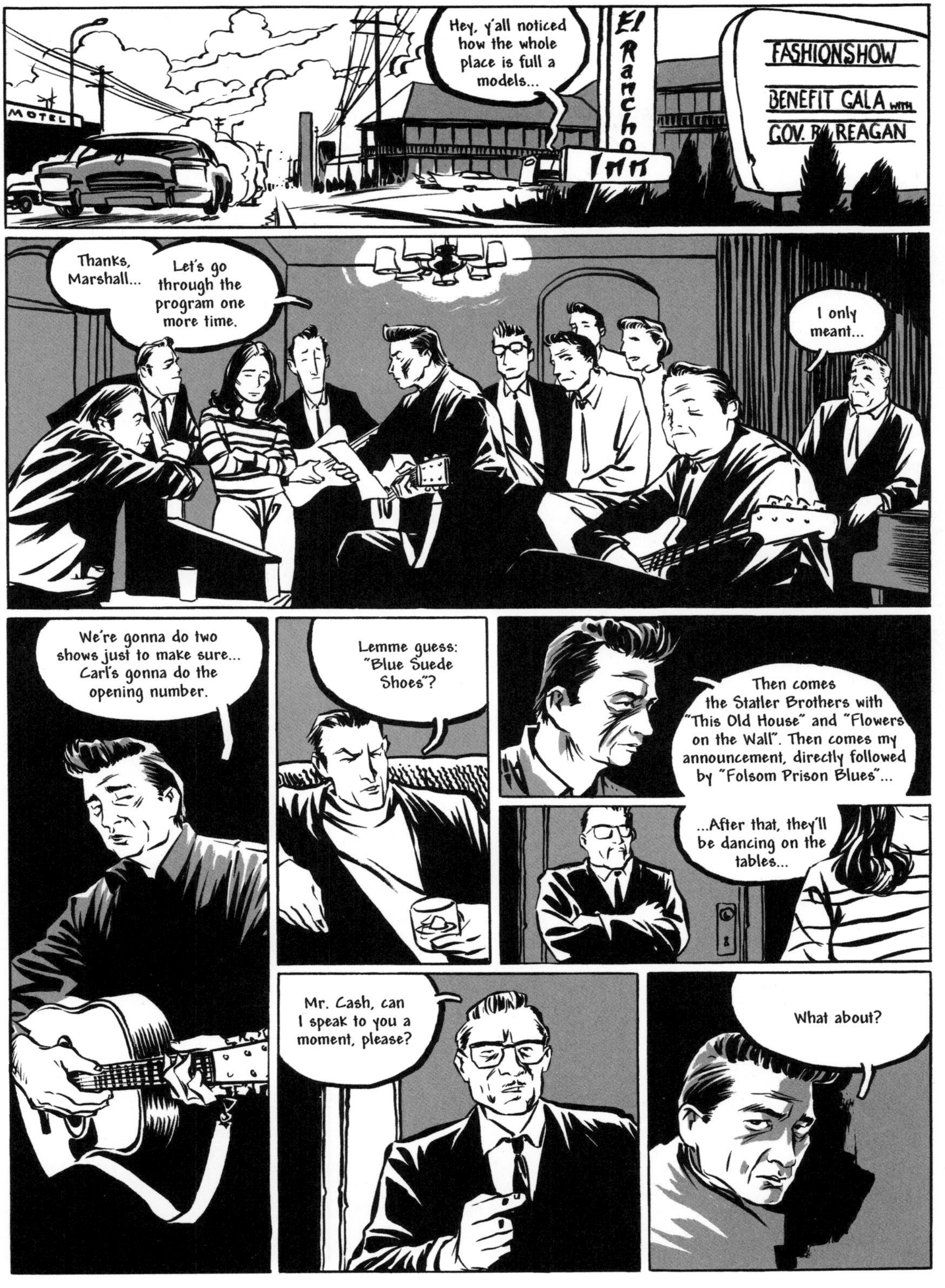

MOTEL
Hey, y'all noticed how the whole place is full a models...
El Rancho Inn
FASHIONSHOW
BENEFIT GALA WITH
GOV. R. REAGAN
Thanks, Marshall...
Let's go through the program one more time.
I only meant...
We're gonna do two shows just to make sure... Carl's gonna do the opening number.
Lemme guess: "Blue Suede Shoes"?
Then comes the Statler Brothers with "This Old House" and "Flowers on the Wall". Then comes my announcement, directly followed by "Folsom Prison Blues"...
...After that, they'll be dancing on the tables...
Mr. Cash, can I speak to you a moment, please?
What about?

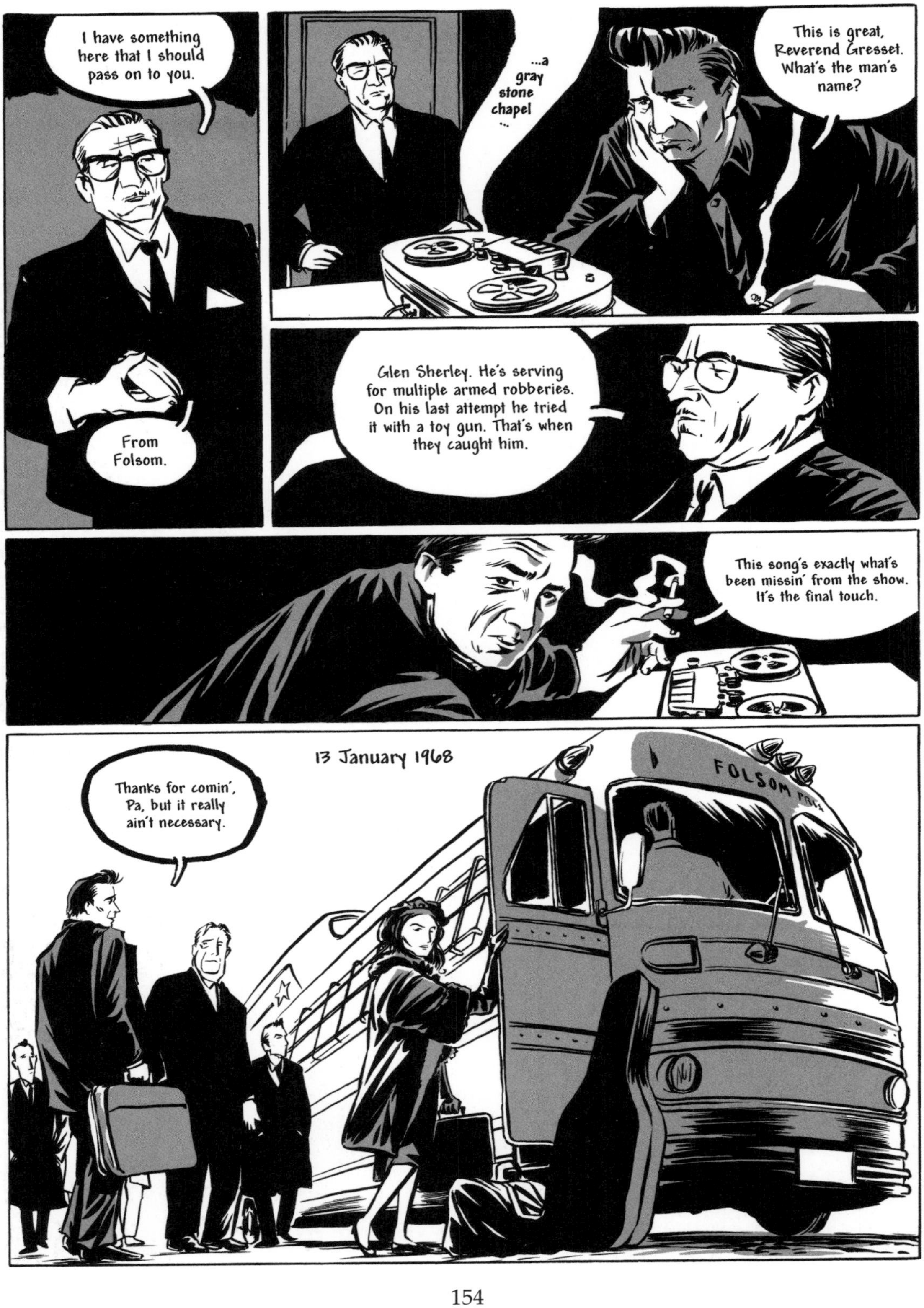
I have something here that I should pass on to you.
From Folsom.
...a gray stone chapel ...
This is great, Reverend Gresset. What's the man's name?
Glen Sherley. He's serving for multiple armed robberies. On his last attempt he tried it with a toy gun. That's when they caught him.
This song's exactly what's been missin' from the show. It's the final touch.
13 January 1968
Thanks for comin', Pa, but it really ain't necessary.
FOLSOM

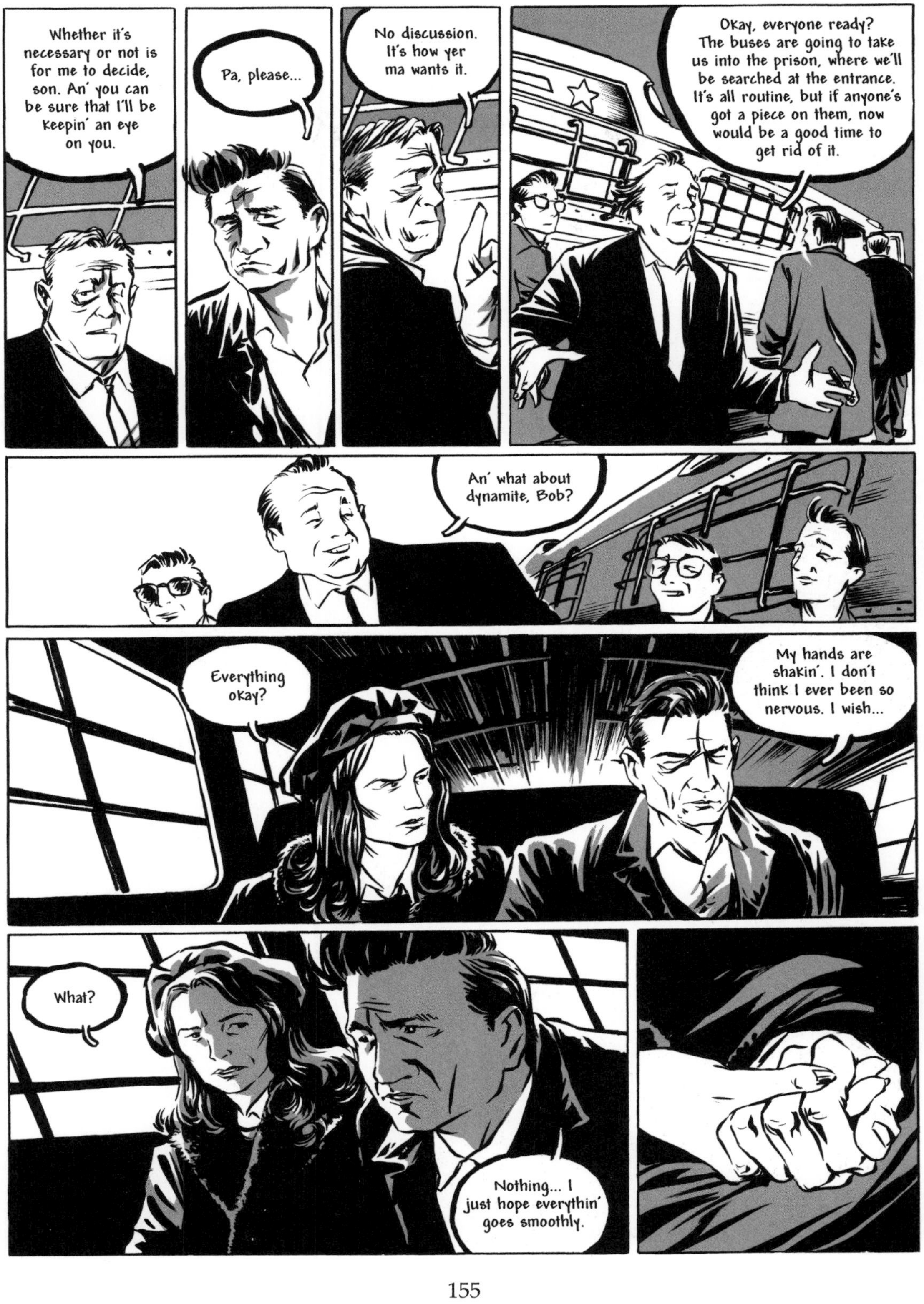
Whether it's necessary or not is for me to decide, son. An' you can be sure that I'll be keepin' an eye on you.
Pa, please...
No discussion. It's how yer ma wants it.
Okay, everyone ready? The buses are going to take us into the prison, where we'll be searched at the entrance. It's all routine, but if anyone's got a piece on them, now would be a good time to get rid of it.
An' what about dynamite, Bob?
Everything okay?
My hands are shakin'. I don't think I ever been so nervous. I wish...
What?
Nothing... I just hope everythin' goes smoothly.

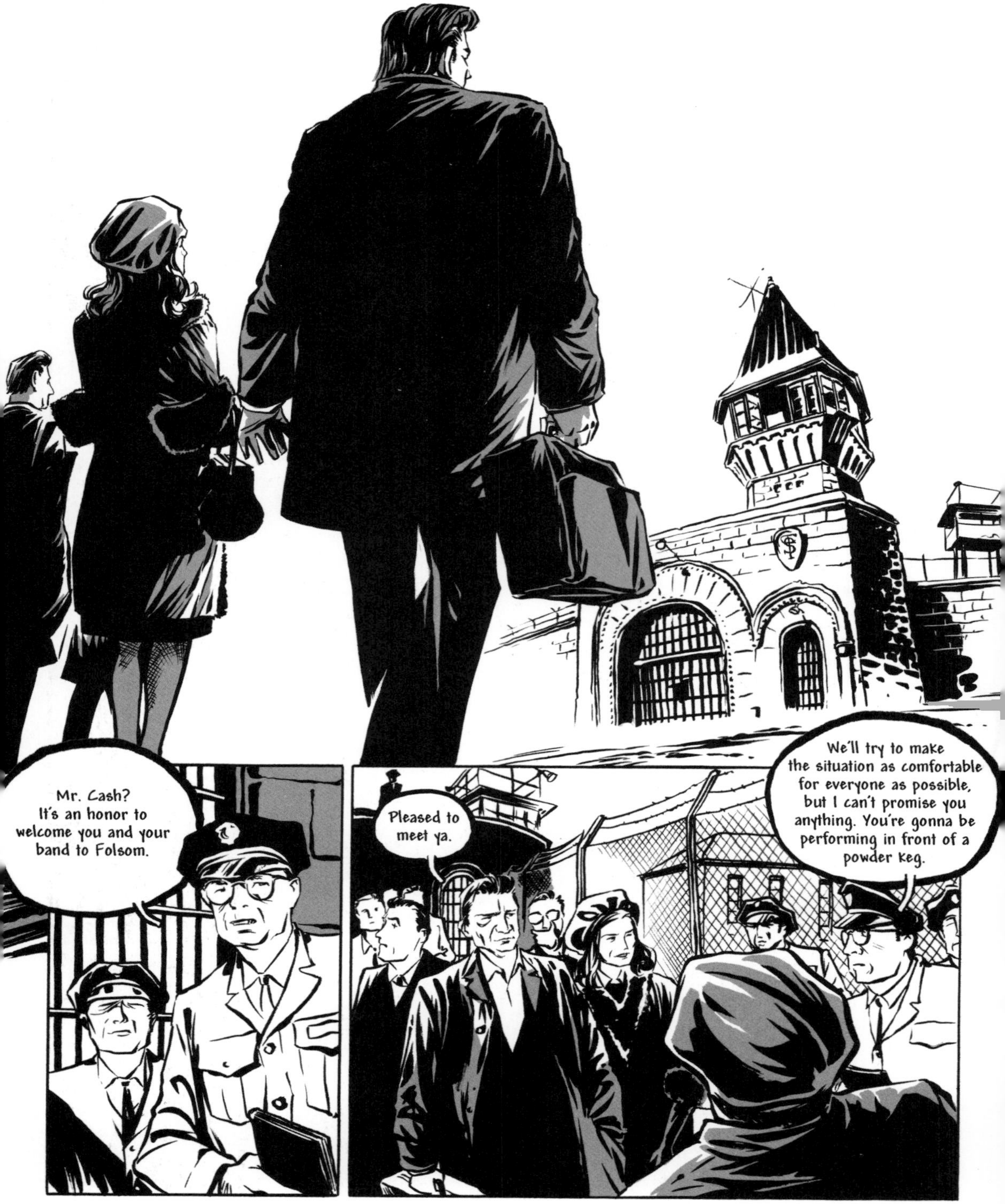
Mr. Cash? It's an honor to welcome you and your band to Folsom.
Pleased to meet ya.
We'll try to make the situation as comfortable for everyone as possible, but I can't promise you anything. You're gonna be performing in front of a powder keg.

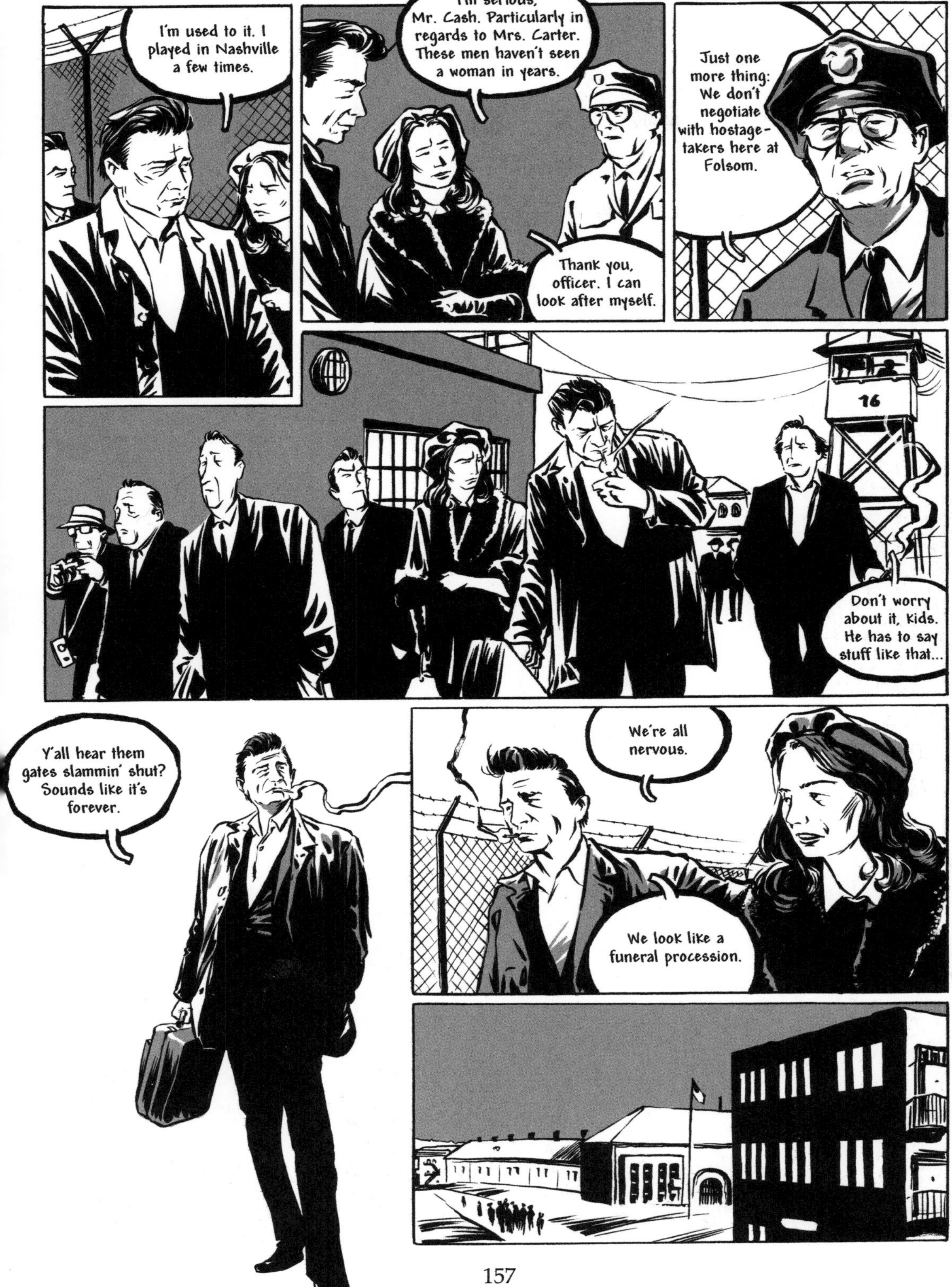
I'm used to it. I played in Nashville a few times.
I'm serious, Mr. Cash. Particularly in regards to Mrs. Carter. These men haven't seen a woman in years.
Thank you, officer. I can look after myself.
Just one more thing: We don't negotiate with hostage-takers here at Folsom.
16
Don't worry about it, kids. He has to say stuff like that...
Y'all hear them gates slammin' shut? Sounds like it's forever.
We're all nervous.
We look like a funeral procession.

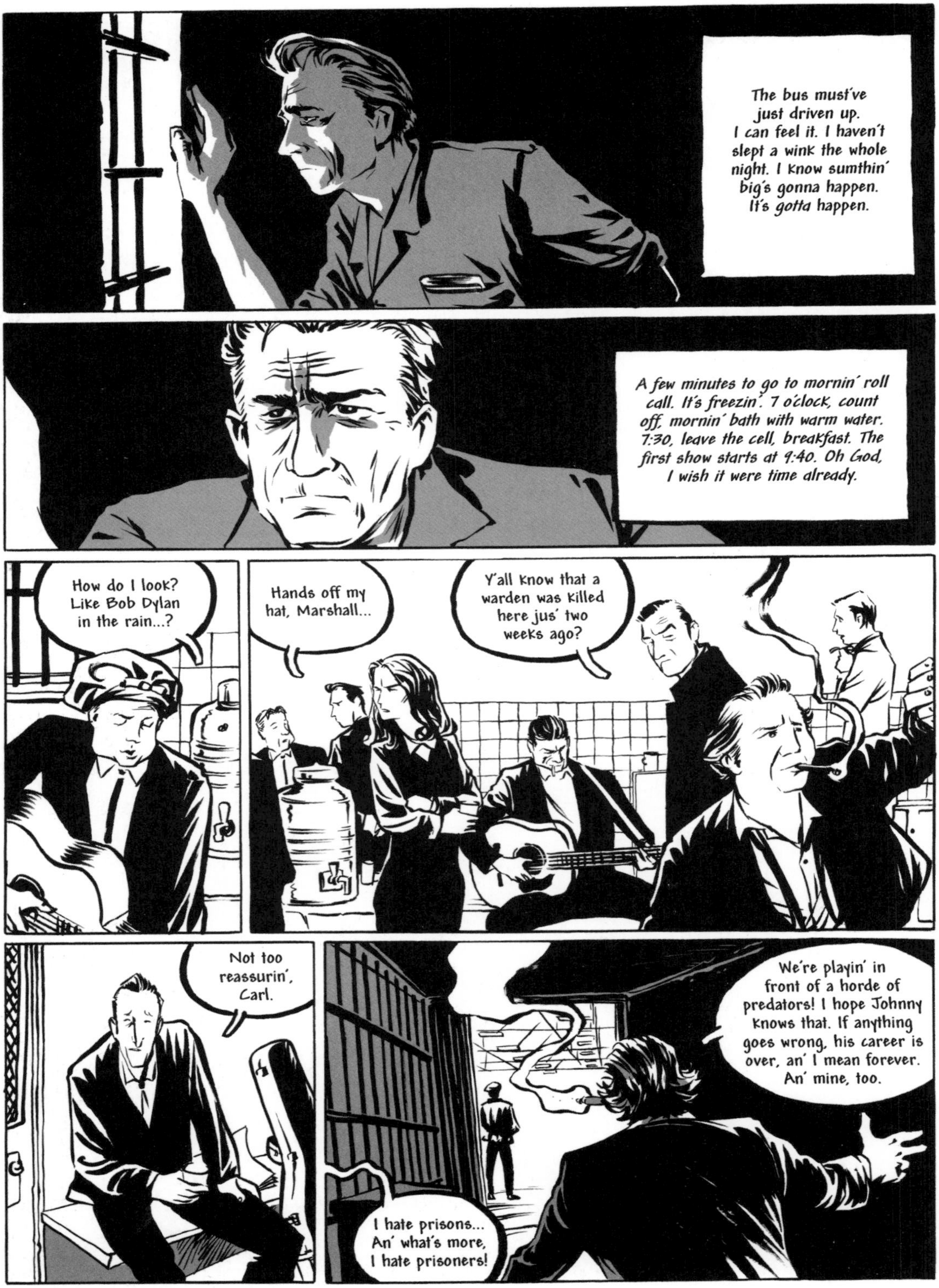
The bus must've just driven up. I can feel it. I haven't slept a wink the whole night. I know sumthin' big's gonna happen. It's *gotta* happen.
A few minutes to go to mornin' roll call. It's freezin'. 7 o'clock, count off, mornin' bath with warm water. 7:30, leave the cell, breakfast. The first show starts at 9:40. Oh God, I wish it were time already.
How do I look? Like Bob Dylan in the rain...?
Hands off my hat, Marshall...
Y'all know that a warden was killed here jus' two weeks ago?
Not too reassurin', Carl.
We're playin' in front of a horde of predators! I hope Johnny knows that. If anything goes wrong, his career is over, an' I mean forever. An' mine, too.
I hate prisons... An' what's more, I hate prisoners!

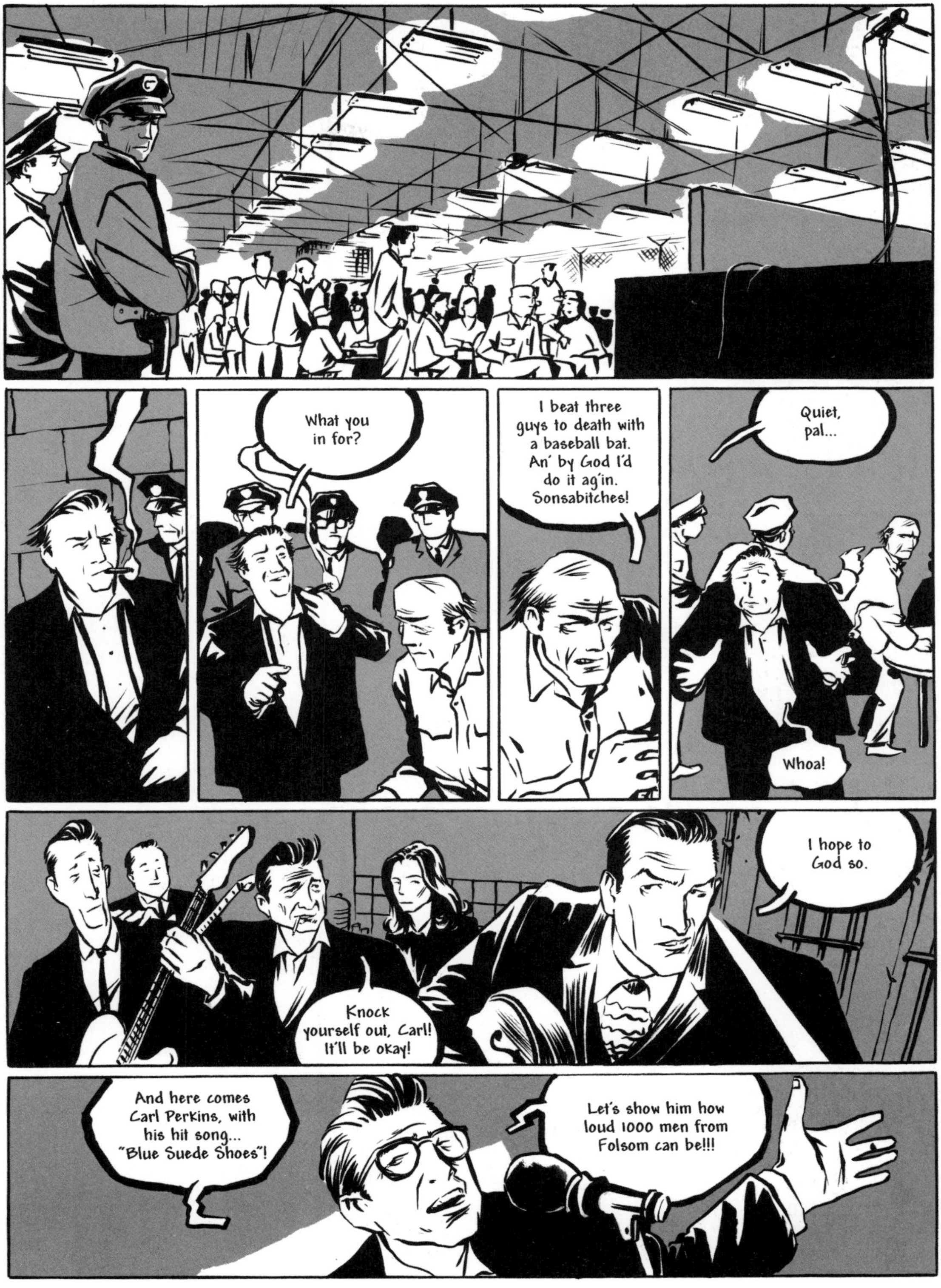

What you in for?
I beat three guys to death with a baseball bat. An' by God I'd do it ag'in. Sonsabitches!
Quiet, pal...
Whoa!
I hope to God so.
Knock yourself out, Carl! It'll be okay!
And here comes Carl Perkins, with his hit song... "Blue Suede Shoes"!
Let's show him how loud 1000 men from Folsom can be!!!

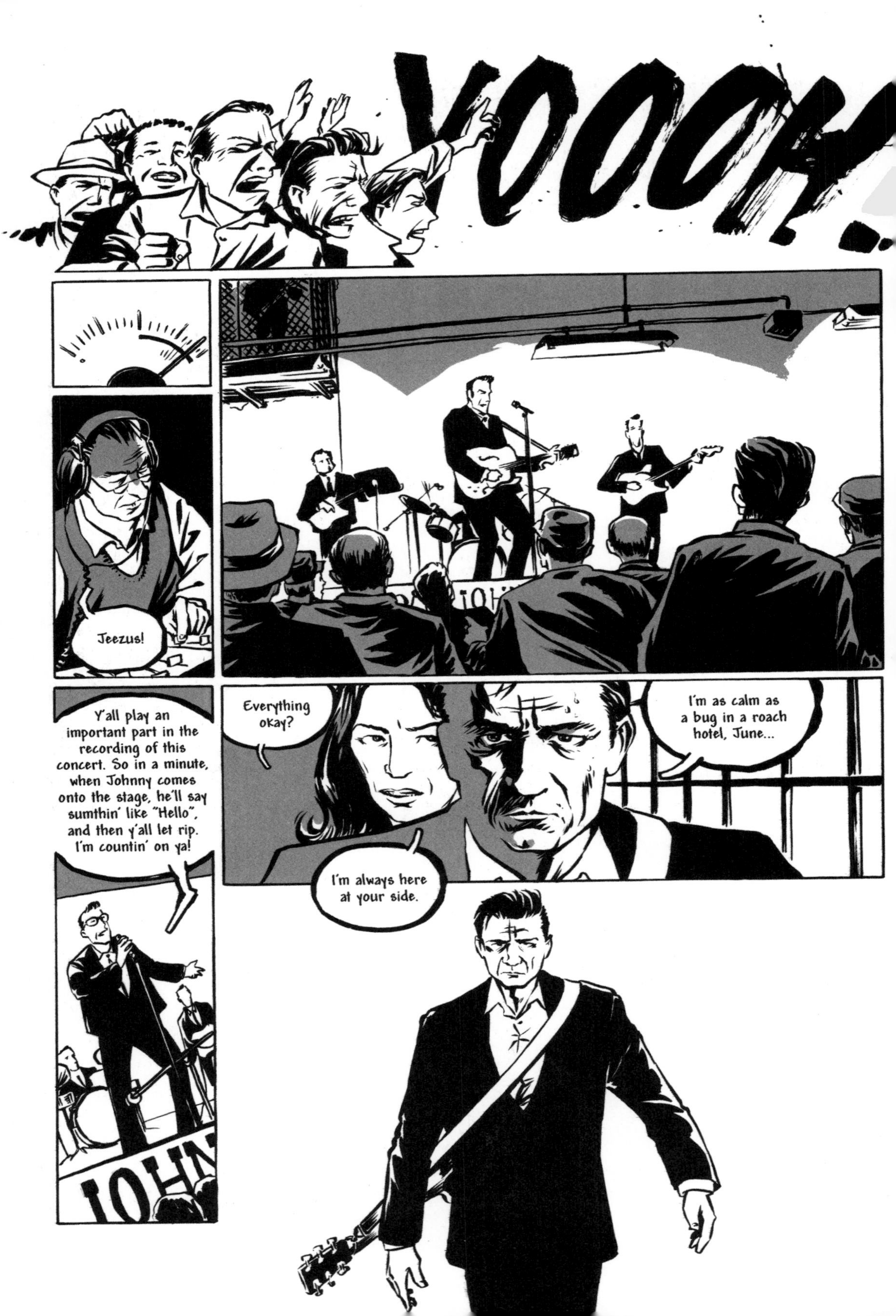
YOOOH!
Jeezus!
Y'all play an important part in the recording of this concert. So in a minute, when Johnny comes onto the stage, he'll say sumthin' like "Hello", and then y'all let rip. I'm countin' on ya!
JOHN
Everything okay?
I'm as calm as a bug in a roach hotel, June...
I'm always here at your side.

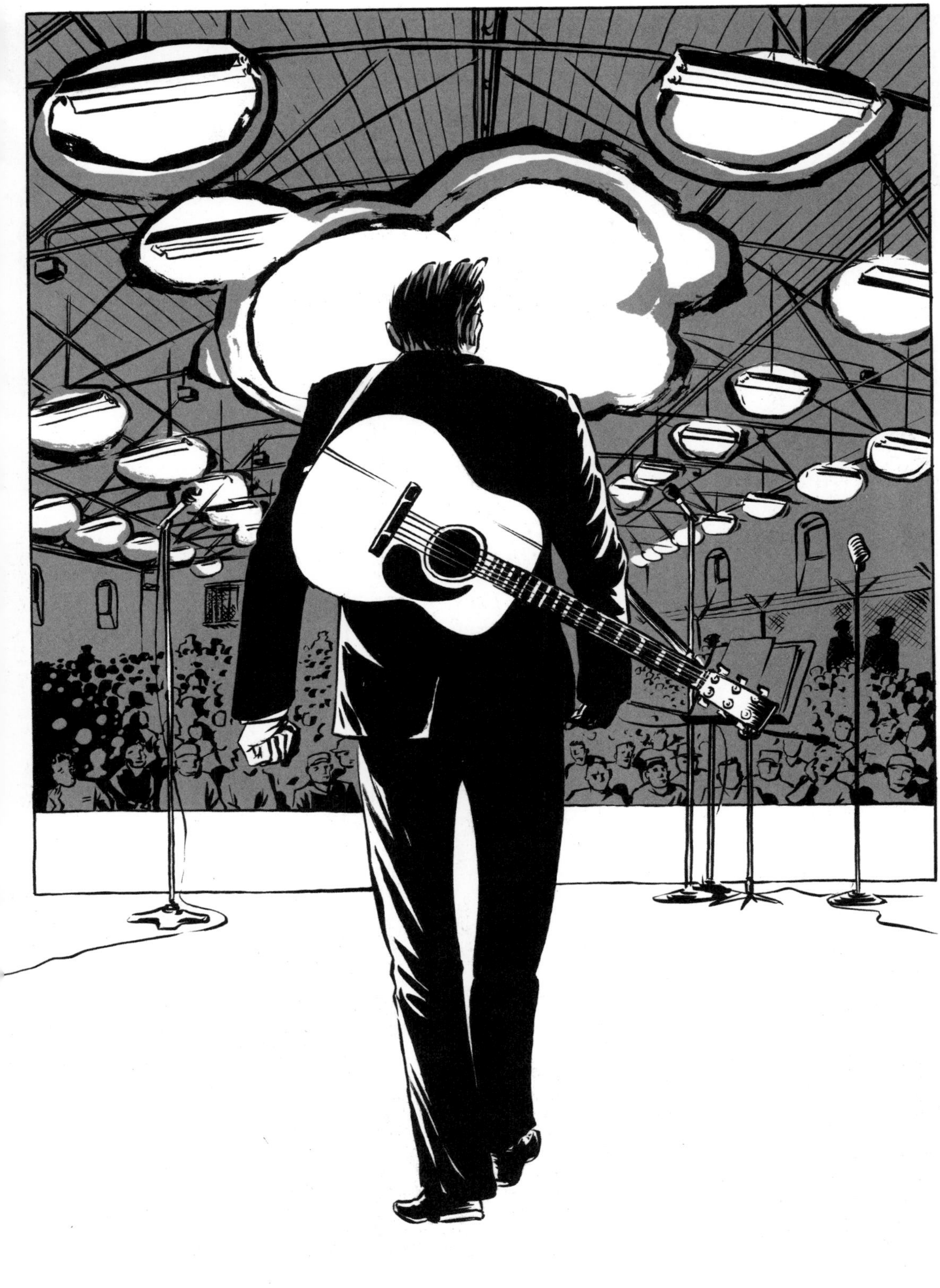

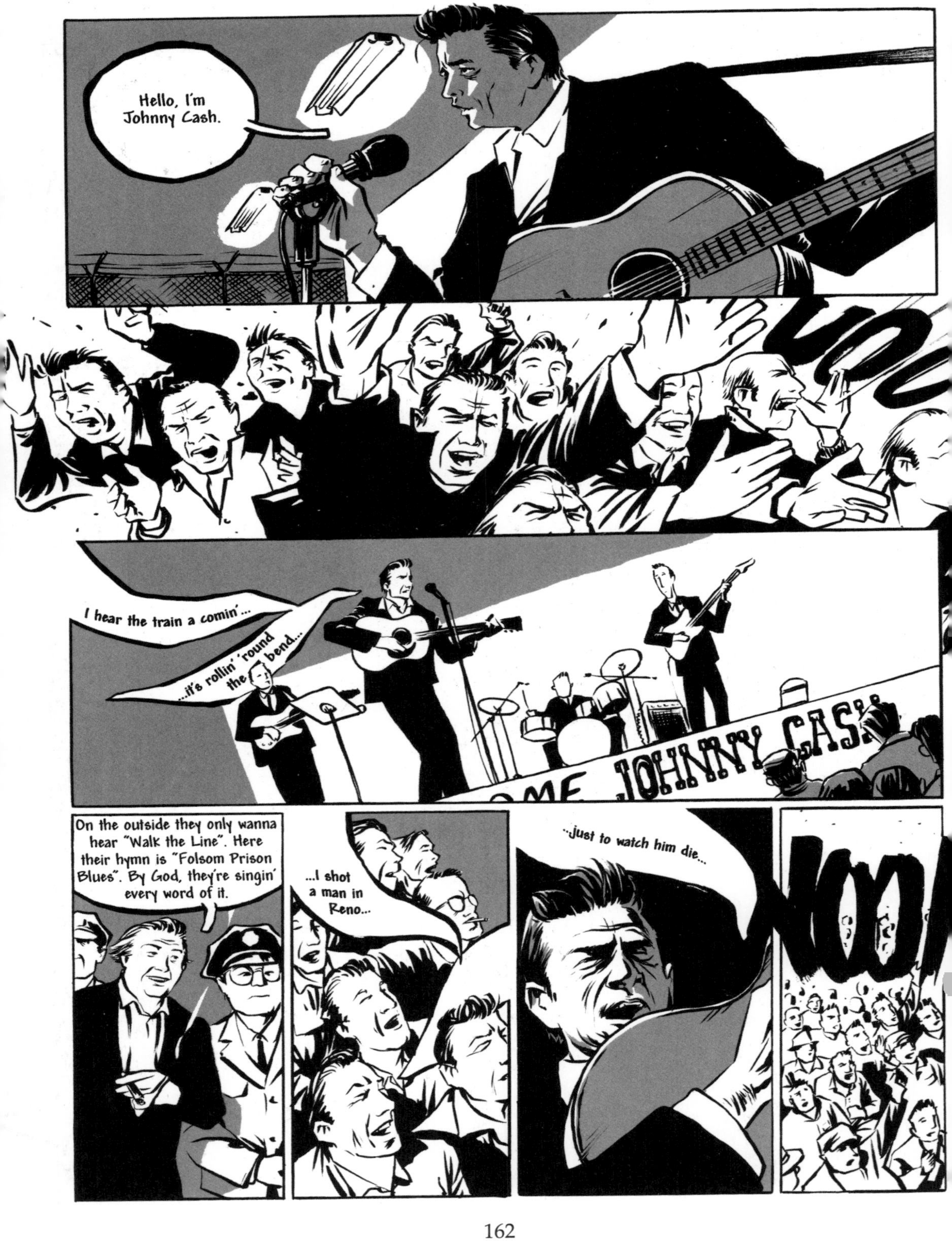
Hello, I'm Johnny Cash.
I hear the train a comin'...
...it's rollin' 'round the bend...
JOHNNY CASH
On the outside they only wanna hear "Walk the Line". Here their hymn is "Folsom Prison Blues". By God, they're singin' every word of it.
...I shot a man in Reno...
...just to watch him die...

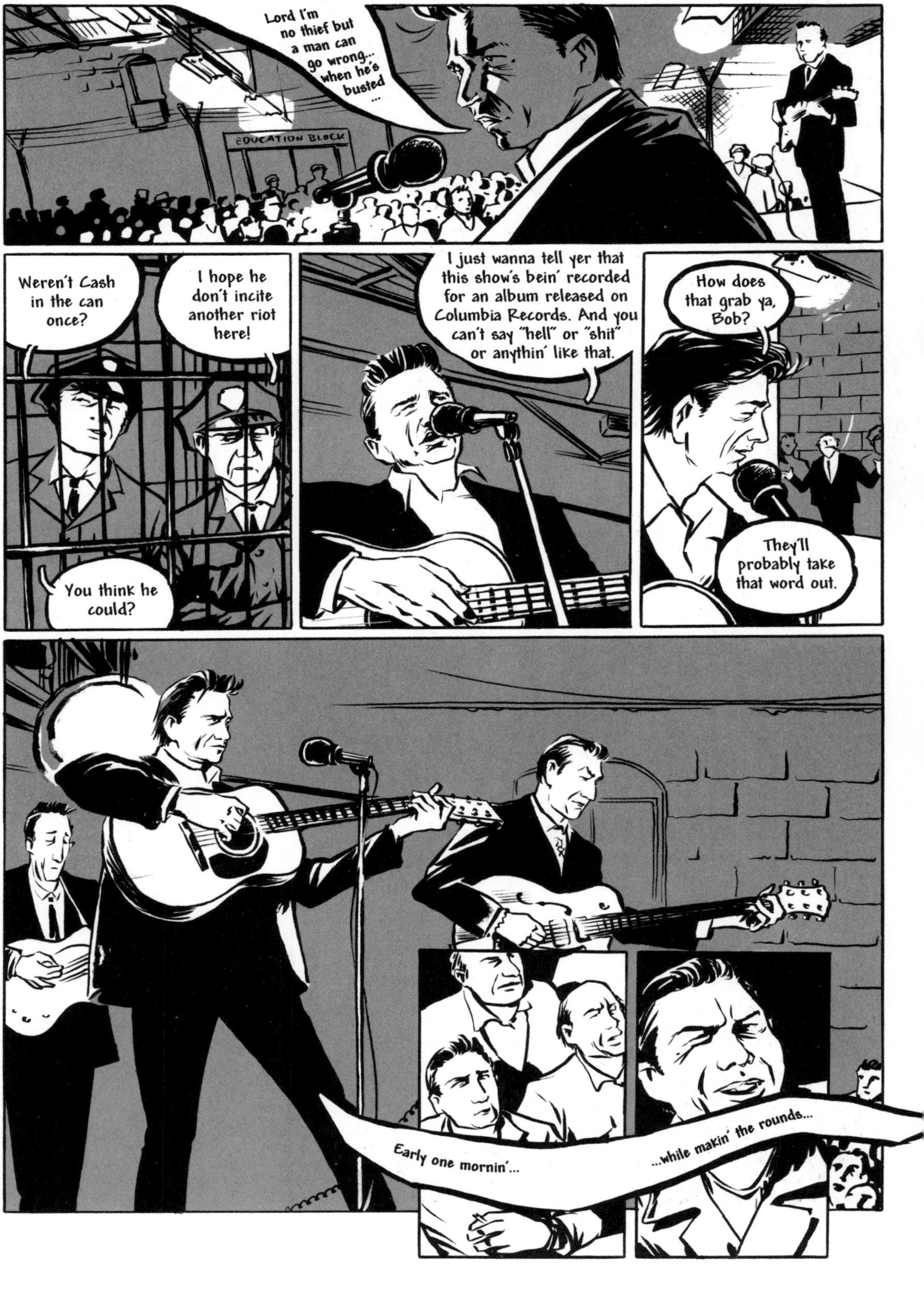
Lord I'm no thief but a man can go wrong... when he's busted ...
EDUCATION BLOCK
Weren't Cash in the can once?
I hope he don't incite another riot here!
You think he could?
I just wanna tell yer that this show's bein' recorded for an album released on Columbia Records. And you can't say "hell" or "shit" or anythin' like that.
How does that grab ya, Bob?
They'll probably take that word out.
Early one mornin'...
...while makin' the rounds...

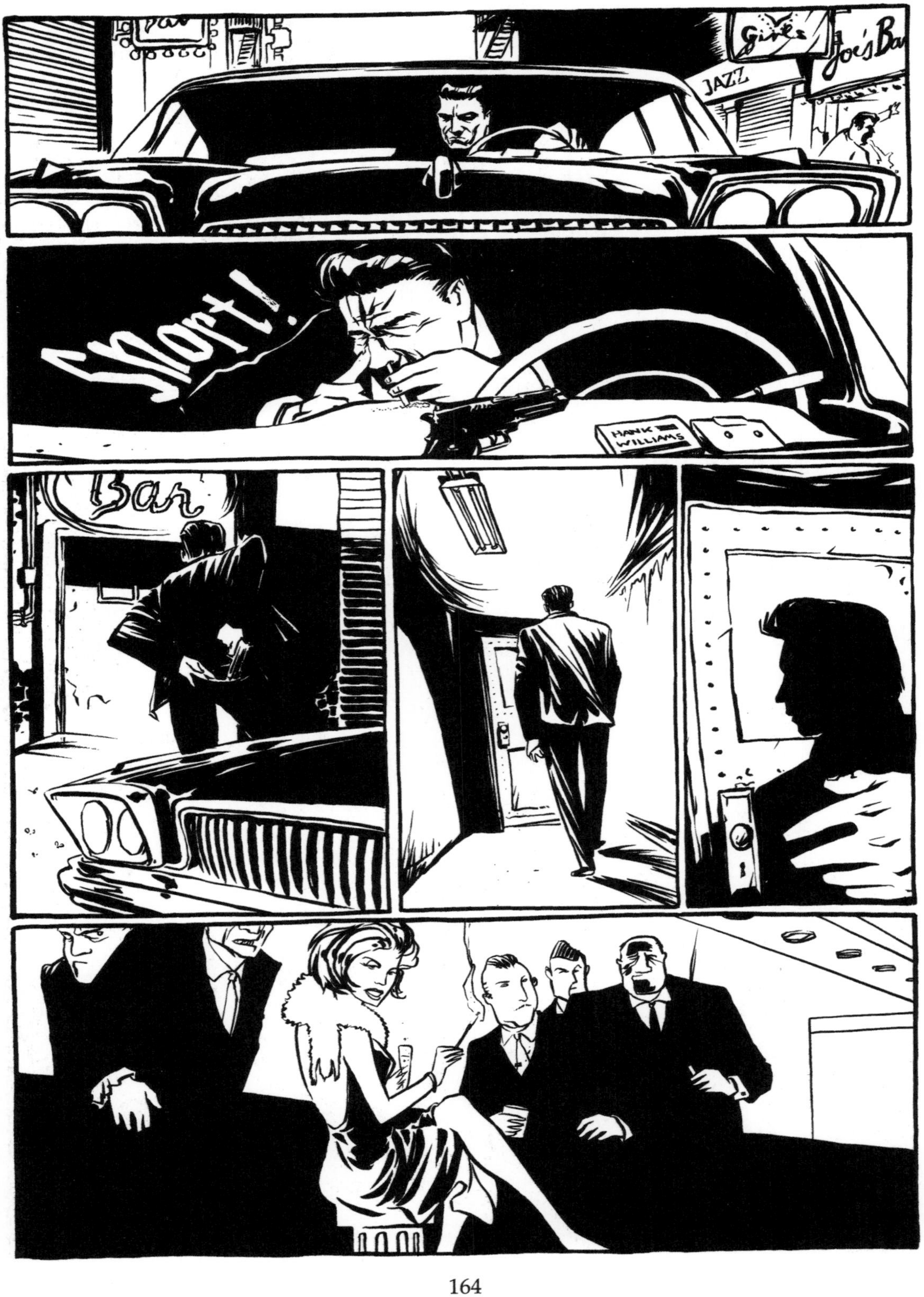
JAZZ
Snort!
HANK WILLIAMS
Bar

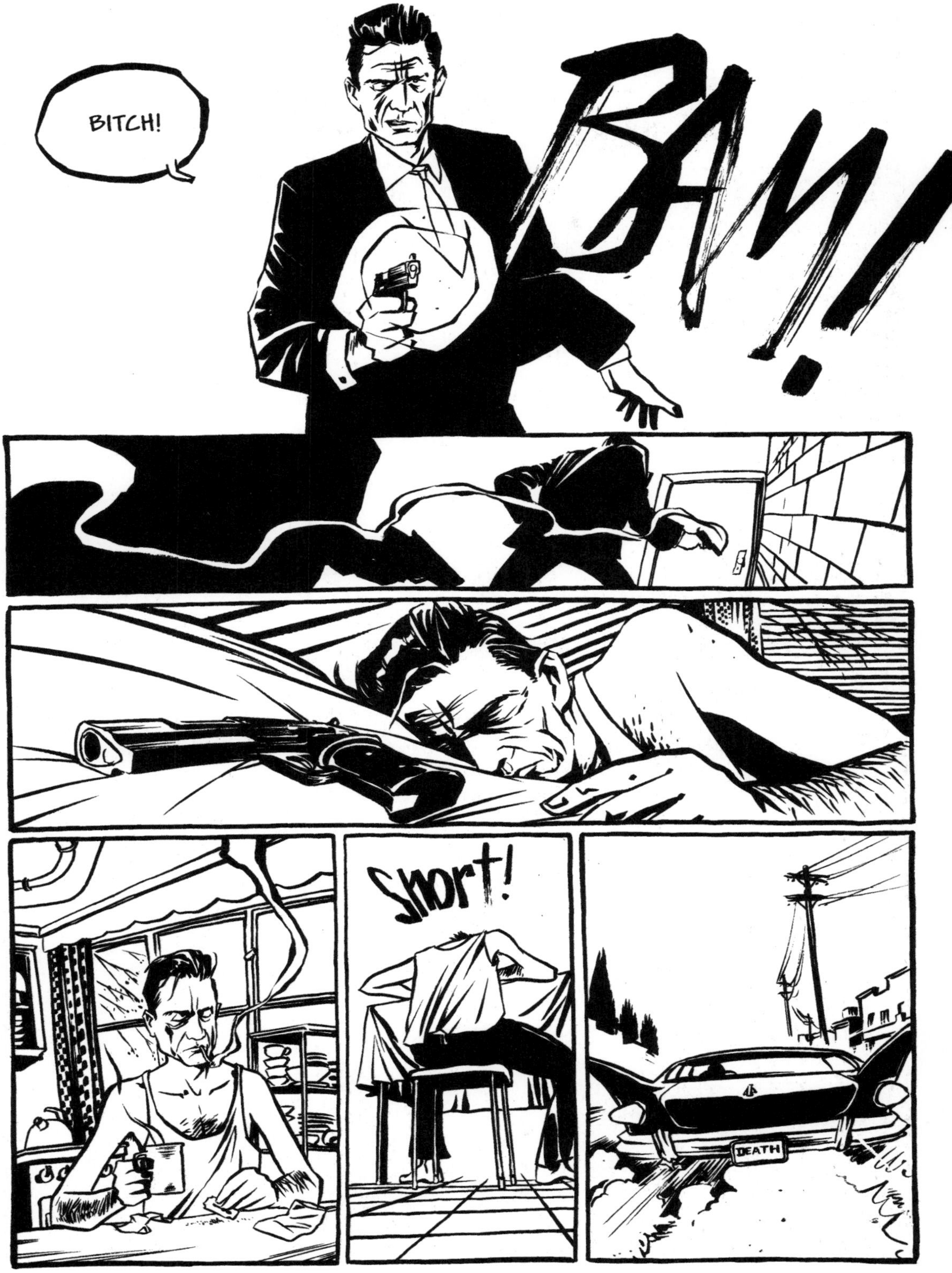
BITCH!
BAM!!
Snort!
DEATH

So ya reckon yer name's Jack Brown, huh? I'll tell ya who ya are. You're Willy Lee...

...the rotten bastard that shot his wife.

Okay, okay, I'm Willy Lee, an' yeah, I killed her.

I thought I was her only guy, but she had five others.

Cough, cough.

So, you bastard, time to go to court.

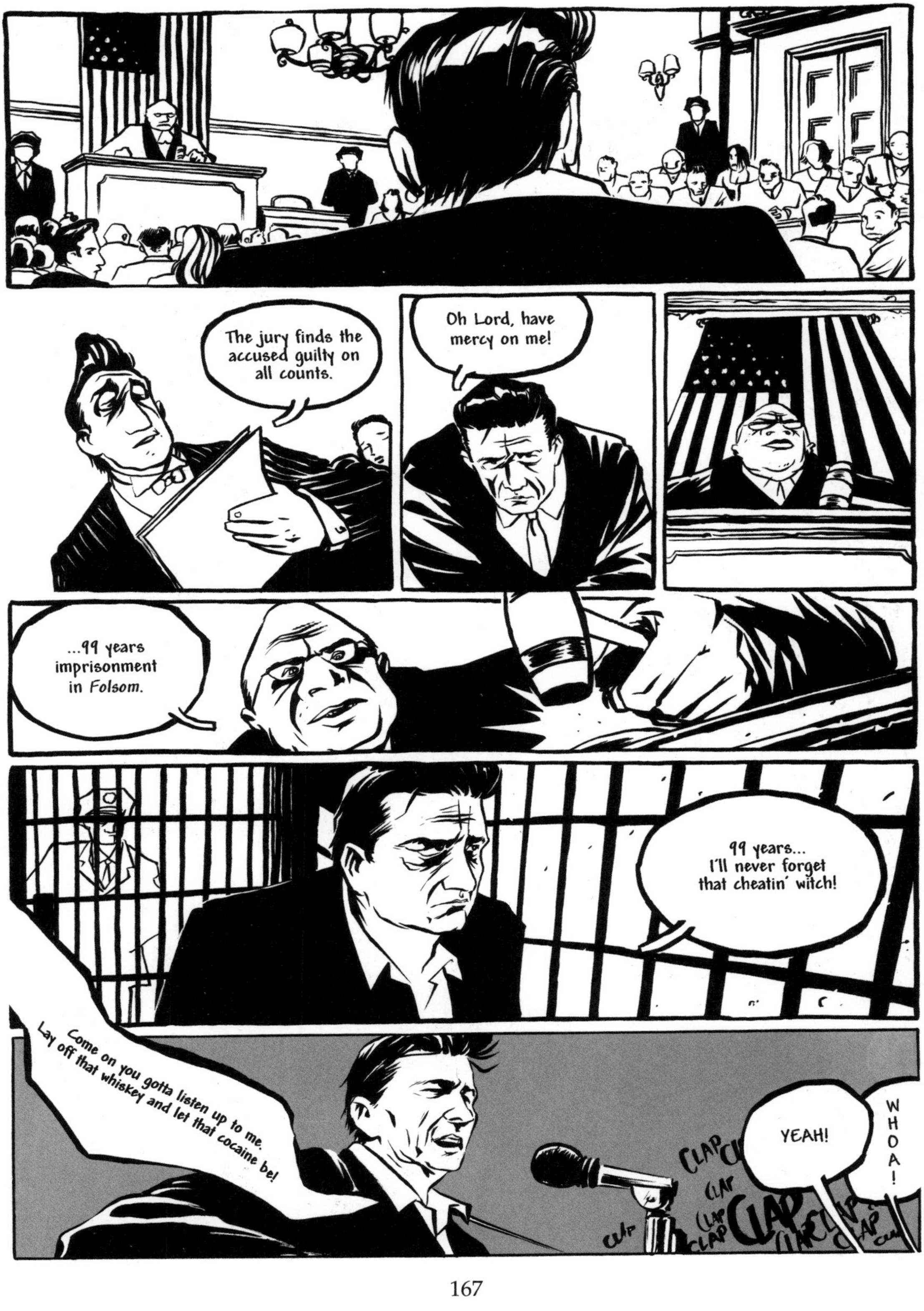
The jury finds the accused guilty on all counts.
Oh Lord, have mercy on me!
...99 years imprisonment in Folsom.
99 years... I'll never forget that cheatin' witch!
Come on you gotta listen up to me. Lay off that whiskey and let that cocaine be!
YEAH!
WHOA!
CLAP CLAP CLAP CLAP CLAP CLAP

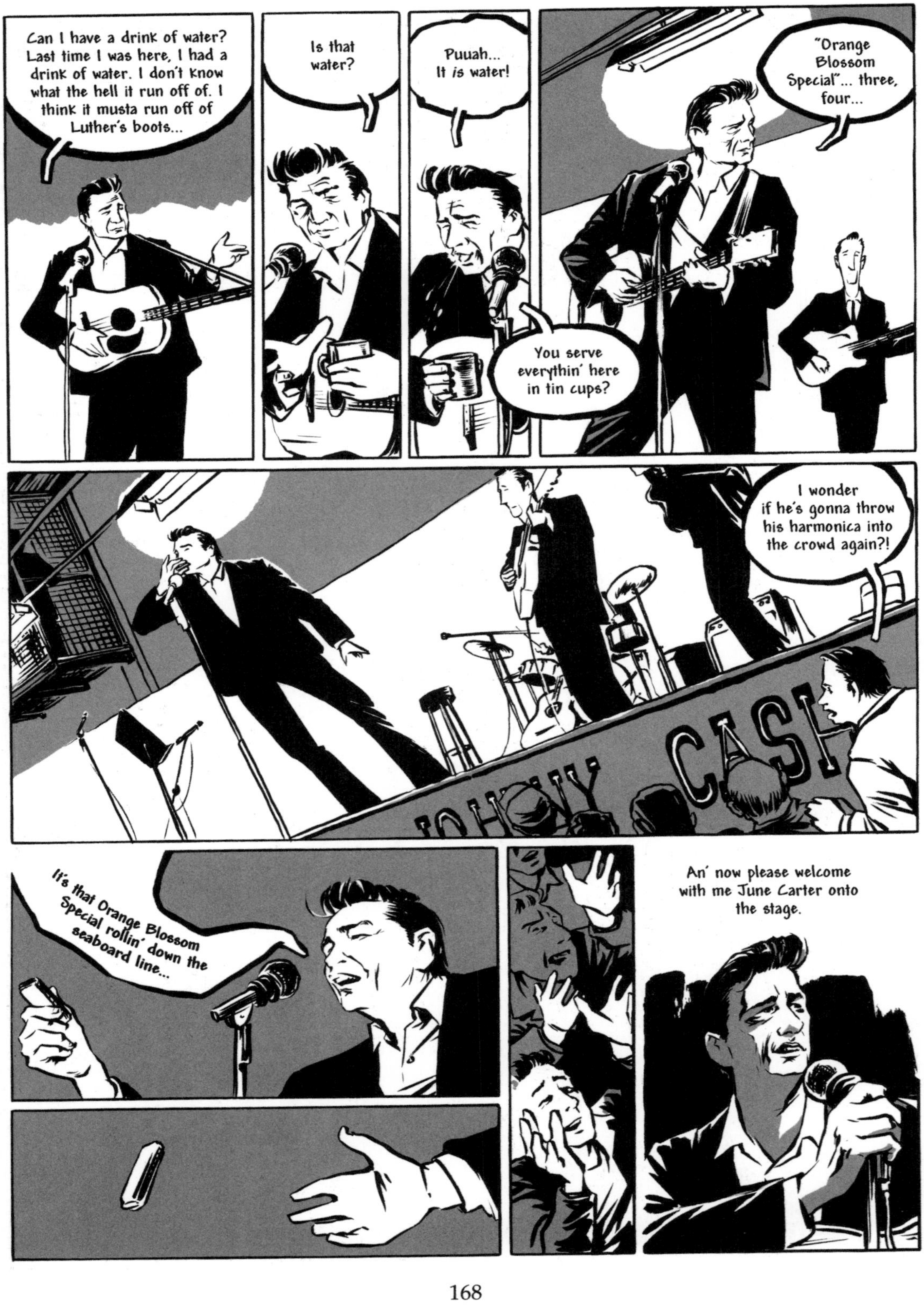
Can I have a drink of water? Last time I was here, I had a drink of water. I don't know what the hell it run off of. I think it musta run off of Luther's boots...
Is that water?
Puuah... It is water!
You serve everythin' here in tin cups?
"Orange Blossom Special"... three, four...
I wonder if he's gonna throw his harmonica into the crowd again?!
JOHNNY CASH
It's that Orange Blossom Special rollin' down the seaboard line...
An' now please welcome with me June Carter onto the stage.

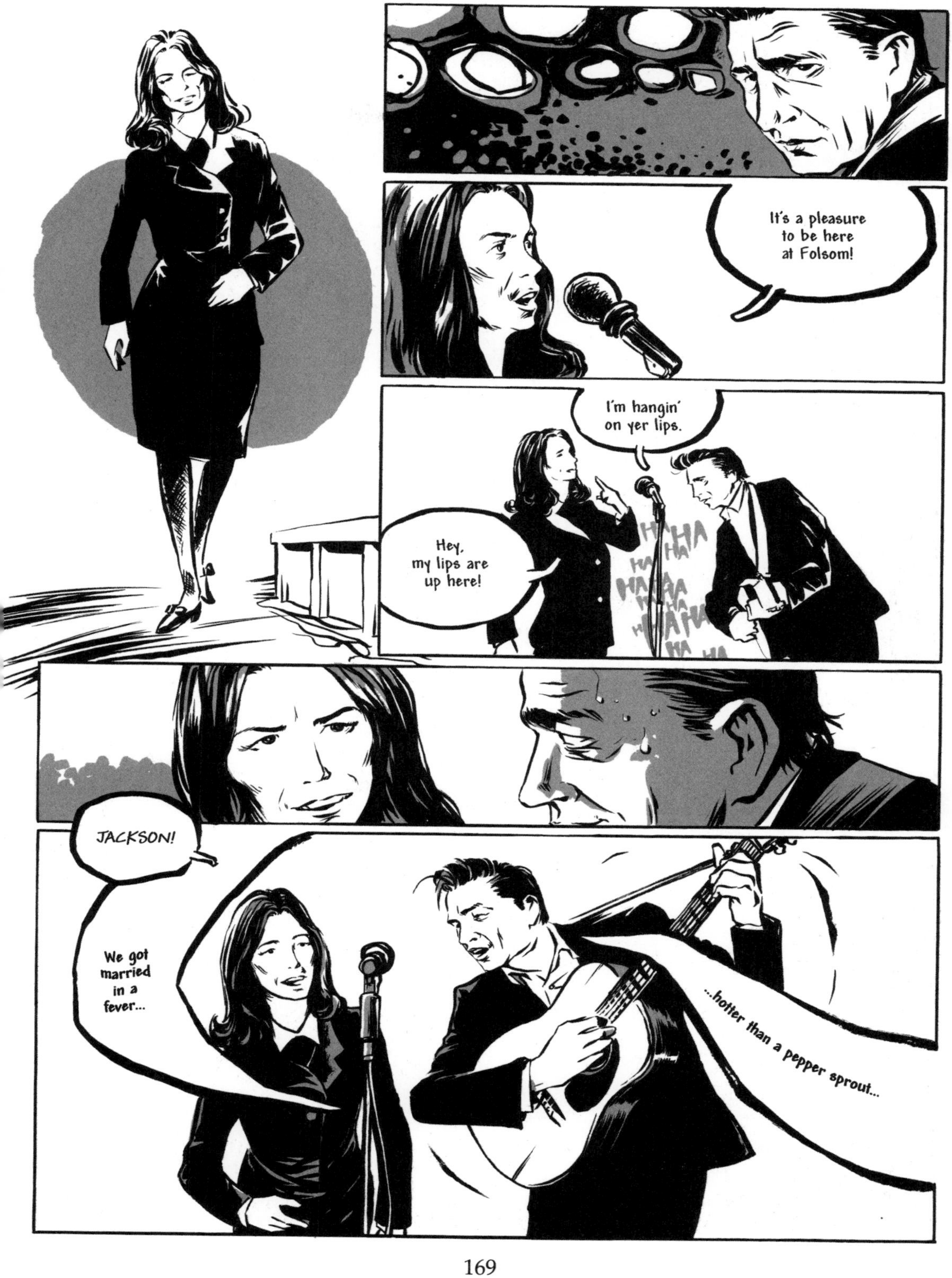

It's a pleasure to be here at Folsom!
I'm hangin' on yer lips.
Hey, my lips are up here!
HA HA HA HA HA HA HA HA HA HA HA
JACKSON!
We got married in a fever...
...hotter than a pepper sprout...

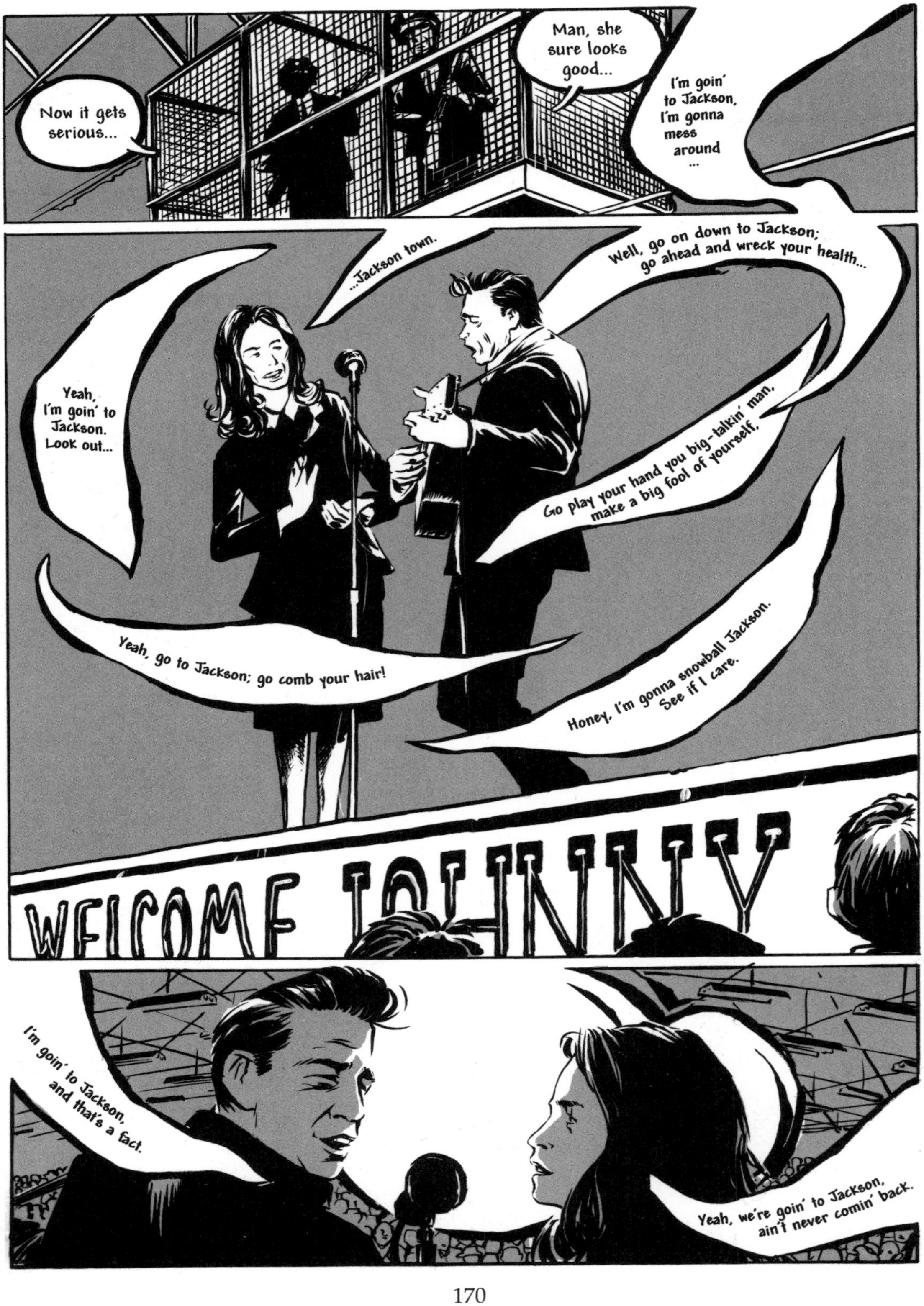
Now it gets serious...
Man, she sure looks good...
I'm goin' to Jackson, I'm gonna mess around ...
...Jackson town.
Well, go on down to Jackson; go ahead and wreck your health...
Yeah, I'm goin' to Jackson. Look out...
Go play your hand you big-talkin' man, make a big fool of yourself.
Yeah, go to Jackson; go comb your hair!
Honey, I'm gonna snowball Jackson. See if I care.
WELCOME JOHNNY
I'm goin' to Jackson, and that's a fact.
Yeah, we're goin' to Jackson, ain't never comin' back.

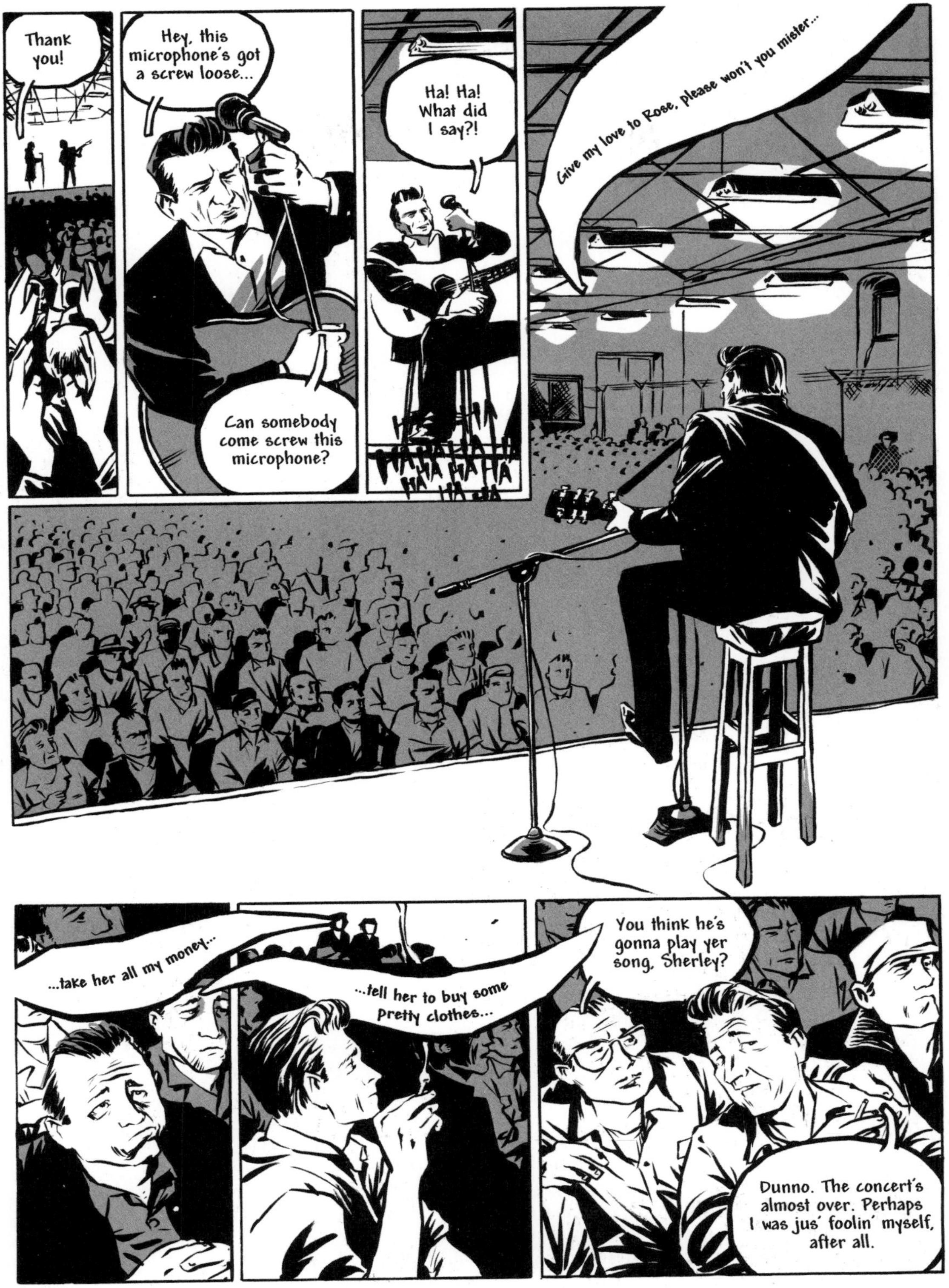
Thank you!
Hey, this microphone's got a screw loose...
Can somebody come screw this microphone?
Ha! Ha! What did I say?!
HA HA HA HA HA HA HA HA HA HA
Give my love to Rose, please won't you mister...
...take her all my money...
...tell her to buy some pretty clothes...
You think he's gonna play yer song, Sherley?
Dunno. The concert's almost over. Perhaps I was jus' foolin' myself, after all.

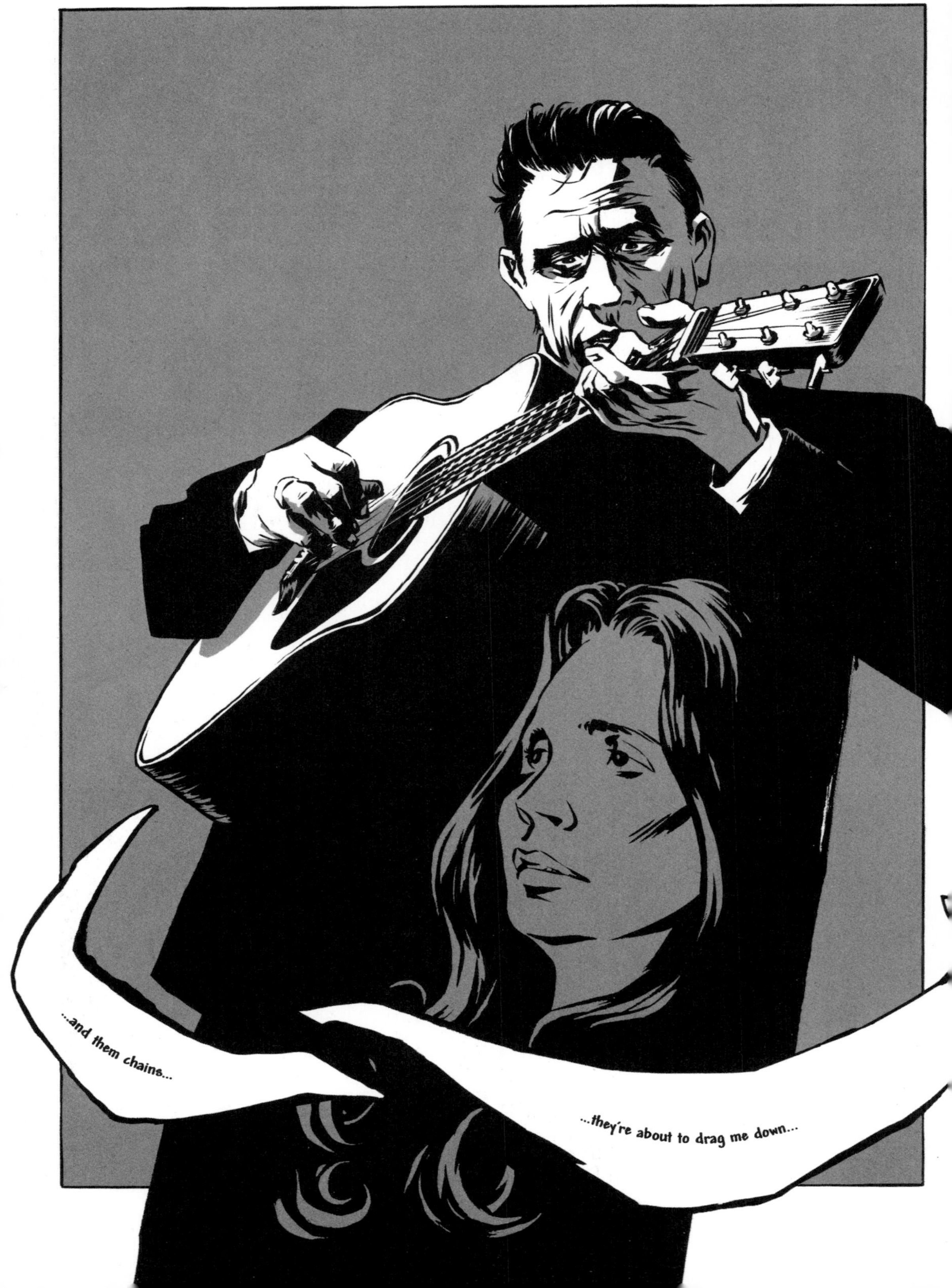
...and them chains...
...they're about to drag me down...

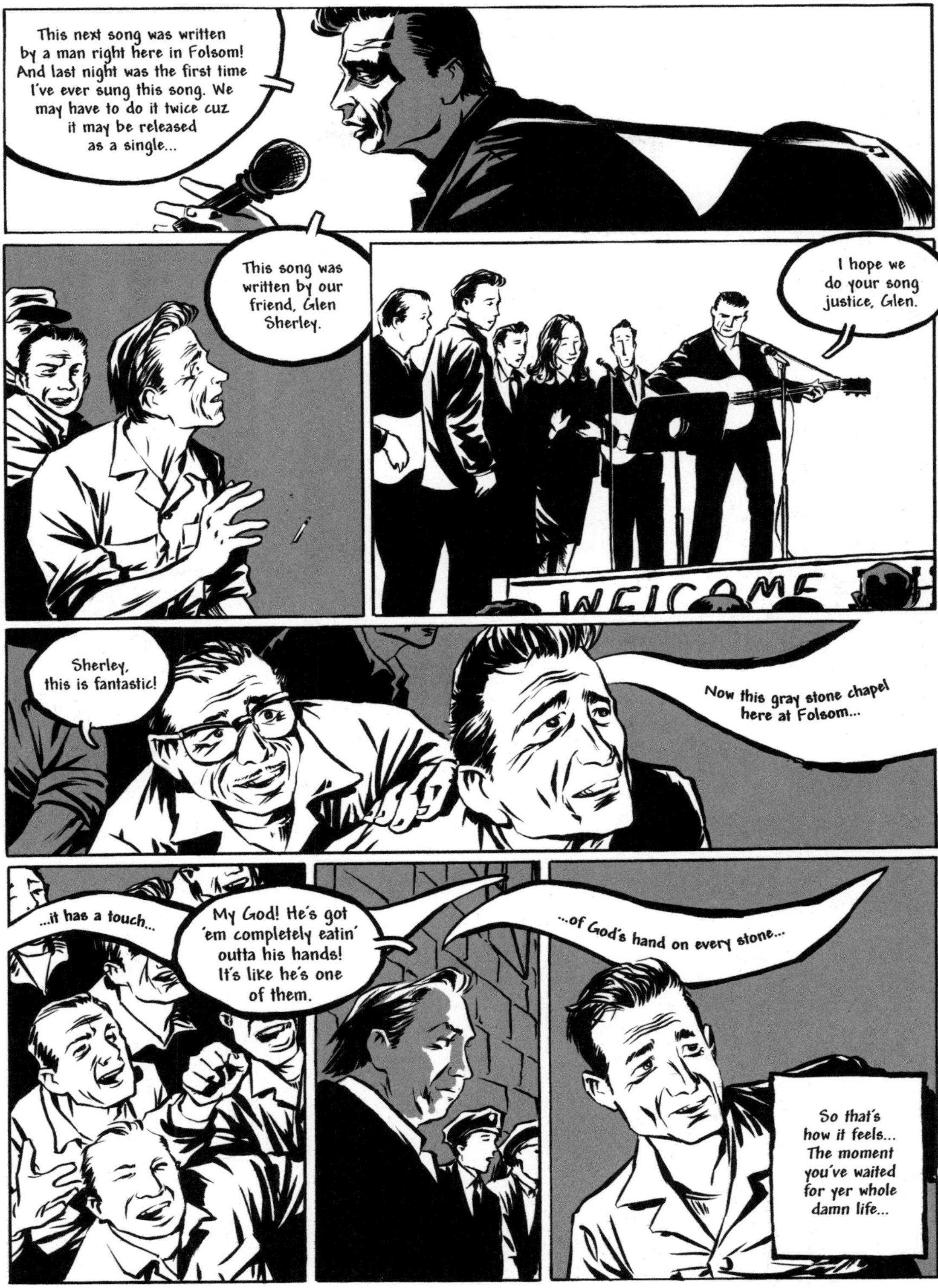

This next song was written by a man right here in Folsom! And last night was the first time I've ever sung this song. We may have to do it twice cuz it may be released as a single...
This song was written by our friend, Glen Sherley.
I hope we do your song justice, Glen.
WELCOME
Sherley, this is fantastic!
Now this gray stone chapel here at Folsom...
...it has a touch...
My God! He's got 'em completely eatin' outta his hands! It's like he's one of them.
...of God's hand on every stone...
So that's how it feels... The moment you've waited for yer whole damn life...

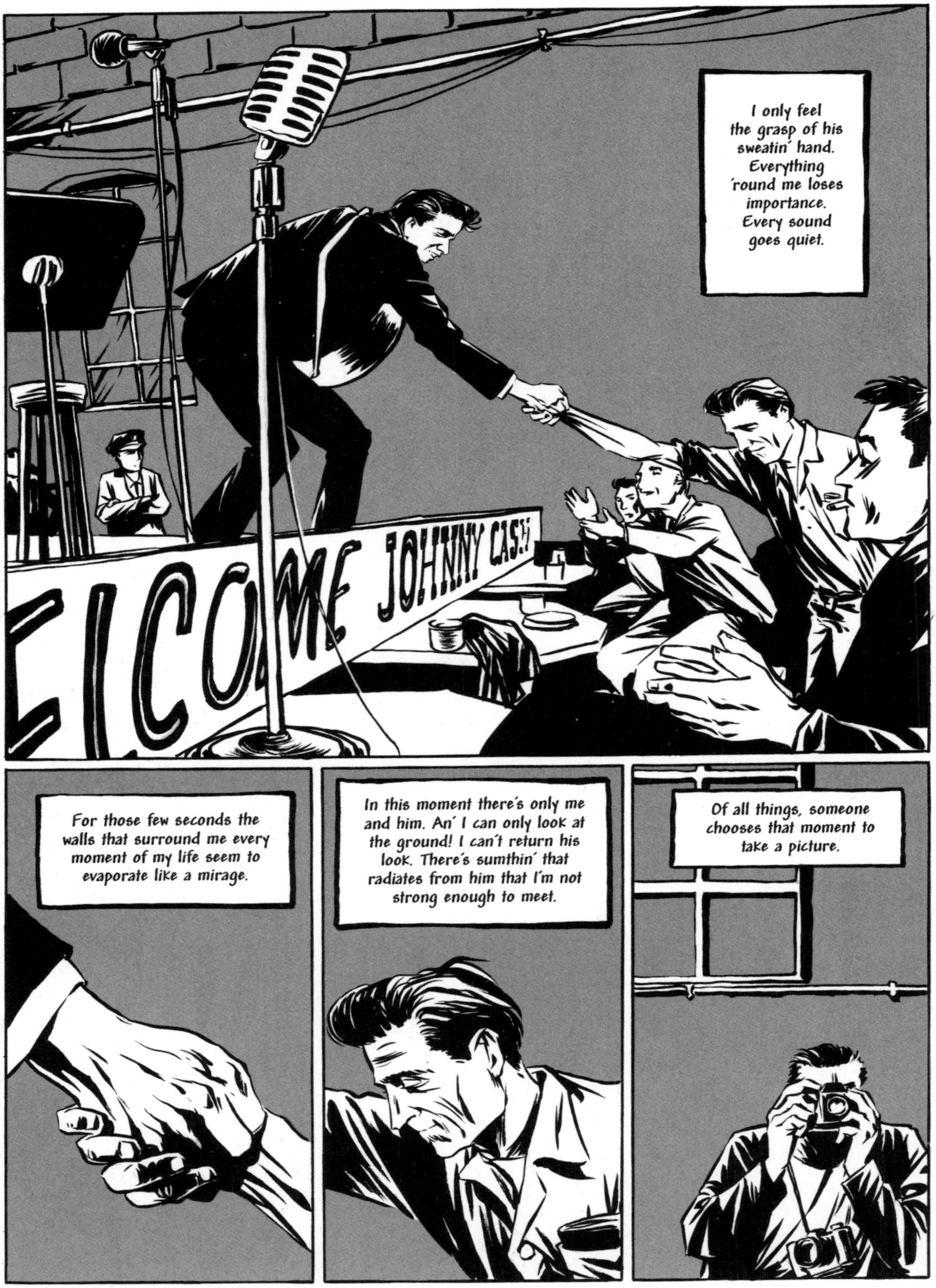
I only feel the grasp of his sweatin´ hand. Everything ´round me loses importance. Every sound goes quiet.
JOHNNY CASH
For those few seconds the walls that surround me every moment of my life seem to evaporate like a mirage.
In this moment there´s only me and him. An´ I can only look at the ground! I can´t return his look. There´s sumthin´ that radiates from him that I´m not strong enough to meet.
Of all things, someone chooses that moment to take a picture.

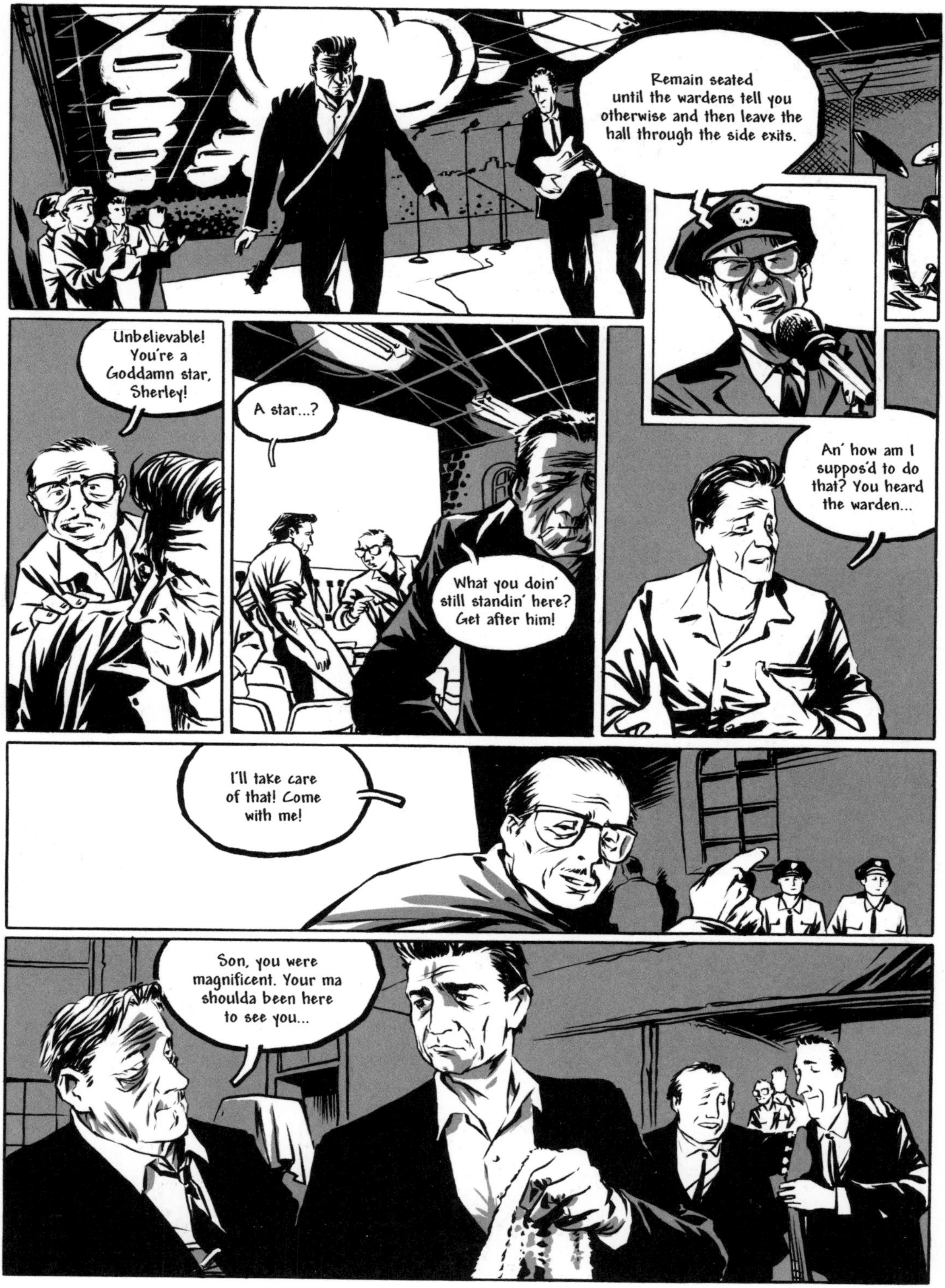
Remain seated until the wardens tell you otherwise and then leave the hall through the side exits.
Unbelievable! You're a Goddamn star, Sherley!
A star...?
What you doin' still standin' here? Get after him!
An' how am I suppos'd to do that? You heard the warden...
I'll take care of that! Come with me!
Son, you were magnificent. Your ma shoulda been here to see you...

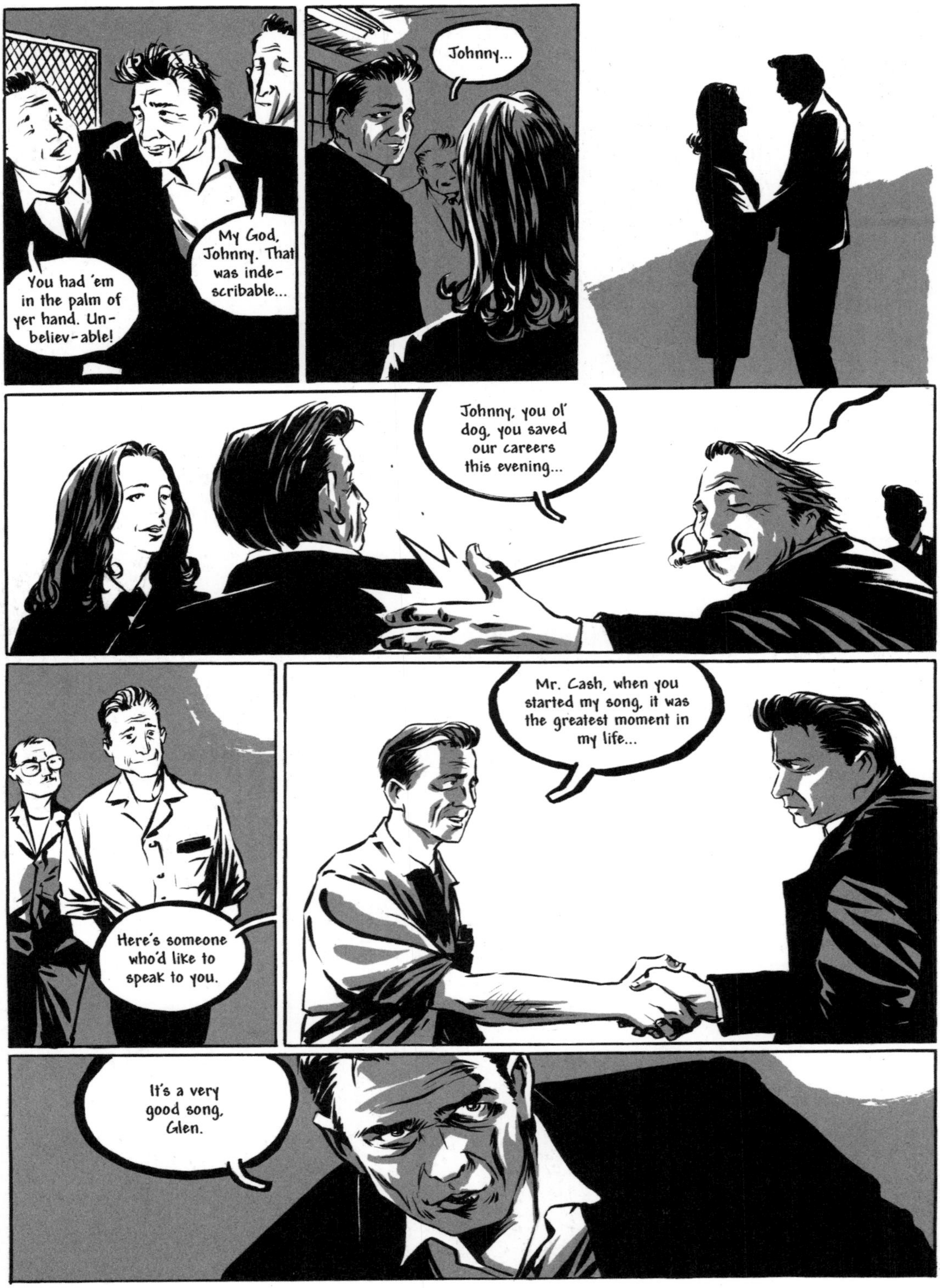
My God, Johnny. That was inde-scribable...
You had 'em in the palm of yer hand. Un-believ-able!
Johnny...
Johnny, you ol' dog, you saved our careers this evening...
Here's someone who'd like to speak to you.
Mr. Cash, when you started my song, it was the greatest moment in my life...
It's a very good song, Glen.

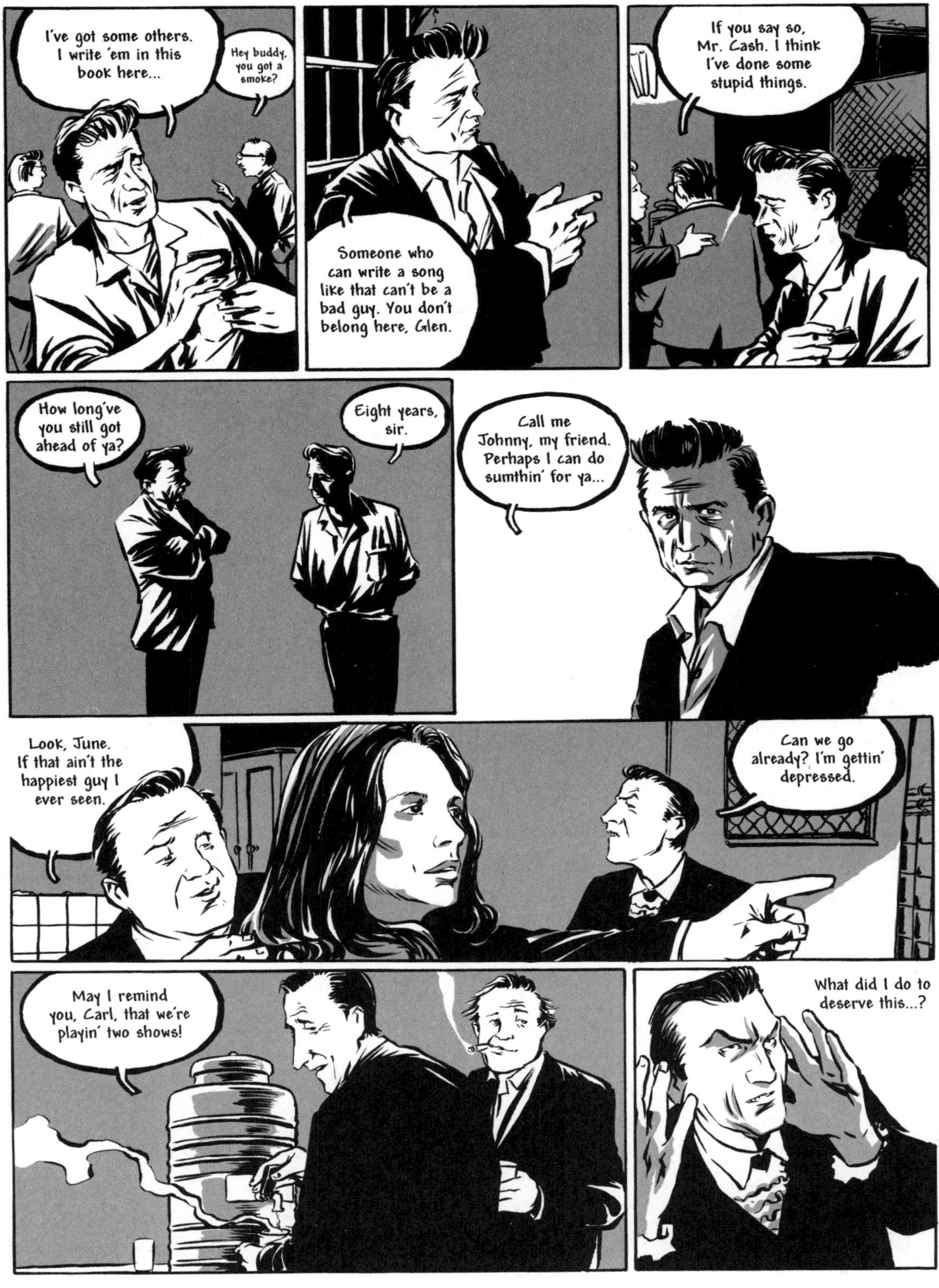

I've got some others. I write 'em in this book here...
Hey buddy, you got a smoke?
Someone who can write a song like that can't be a bad guy. You don't belong here, Glen.
If you say so, Mr. Cash. I think I've done some stupid things.
How long've you still got ahead of ya?
Eight years, sir.
Call me Johnny, my friend. Perhaps I can do sumthin' for ya...
Look, June. If that ain't the happiest guy I ever seen.
Can we go already? I'm gettin' depressed.
May I remind you, Carl, that we're playin' two shows!
What did I do to deserve this...?

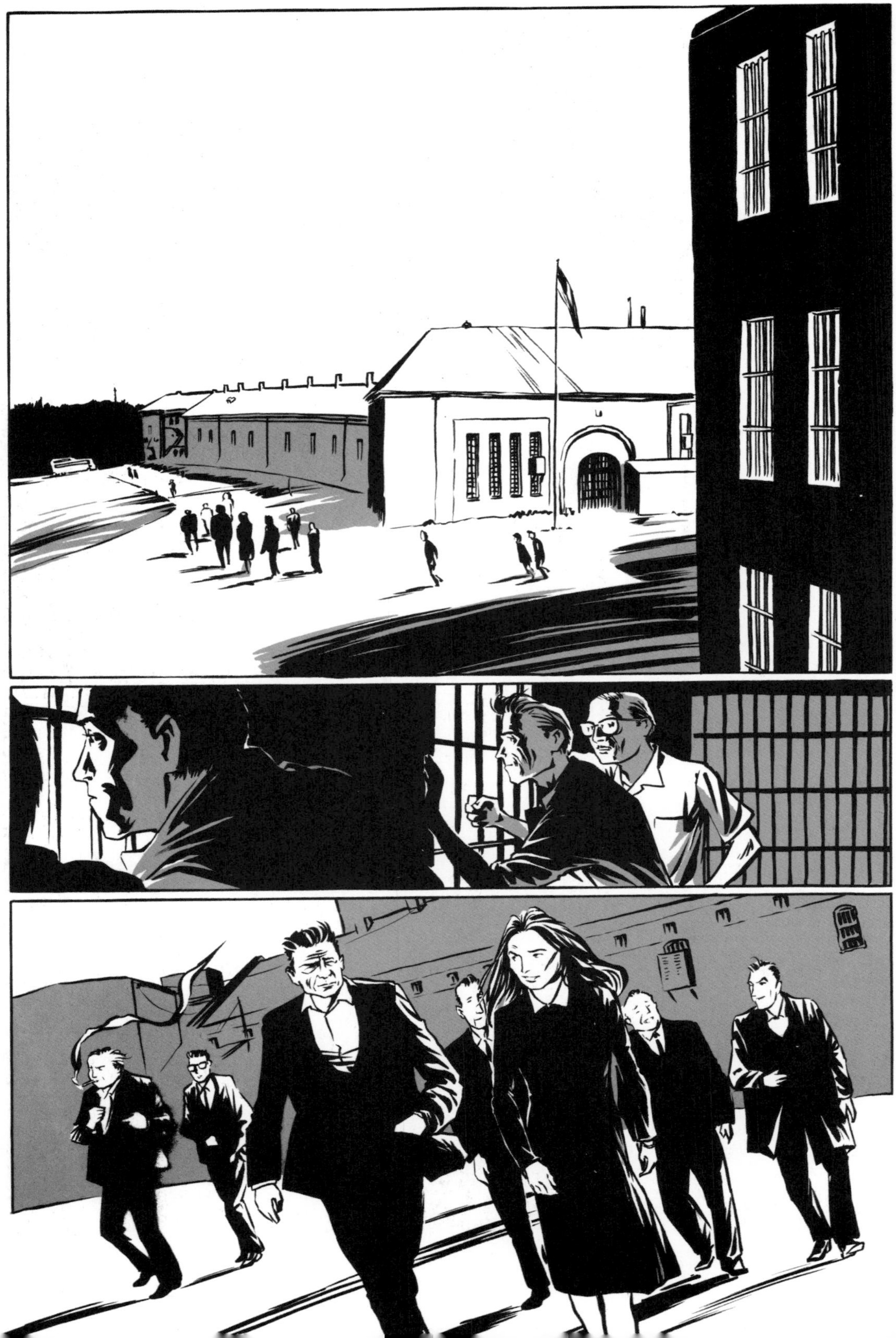

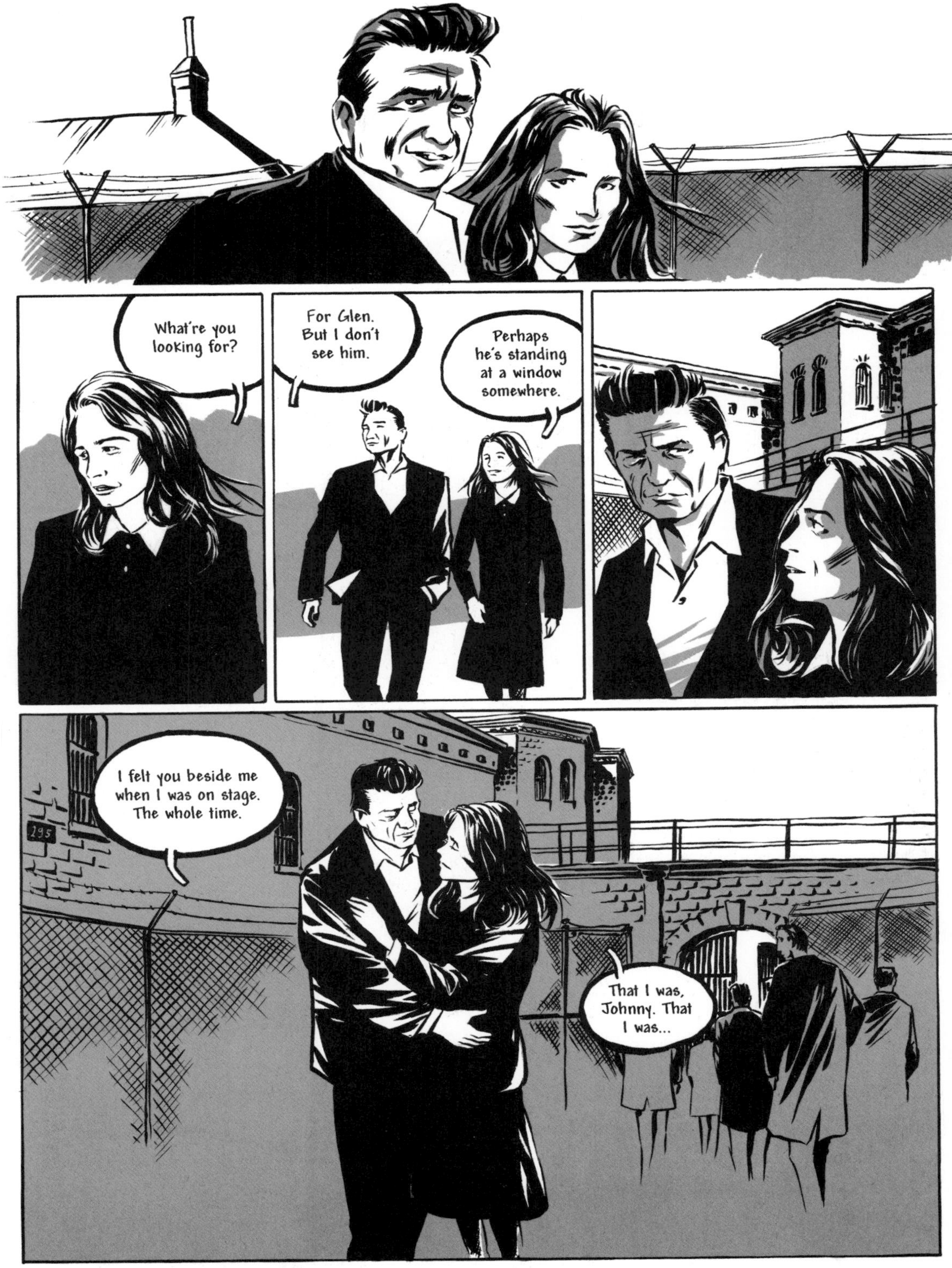
What're you looking for?
For Glen. But I don't see him.
Perhaps he's standing at a window somewhere.
295
I felt you beside me when I was on stage. The whole time.
That I was, Johnny. That I was...

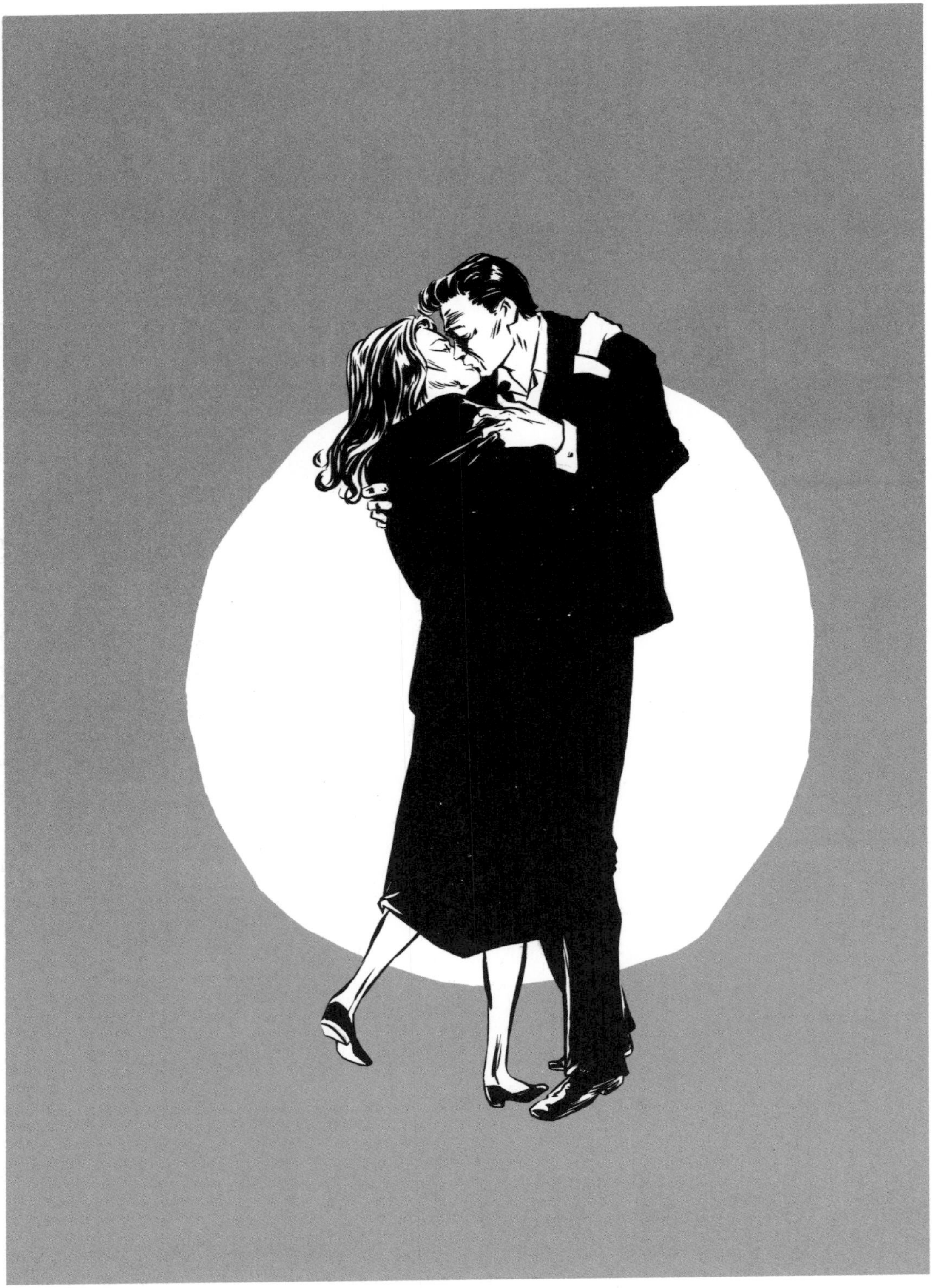

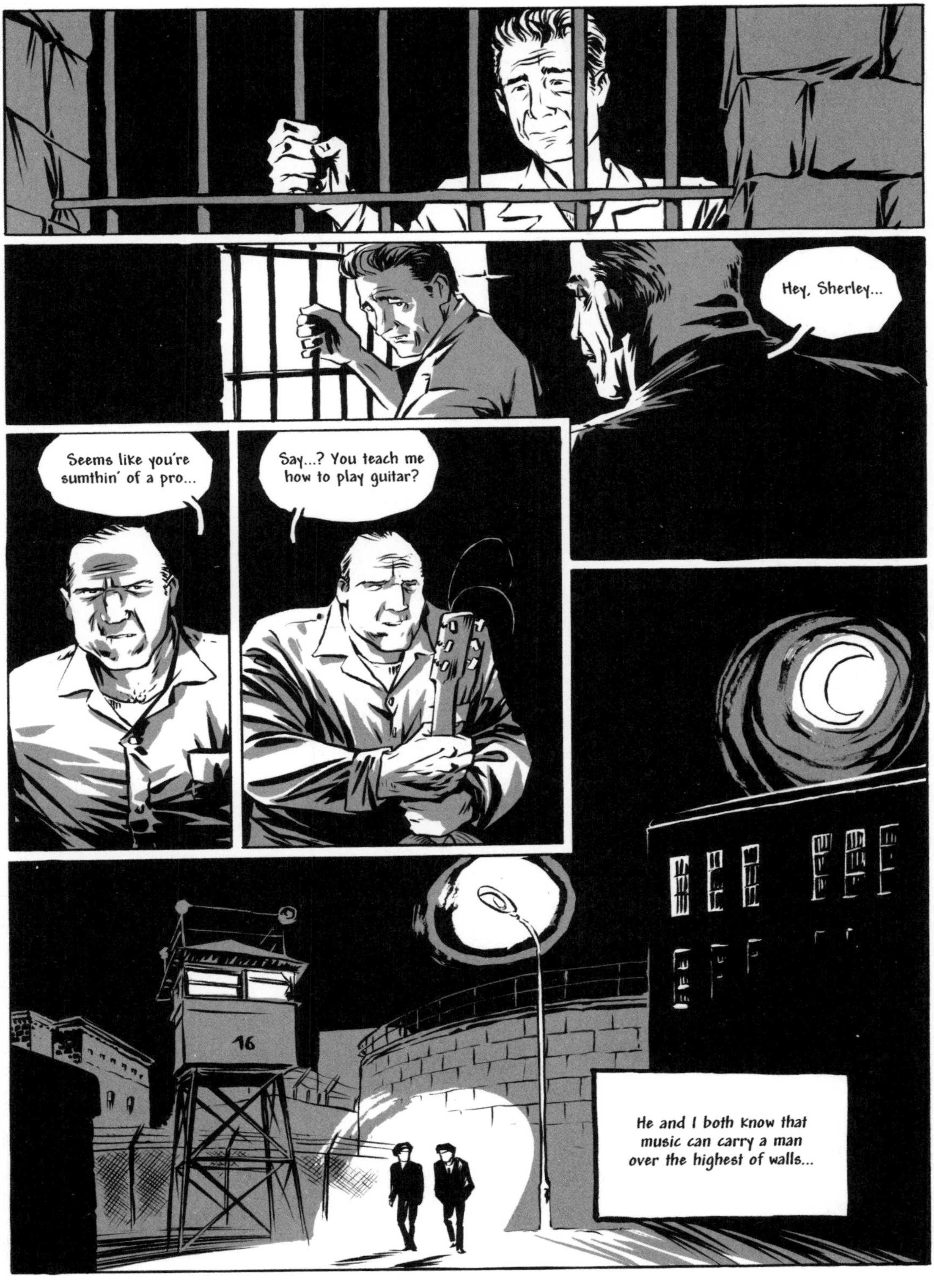
Hey, Sherley...
Seems like you're sumthin' of a pro...
Say...? You teach me how to play guitar?
16
He and I both know that music can carry a man over the highest of walls...

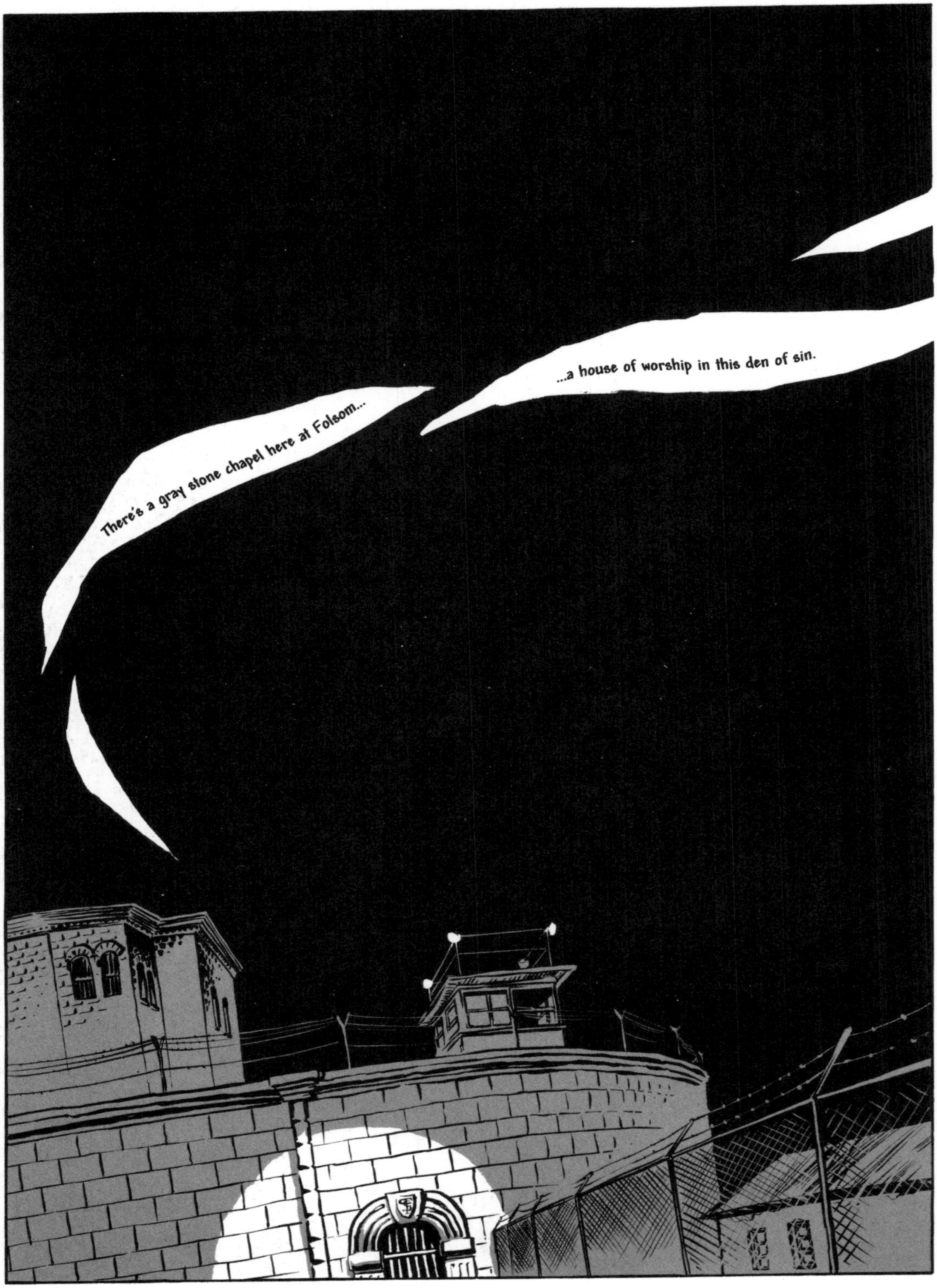
There's a gray stone chapel here at Folsom...
...a house of worship in this den of sin.

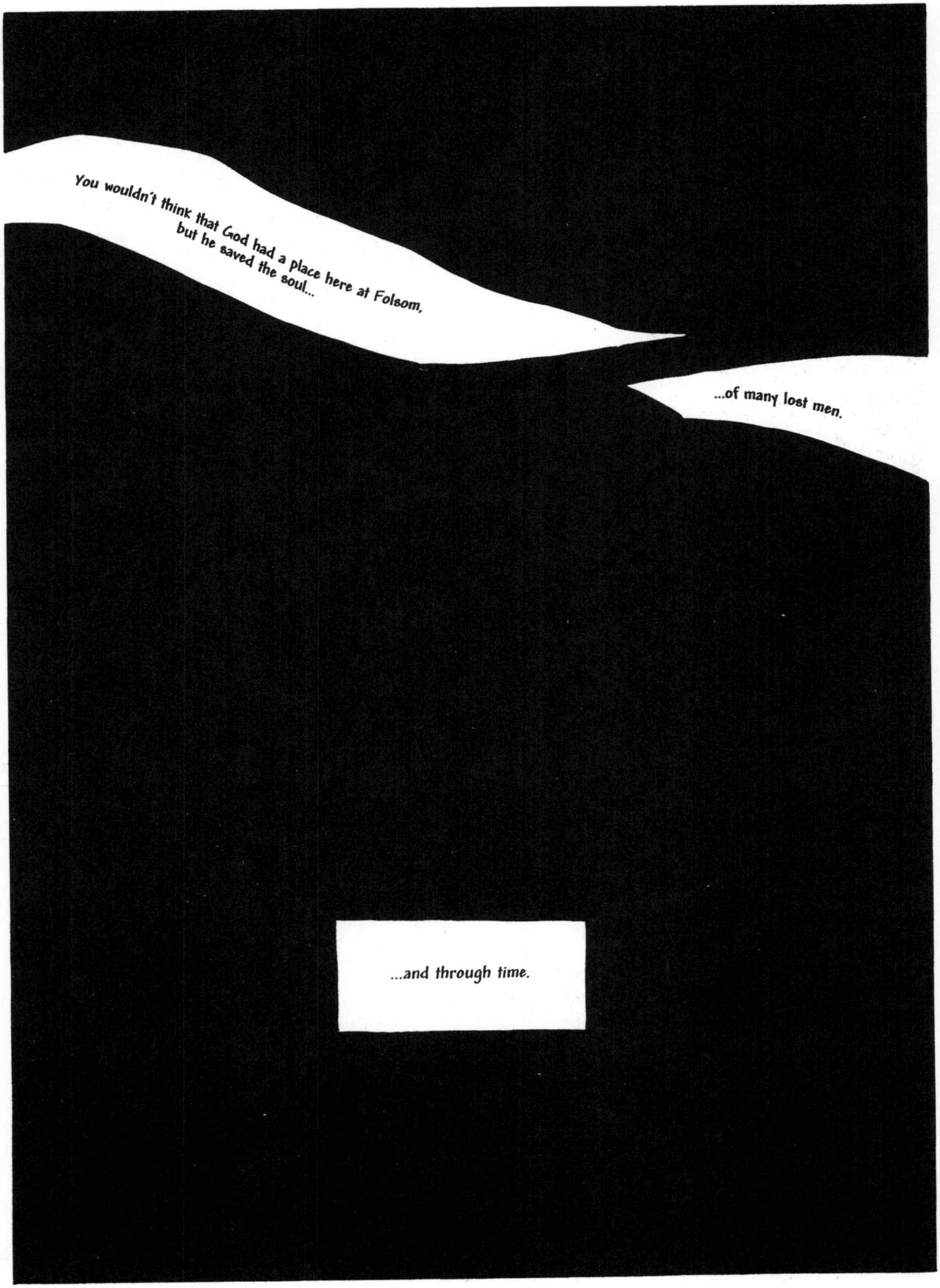
You wouldn't think that God had a place here at Folsom,
but he saved the soul...
...of many lost men.
...and through time.

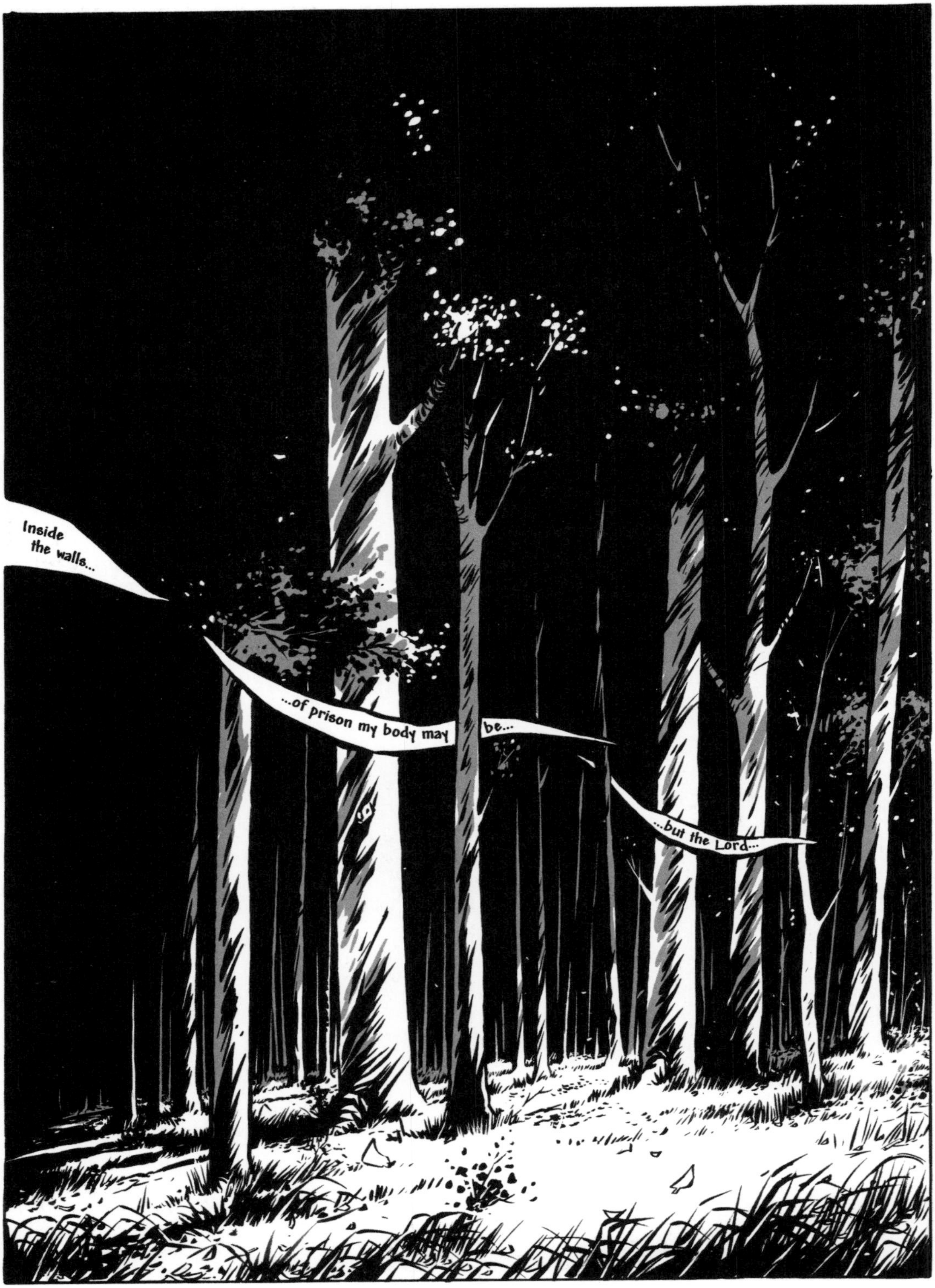

Inside the walls...
...of prison my body may be...
...but the Lord...

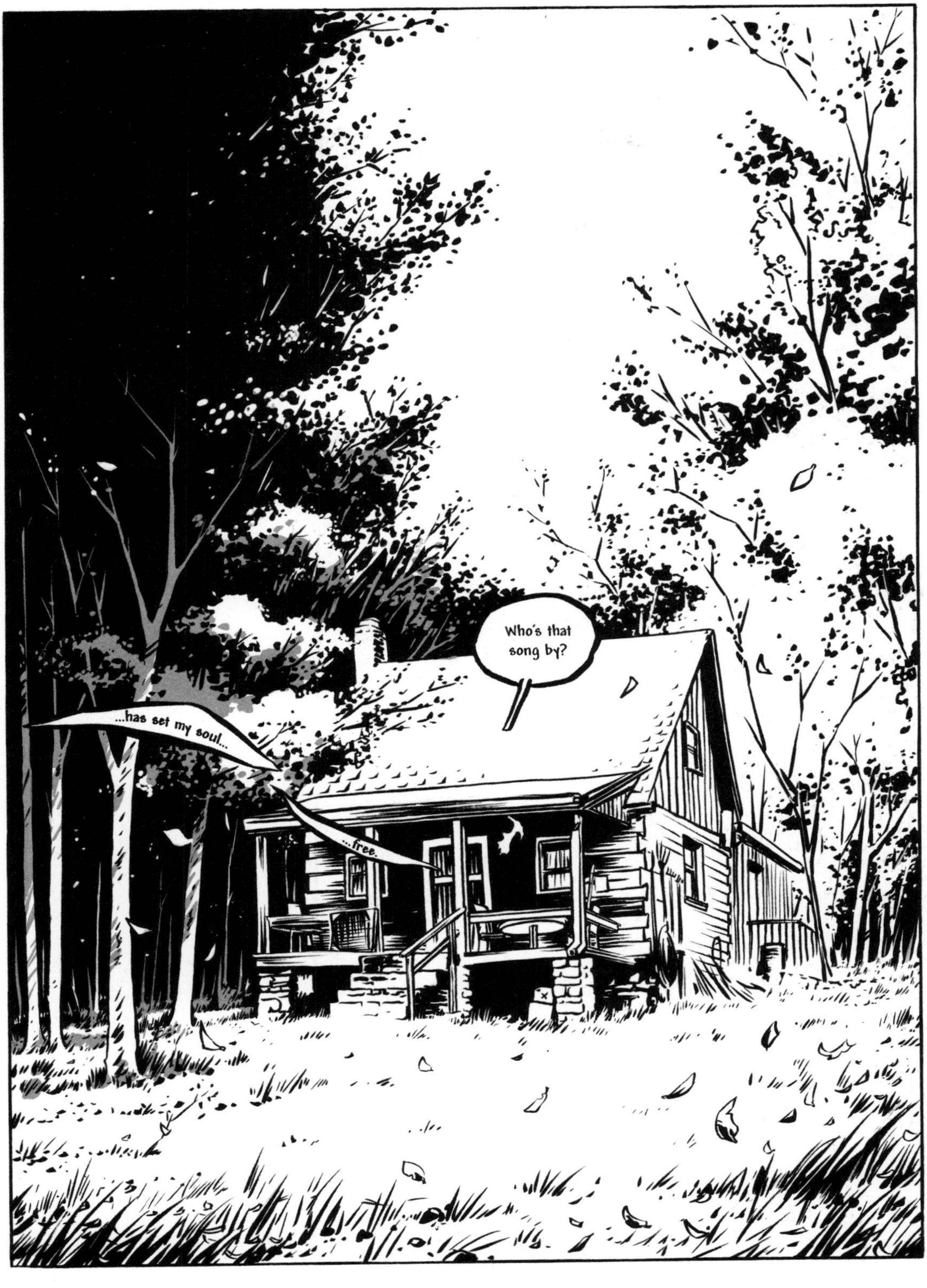
...has set my soul...
...free.
Who's that song by?

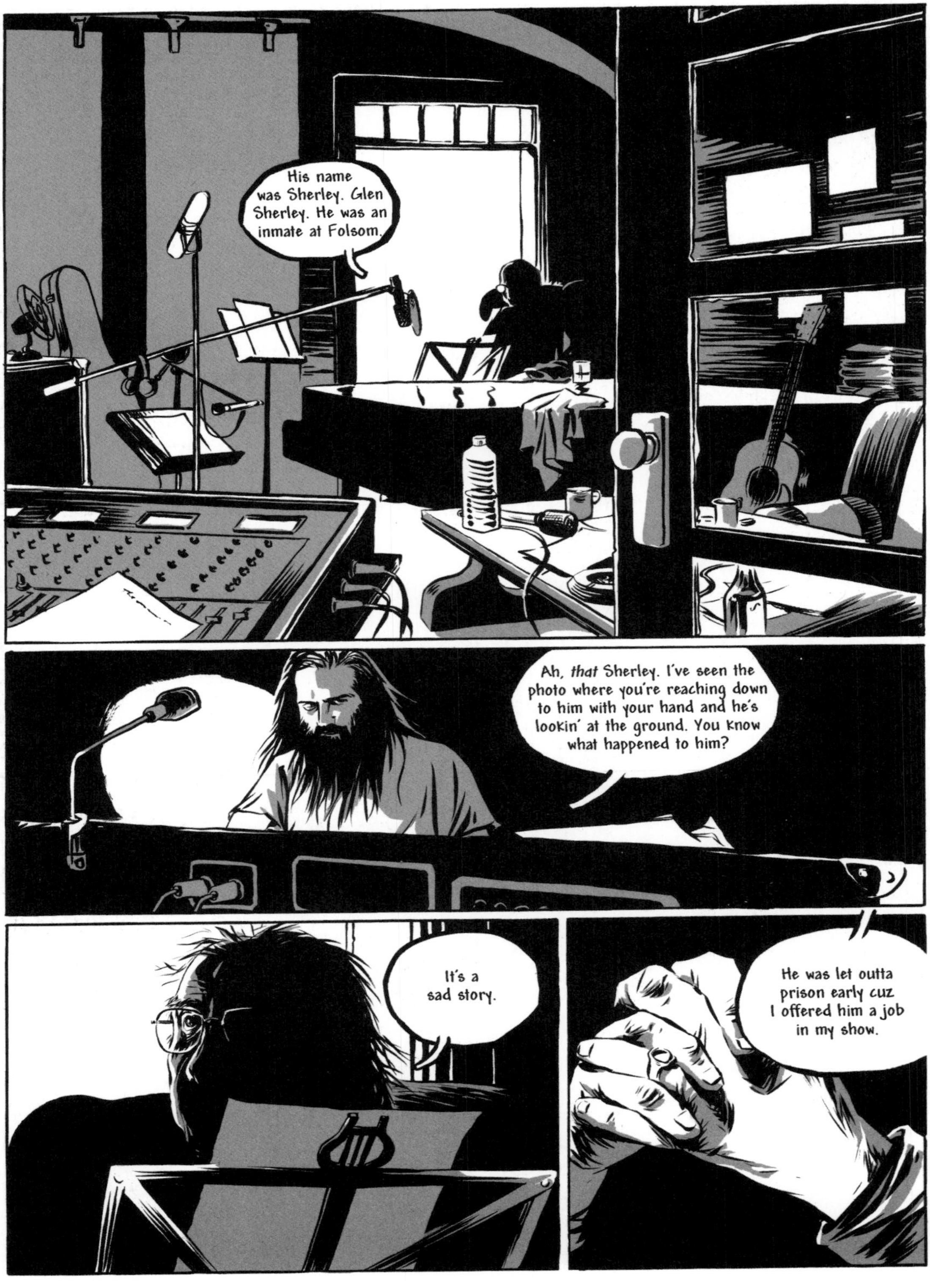
His name was Sherley. Glen Sherley. He was an inmate at Folsom.
Ah, *that* Sherley. I've seen the photo where you're reaching down to him with your hand and he's lookin' at the ground. You know what happened to him?
It's a sad story.
He was let outta prison early cuz I offered him a job in my show.

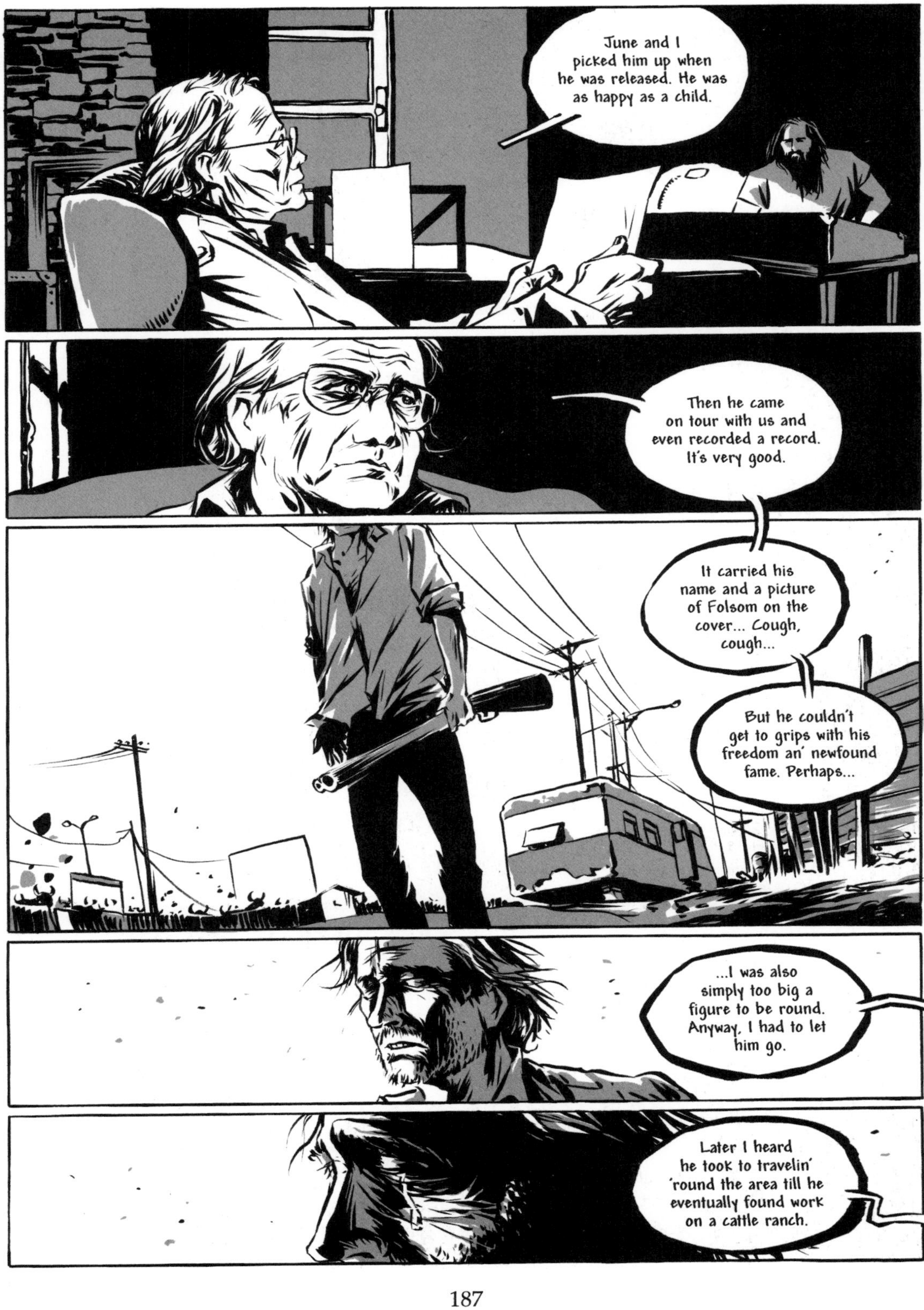
June and I picked him up when he was released. He was as happy as a child.
Then he came on tour with us and even recorded a record. It's very good.
It carried his name and a picture of Folsom on the cover... Cough, cough...
But he couldn't get to grips with his freedom an' newfound fame. Perhaps...
...I was also simply too big a figure to be round. Anyway, I had to let him go.
Later I heard he took to travelin' 'round the area till he eventually found work on a cattle ranch.

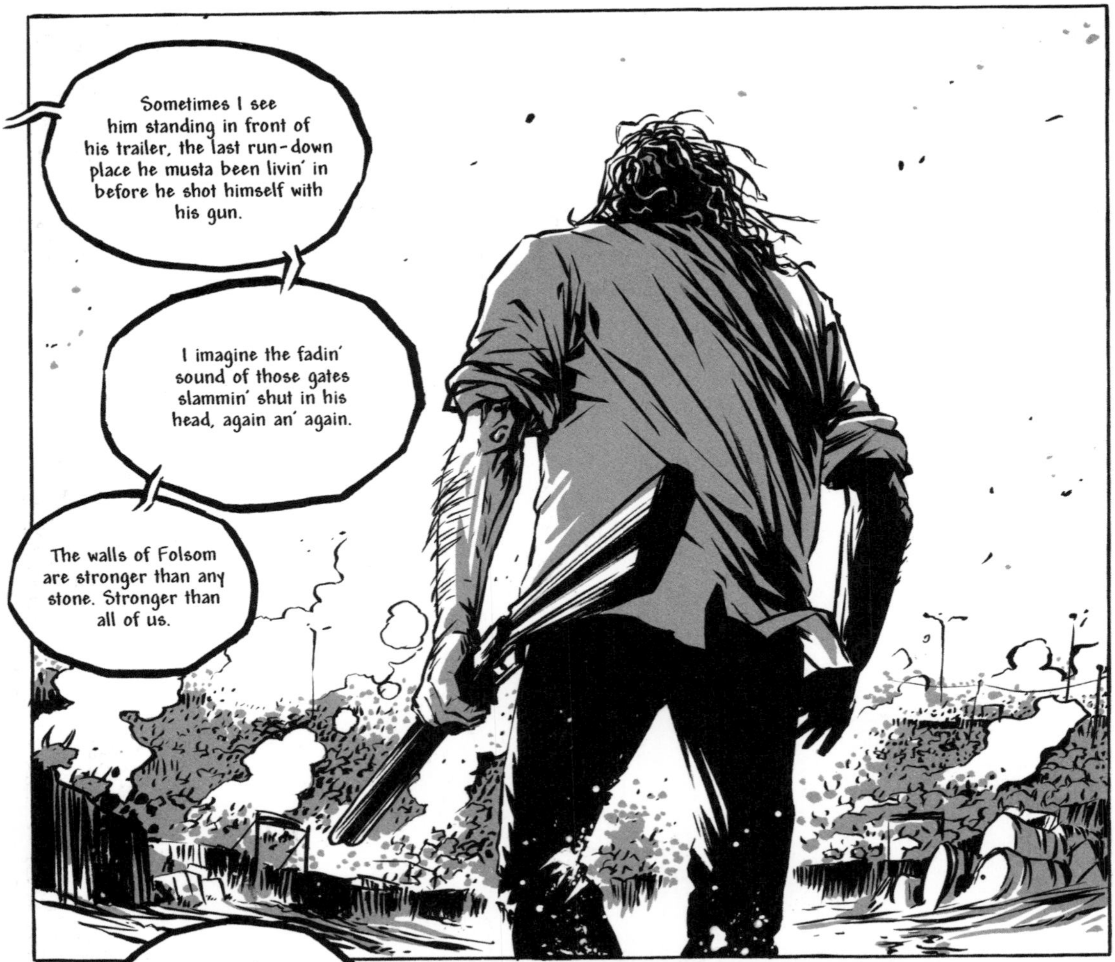
Sometimes I see him standing in front of his trailer, the last run-down place he musta been livin' in before he shot himself with his gun.
I imagine the fadin' sound of those gates slammin' shut in his head, again an' again.
The walls of Folsom are stronger than any stone. Stronger than all of us.

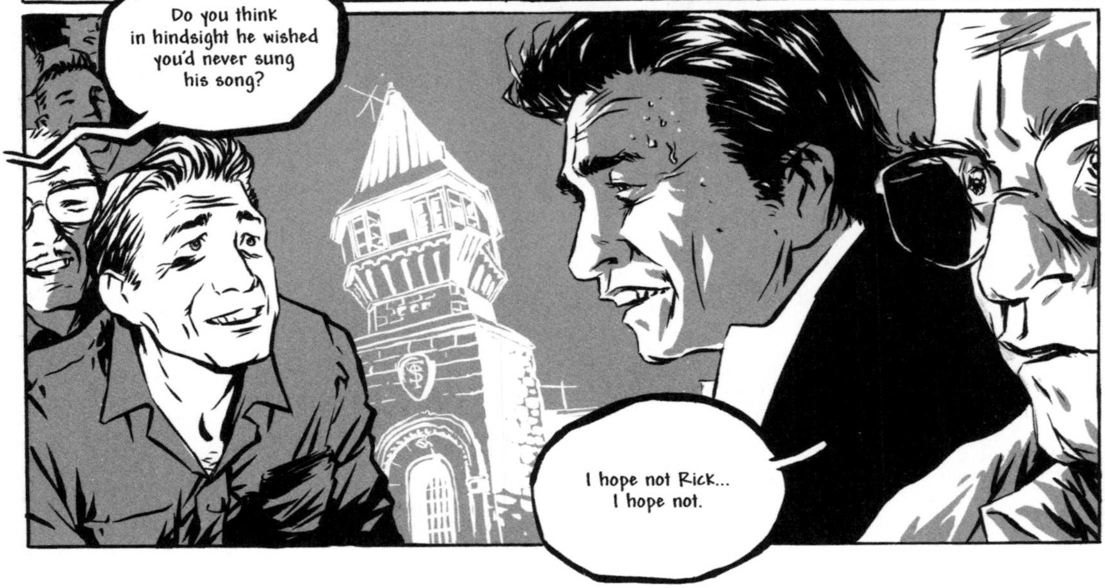
Do you think in hindsight he wished you'd never sung his song?
I hope not Rick... I hope not.

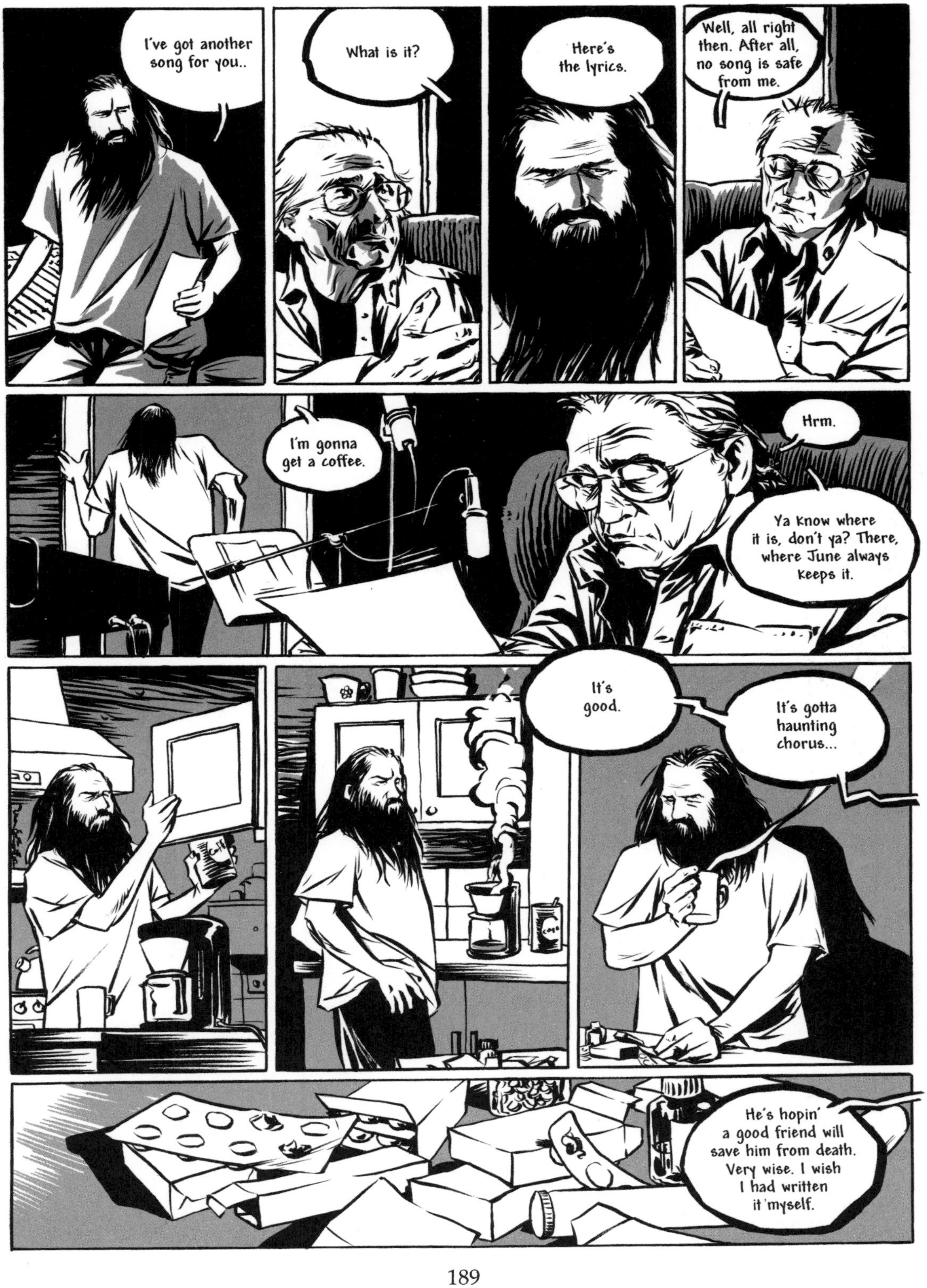
I've got another song for you..
What is it?
Here's the lyrics.
Well, all right then. After all, no song is safe from me.
I'm gonna get a coffee.
Hrm.
Ya know where it is, don't ya? There, where June always keeps it.
It's good.
It's gotta haunting chorus...
He's hopin' a good friend will save him from death. Very wise. I wish I had written it myself.

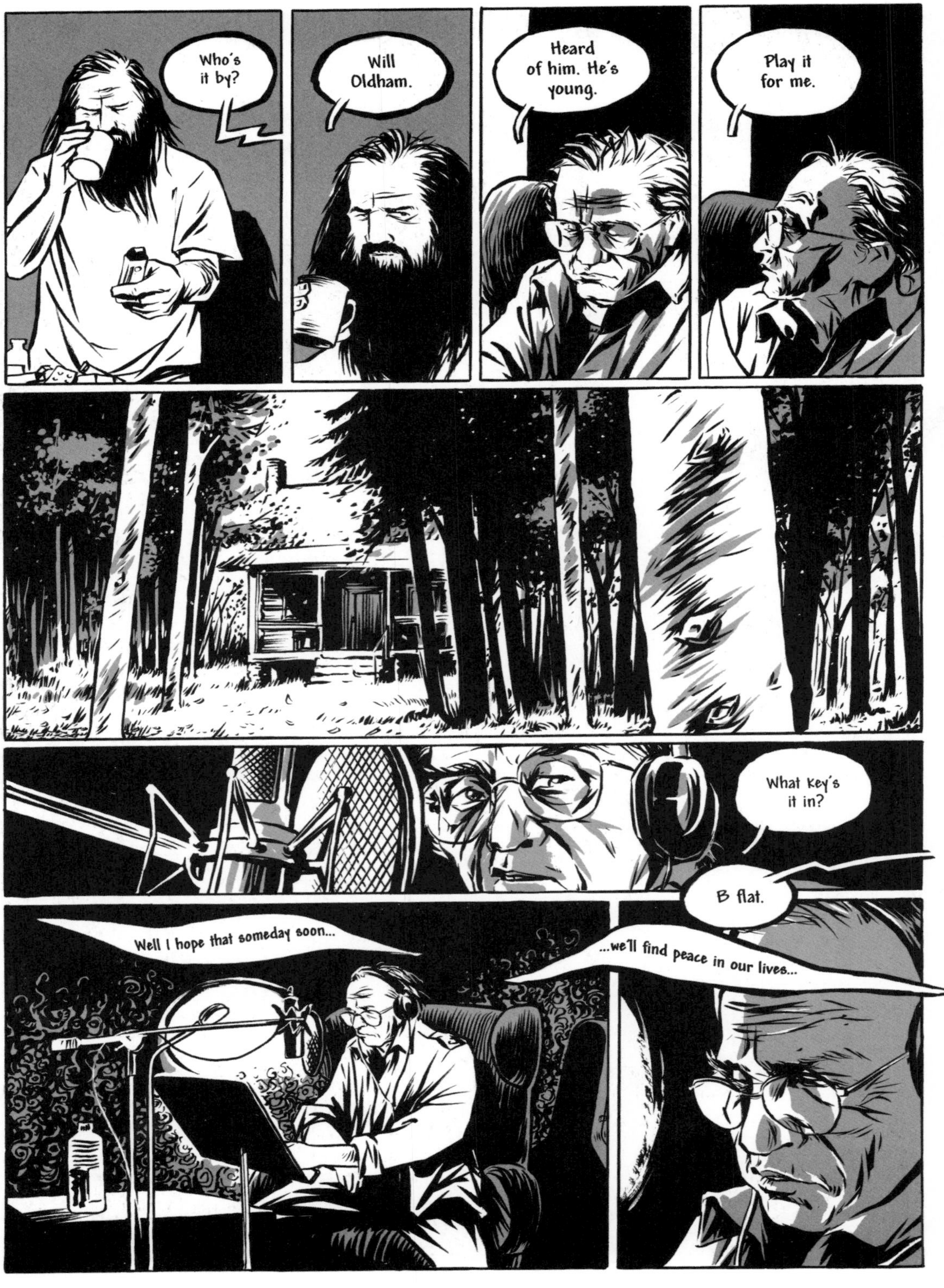
Who's it by?
Will Oldham.
Heard of him. He's young.
Play it for me.
What key's it in?
B flat.
Well I hope that someday soon...
...we'll find peace in our lives...

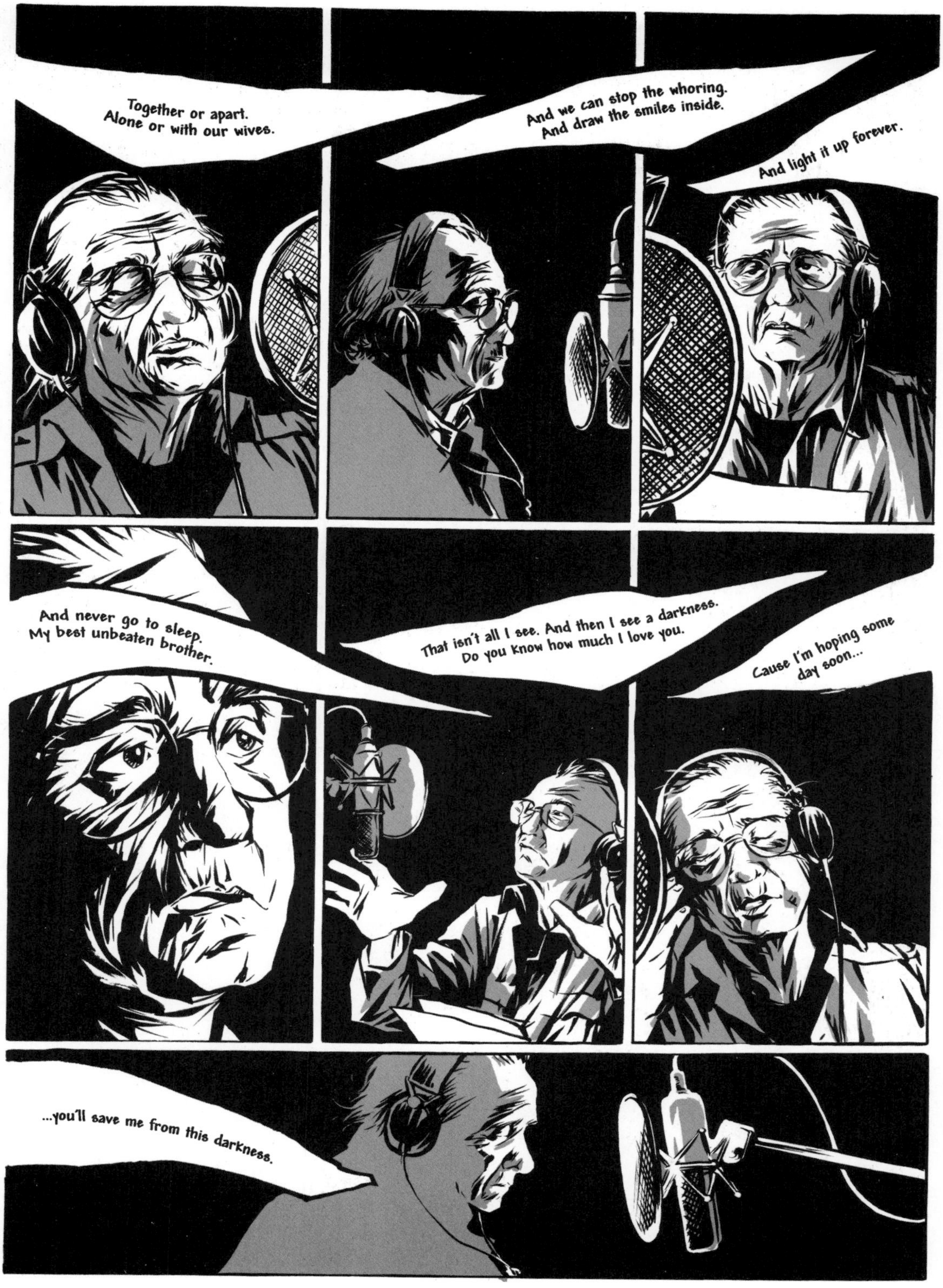
Together or apart.
Alone or with our wives.
And we can stop the whoring.
And draw the smiles inside.
And light it up forever.
And never go to sleep.
My best unbeaten brother.
That isn't all I see. And then I see a darkness.
Do you know how much I love you.
Cause I'm hoping some day soon...
...you'll save me from this darkness.

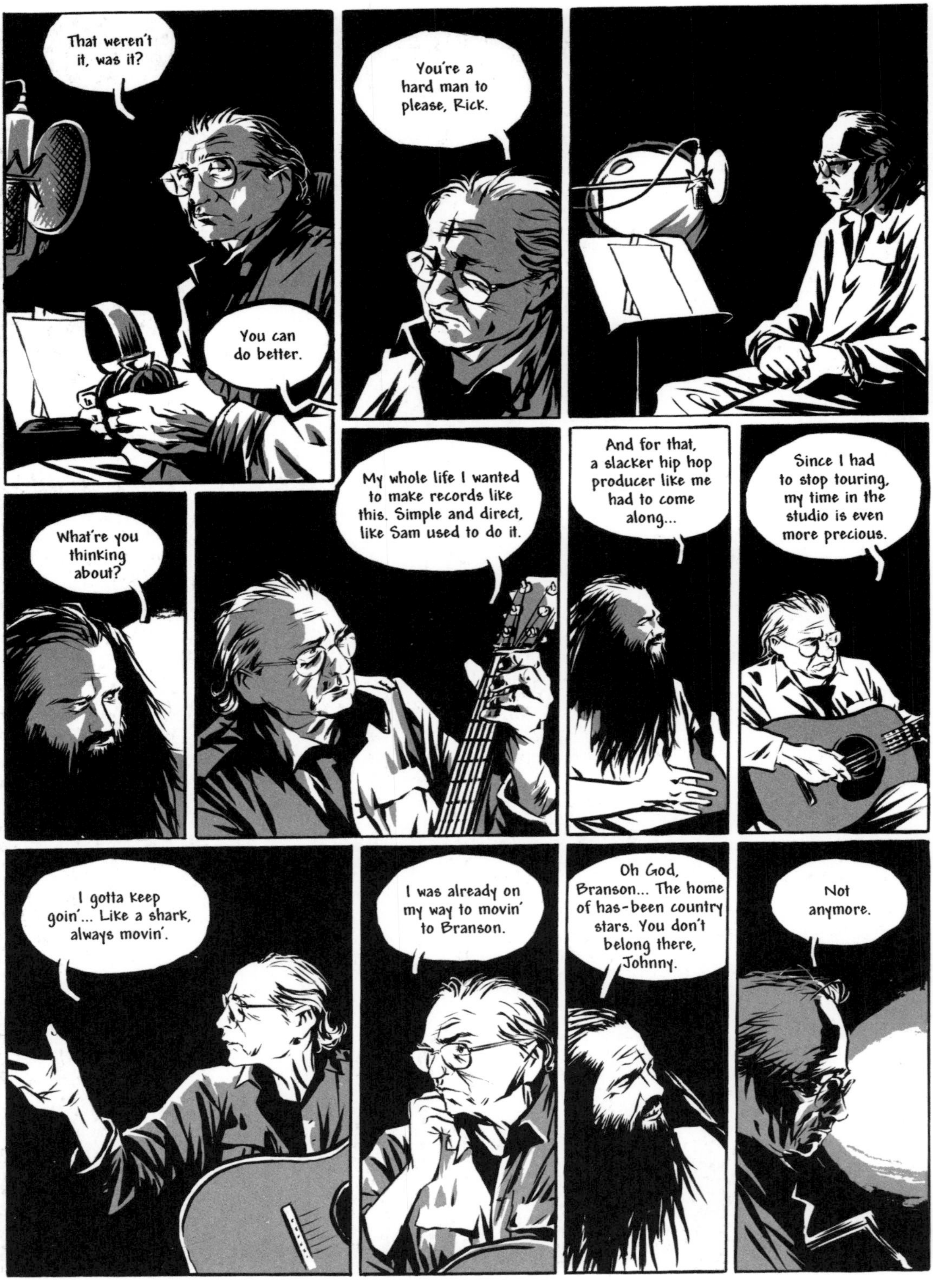
That weren't it, was it?
You can do better.
You're a hard man to please, Rick.
What're you thinking about?
My whole life I wanted to make records like this. Simple and direct, like Sam used to do it.
And for that, a slacker hip hop producer like me had to come along...
Since I had to stop touring, my time in the studio is even more precious.
I gotta keep goin'... Like a shark, always movin'.
I was already on my way to movin' to Branson.
Oh God, Branson... The home of has-been country stars. You don't belong there, Johnny.
Not anymore.

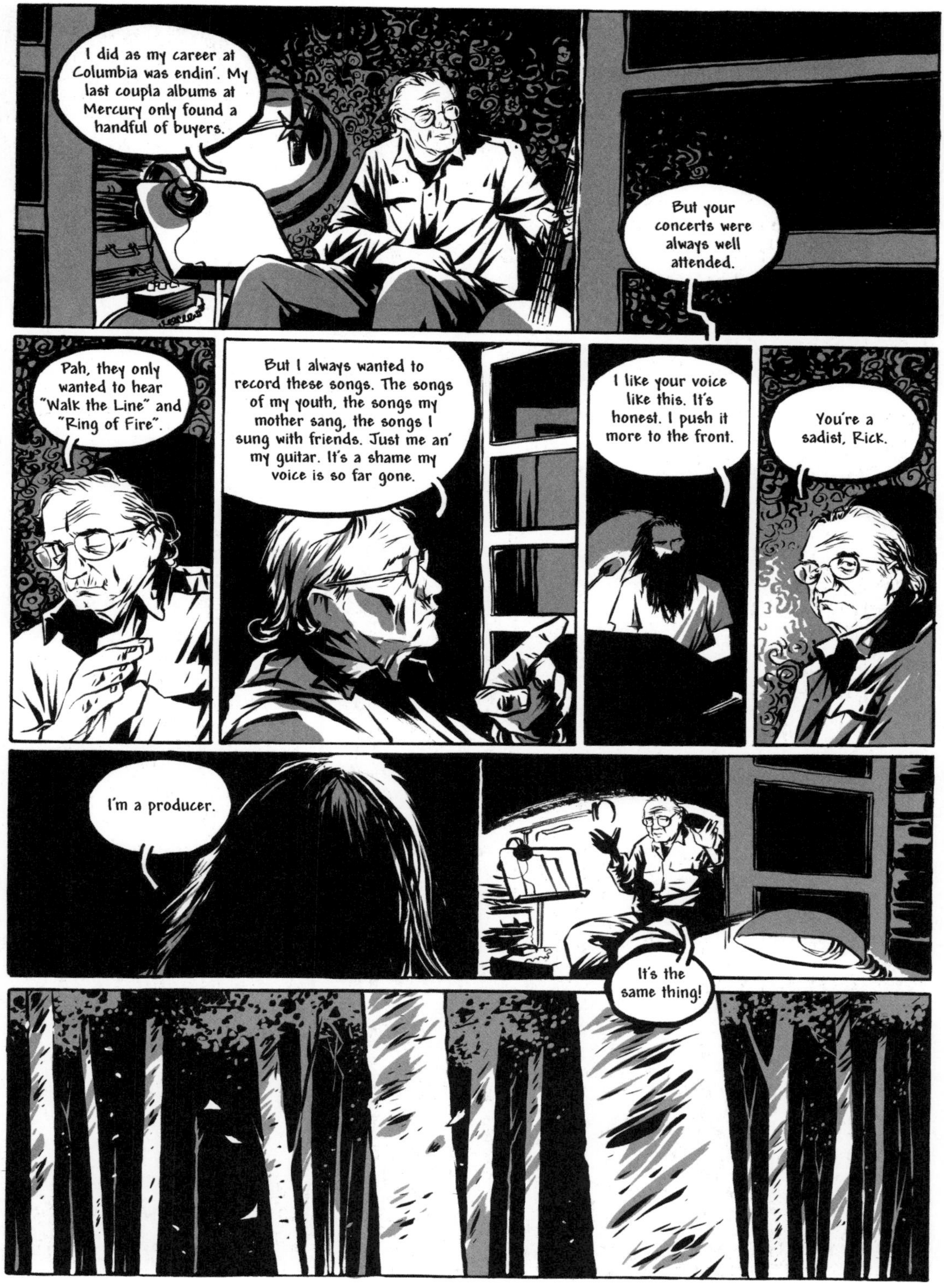
I did as my career at Columbia was endin'. My last coupla albums at Mercury only found a handful of buyers.
But your concerts were always well attended.
Pah, they only wanted to hear "Walk the Line" and "Ring of Fire".
But I always wanted to record these songs. The songs of my youth, the songs my mother sang, the songs I sung with friends. Just me an' my guitar. It's a shame my voice is so far gone.
I like your voice like this. It's honest. I push it more to the front.
You're a sadist, Rick.
I'm a producer.
It's the same thing!

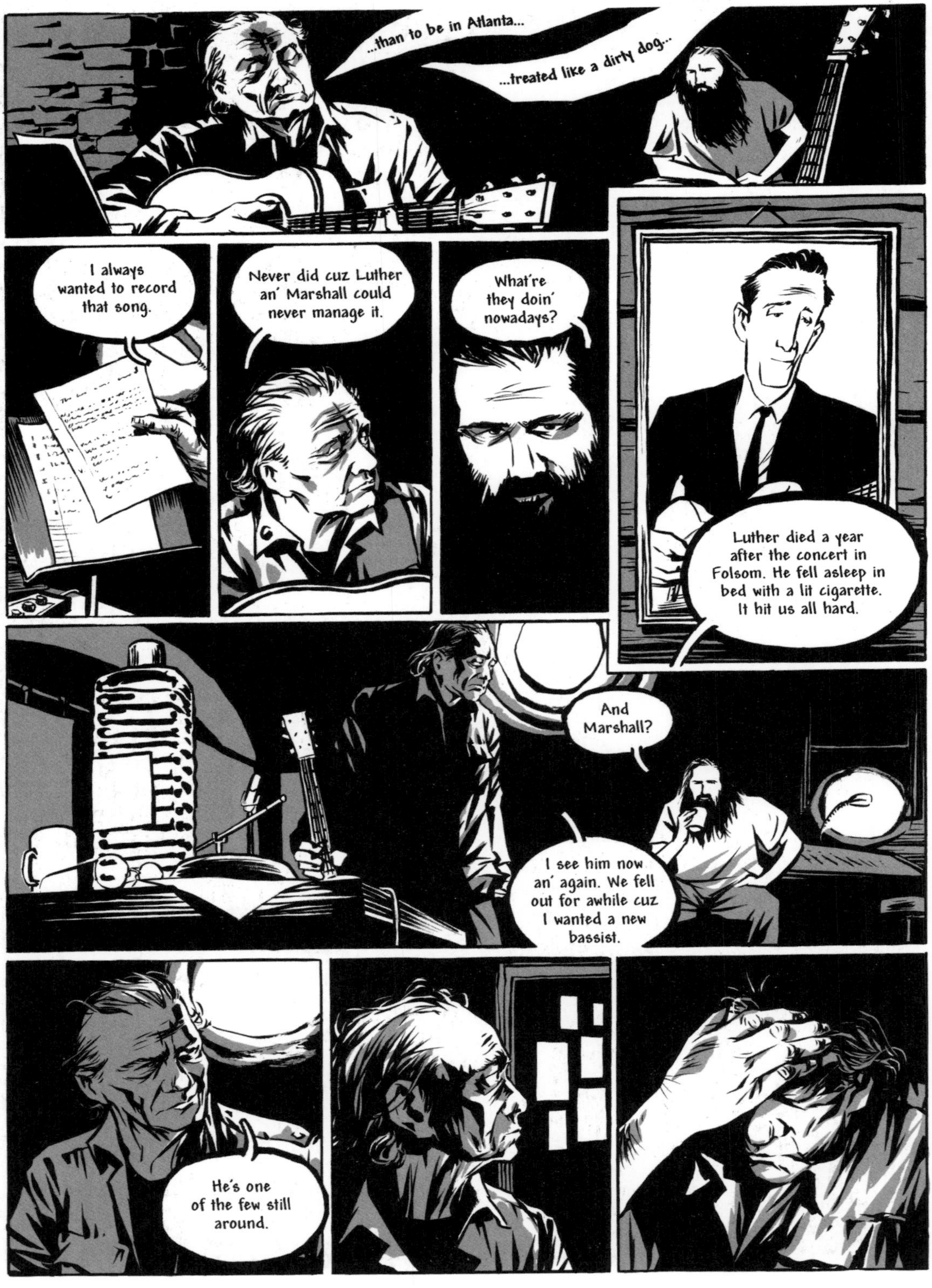

...than to be in Atlanta...
...treated like a dirty dog...
I always wanted to record that song.
Never did cuz Luther an' Marshall could never manage it.
What're they doin' nowadays?
Luther died a year after the concert in Folsom. He fell asleep in bed with a lit cigarette. It hit us all hard.
And Marshall?
I see him now an' again. We fell out for awhile cuz I wanted a new bassist.
He's one of the few still around.

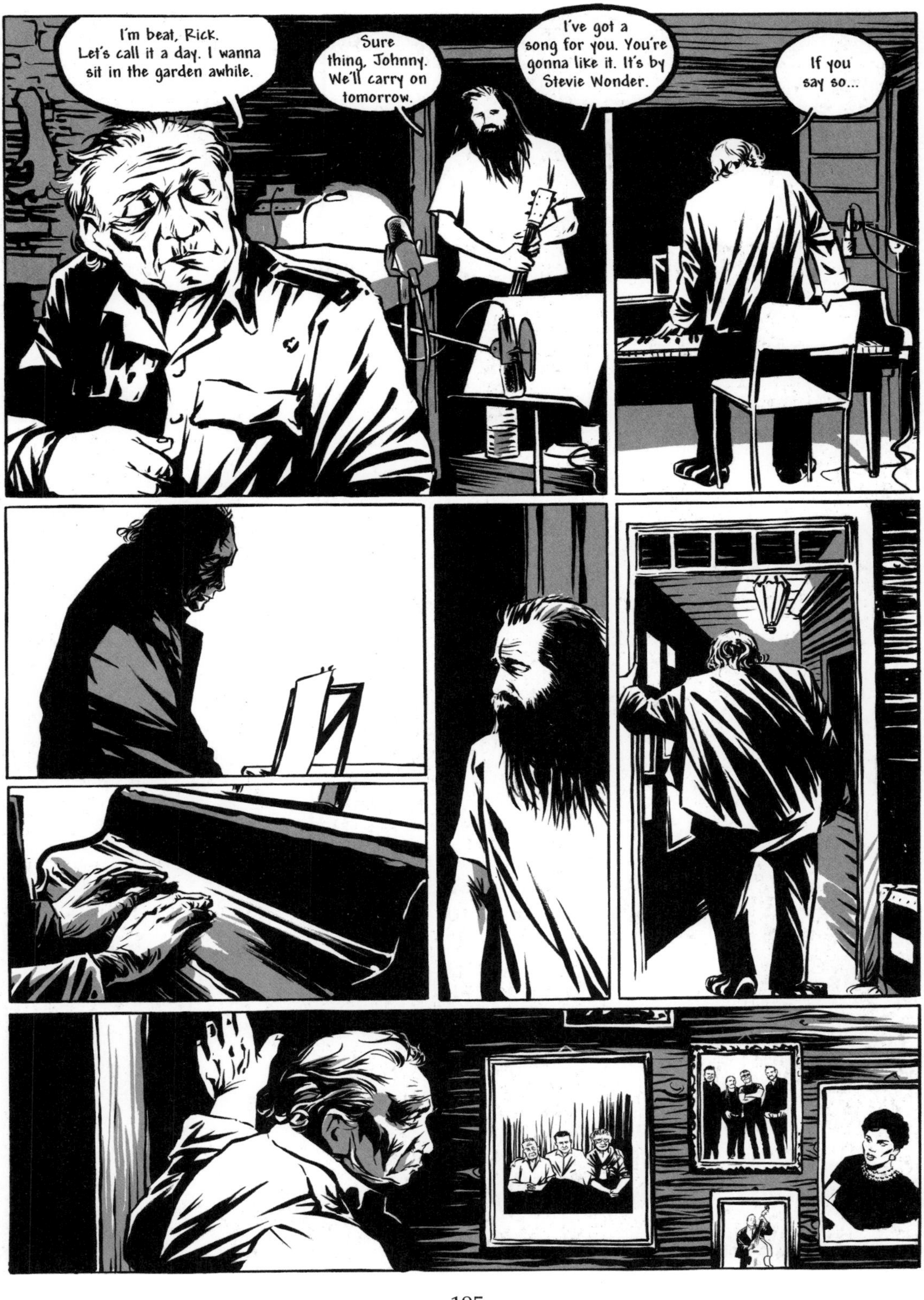
I'm beat, Rick.
Let's call it a day. I wanna sit in the garden awhile.
Sure thing, Johnny. We'll carry on tomorrow.
I've got a song for you. You're gonna like it. It's by Stevie Wonder.
If you say so...

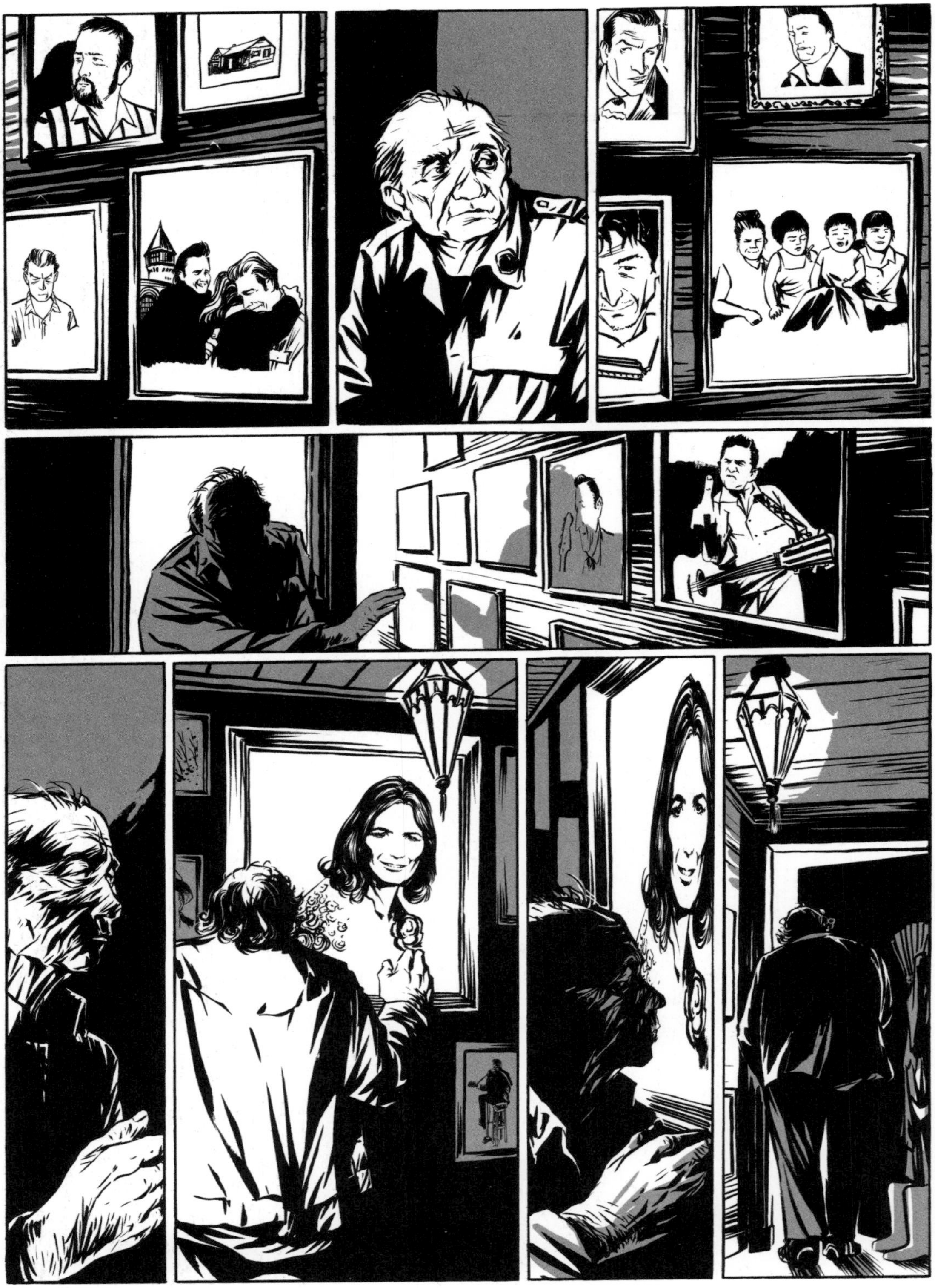

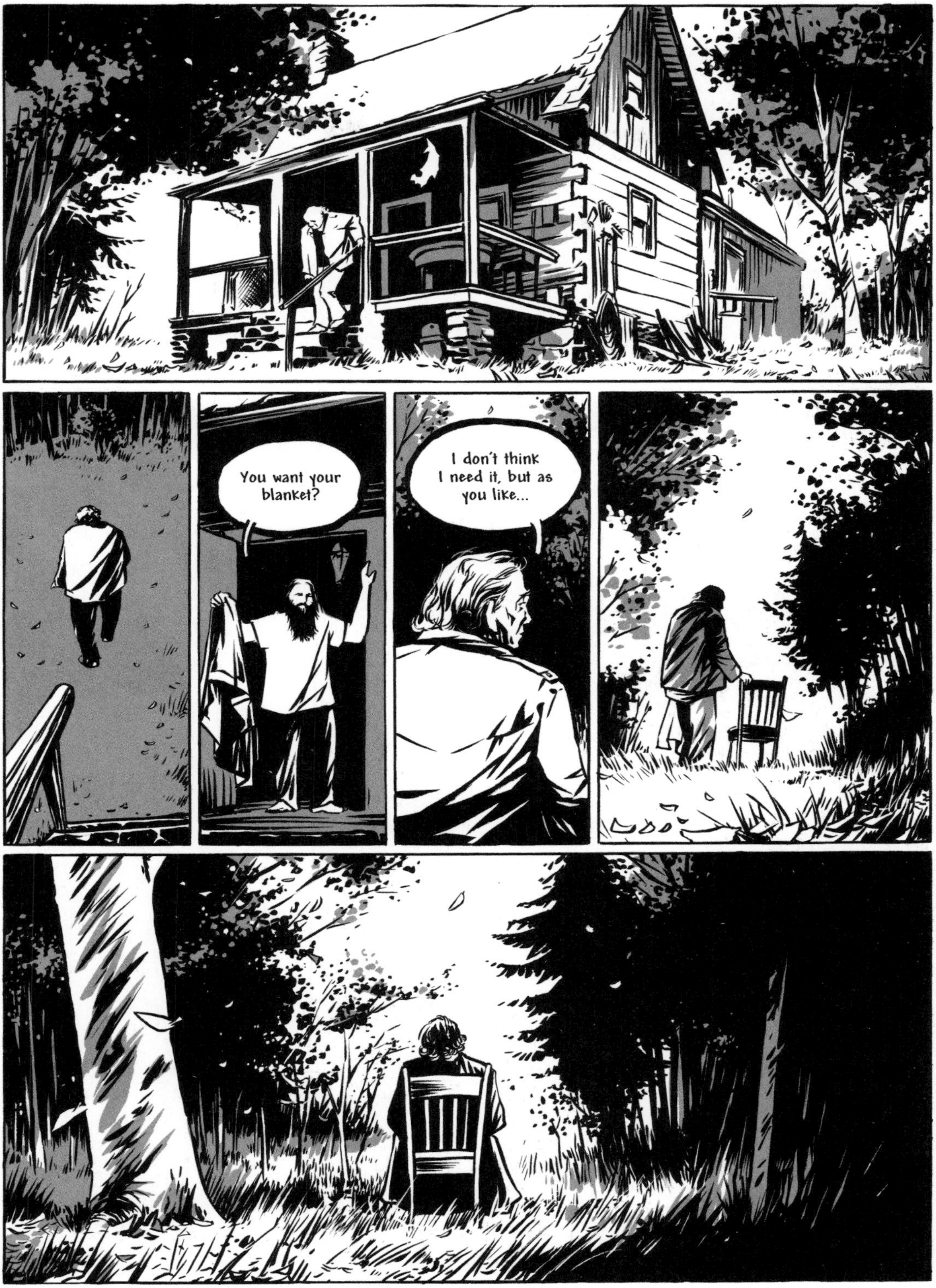
You want your blanket?
I don't think I need it, but as you like...

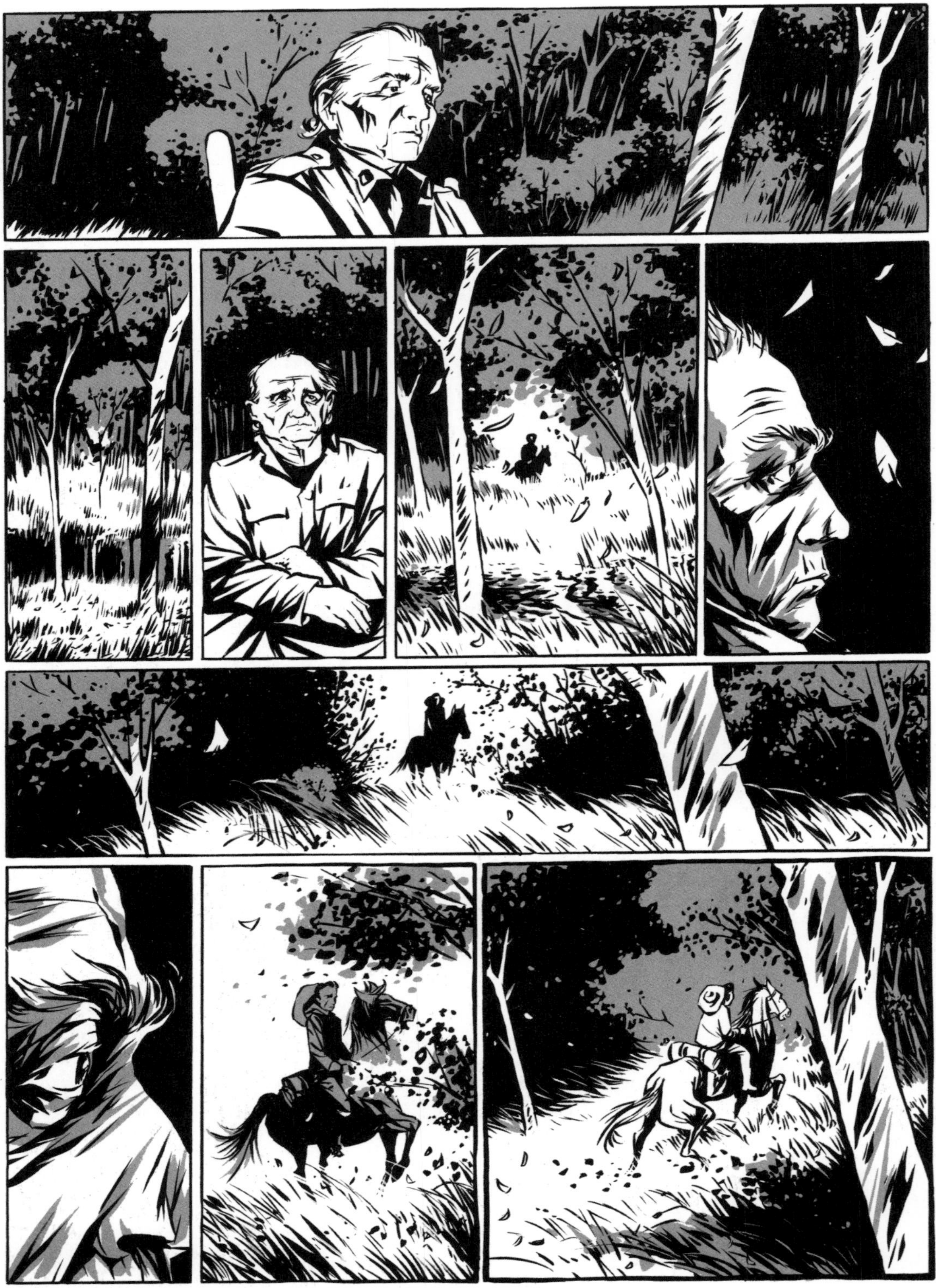

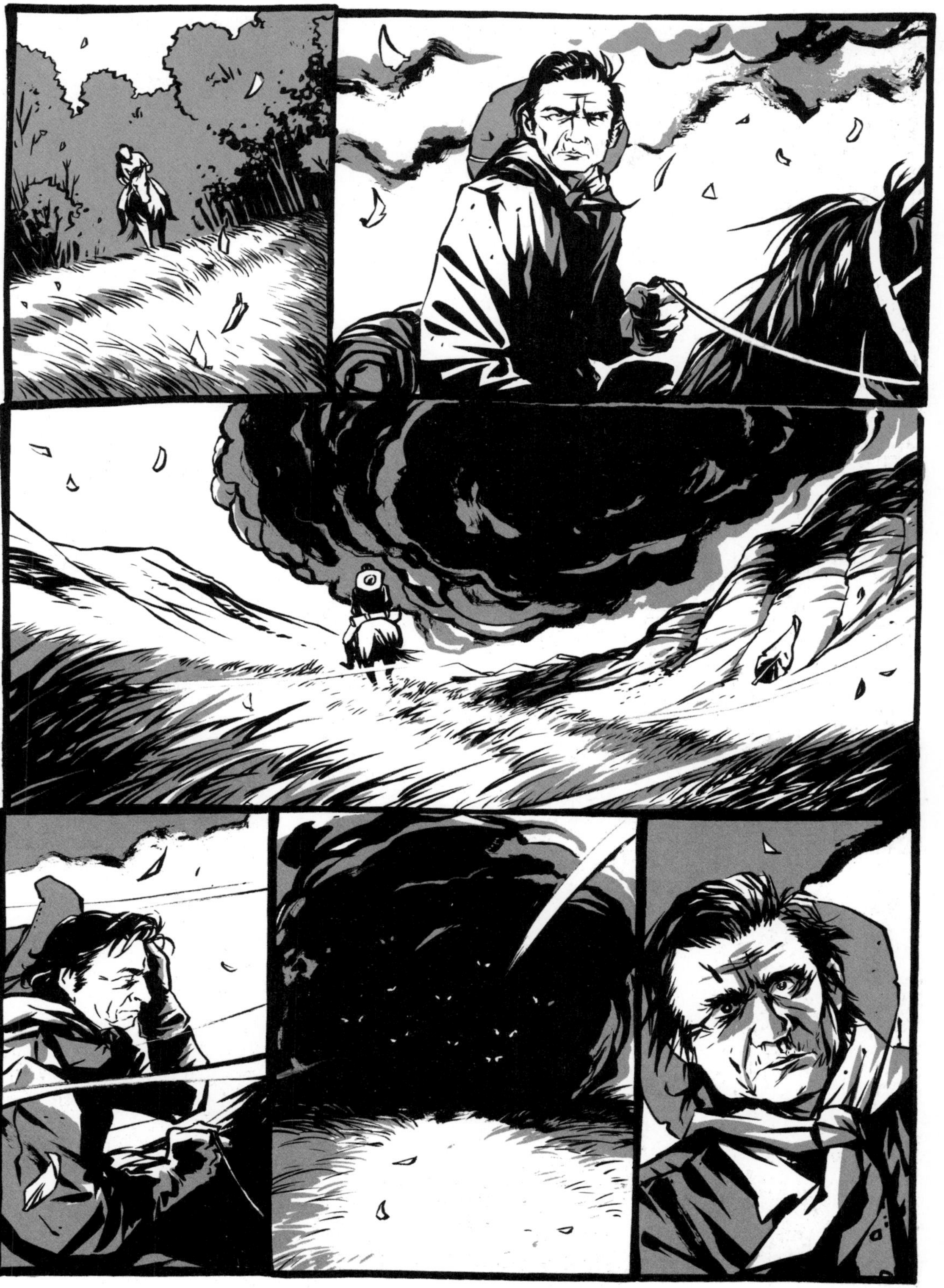

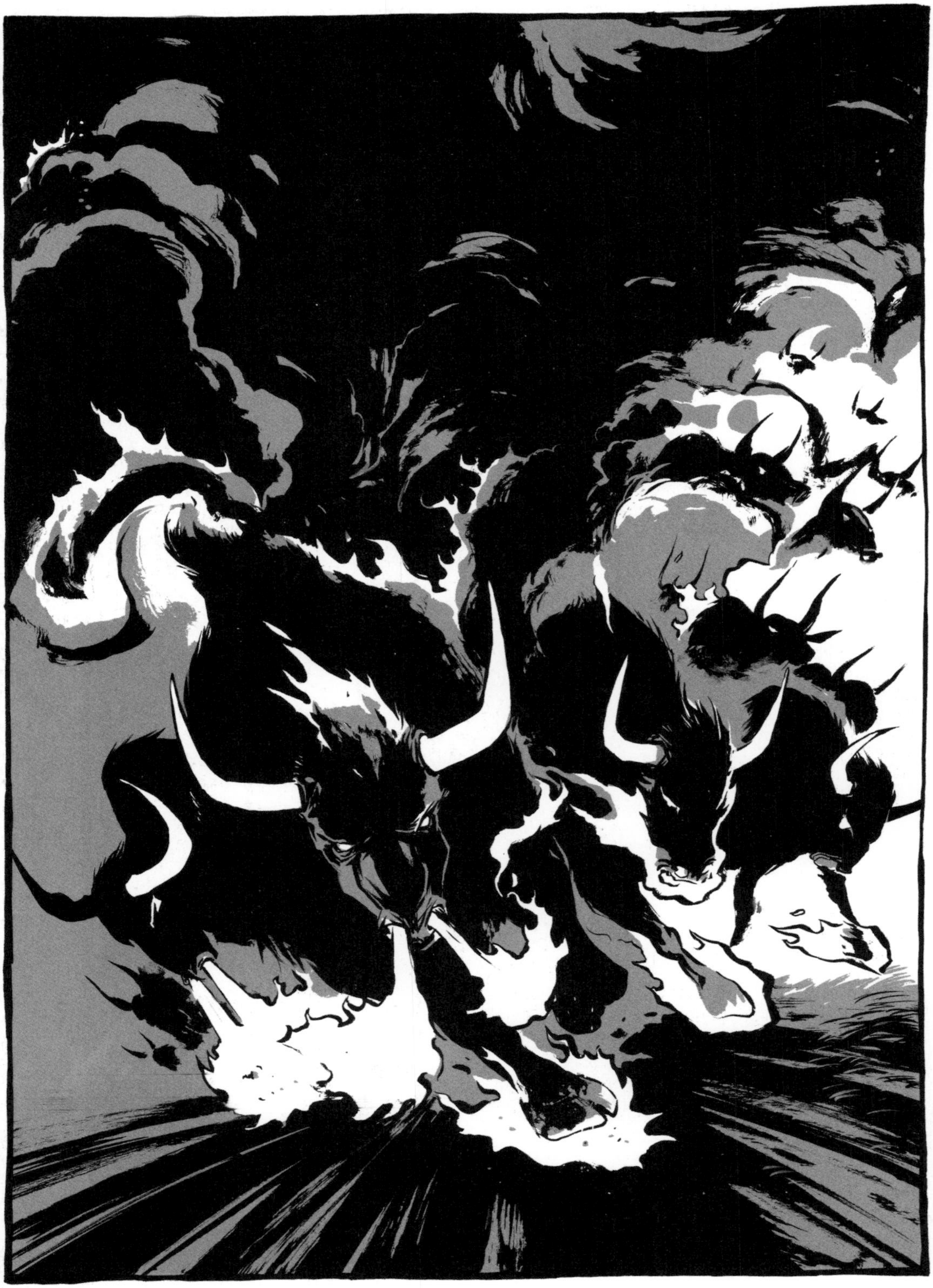

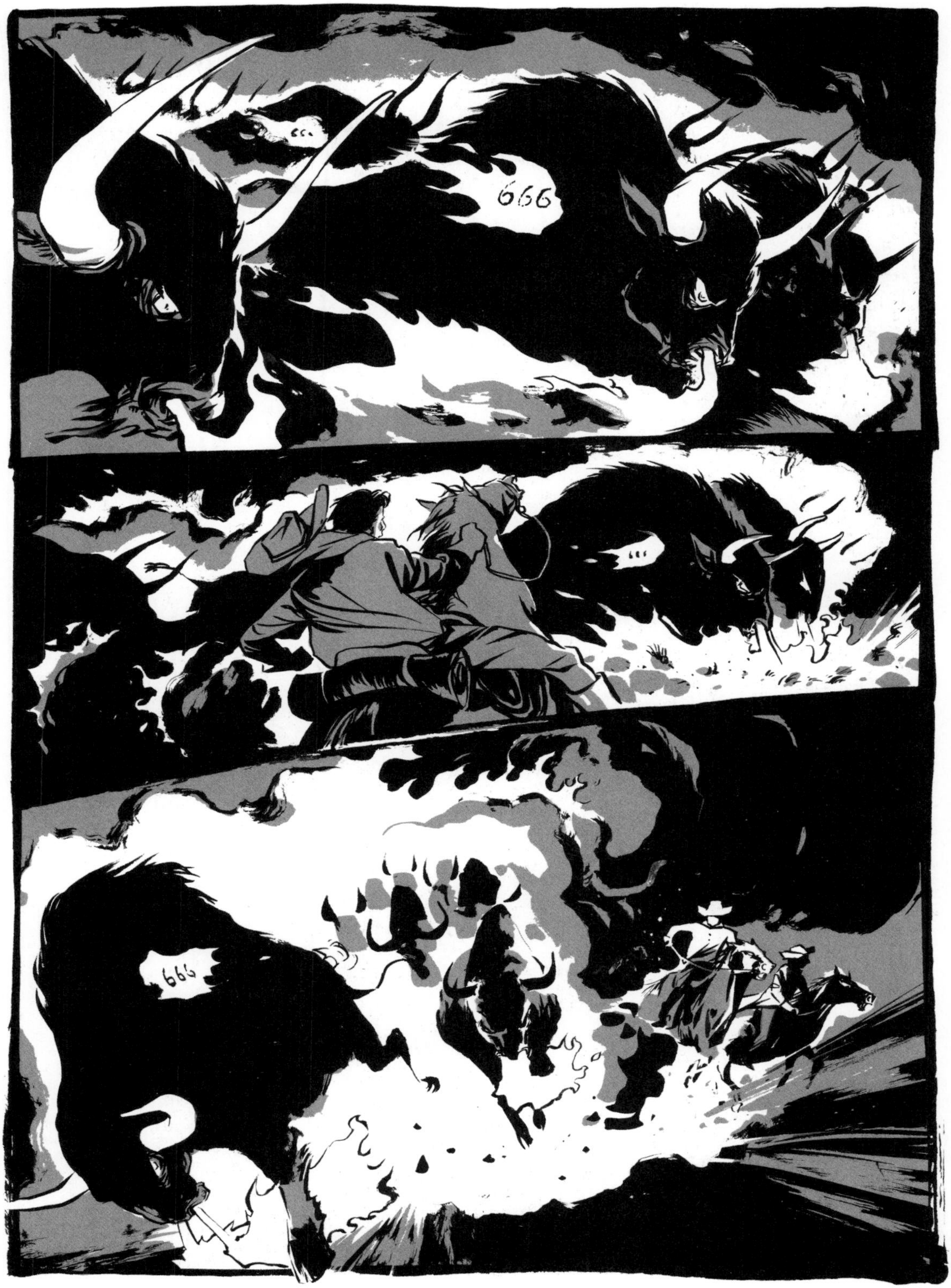
666
666

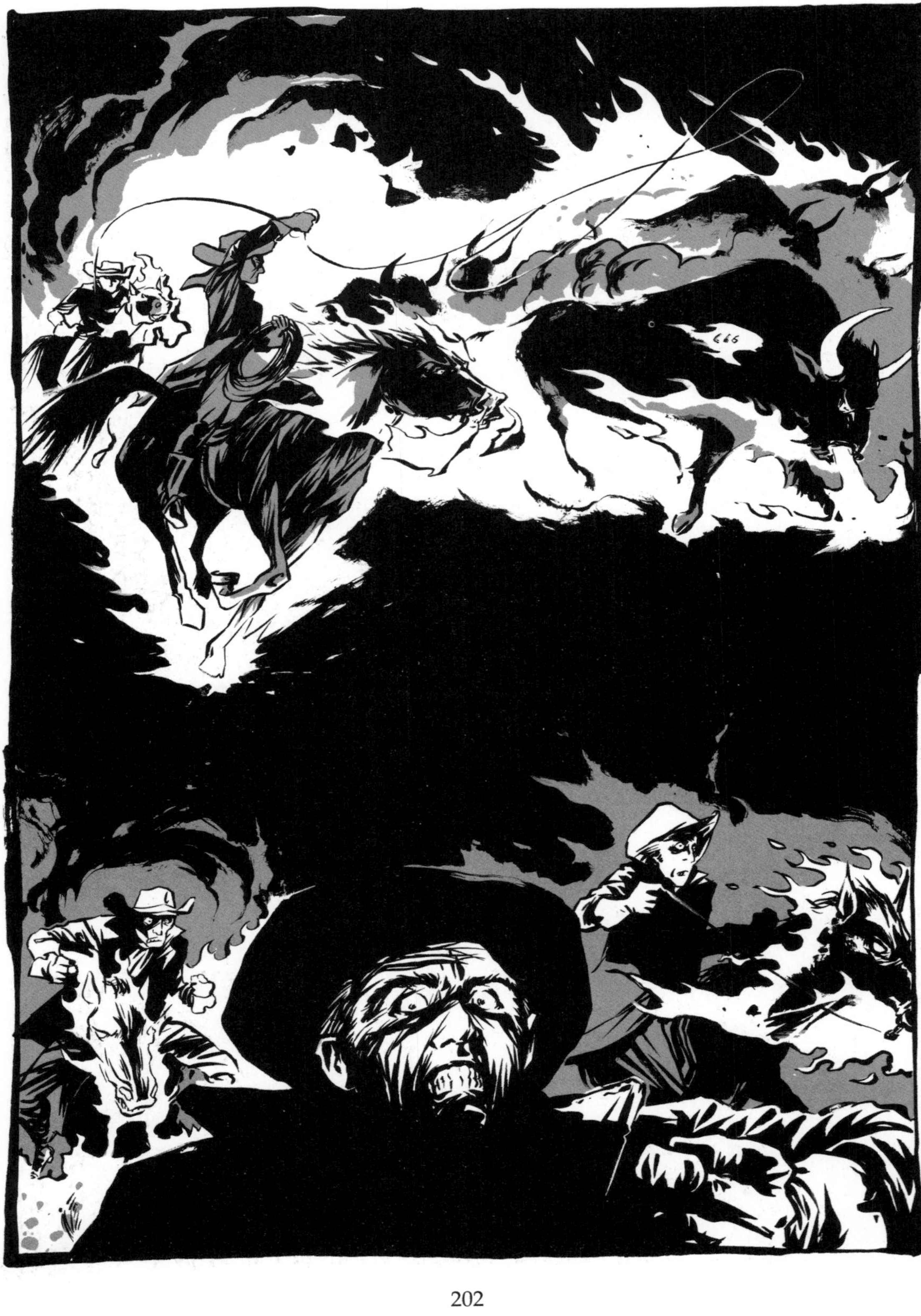

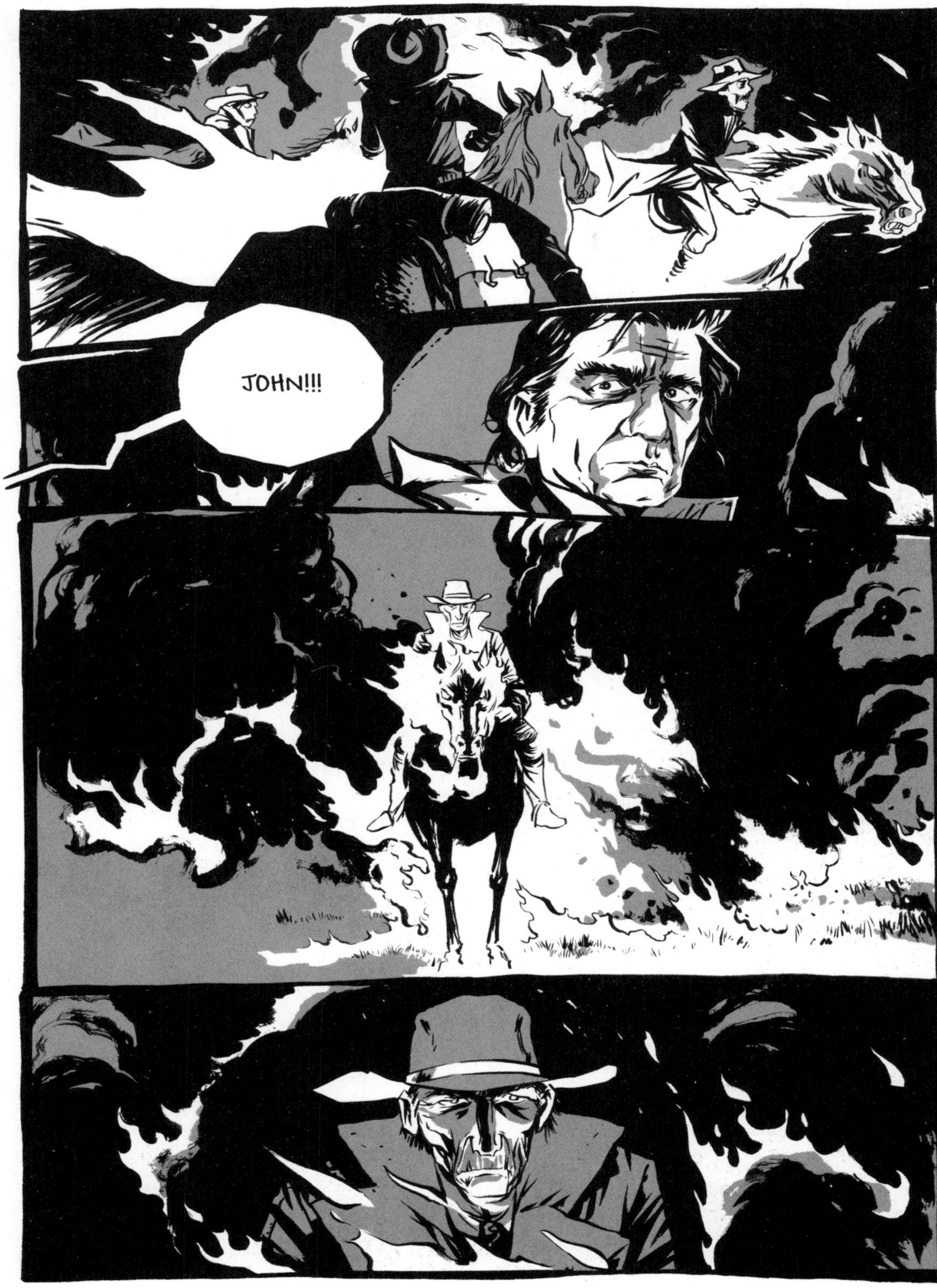
JOHN!!!

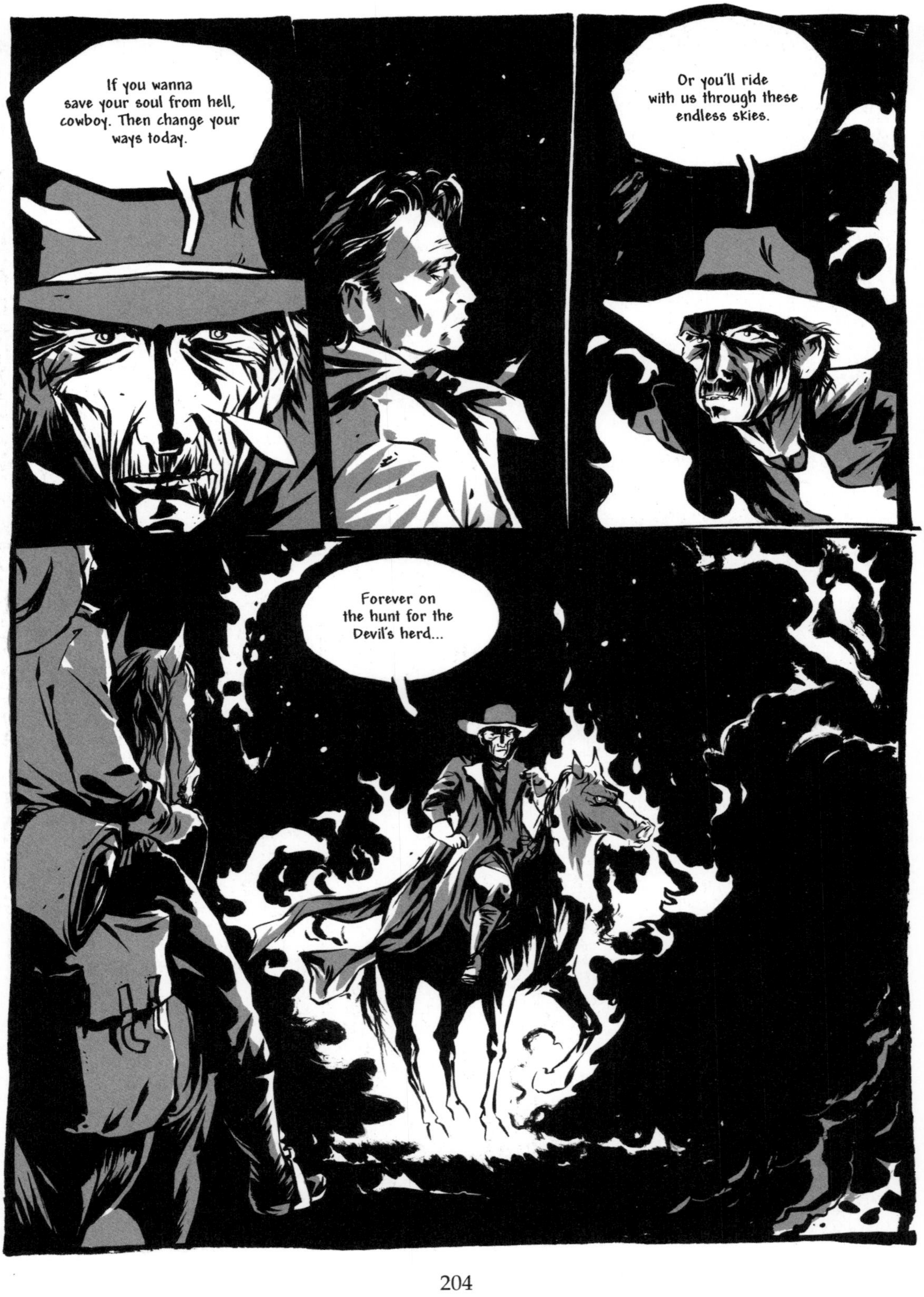
If you wanna save your soul from hell, cowboy. Then change your ways today.
Or you'll ride with us through these endless skies.
Forever on the hunt for the Devil's herd...

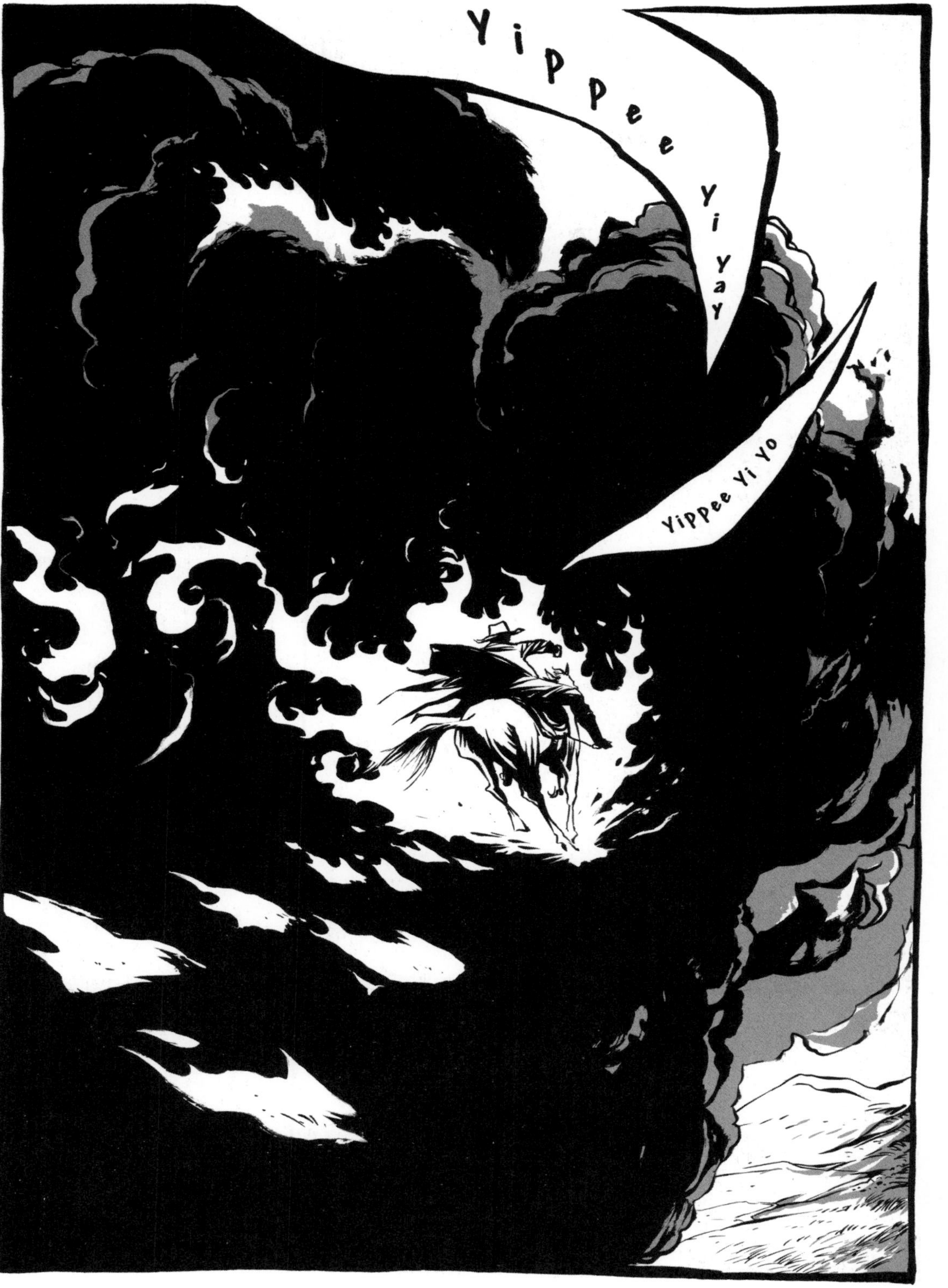
Yippee Yi Yay
Yippee Yi Yo

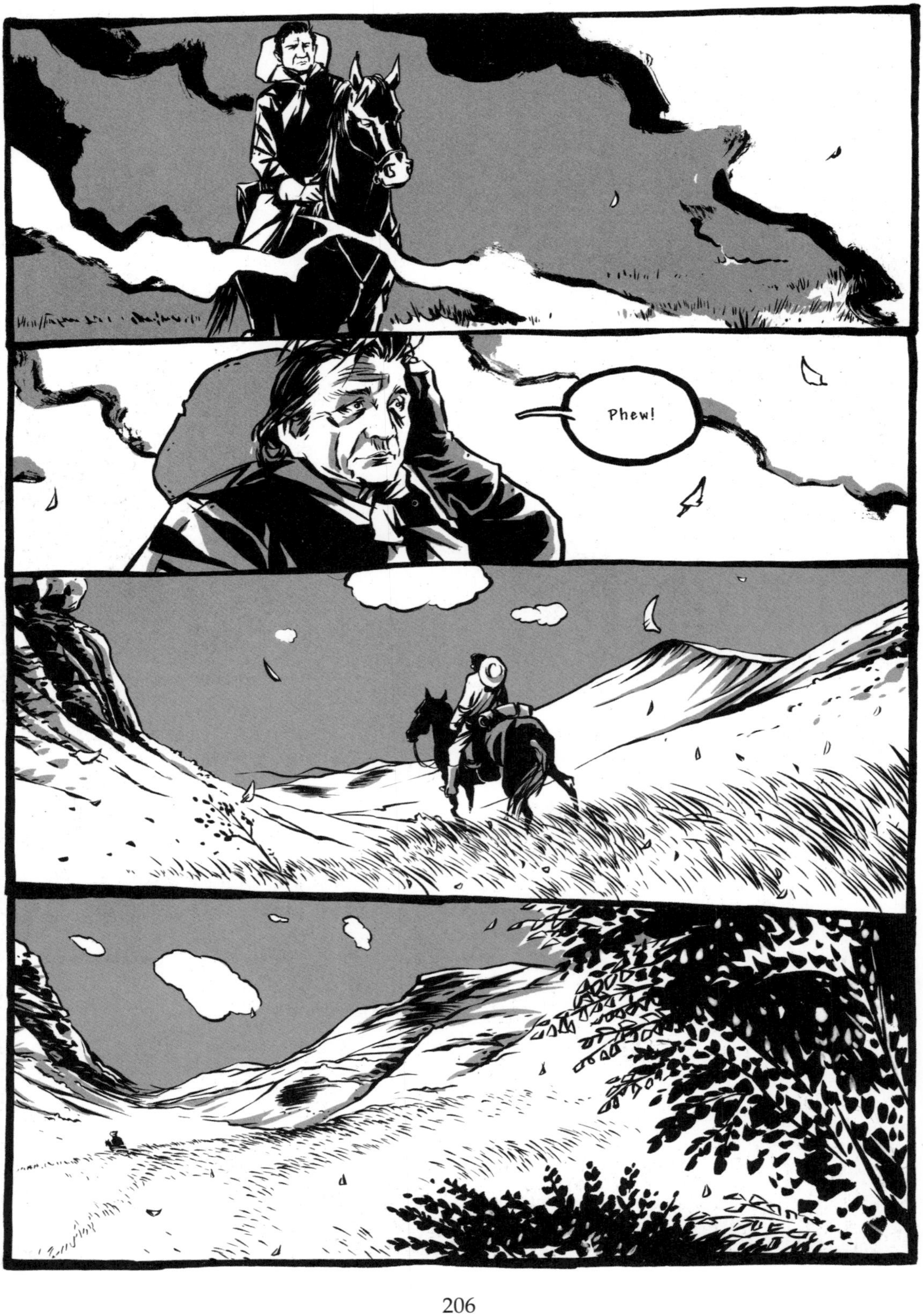
Phew!

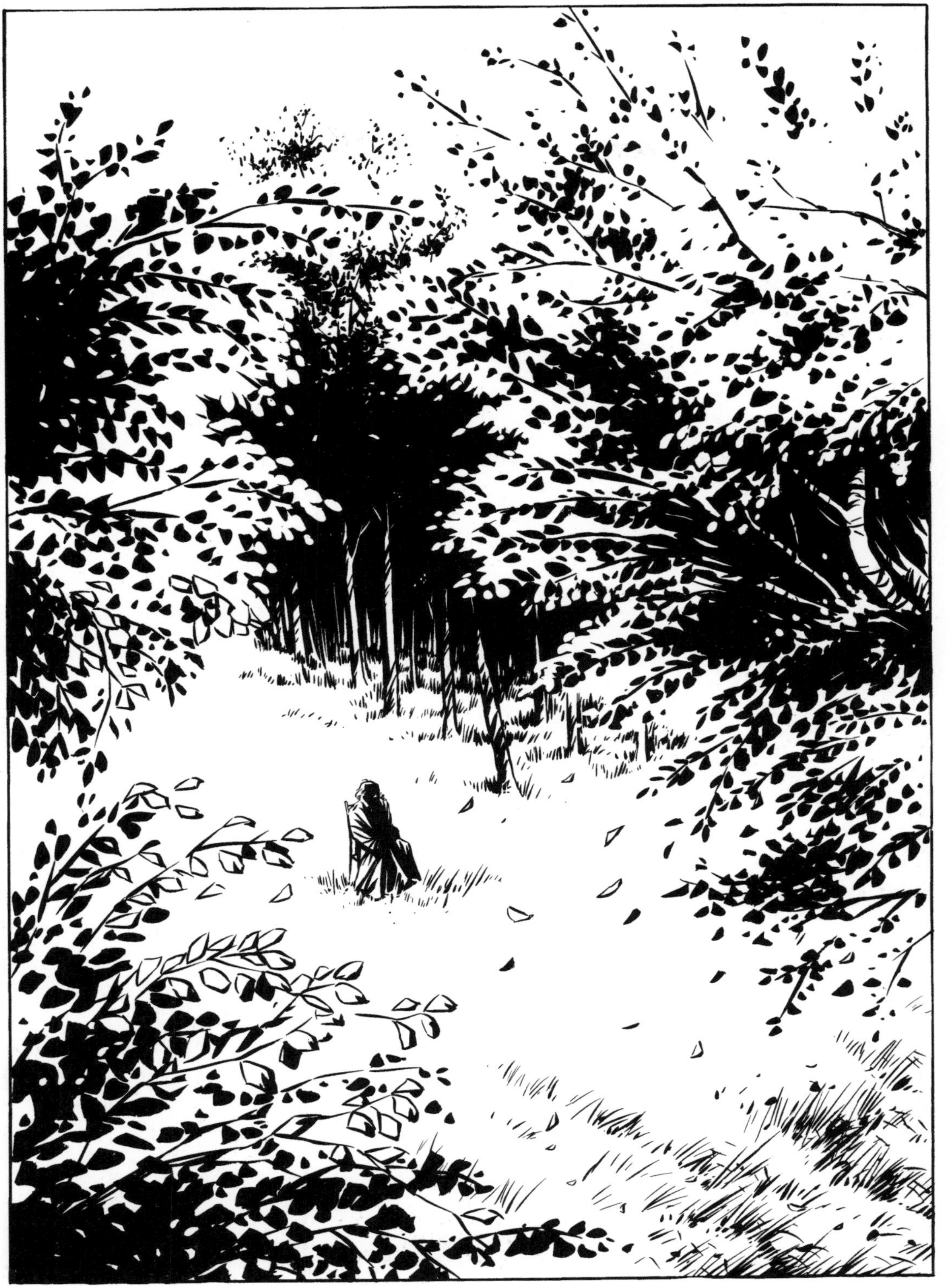

CASH GALLERY

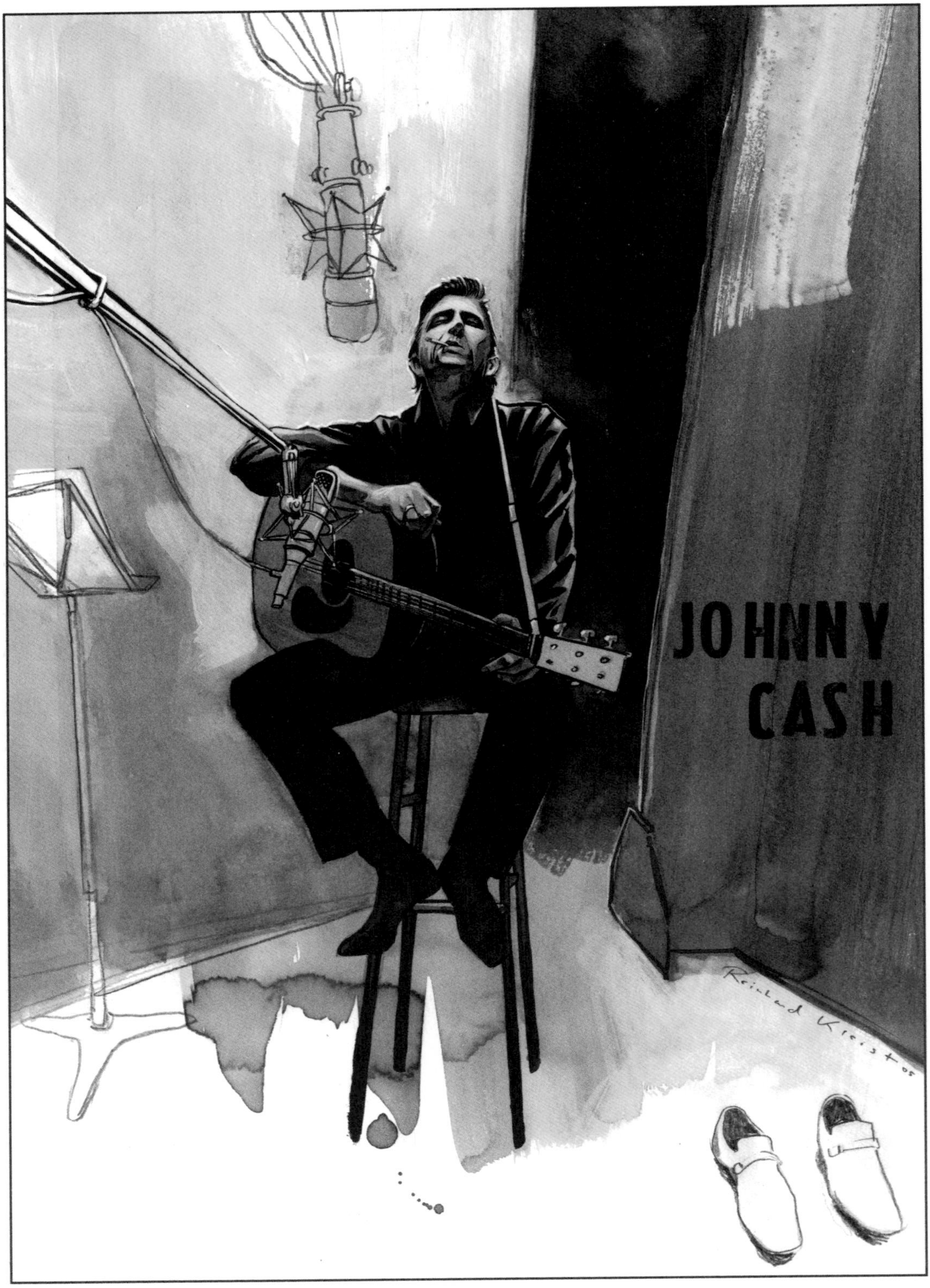
JOHNNY
CASH

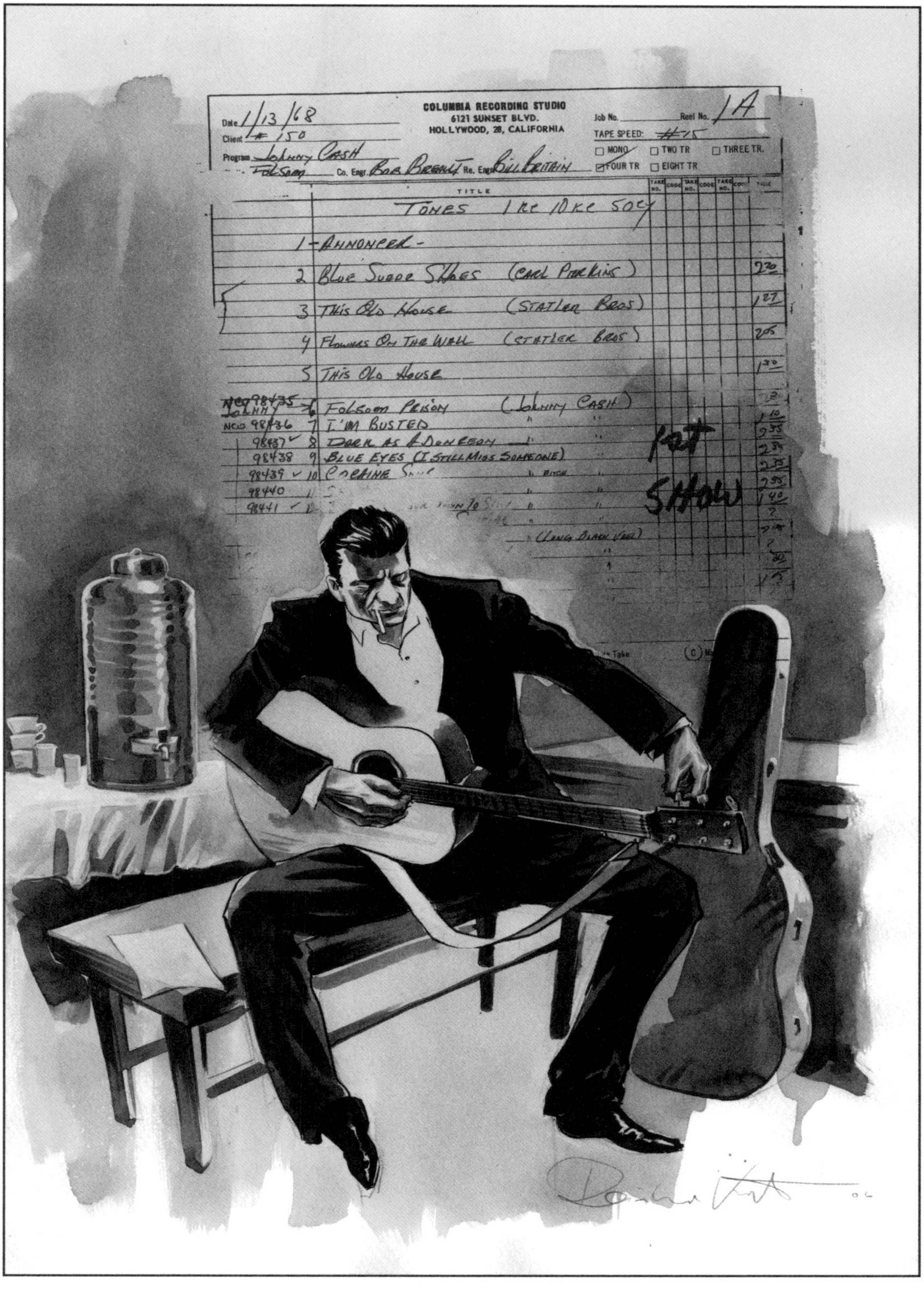
COLUMBIA RECORDING STUDIO
6121 SUNSET BLVD.
HOLLYWOOD, 28, CALIFORNIA
Date 1/13/68
Client #150
Program Johnny Cash
Folsom
Co. Engr. Bob Breault
Re. Engr. Bill Britain
Job No.
Reel No. 1A
TAPE SPEED: #15
MONO
TWO TR
THREE TR.
FOUR TR
EIGHT TR
TITLE
TAKE NO.
CODE
TONES 1 kc 10 kc 50 c
1 - ANNONCER -
2 Blue Suede Shoes (Carl Perkins) 2:30
3 This Old House (Statler Bros) 1:27
4 Flowers On The Wall (Statler Bros) 2:05
5 This Old House 1:30
6 Folsom Prison (Johnny Cash)
7 I'M BUSTED
8 DARK AS A DUNGEON
9 BLUE EYES (I STILL MISS SOMEONE)
10 COCAINE
(Long Black Veil)
1st SHOW

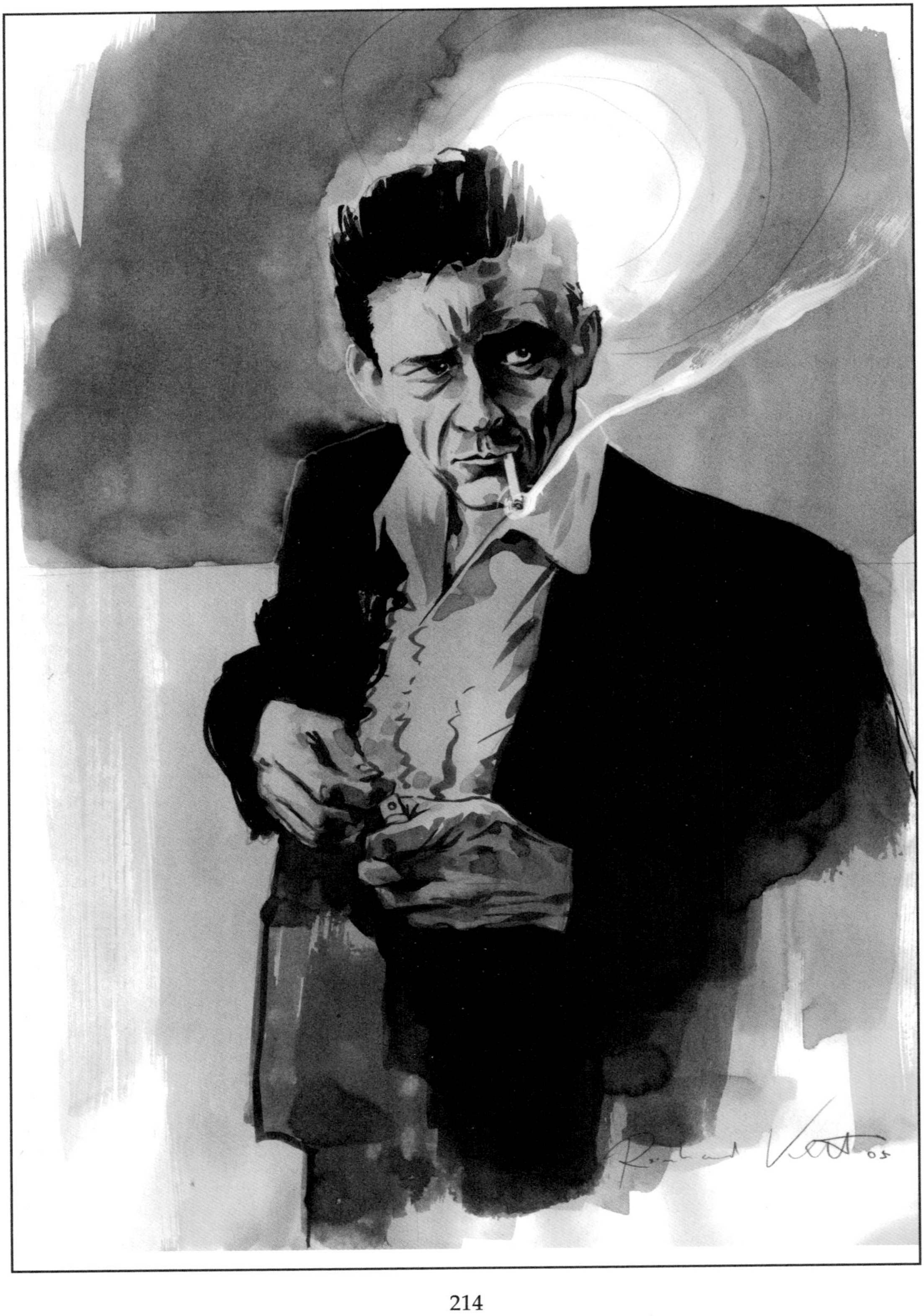

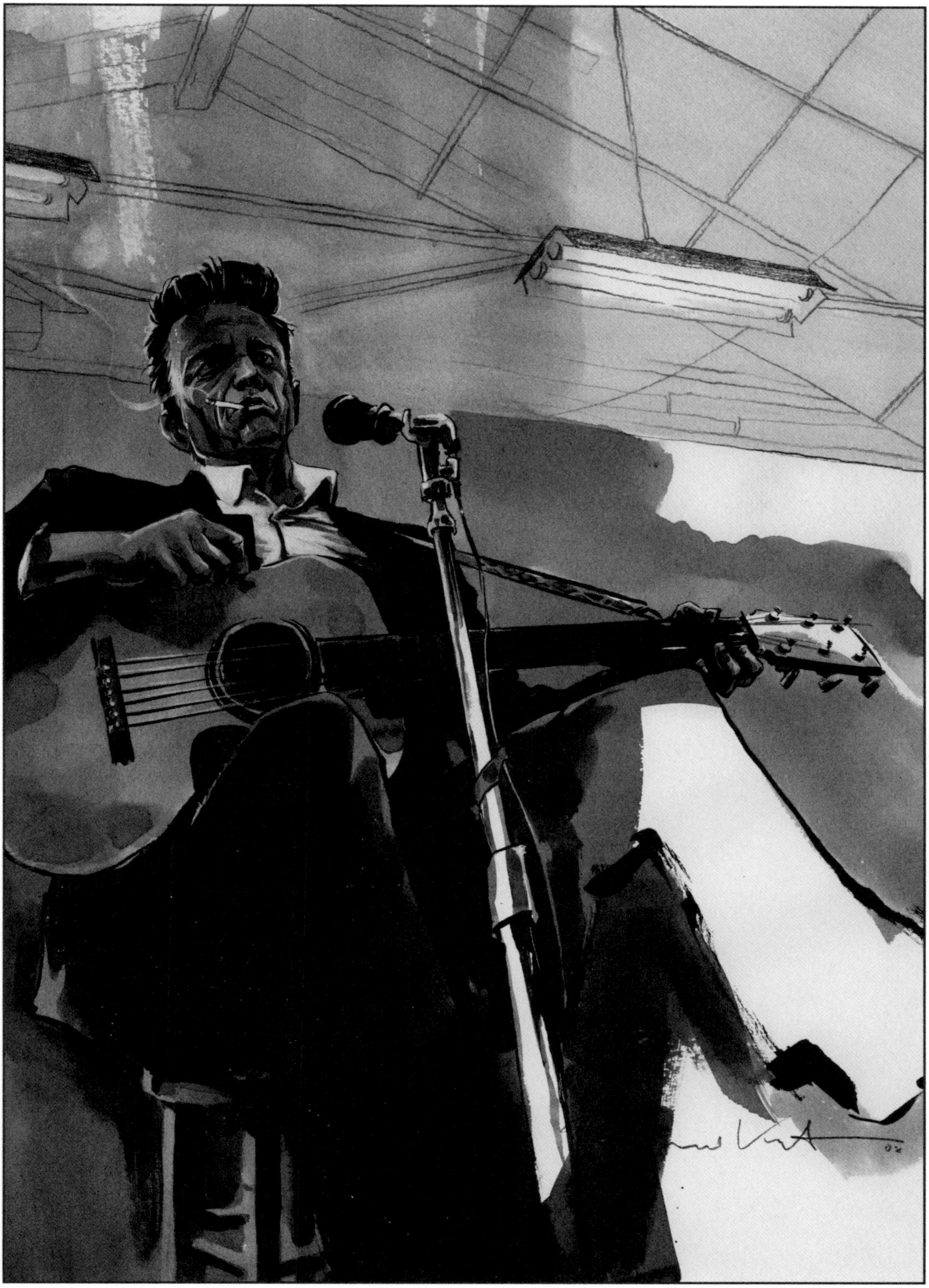

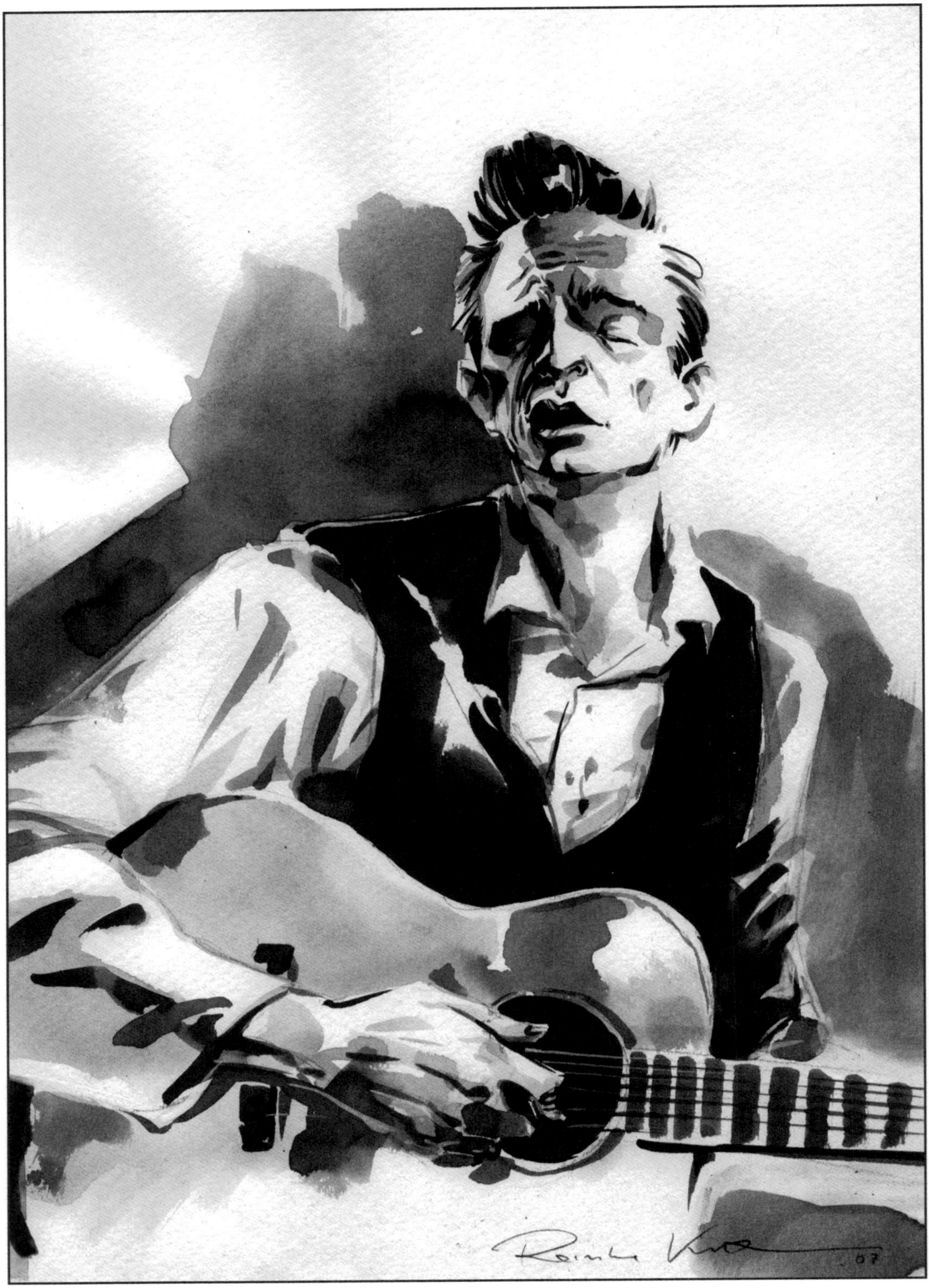

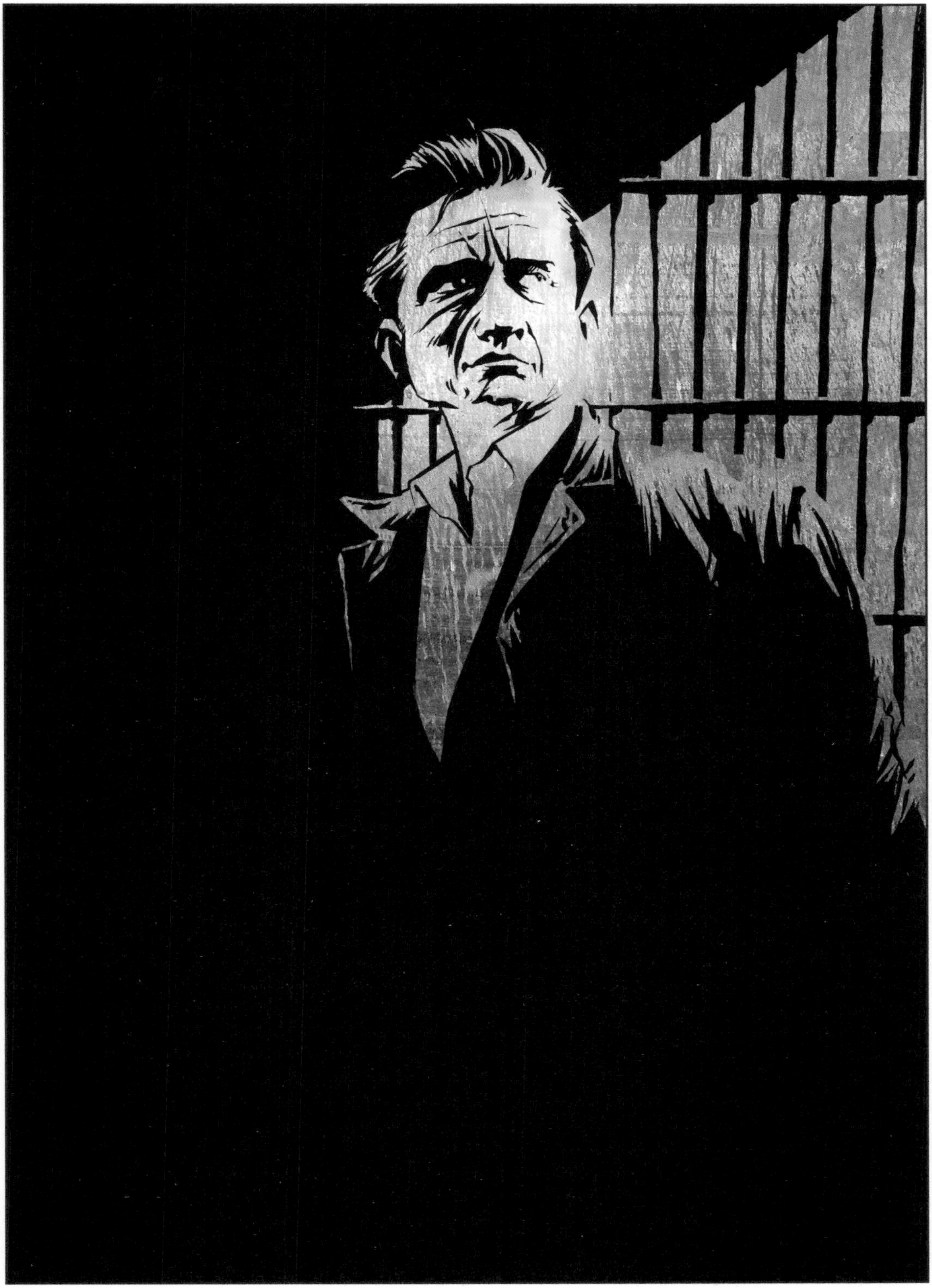

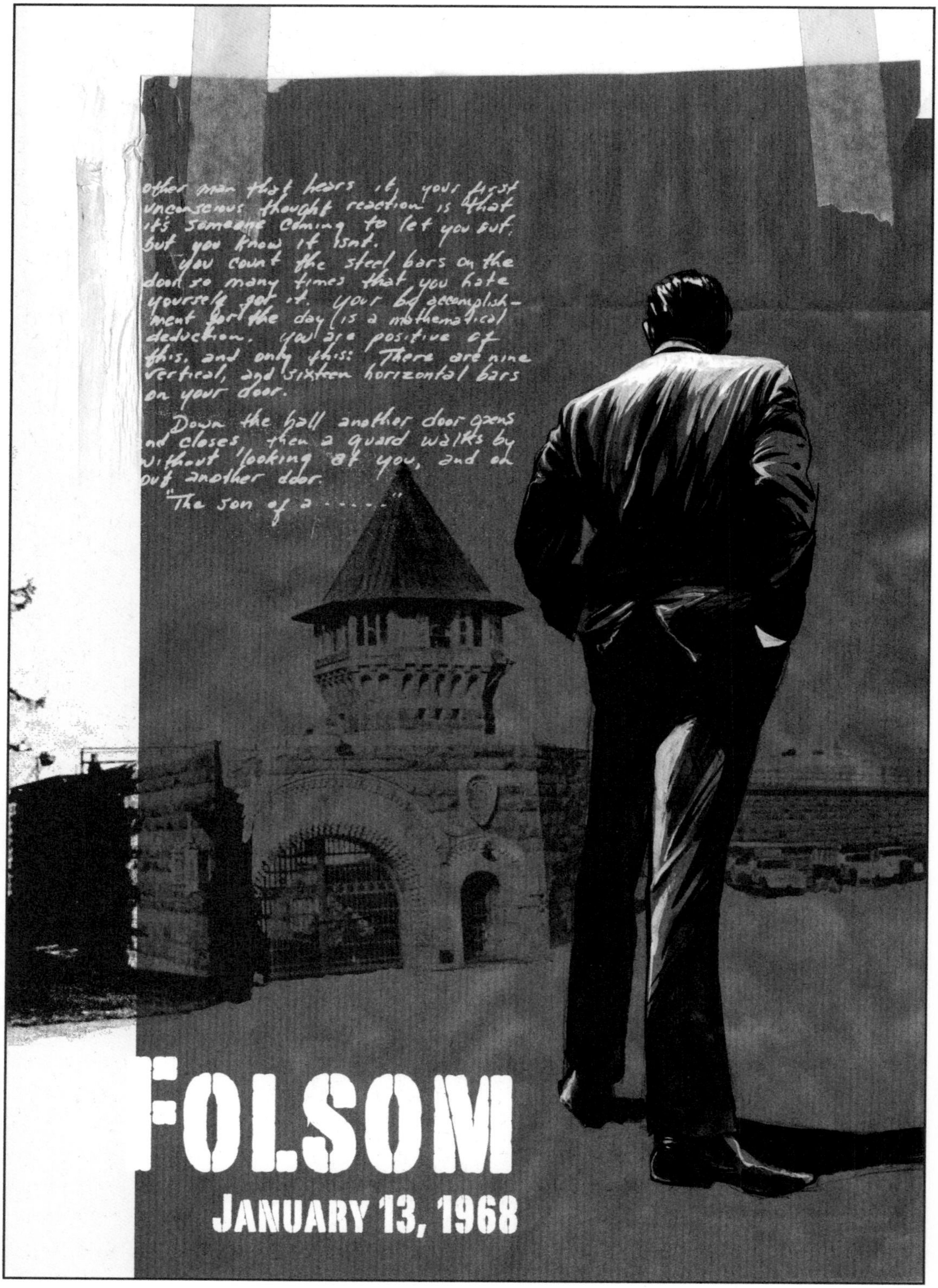
other man that hears it, your first
unconscious thought reaction is that
it's someone coming to let you out,
but you know it isnt.
You count the steel bars on the
door so many times that you hate
yourself for it. Your big accomplish-
ment for the day (is a mathematical
deduction. You are positive of
this, and only this: There are nine
vertical, and sixteen horizontal bars
on your door.
Down the hall another door opens
and closes, then a guard walks by
without looking at you, and on
out another door.
"The son of a ......"
FOLSOM
JANUARY 13, 1968

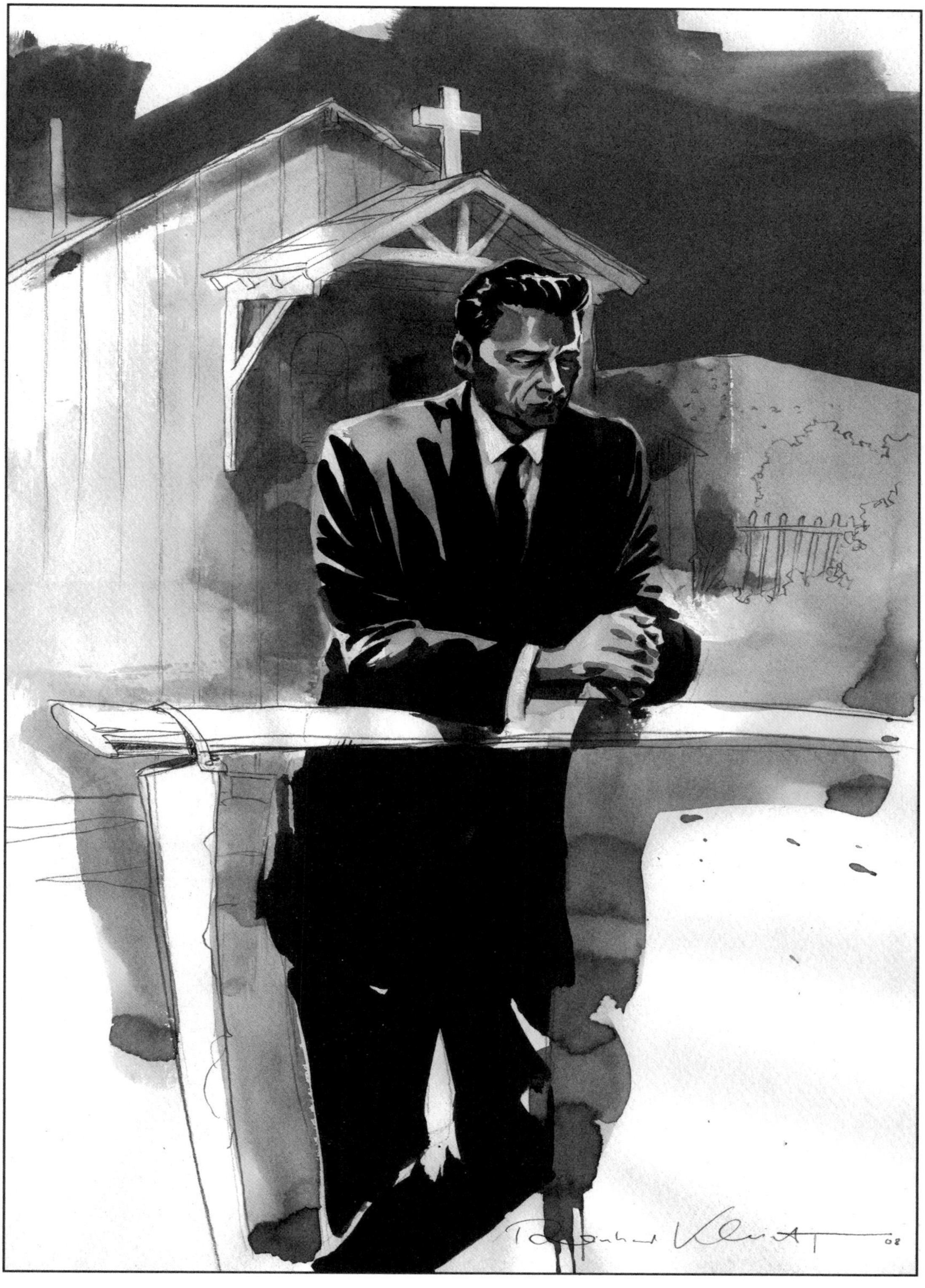

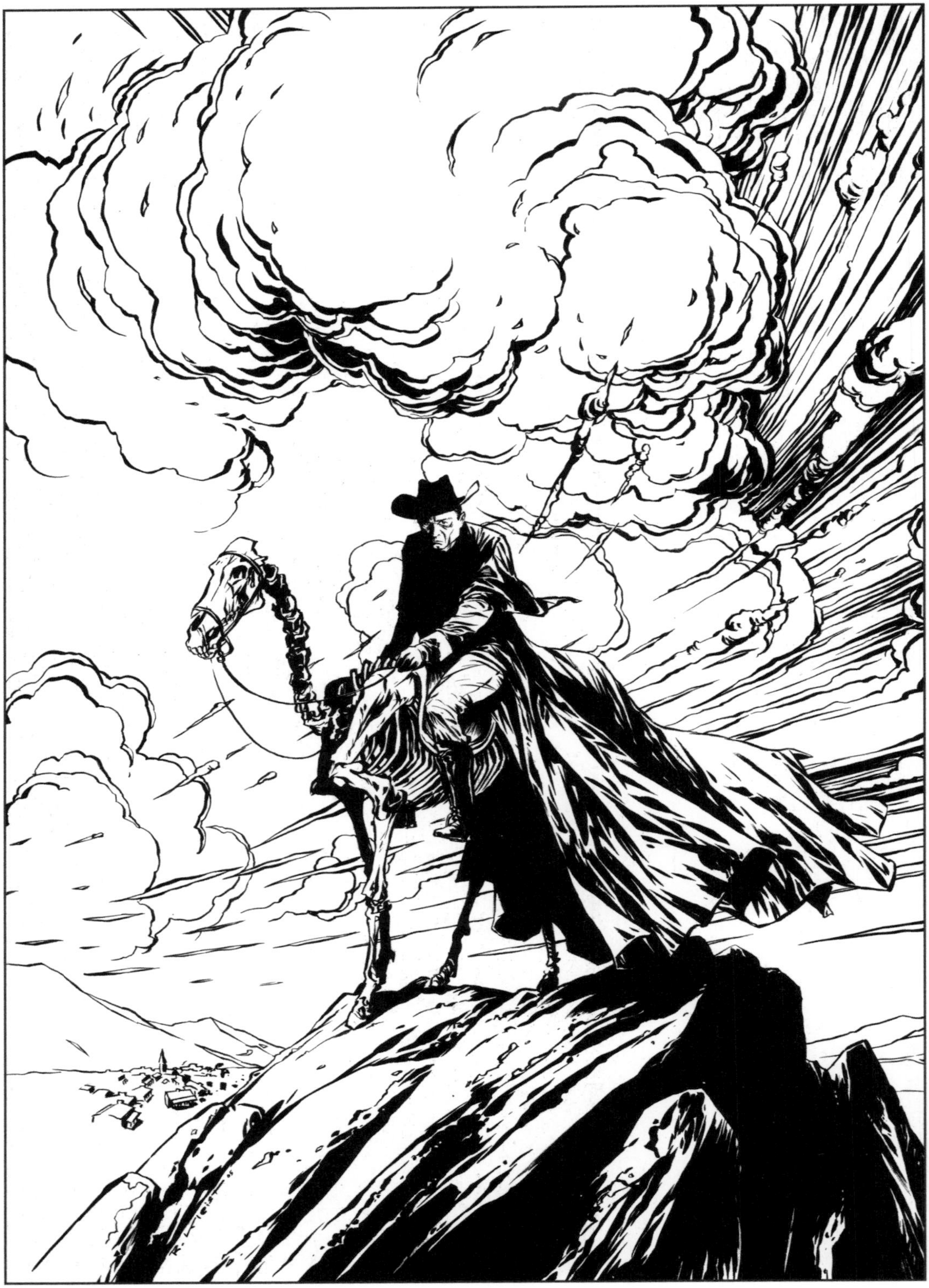

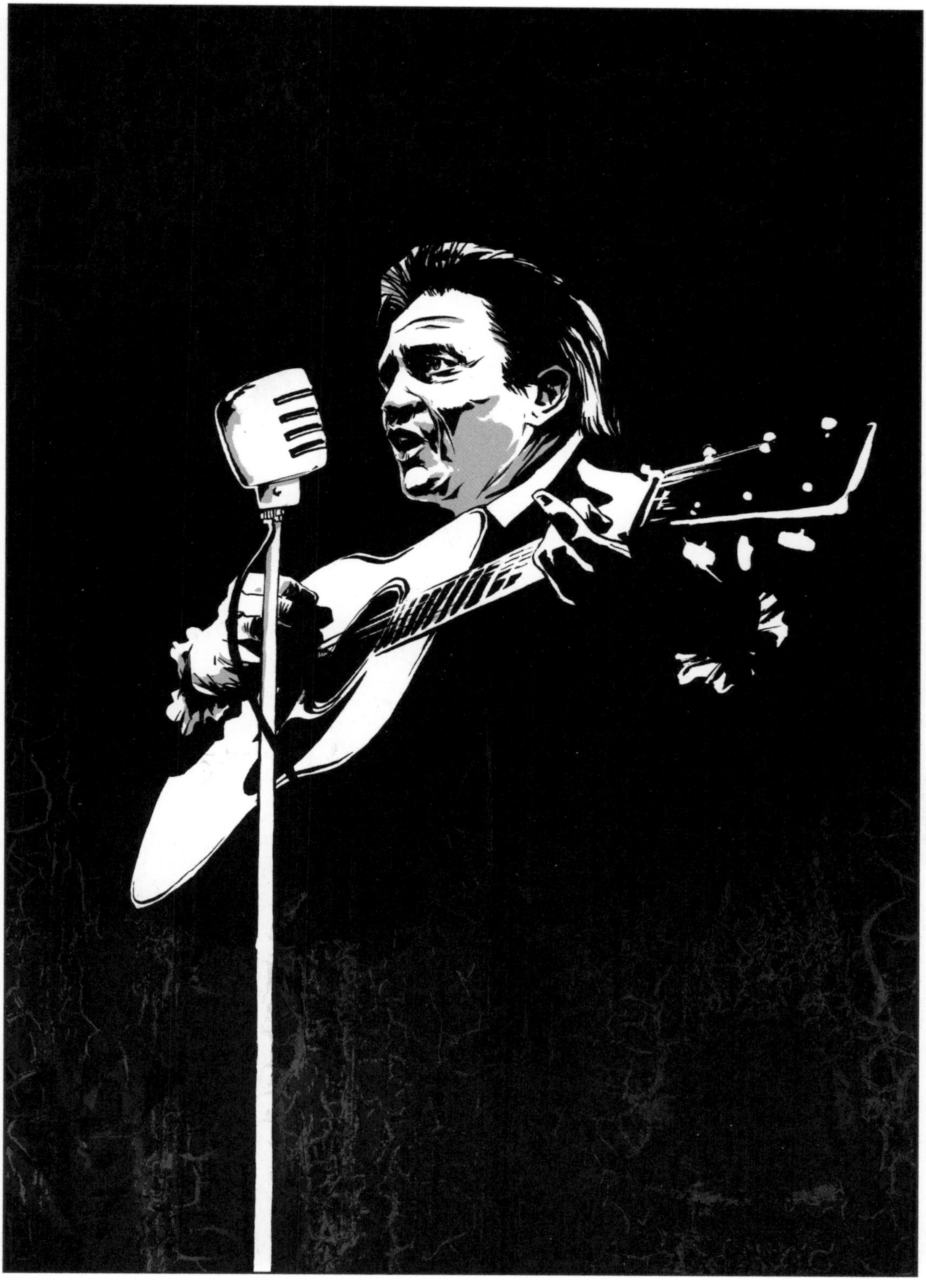

BIBLIOGRAPHY
This book primarily drew on the following sources:

LITERATURE

Cash: The Autobiography
by Patrick Carr and Johnny Cash (Harper Collins, 1997)

The beast in me - Johnny Cash und die seltsame und schöne Welt der Countrymusik
by Franz Dobler (Heyne, 2004)

Johnny Cash at Folsom Prison: The Making of a Masterpiece
by Michael Streissguth, with photographs by Jim Marshall
(Da Capo Press, 2004)

Johnny Cash: The Life of an American Icon
by Stephen Miller (Music Sales, 2006)

Cash
published by Jason Fine, with photographs from *Rolling Stone* (Crown, 2004)

FILM DOCUMENTATION

The Man, His World, His Music
by Robert Elfstrom, 1969 (DVD from Sony BMG, 2003)